D0843316

INTRODUCTION TO STATISTICS
AND ECONOMETRICS

INTRODUCTION TO STATISTICS AND ECONOMETRICS

TAKESHI AMEMIYA

Harvard University Press

Cambridge, Massachusetts

London, England

This book has been digitally reprinted. The content remains
identical to that of previous printings.

Library of Congress Cataloging-in-Publication Data

Amemiya, Takeshi.
  Introduction to statistics and econometrics / Takeshi Amemiya.
    p. cm.
  Includes bibliographical references and index.
  ISBN 0-674-46225-4 (alk. paper)
  1. Econometrics. 2. Statistics. I. Title.
HB139.A513 1993
330'.01'5195—dc20
                                                    93-3777
                                                      CIP

To Yoshiko

CONTENTS

PREFACE

Although there are many textbooks on statistics, they usually contain only a cursory discussion of regression analysis and seldom cover various generalizations of the classical regression model important in econometrics and other social science applications. Moreover, in most of these textbooks the selection of topics is far from ideal from an econometrician's point of view. At the same time, there are many textbooks on econometrics, but either they do not include statistics proper, or they give it a superficial treatment. The present book is aimed at filling that gap.

Chapters 1 through 9 cover probability and statistics and can be taught in a semester course for advanced undergraduates or first-year graduate students. My own course on this material has been taken by both undergraduate and graduate students in economics, statistics, and other social science disciplines. The prerequisites are one year of calculus and an ability to think mathematically.

In these chapters I emphasize certain topics which are important in econometrics but which are often overlooked by statistics textbooks at this level. Examples are best prediction and best linear prediction, conditional density of the form $f(x \mid x < y)$, the joint distribution of a continuous and a discrete random variable, large sample theory, and the properties of the maximum likelihood estimator. I discuss these topics without undue use of mathematics and with many illustrative examples and diagrams. In addition, many exercises are given at the end of each chapter (except Chapters 1 and 13). I devote a lot of space to these and other fundamental concepts because I believe that it is far better for a student to have a solid knowledge of the basic facts about random variables than to have a superficial knowledge of the latest techniques.

I also believe that students should be trained to question the validity and reasonableness of conventional statistical techniques. Therefore, I give a thorough analysis of the problem of choosing estimators, including a comparison of various criteria for ranking estimators. I also present a critical evaluation of the classical method of hypothesis testing, especially in the realistic case of testing a composite null against a composite alternative. In discussing these issues as well as other problematic areas of classical statistics, I frequently have recourse to Bayesian statistics. I do so not because I believe it is superior (in fact, this book is written mainly from the classical point of view) but because it provides a pedagogically useful framework for consideration of many fundamental issues in statistical inference.

Chapter 10 presents the bivariate classical regression model in the conventional summation notation. Chapter 11 is a brief introduction to matrix analysis. By studying it in earnest, the reader should be able to understand Chapters 12 and 13 as well as the brief sections in Chapters 5 and 9 that use matrix notation. Chapter 12 gives the multiple classical regression model in matrix notation. In Chapters 10 and 12 the concepts and the methods studied in Chapters 1 through 9 in the framework of the i.i.d. (independent and identically distributed) sample are extended to the regression model. Finally, in Chapter 13, I discuss various generalizations of the classical regression model (Sections 13.1 through 13.4) and certain other statistical models extensively used in econometrics and other social science applications (13.5 through 13.7). The first part of the chapter is a quick overview of the topics. The second part, which discusses qualitative response models, censored and truncated regression models, and duration models, is a more extensive introduction to these important subjects.

Chapters 10 through 13 can be taught in the semester after the semester that covers Chapters 1 through 9. Under this plan, the material in Sections 13.1 through 13.4 needs to be supplemented by additional readings. Alternatively, for students with less background, Chapters 1 through 12 may be taught in a year, and Chapter 13 studied independently. At Stanford about half of the students who finish a year-long course in statistics and econometrics go on to take a year's course in advanced econometrics, for which I use my *Advanced Econometrics* (Harvard University Press, 1985).

It is expected that those who complete the present textbook will be able to understand my advanced textbook.

I am grateful to Gene Savin, Peter Robinson, and James Powell, who read all or part of the manuscript and gave me valuable comments. I am also indebted to my students Fumihiro Goto and Dongseok Kim for carefully checking the entire manuscript for typographical and more substantial errors. I alone, however, take responsibility for the remaining errors. Dongseok Kim also prepared all the figures in the book. I also thank Michael Aronson, general editor at Harvard University Press, for constant encouragement and guidance, and Elizabeth Gretz and Vivian Wheeler for carefully checking the manuscript and suggesting numerous stylistic changes that considerably enhanced its readability.

I dedicate this book to my wife, Yoshiko, who for over twenty years has made a steadfast effort to bridge the gap between two cultures. Her work, though perhaps not conspicuous in the short run, will, I am sure, have a long-lasting effect.

INTRODUCTION TO STATISTICS
AND ECONOMETRICS

1 | INTRODUCTION

1.1 WHAT IS PROBABILITY?

As a common word in everyday usage, *probability* expresses a degree of belief a person has about an event or statement by a number between zero and one. Probability also has a philosophical meaning, which will not be discussed here. The two major schools of statistical inference—the Bayesian and the classical—hold two different interpretations of probability. The *Bayesian* (after Thomas Bayes, an eighteenth-century English clergyman and probabilist) interpretation of probability is essentially that of everyday usage. The *classical* school refers to an approach that originated at the beginning of the twentieth century under the leadership of R. A. Fisher and is still prevalent. The classical statistician uses the word *probability* only for an event which can be repeated, and interprets it as the limit of the empirical frequency of the event as the number of repetitions increases indefinitely. For example, suppose we toss a coin n times, and a head comes up r times. The classical statistician interprets the probability of heads as a limit (in the sense that will be defined later) of the empirical frequency r/n as n goes to infinity. Because a coin cannot be tossed infinitely many times, we will never know this probability exactly and can only guess (or estimate) it.

To consider the difference between the two interpretations, examine the following three events or statements:

(1) A head comes up when we toss a particular coin.

(2) Atlantis, described by Plato, actually existed.

(3) The probability of obtaining heads when we toss a particular
    coin is $\frac{1}{2}$.

A Bayesian can talk about the probability of any one of these events or
statements; a classical statistician can do so only for the event (1), because
only (1) is concerned with a repeatable event. Note that (1) is sometimes
true and sometimes false as it is repeatedly observed, whereas statement
(2) or (3) is either true or false as it deals with a particular thing—one of
a kind. It may be argued that a frequency interpretation of (2) is possible
to the extent that some of Plato's assertions have been proved true by a
later study and some false. But in that case we are considering any asser-
tion of Plato's, rather than the particular one regarding Atlantis.

As we shall see in later chapters, these two interpretations of probability
lead to two different methods of statistical inference. Although in this
book I present mainly the classical method, I will present Bayesian method
whenever I believe it offers more attractive solutions. The two methods
are complementary, and different situations call for different methods.

1.2   WHAT IS STATISTICS?

In our everyday life we must continuously make decisions in the face of
uncertainty, and in making decisions it is useful for us to know the probability of certain events. For example, before deciding to gamble, we would
want to know the probability of winning. We want to know the probability
of rain when we decide whether or not to take an umbrella in the morn-
ing. In determining the discount rate, the Federal Reserve Board needs
to assess the probabilistic impact of a change in the rate on the unemployment rate and on inflation. It is advisable to determine these probabilities
in a reasonable way; otherwise we will lose in the long run, although in
the short run we may be lucky and avoid the consequences of a haphazard
decision. A reasonable way to determine a probability should take into
account the past record of an event in question or, whenever possible, the
results of a deliberate experiment.

We are ready for our first working definition of statistics: *Statistics is the
science of assigning a probability to an event on the basis of experiments.*

Consider estimating the probability of heads by tossing a particular coin
many times. Most people will think it reasonable to use the ratio of heads

over tosses as an estimate. In statistics we study whether it is indeed reasonable and, if so, in what sense.

Tossing a coin with the probability of heads equal to p is identical to choosing a ball at random from a box that contains two types of balls, one of which corresponds to heads and the other to tails, with p being the proportion of heads balls. The statistician regards every event whose outcome is unknown to be like drawing a ball at random from a box that contains various types of balls in certain proportions.

For example, consider the question of whether or not cigarette smoking is associated with lung cancer. First, we need to paraphrase the question to make it more readily accessible to statistical analysis. One way is to ask, What is the probability that a person who smokes more than ten cigarettes a day will contract lung cancer? (This may not be the optimal way, but we choose it for the sake of illustration.) To apply the box-ball analogy to this example, we should imagine a box that contains balls, corresponding to cigarette smokers; some of the balls have lung cancer marked on them and the rest do not. Drawing a ball at random corresponds to choosing a cigarette smoker at random and observing him until he dies to see whether or not he contracts lung cancer. (Such an experiment would be a costly one. If we asked a related but different question—what is the probability that a man who died of lung cancer was a cigarette smoker?— the experiment would be simpler.)

This example differs from the example of coin tossing in that in coin tossing we create our own sample, whereas in this example it is as though God (or a god) has tossed a coin and we simply observe the outcome. This is not an essential difference. Its only significance is that we can toss a coin as many times as we wish, whereas in the present example the statistician must work with whatever sample God has provided. In the physical sciences we are often able to conduct our own experiments, but in economics or other behavioral sciences we must often work with a limited sample, which may require specific tools of analysis.

A statistician looks at the world as full of balls that have been drawn by God and examines the balls in order to estimate the characteristics ("proportion") of boxes from which the balls have been drawn. This mode of thinking is indispensable for a statistician. Thus we state a second working definition of statistics: *Statistics is the science of observing data and making inferences about the characteristics of a random mechanism that has generated the data.*

Coin tossing is an example of a random mechanism whose outcomes are objects called heads and tails. In order to facilitate mathematical analysis, the statistician assigns numbers to objects: for example, 1 to heads and 0 to tails. A random mechanism whose outcomes are real numbers is called a *random variable.* The random mechanism whose outcome is the height (measured in feet) of a Stanford student is another random variable. The first is called a *discrete random variable,* and the second, a *continuous random variable* (assuming hypothetically that height can be measured to an infinite degree of accuracy). A discrete random variable is characterized by the probabilities of the outcomes. The characteristics of a continuous random variable are captured by a *density function,* which is defined in such a way that the probability of any interval is equal to the area under the density function over that interval. We use the term *probability distribution* as a broader concept which refers to either a set of discrete probabilities or a density function. Now we can compose a third and final definition: *Statistics is the science of estimating the probability distribution of a random variable on the basis of repeated observations drawn from the same random variable.*

2 | PROBABILITY

2.1 INTRODUCTION

In this chapter we shall define probability mathematically and learn how to calculate the probability of a complex event when the probabilities of simple events are given. For example, what is the probability that a head comes up twice in a row when we toss an unbiased coin? We shall learn that the answer is $\frac{1}{4}$. As a more complicated example, what is the probability that a student will be accepted by at least one graduate school if she applies to ten schools for each of which the probability of acceptance is 0.1? The answer is $1 - 0.9^{10} \cong 0.65$. (The answer is derived under the assumption that the ten schools make independent decisions.) Or what is the probability a person will win a game in tennis if the probability of his winning a point is p? The answer is

$$p^4\{1 + 4(1 - p) + 10(1 - p)^2 + 20p(1 - p)^3/[1 - 2p(1 - p)]\}.$$

For example, if $p = 0.51$, the formula gives 0.525.

In these calculations we have not engaged in any statistical inference. Probability is a subject which can be studied independently of statistics; it forms the foundation of statistics.

2.2 AXIOMS OF PROBABILITY

Definitions of a few commonly used terms follow. These terms inevitably remain vague until they are illustrated; see Examples 2.2.1 and 2.2.2.

Sample space. The set of all the possible outcomes of an experiment.

Event. A subset of the sample space.

Simple event. An event which cannot be a union of other events.

Composite event. An event which is not a simple event.

EXAMPLE 2.2.1

Experiment: Tossing a coin twice.

Sample space: {HH, HT, TH, TT}.

The event that a head occurs at least once: HH ∪ HT ∪ TH.

EXAMPLE 2.2.2

Experiment: Reading the temperature (F) at Stanford at noon on October 1.

Sample space: Real interval (0, 100).

Events of interest are intervals contained in the above interval.

A probability is a nonnegative number we assign to every event. The axioms of probability are the rules we agree to follow when we assign probabilities.

Axioms of Probability

(1) $P(A) \geq 0$ for any event A.

(2) $P(S) = 1$, where S is the sample space.

(3) If $\{A_i\}$, $i = 1, 2, \ldots$, are mutually exclusive (that is, $A_i \cap A_j = \varnothing$ for all $i \neq j$), then $P(A_1 \cup A_2 \cup \ldots) = P(A_1) + P(A_2) + \ldots$.

The first two rules are reasonable and consistent with the everyday use of the word probability. The third rule is consistent with the frequency interpretation of probability, for relative frequency follows the same rule. If, at the roll of a die, A is the event that the die shows 1 and B the event that it shows 2, the relative frequency of $A \cup B$ (either 1 or 2) is clearly the sum of the relative frequencies of A and B. We want probability to follow the same rule.

When the sample space is discrete, as in Example 2.2.1, it is possible to assign probability to every event (that is, every possible subset of the sample space) in a way which is consistent with the probability axioms. When the sample space is continuous, however, as in Example 2.2.2, it is not possible to do so. In such a case we restrict our attention to a smaller class of events to which we can assign probabilities in a manner consistent with the axioms. For example, the class of all the intervals contained in (0, 100) and their unions satisfies the condition. In the subsequent discussion we shall implicitly be dealing with such a class. The reader who wishes to study this problem is advised to consult a book on the theory of probability, such as Chung (1974).

2.3 COUNTING TECHNIQUES

2.3.1 Simple Events with Equal Probabilities

Axiom (3) suggests that often the easiest way to calculate the probability of a composite event is to sum the probabilities of all the simple events that constitute it. The calculation is especially easy when the sample space consists of a finite number of simple events with equal probabilities, a situation which often occurs in practice. Let $n(A)$ be the number of the simple events contained in subset A of the sample space S. Then we have

$$P(A) = \frac{n(A)}{n(S)}.$$

Two examples of this rule follow.

EXAMPLE 2.3.1 What is the probability that an even number will show in a roll of a fair die?
   We have $n(S) = 6$; $A = \{2, 4, 6\}$ and hence $n(A) = 3$. Therefore, $P(A) = 0.5$.

EXAMPLE 2.3.2 A pair of fair dice are rolled once. Compute the probability that the sum of the two numbers is equal to each of the integers 2 through 12.
   Let the ordered pair (i, j) represent the event that i shows on the first die and j on the second. Then $S = \{(i, j) \mid i, j = 1, 2, \ldots, 6\}$, so that $n(S) = 36$. We have

$$n(i + j = 2) = n[(1, 1)] = 1,$$

$$n(i + j = 3) = n[(1, 2), (2, 1)] = 2,$$

$$n(i + j = 4) = n[(1, 3), (3, 1), (2, 2)] = 3,$$

and so on. See Exercise 2.

2.3.2 Permutations and Combinations

The formulae for the numbers of permutations and combinations are useful for counting the number of simple events in many practical problems.

DEFINITION 2.3.1 The number of *permutations* of taking r elements from n elements is the number of distinct ordered sets consisting of r distinct elements which can be formed out of a set of n distinct elements and is denoted by P_r^n.

For example, the permutations of taking two numbers from the three numbers 1, 2, and 3 are $(1, 2), (1, 3), (2, 1), (2, 3), (3, 1), (3, 2)$; therefore, we have $P_2^3 = 6$.

THEOREM 2.3.1 $P_r^n = n!/(n - r)!$, where $n!$ reads n factorial and denotes $n(n - 1)(n - 2) \cdots 2 \cdot 1$. (We define $0! = 1$.)

Proof. In the first position we can choose any one of n elements and in the second position $n - 1$ and so on, and finally in the rth position we can choose one of $n - r + 1$ elements. Therefore, the number of permutations is the product of all these numbers. ❑

DEFINITION 2.3.2 The number of *combinations* of taking r elements from n elements is the number of distinct sets consisting of r distinct elements which can be formed out of a set of n distinct elements and is denoted by C_r^n.

Note that the order of the elements matters in permutation but not in combination. Thus in the example of taking two numbers from three, $(1, 2)$ and $(2, 1)$ make the same combination.

THEOREM 2.3.2

$$C_r^n = \frac{n!}{(n-r)!\,r!}.$$

Proof. It follows directly from the observation that for each combination, $r!$ different permutations are possible. ❑

EXAMPLE 2.3.3 Compute the probability of getting two of a kind and three of a kind (a "full house") when five dice are rolled.

Let n_i be the number on the ith die. We shall take as the sample space the set of all the distinct ordered 5-tuples $(n_1, n_2, n_3, n_4, n_5)$, so that $n(S) = 6^5$. Let the ordered pair (i, j) mean that i is the number that appears twice and j is the number that appears three times. The number of the distinct ordered pairs, therefore, is P_2^6. Given a particular (i, j), we can choose two dice out of five which show i: there are C_2^5 ways to do so. Therefore we conclude that the desired probability P is given by

$$P = \frac{P_2^6 \cdot C_2^5}{6^5} \cong 0.03858.$$

EXAMPLE 2.3.4 If a poker hand of five cards is drawn from a deck, what is the probability that it will contain three aces?

We shall take as the sample space the set of distinct poker hands without regard to a particular order in which the five cards are drawn. Therefore, $n(S) = C_5^{52}$. Of these, the number of the hands that contain three aces but not the ace of clubs is equal to the number of ways of choosing the two remaining cards out of the 48 nonaces: namely, C_2^{48}. We must also count the number of the hands that contain three aces but not the ace of spades, which is also C_2^{48}, and similarly for hearts and diamonds. Therefore, we must multiply C_2^{48} by four. The desired probability P is thus given by

$$P = \frac{4C_2^{48}}{C_5^{52}} = \frac{94}{54145} \cong 0.001736.$$

In Example 2.5.1 we shall solve the same problem in an alternative way.

2.4 CONDITIONAL PROBABILITY AND INDEPENDENCE

2.4.1 Axioms of Conditional Probability

The concept of conditional probability is intuitively easy to understand. For example, it makes sense to talk about the conditional probability that number one will show in a roll of a die given that an odd number has occurred. In the frequency interpretation, this conditional probability can be regarded as the limit of the ratio of the number of times one occurs to the number of times an odd number occurs. In general we shall consider the "conditional probability of A given B," denoted by $P(A \mid B)$, for any pair of events A and B in a sample space, provided $P(B) > 0$, and establish axioms that govern the calculation of conditional probabilities.

Axioms of Conditional Probability
(In the following axioms it is assumed that $P(B) > 0$.)

(1) $P(A \mid B) \geq 0$ for any event A.

(2) $P(A \mid B) = 1$ for any event $A \supset B$.

(3) If $\{A_i \cap B\}$, $i = 1, 2, \ldots$, are mutually exclusive, then
$P(A_1 \cup A_2 \cup \ldots \mid B) = P(A_1 \mid B) + P(A_2 \mid B) + \ldots$.

(4) If $B \supset H$ and $B \supset G$ and $P(G) \neq 0$, then

$$\frac{P(H \mid B)}{P(G \mid B)} = \frac{P(H)}{P(G)} .$$

Axioms (1), (2), and (3) are analogous to the corresponding axioms of probability. They mean that we can treat conditional probability just like probability by regarding B as the sample space. Axiom (4) is justified by observing that the relative frequency of H versus G remains the same before and after B is known to have happened. Using the four axioms of conditional probability, we can prove

THEOREM 2.4.1 $P(A \mid B) = P(A \cap B)/P(B)$ for any pair of events A and B such that $P(B) > 0$.

Proof. From axiom (3) we have

(2.4.1) $P(A \mid B) = P(A \cap B \mid B) + P(A \cap \bar{B} \mid B),$

where $\bar{B}$ denotes the complement of B. But from axioms (2) and (3) we can easily deduce that $P(C \mid B) = 0$ if $C \cap B = \varnothing$. Therefore we can eliminate the last term of (2.4.1) to obtain

(2.4.2) $\qquad P(A \mid B) = P(A \cap B \mid B).$

The theorem follows by putting $H = A \cap B$ and $G = B$ in axiom (4) and noting $P(B \mid B) = 1$ because of axiom (2). $\quad\square$

The reason axiom (1) was not used in the above proof is that axiom (1) follows from the other three axioms. Thus we have proved that (2), (3), and (4) imply Theorem 2.4.1. It is easy to show the converse. Therefore we may postulate either axioms (2), (3), and (4) or, more simply, Theorem 2.4.1 as the only axiom of conditional probability. Most textbooks adopt the latter approach.

If the conditioning event B consists of simple events with equal probability, Theorem 2.4.1 shows $P(A \mid B) = n(A \cap B)/n(B)$. Therefore, the counting techniques of Section 2.3 may be used to calculate a conditional probability in this case.

2.4.2 Bayes' Theorem

Bayes' theorem follows easily from the rules of probability but is listed separately here because of its special usefulness.

THEOREM 2.4.2 (Bayes) Let events $A_1, A_2, \ldots, A_n$ be mutually exclusive such that $P(A_1 \cup A_2 \cup \ldots \cup A_n) = 1$ and $P(A_i) > 0$ for each i. Let E be an arbitrary event such that $P(E) > 0$. Then

$$P(A_i \mid E) = \frac{P(E \mid A_i)P(A_i)}{\displaystyle\sum_{j=1}^{n} P(E \mid A_j)P(A_j)}, \qquad i = 1, 2, \ldots, n.$$

Proof. From Theorem 2.4.1, we have

(2.4.3) $\qquad P(A_i \mid E) = \frac{P(E \mid A_i)P(A_i)}{P(E)}.$

Since $E \cap A_1, E \cap A_2, \ldots, E \cap A_n$ are mutually exclusive and their union is equal to E, we have, from axiom (3) of probability,

(2.4.4) $P(E) = \sum_{j=1}^{n} P(E \cap A_j).$

Thus the theorem follows from (2.4.3) and (2.4.4) and by noting that $P(E \cap A_j) = P(E \mid A_j)P(A_j)$ by Theorem 2.4.1. ❏

2.4.3 Statistical Independence

We shall first define the concept of statistical (stochastic) independence for a pair of events. Henceforth it will be referred to simply as "independence."

DEFINITION 2.4.1 Events A and B are said to be *independent* if $P(A) = P(A \mid B)$.

The term "*independence*" has a clear intuitive meaning. It means that the probability of occurrence of A is not affected by whether or not B has occurred. Because of Theorem 2.4.1, the above equality is equivalent to $P(A)P(B) = P(A \cap B)$ or to $P(B) = P(B \mid A)$.

Since the outcome of the second toss of a coin can be reasonably assumed to be independent of the outcome of the first, the above formula enables us to calculate the probability of obtaining heads twice in a row when tossing a fair coin to be $\frac{1}{4}$.

Definition 2.4.1 needs to be generalized in order to define the mutual independence of three or more events. First we shall ask what we mean by the mutual independence of three events, A, B, and C. Clearly we mean *pairwise independence*, that is, independence in the sense of Definition 2.4.1 between any pair. But that is not enough. We do not want A and B put together to influence C, which may be stated as the independence between $A \cap B$ and C, that is, $P(A \cap B) = P(A \cap B \mid C)$. Thus we should have

$$P(A \cap B \cap C) = P[(A \cap B) \mid C]P(C) = P(A \cap B)P(C)$$

$$= P(A)P(B)P(C).$$

Note that independence between $A \cap C$ and B or between $B \cap C$ and A follows from the above. To summarize,

DEFINITION 2.4.2 Events A, B, and C are said to be *mutually independent* if the following equalities hold:

(2.4.5) $P(A \cap B) = P(A)P(B).$

(2.4.6) $P(A \cap C) = P(A)P(C).$

(2.4.7) $P(B \cap C) = P(B)P(C).$

(2.4.8) $P(A \cap B \cap C) = P(A)P(B)P(C).$

We can now recursively define mutual independence for any number of events:

DEFINITION 2.4.3 Events $A_1, A_2, \ldots, A_n$ are said to be mutually independent if any proper subset of the events are mutually independent and

$$P(A_1 \cap A_2 \cap \ldots \cap A_n) = P(A_1)P(A_2) \cdots P(A_n).$$

The following example shows that pairwise independence does not imply mutual independence. Let A be the event that a head appears in the first toss of a coin, let B be the event that a head appears in the second toss, and let C be the event that either both tosses yield heads or both tosses yield tails. Then A, B, and C are pairwise independent but not mutually independent, because $P(A \cap B \cap C) = P(A \cap B) = \frac{1}{4}$, whereas $P(A)P(B)P(C) = \frac{1}{8}$.

2.5 PROBABILITY CALCULATIONS

We have now studied all the rules of probability for discrete events: the axioms of probability and conditional probability and the definition of independence. The following are examples of calculating probabilities using these rules.

EXAMPLE 2.5.1 Using the axioms of conditional probability, we shall solve the same problem that appears in Example 2.3.4. In the present approach we recognize only two types of cards, aces and nonaces, without paying any attention to the other characteristics—suits or numbers. We shall first compute the probability that three aces turn up in a particular sequence: for example, suppose the first three cards are aces and the last two nonaces. Let A_i denote the event that the ith card is an ace and let N_i denote the event that the ith card is a nonace. Then, by the repeated application of Theorem 2.4.1, we have

(2.5.1) $P(A_1 \cap A_2 \cap A_3 \cap N_4 \cap N_5)$

$$= P(N_5 \mid A_1 \cap A_2 \cap A_3 \cap N_4) P(A_1 \cap A_2 \cap A_3 \cap N_4)$$

$$= P(N_5 \mid A_1 \cap A_2 \cap A_3 \cap N_4) P(N_4 \mid A_1 \cap A_2 \cap A_3)$$

$$\cdot P(A_1 \cap A_2 \cap A_3)$$

$$= \ldots$$

$$= P(A_1) P(A_2 \mid A_1) P(A_3 \mid A_1 \cap A_2) P(N_4 \mid A_1 \cap A_2 \cap A_3)$$

$$\cdot P(N_5 \mid A_1 \cap A_2 \cap A_3 \cap N_4)$$

$$= \frac{4}{52} \cdot \frac{3}{51} \cdot \frac{2}{50} \cdot \frac{48}{49} \cdot \frac{47}{48}.$$

There are C_3^5 ways in which three aces can appear in five cards, and each way has the same probability as (2.5.1). Therefore the answer to the problem is obtained by multiplying (2.5.1) by C_3^5.

EXAMPLE 2.5.2 Suppose that three events, A, B, and C, affect each other in the following way: $P(B \mid C) = \frac{1}{2}$, $P(B \mid \bar{C}) = \frac{1}{3}$, $P(A \mid B) = \frac{1}{2}$, $P(A \mid \bar{B}) = \frac{1}{3}$. Furthermore, assume that $P(A \mid B \cap C) = P(A \mid B)$ and that $P(A \mid \bar{B} \cap C) = P(A \mid \bar{B})$. (In other words, if B or $\bar{B}$ is known, C or $\bar{C}$ does not affect the probability of A.) Calculate $P(A \mid C)$ and $P(A \mid \bar{C})$.

Since $A = (A \cap B) \cup (A \cap \bar{B})$, we have by axiom (3) of conditional probability

(2.5.2) $P(A \mid C) = P(A \cap B \mid C) + P(A \cap \bar{B} \mid C)$.

By repeated application of Theorem 2.4.1, we have

(2.5.3) $P(A \cap B \mid C) = \dfrac{P(A \cap B \cap C)}{P(C)}$

$$= \frac{P(A \mid B \cap C) P(B \cap C)}{P(C)}$$

$$= P(A \mid B \cap C) P(B \mid C).$$

Therefore, by our assumptions,

(2.5.4) $P(A \cap B \mid C) = P(A \mid B) P(B \mid C) = \dfrac{1}{2} \cdot \dfrac{1}{2} = \dfrac{1}{4}.$

Similarly,

(2.5.5) $P(A \cap \bar{B} \mid C) = P(A \mid \bar{B})P(\bar{B} \mid C) = \dfrac{1}{3} \cdot \dfrac{1}{2} = \dfrac{1}{6}$.

Finally, from (2.5.2), (2.5.4), and (2.5.5) we obtain $P(A \mid C) = \frac{5}{12}$. Calculating $P(A \mid \bar{C})$ is left as a simple exercise.

EXAMPLE 2.5.3 Probability calculation may sometimes be counterintuitive. Suppose that there are four balls in a box with the numbers 1 through 4 written on them, and we pick two balls at random. What is the probability that 1 and 2 are drawn given that 1 or 2 is drawn? What is the probability that 1 and 2 are drawn given that 1 is drawn?

By Theorem 2.4.1 we have

(2.5.6) $P(1 \text{ and } 2 \mid 1 \text{ or } 2) = \dfrac{P[(1 \text{ and } 2) \cap (1 \text{ or } 2)]}{P(1 \text{ or } 2)}$

$= \dfrac{P(1 \text{ and } 2)}{P(1 \text{ or } 2)}$

$= \dfrac{1}{5}$.

Similarly,

(2.5.7) $P(1 \text{ and } 2 \mid 1) = \dfrac{P[(1 \text{ and } 2) \cap 1]}{P(1)}$

$= \dfrac{P(1 \text{ and } 2)}{P(1)}$

$= \dfrac{1}{3}$.

The result of Example 2.5.3 is somewhat counterintuitive: once we have learned that 1 or 2 has been drawn, learning further that 1 has been drawn does not seem to contain any more relevant information about the event that 1 and 2 are drawn. But it does. Figure 2.1 illustrates the relationship among the relevant events in this example.

EXAMPLE 2.5.4 There is an experiment for which there are three outcomes, A, B, and C, with respective probabilities p_A, p_B, and p_C. If we try

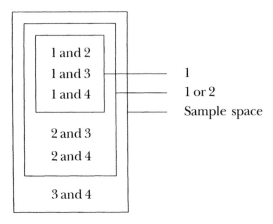

1 and 2
1 and 3 ———— 1
1 and 4 ———— 1 or 2
———— Sample space

2 and 3
2 and 4

3 and 4

FIGURE 2.1   Characterization of events

this experiment repeatedly, what is the probability that A occurs before B does? Assume $p_C \neq 0$.

We shall solve this problem by two methods.

(1)   Let A_i be the event that A happens in the ith trial, and define B_i and C_i similarly. Let P be the desired probability. Then we have

$$(2.5.8) \qquad P = P(A_1) + P(C_1 \cap A_2) + P(C_1 \cap C_2 \cap A_3) + \ldots$$

$$= P(A_1) + P(C_1)P(A_2) + P(C_1)P(C_2)P(A_3) + \ldots$$

$$= p_A + p_C p_A + p_C^2 p_A + \ldots$$

$$= \frac{p_A}{1 - p_c}.$$

(2)   We claim that the desired probability is essentially the same thing as the conditional probability of A given that A or B has occurred. Thus

$$(2.5.9) \qquad P = \frac{p_A}{p_A + p_B},$$

which gives the same answer as the first method. The second method is an intuitive approach, which in this case has turned out to be correct, substantiated by the result of the rigorous first approach.

EXAMPLE 2.5.5   This is an application of Bayes' theorem. Suppose that a cancer diagnostic test is 95% accurate both on those who do have cancer and on those who do not have cancer. Assuming that 0.005 of the population actually has cancer, compute the probability that a particular individual has cancer, given that the test says he has cancer.

Let C indicate the event that this individual actually has cancer and let T be the event that the test shows he has cancer. Then we have by Theorem 2.4.2 (Bayes)

$$(2.5.10) \qquad P(C \mid T) = \frac{P(T \mid C)P(C)}{P(T \mid C)P(C) + P(T \mid \bar{C})P(\bar{C})}$$

$$= \frac{0.95 \cdot 0.005}{0.95 \cdot 0.005 + 0.05 \cdot 0.995}$$

$$= \frac{475}{5450}$$

$$\cong 0.087.$$

EXERCISES

1. (Section 2.2)
   Prove
   (a) $A \cap (B \cup C) = (A \cap B) \cup (A \cap C)$.
   (b) $A \cup (B \cap C) = (A \cup B) \cap (A \cup C)$.
   (c) $(A - C) \cap (B - C) = (A \cap B) - C$.

2. (Section 2.3.1)
   Complete Example 2.3.2.

3. (Section 2.4.1)
   Show that Theorem 2.4.1 implies (2), (3), and (4) of the axioms of conditional probability.

4. (Section 2.4.2)
   Suppose that the Stanford faculty consists of 40 percent Democrats and 60 percent Republicans. If 10 percent of the Democrats and 70 percent of the Republicans vote for Bush, what is the probability that a Stanford faculty member who voted for Bush is a Republican?

5. (Section 2.4.3)
   Fill each of the seven disjoint regions described in the figure below

by an integer representing the number of simple events with equal probabilities in such a way that

(a) (2.4.8) is satisfied but (2.4.5), (2.4.6), and (2.4.7) are not.

(b) (2.4.5), (2.4.6), and (2.4.7) are satisfied but (2.4.8) is not.

(c) (2.4.5), (2.4.6), (2.4.7), and (2.4.8) are all satisfied.

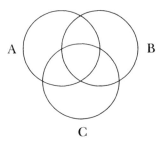

6. (Section 2.5)

Calculate $P(A \mid \bar{C})$ in Example 2.5.2.

7. (Section 2.5)

If the probability of winning a point is p, what is the probability of winning a tennis game under the "no-ad" scoring? (The first player who wins four points wins the game.)

8. (Section 2.5)

Compute the probability of obtaining four of a kind when five dice are rolled.

9. (Section 2.5)

If the probability of being admitted into a graduate school is $1/n$ and you apply to n schools, what is the probability that you will be admitted into at least one school? Find the limit of this probability as n goes to infinity.

10. (Section 2.5)

A die is rolled successively until the ace turns up. How many rolls are necessary before the probability is at least 0.5 that the ace will turn up at least once?

3 RANDOM VARIABLES AND PROBABILITY DISTRIBUTIONS

3.1 DEFINITIONS OF A RANDOM VARIABLE

We have already loosely defined the term *random variable* in Section 1.2 as a random mechanism whose outcomes are real numbers. We have mentioned *discrete* and *continuous* random variables: the discrete random variable takes a countable number of real numbers with preassigned probabilities, and the continuous random variable takes a continuum of values in the real line according to the rule determined by a density function. Later in this chapter we shall also mention a random variable that is a mixture of these two types. In general, we can simply state

DEFINITION 3.1.1 A *random variable* is a variable that takes values according to a certain probability distribution.

When we speak of a "variable," we think of all the possible values it can take; when we speak of a "random variable," we think in addition of the probability distribution according to which it takes all possible values. The customary textbook definition of a random variable is as follows:

DEFINITION 3.1.2 A *random variable* is a real-valued function defined over a sample space.

Defining a random variable as a function has a certain advantage which becomes apparent at a more advanced stage of probability theory. At our level of study, Definition 3.1.1 is just as good. Note that the idea of a probability distribution is firmly embedded in Definition 3.1.2 as well, for a sample space always has a probability function associated with it and this determines the probability distribution of a particular random variable. In the next section, we shall illustrate how a probability function defined over the events in a sample space determines the probability distribution of a random variable.

3.2 DISCRETE RANDOM VARIABLES

3.2.1 Univariate Random Variables

The following are examples of several random variables defined over a given sample space.

EXAMPLE 3.2.1 Experiment: A throw of a fair die.

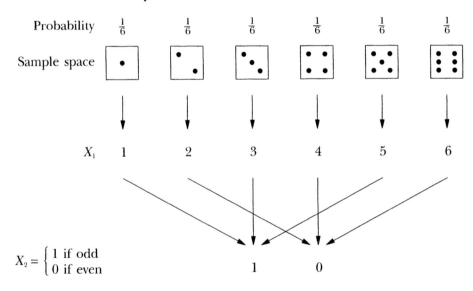

Note that X_1 can hardly be distinguished from the sample space itself. It indicates the little difference there is between Definition 3.1.1 and Definition 3.1.2. The arrows indicate mappings from the sample space to the random variables. Note that the probability distribution of X_2 can be derived from the sample space: $P(X_2 = 1) = \frac{1}{2}$ and $P(X_2 = 0) = \frac{1}{2}$.

EXAMPLE 3.2.2   Experiment: Tossing a fair coin twice.

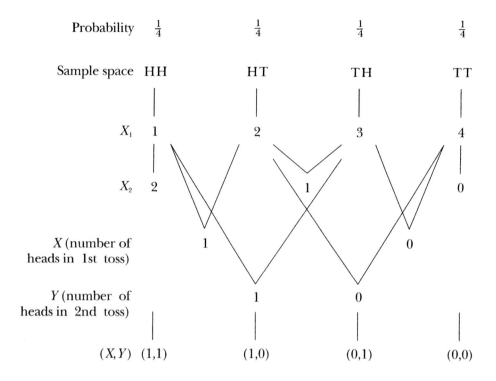

In almost all our problems involving random variables, we can forget about the original sample space and pay attention only to what values a random variable takes with what probabilities. We specialize Definition 3.1.1 to the case of a discrete random variable as follows:

DEFINITION 3.2.1   A *discrete random variable* is a variable that takes a countable number of real numbers with certain probabilities.

The probability distribution of a discrete random variable is completely characterized by the equation $P(X = x_i) = p_i$, $i = 1, 2, \ldots, n$. It means the random variable X takes value x_i with probability p_i. We must, of course, have $\Sigma_{i=1}^{n} p_i = 1$; n may be ∞ in some cases. It is customary to denote a random variable by a capital letter and the values it takes by lowercase letters.

3.2.2 Bivariate Random Variables

The last row in Example 3.2.2 shows the values taken jointly by two random variables X and Y. Since a quantity such as $(1, 1)$ is not a real number, we do not have a random variable here as defined in Definition 3.2.1. But it is convenient to have a name for a pair of random variables put together. Thus we have

DEFINITION 3.2.2 A *bivariate discrete random variable* is a variable that takes a countable number of points on the plane with certain probabilities.

The probability distribution of a bivariate random variable is determined by the equations $P(X = x_i, Y = y_j) = p_{ij}, i = 1, 2, \ldots, n, j = 1, 2, \ldots, m$. We call p_{ij} the joint probability; again, n and/or m may be ∞ in some cases.

When we have a bivariate random variable in mind, the probability distribution of one of the univariate random variables is given a special name: *marginal probability distribution*. Because of probability axiom (3) of Section 2.2, the marginal probability is related to the joint probabilities by the following relationship.

Marginal probability

$$P(X = x_i) = \sum_{j=1}^{m} P(X = x_i, Y = y_j), \quad i = 1, 2, \ldots, n.$$

Using Theorem 2.4.1, we can define

Conditional probability

$$P(X = x_i \mid Y = y_j) = \frac{P(X = x_i, Y = y_j)}{P(Y = y_j)} \quad \text{if } P(Y = y_j) > 0.$$

In Definition 2.4.1 we defined independence between a pair of events. Here we shall define independence between a pair of two discrete random variables.

DEFINITION 3.2.3 Discrete random variables are said to be independent if the event $(X = x_i)$ and the event $(Y = y_j)$ are independent for all i, j. That is to say, $P(X = x_i, Y = y_j) = P(X = x_i)P(Y = y_j)$ for all i, j.

TABLE 3.1   Probability distribution of a bivariate random variable

X \ Y	y_1	y_2	$\cdots$	y_m	
x_1	p_{11}	p_{12}		p_{1m}	p_{1o}
x_2	p_{21}	p_{22}		p_{2m}	p_{2o}
.					
.					
.					
x_n	p_{n1}	p_{n2}		p_{nm}	p_{no}
	p_{o1}	p_{o2}		p_{om}	

It is instructive to represent the probability distribution of a bivariate random variable in an $n \times m$ table. See Table 3.1. Affixed to the end of Table 3.1 are a column and a row representing marginal probabilities calculated by the rules $p_{io} = \Sigma_{j=1}^{m} p_{ij}$ and $p_{oj} = \Sigma_{i=1}^{n} p_{ij}$. (The word marginal comes from the positions of the marginal probabilities in the table.) By looking at the table we can quickly determine whether X and Y are independent or not according to the following theorem.

THEOREM 3.2.1   Discrete random variables X and Y with the probability distribution given in Table 3.1 are independent if and only if every row is proportional to any other row, or, equivalently, every column is proportional to any other column.

Proof. ("only if" part). Consider, for example, the first two rows. We have

$$(3.2.1) \quad \frac{p_{1j}}{p_{2j}} = \frac{P(x_1 \mid y_j)P(y_j)}{P(x_2 \mid y_j)P(y_j)} = \frac{P(x_1 \mid y_j)}{P(x_2 \mid y_j)} \quad \text{for every } j.$$

If X and Y are independent, we have by Definition 3.2.3

$$(3.2.2) \quad \frac{P(x_1 \mid y_j)}{P(x_2 \mid y_j)} = \frac{P(x_1)}{P(x_2)},$$

which does not depend on j. Therefore, the first two rows are proportional to each other. The same argument holds for any pair of rows and any pair of columns.

("if" part). Suppose all the rows are proportional to each other. Then from (3.2.1) we have

(3.2.3) $P(x_i \mid y_j) = c_{ik} \cdot P(x_k \mid y_j)$ for every i, k, and j.

Multiply both sides of (3.2.3) by $P(y_j)$ and sum over j to get

(3.2.4) $P(x_i) = c_{ik} \cdot P(x_k)$ for every i and k.

From (3.2.3) and (3.2.4) we have

(3.2.5) $\dfrac{P(x_i \mid y_j)}{P(x_i)} = \dfrac{P(x_k \mid y_j)}{P(x_k)}$ for every i, j, and k.

Therefore

(3.2.6) $P(x_i \mid y_j) = c_j \cdot P(x_i)$ for every i and j.

Summing both sides over i, we determine c_j to be unity for every j. Therefore X and Y are independent. ❑

We shall give two examples of nonindependent random variables.

EXAMPLE 3.2.3 Let the joint probability distribution of X and Y be given by

Y			
X	1	0	
1	$\frac{2}{8}$	$\frac{1}{8}$	$\frac{3}{8}$
0	$\frac{2}{8}$	$\frac{3}{8}$	$\frac{5}{8}$
	$\frac{4}{8}$	$\frac{4}{8}$	

Then we have $P(Y = 1 \mid X = 1) = (\frac{2}{8})/(\frac{3}{8}) = \frac{2}{3}$ and $P(Y = 1 \mid X = 0) = (\frac{2}{8})/(\frac{5}{8}) = \frac{2}{5}$, which shows that X and Y are not independent.

EXAMPLE 3.2.4 Random variables X and Y defined below are not independent, but X^2 and Y^2 are independent.

$P(X = 1) = p$, $0 < p < 1$

$P(X = 0) = 1 - p$

$P(Y = 1 \mid X = 1) = \frac{1}{2}$

$P(Y = 0 \mid X = 1) = \frac{1}{4}$

$$P(Y = -1 \mid X = 1) = \frac{1}{4}$$

$$P(Y = 1 \mid X = 0) = \frac{1}{4}$$

$$P(Y = 0 \mid X = 0) = \frac{1}{4}$$

$$P(Y = -1 \mid X = 0) = \frac{1}{2}.$$

Note that this example does not contradict Theorem 3.5.1. The word *function* implies that each value of the domain is mapped to a *unique* value of the range, and therefore X cannot be regarded as a function of X^2.

3.2.3 Multivariate Random Variables

We can generalize Definition 3.2.2 as follows.

DEFINITION 3.2.4 A T-variate discrete random variable is a variable that takes a countable number of points on the T-dimensional Euclidean space with certain probabilities.

The probability distribution of a trivariate random variable is determined by the equations $P(X = x_i, Y = y_j, Z = z_k) = p_{ijk}$, $i = 1, 2, \ldots, n$, $j = 1, 2, \ldots, m$, $k = 1, 2, \ldots, q$. As in Section 3.2.2, we can define

Marginal probability

$$P(X = x_i) = \sum_{j=1}^{m} \sum_{k=1}^{q} P(X = x_i, Y = y_j, Z = z_k), \qquad i = 1, 2, \ldots, n.$$

Conditional probability

$$P(X = x_i, Y = y_j \mid Z = z_k) = \frac{P(X = x_i, Y = y_j, Z = z_k)}{P(Z = z_k)}$$

$$\text{if } P(Z = z_k) > 0$$

$$P(X = x_i \mid Y = y_j, Z = z_k) = \frac{P(X = x_i, Y = y_j, Z = z_k)}{P(Y = y_j, Z = z_k)}$$

$$\text{if } P(Y = y_j, Z = z_k) > 0.$$

Definition 3.2.5 generalizes Definition 3.2.3.

DEFINITION 3.2.5 A finite set of discrete random variables $X, Y, Z, \ldots$ are mutually independent if

$$P(X = x_i, Y = y_j, Z = z_k, \ldots)$$
$$= P(X = x_i)P(Y = y_j)P(Z = z_k) \ldots \quad \text{for all } i, j, k, \ldots.$$

It is important to note that pairwise independence does not imply mutual independence, as illustrated by Example 3.2.5.

EXAMPLE 3.2.5 Suppose X and Y are independent random variables which each take values 1 or -1 with probability 0.5 and define $Z = XY$. Then Z is independent of either X or Y, but $X, Y,$ and Z are not mutually independent because

$$P(X = 1, Y = 1, Z = 1) = P(Z = 1 \mid X = 1, Y = 1)P(X = 1, Y = 1)$$
$$= P(X = 1, Y = 1) = \tfrac{1}{4},$$

whereas

$$P(X = 1)P(Y = 1)P(Z = 1) = \tfrac{1}{8}.$$

An example of mutually independent random variables follows.

EXAMPLE 3.2.6 Let the sample space S be the set of eight integers 1 through 8 with the equal probability of $\frac{1}{8}$ assigned to each of the eight integers. Find three random variables (real-valued functions) defined over S which are mutually independent.

There are many possible answers, but we can, for example, define

$$\begin{aligned} X &= 1 \quad \text{for } i \le 4, \\ &= 0 \quad \text{otherwise.} \end{aligned}$$

$$\begin{aligned} Y &= 1 \quad \text{for } 3 \le i \le 6, \\ &= 0 \quad \text{otherwise.} \end{aligned}$$

$$\begin{aligned} Z &= 1 \quad \text{for } i \text{ even,} \\ &= 0 \quad \text{otherwise.} \end{aligned}$$

Then $X, Y,$ and Z are mutually independent because

$$P(X = 1, Y = 1, Z = 1) = P(i = 4) = \tfrac{1}{8}$$
$$= P(X = 1)P(Y = 1)P(Z = 1),$$

$$P(X = 1, Y = 1, Z = 0) = P(i = 3) = \frac{1}{8}$$
$$= P(X = 1)P(Y = 1)P(Z = 0),$$

and so on for all eight possible outcomes.

3.3 UNIVARIATE CONTINUOUS RANDOM VARIABLES

3.3.1 Density Function

In Chapter 2 we briefly discussed a continuous sample space. Following Definition 3.1.2, we define a continuous random variable as a real-valued function defined over a continuous sample space. Or we can define it in a way analogous to Definition 3.2.1: A continuous random variable is a variable that takes a continuum of values in the real line according to the rule determined by a density function. We need to make this definition more precise, however. The following defines a continuous random variable and a density at the same time.

DEFINITION 3.3.1 If there is a nonnegative function $f(x)$ defined over the whole line such that

(3.3.1) $\qquad P(x_1 \leq X \leq x_2) = \int_{x_1}^{x_2} f(x)dx$

for any x_1, x_2 satisfying $x_1 \leq x_2$, then X is a continuous random variable and $f(x)$ is called its *density function*.

We assume that the reader is familiar with the *Riemann integral*. For a precise definition, see, for example, Apostol (1974). For our discussion it is sufficient for the reader to regard the right-hand side of (3.3.1) simply as the area under $f(x)$ over the interval $[x_1, x_2]$.

We shall allow $x_1 = -\infty$ and/or $x_2 = \infty$. Then, by axiom (2) of probability, we must have $\int_{-\infty}^{\infty} f(x)dx = 1$. It follows from Definition 3.3.1 that the probability that a continuous random variable takes any single value is zero, and therefore it does not matter whether $<$ or $\leq$ is used within the probability bracket. In most practical applications, $f(x)$ will be continuous except possibly for a finite number of discontinuities. For such a function the Riemann integral on the right-hand side of (3.3.1) exists, and therefore $f(x)$ can be a density function.

3.3.2 Conditional Density Function

Suppose that a random variable X has density $f(x)$ and that $[a, b]$ is a certain closed interval such that $P(a \leq X \leq b) > 0$. Then, for any closed interval $[x_1, x_2]$ contained in $[a, b]$, we have from Theorem 2.4.1

$$(3.3.2) \qquad P(x_1 \leq X \leq x_2 \mid a \leq X \leq b) = \frac{P(x_1 \leq X \leq x_2)}{P(a \leq X \leq b)}.$$

Now we want to ask the question: Is there a function such that its integral over $[x_1, x_2]$ is equal to the conditional probability given in (3.3.2)? The answer is yes, and the details are provided by Definition 3.3.2.

DEFINITION 3.3.2 Let X have density $f(x)$. The *conditional density* of X given $a \leq X \leq b$, denoted by $f(x \mid a \leq X \leq b)$, is defined by

$$(3.3.3) \qquad f(x \mid a \leq X \leq b) = \frac{f(x)}{\displaystyle\int_a^b f(x)dx} \qquad \text{for } a \leq x \leq b,$$

$$= 0 \qquad \text{otherwise,}$$

provided that $\int_a^b f(x)dx \neq 0$.

We can easily verify that $f(x \mid a \leq X \leq b)$ defined above satisfies

$$(3.3.4) \qquad P(x_1 \leq X \leq x_2 \mid a \leq X \leq b) = \int_{x_1}^{x_2} f(x \mid a \leq X \leq b)dx$$

whenever $[a, b] \supset [x_1, x_2]$, as desired. From the above result it is not difficult to understand the following generalization of Definition 3.3.2.

DEFINITION 3.3.3 Let X have the density $f(x)$ and let S be a subset of the real line such that $P(X \in S) > 0$. Then the conditional density of X given $X \in S$, denoted by $f(x \mid S)$, is defined by

$$(3.3.5) \qquad f(x \mid S) = \frac{f(x)}{P(X \in S)} \qquad \text{for } x \in S,$$

$$= 0 \qquad \text{otherwise.}$$

3.4 BIVARIATE CONTINUOUS RANDOM VARIABLES

3.4.1 Bivariate Density Function

We may loosely say that the bivariate continuous random variable is a variable that takes a continuum of values on the plane according to the rule determined by a joint density function defined over the plane. The rule is that the probability that a bivariate random variable falls into any region on the plane is equal to the volume of the space under the density function over that region. We shall give a more precise definition similar to Definition 3.3.1, which was given for a univariate continuous random variable.

DEFINITION 3.4.1   If there is a nonnegative function $f(x, y)$ defined over the whole plane such that

$$(3.4.1) \qquad P(x_1 \leq X \leq x_2, y_2 \leq Y \leq y_2) = \int_{y_1}^{y_2} \int_{x_1}^{x_2} f(x, y) dx dy$$

for any x_1, x_2, y_1, y_2 satisfying $x_1 \leq x_2, y_1 \leq y_2$, then (X, Y) is a *bivariate continuous random variable* and $f(x, y)$ is called the *joint density function*.

In order for a function $f(x, y)$ to be a joint density function, it must be nonnegative and the total volume under it must be equal to 1 because of the probability axioms. The second condition may be mathematically expressed as

$$(3.4.2) \qquad \int_{-\infty}^{\infty} \int_{-\infty}^{\infty} f(x, y) dx dy = 1.$$

If $f(x, y)$ is continuous except possibly over a finite number of smooth curves on the plane, in addition to satisfying the above two conditions, it will satisfy (3.4.1) and hence qualify as a joint density function. For such a function we may change the order of integration so that we have

$$(3.4.3) \qquad \int_{y_1}^{y_2} \int_{x_1}^{x_2} f(x, y) dx dy = \int_{x_1}^{x_2} \int_{y_1}^{y_2} f(x, y) dy dx .$$

We shall give a few examples concerning the joint density and the evaluation of the joint probability of the form given in (3.4.1).

EXAMPLE 3.4.1 If $f(x, y) = xye^{-(x+y)}$, $x > 0$, $y > 0$, and 0 otherwise, what is $P(X > 1, Y < 1)$?

By (3.4.1) we have

(3.4.4) $P(X > 1, Y < 1) = \int_0^1 \int_1^\infty xye^{-(x+y)} dxdy$

$$= \int_1^\infty xe^{-x} dx \cdot \int_0^1 ye^{-y} dy.$$

To evaluate each of the single integrals that appear in (3.4.4), we need the following formula for *integration by parts:*

(3.4.5) $\int_a^b \dfrac{dU}{dx} V dx = U(b)V(b) - U(a)V(a) - \int_a^b U \dfrac{dV}{dx} dx,$

where U and V are functions of x. Putting $U = -e^{-x}$, $V = x$, $a = 1$, and $b = \infty$ in (3.4.5), we have

(3.4.6) $\int_1^\infty xe^{-x} dx = [-xe^{-x}]_1^\infty + \int_1^\infty e^{-x} dx = e^{-1} + [-e^{-x}]_1^\infty = 2e^{-1}.$

Putting $U = -e^{-y}$, $V = y$, $a = 0$, and $b = 1$ in (3.4.5) we have

(3.4.7) $\int_0^1 ye^{-y} dy = [-ye^{-y}]_0^1 + \int_0^1 e^{-y} dy = -e^{-1} + [-e^{-y}]_0^1 = 1 - 2e^{-1}.$

Therefore from (3.4.4), (3.4.6), and (3.4.7) we obtain

(3.4.8) $P(X > 1, Y < 1) = 2e^{-1}(1 - 2e^{-1}).$

If a function $f(x, y)$ is a joint density function of a bivariate random variable (X, Y), the probability that (X, Y) falls into a more general region (for example, the inside of a circle) can be also evaluated as a double integral of $f(x, y)$. We write this statement mathematically as

(3.4.9) $P[(X, Y) \in S] = \iint_S f(x, y)dxdy,$

where S is a subset of the plane. The double integral on the right-hand side of (3.4.9) may be intuitively interpreted as the volume of the space under $f(x, y)$ over S. If $f(x, y)$ is a simple function, this intuitive interpretation will enable us to calculate the double integral without actually

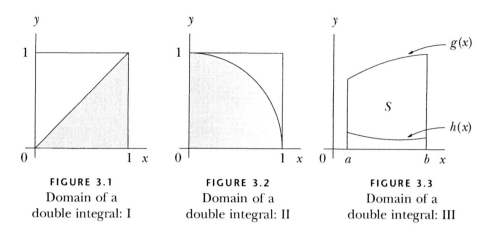

FIGURE 3.1
Domain of a
double integral: I

FIGURE 3.2
Domain of a
double integral: II

FIGURE 3.3
Domain of a
double integral: III

performing the mathematical operation of integration, as in the following example.

EXAMPLE 3.4.2 Assuming $f(x, y) = 1$ for $0 < x < 1$, $0 < y < 1$ and $= 0$ otherwise, calculate $P(X > Y)$ and $P(X^2 + Y^2 < 1)$.

The event $(X > Y)$ means that (X, Y) falls into the shaded triangle in Figure 3.1. Since $P(X > Y)$ is the volume under the density over the triangle, it must equal the area of the triangle times the height of the density, which is 1. Therefore, $P(X > Y) = \frac{1}{2}$. The event $(X^2 + Y^2 < 1)$ means that (X, Y) falls into the shaded quarter of the unit circle in Figure 3.2. Therefore, $P(X^2 + Y^2 < 1) = \pi/4$. Note that the square in each figure indicates the total range of (X, Y).

This geometric approach of evaluating the double integral (3.4.9) may not work if $f(x, y)$ is a complicated function. We shall show the algebraic approach to evaluating the double integral (3.4.9), which will have a much more general usage than the geometric approach. We shall consider only the case where S is a region surrounded by two vertical line segments and two functions of x on the (x, y) plane, as shown in Figure 3.3.

A region surrounded by two horizontal line segments and two functions of y may be similarly treated. Once we know how to evaluate the double integral over such a region, we can treat any general region of practical interest since it can be expressed as a union of such regions.

Let S be as in Figure 3.3. Then we have

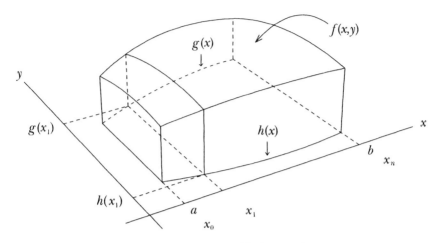

FIGURE 3.4   Double integral

(3.4.10) $\iint_S f(x, y)dxdy = \int_a^b \left[\int_{h(x)}^{g(x)} f(x, y)dy \right] dx.$

We shall show graphically why the right-hand side of (3.4.10) indeed gives the volume under $f(x, y)$ over S. In Figure 3.4 the volume to be evaluated is drawn as a loaf-like figure.

The first slice of the loaf is also described in the figure. We have approximately

(3.4.11)   Volume of the ith slice $\cong \int_{h(x_i)}^{g(x_i)} f(x_i, y)dy \cdot (x_i - x_{i-1}),$

$$i = 1, 2, \ldots, n.$$

Summing both sides of (3.4.11) over i, we get

(3.4.12)   Volume $\cong \sum_{i=1}^{n} \int_{h(x_i)}^{g(x_i)} f(x_i, y)dy \cdot (x_i - x_{i-1}).$

But the limit of the right-hand side of (3.4.12) as n goes to ∞ is clearly equal to the right-hand side of (3.4.10).

The following examples use (3.4.10) to evaluate the joint probability.

EXAMPLE 3.4.3 We shall calculate the two probabilities asked for in Example 3.4.2 using formula (3.4.10). Note that the shaded regions in

Figures 3.1 and 3.2 are special cases of region S depicted in Figure 3.3. To evaluate $P(X > Y)$, we put $f(x, y) = 1$, $a = 0$, $b = 1$, $g(x) = x$, and $h(x) = 0$ in (3.4.10) so that we have

$$(3.4.13) \qquad P(X > Y) = \int_0^1 \left(\int_0^x dy \right) dx = \int_0^1 x \, dx = \frac{1}{2}.$$

To evaluate $P(X^2 + Y^2 < 1)$, we put $f(x, y) = 1$, $a = 0$, $b = 1$, $g(x) = \sqrt{1 - x^2}$, and $h(x) = 0$ so that we have

$$(3.4.14) \qquad P(X^2 + Y^2 < 1) = \int_0^1 \left(\int_0^{\sqrt{1-x^2}} dy \right) dx = \int_0^1 \sqrt{1 - x^2} \, dx.$$

To evaluate the last integral above, we need the following formula for *integration by change of variables:*

$$(3.4.15) \qquad \int_{x_1}^{x_2} f(x) dx = \int_{t_1}^{t_2} f[\phi(t)] \phi'(t) dt,$$

if ϕ is a monotonic function such that $\phi(t_1) = x_1$ and $\phi(t_2) = x_2$. Here, $\phi'(t)$ denotes the derivative of ϕ with respect to t. Next, we shall put $x = \cos \theta$. Then, since $dx/d\theta = -\sin \theta$ and $\sin^2\theta + \cos^2\theta = 1$, we have

$$(3.4.16) \qquad \int_0^1 \sqrt{1 - x^2} \, dx = \int_0^{\pi/2} \sin^2\theta \, d\theta = \left[-\frac{1}{2} \sin \theta \cos \theta + \frac{1}{2} \theta \right]_0^{\pi/2} = \frac{\pi}{4}.$$

EXAMPLE 3.4.4 Suppose $f(x, y) = 24 xy$ for $0 < x < 1$, $0 < y < 1 - x$ and $= 0$ otherwise. Calculate $P(Y < \frac{1}{2})$.

Event $(Y < \frac{1}{2})$ means that (X, Y) falls into the shaded region of Figure 3.5. In order to apply (3.4.10) to this problem, we must reverse the role of x and y and put $a = 0$, $b = \frac{1}{2}$, $g(y) = 1 - y$, $h(y) = 0$ in (3.4.10) so that we have

$$(3.4.17) \qquad P\left(Y < \frac{1}{2}\right) = 24 \int_0^{1/2} y \left(\int_0^{1-y} x \, dx \right) dy = 12 \int_0^{1/2} y (1 - y)^2 dy = \frac{11}{16}.$$

3.4.2 Marginal Density

When we are considering a bivariate random variable (X, Y), the probability pertaining to one of the variables, such as $P(x_1 \leq X \leq x_2)$ or $P(y_1 \leq Y \leq y_2)$, is called the *marginal probability*. The following relationship between a marginal probability and a joint probability is obviously true.

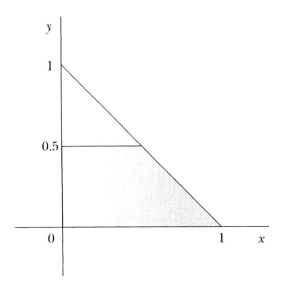

FIGURE 3.5   Domain of a double integral for Example 3.4.4

(3.4.18) $P(x_1 \leq X \leq x_2) = P(x_1 \leq X \leq x_2, -\infty < Y < \infty).$

More generally, one may replace $x_1 \leq X \leq x_2$ in both sides of (3.4.18) by $x \in S$ where S is an arbitrary subset of the real line.

Similarly, when we are considering a bivariate random variable (X, Y), the density function of one of the variables is called the *marginal density*. Theorem 3.4.1 shows how a marginal density is related to a joint density.

THEOREM 3.4.1   Let $f(x, y)$ be the joint density of X and Y and let $f(x)$ be the marginal density of X. Then

(3.4.19) $f(x) = \displaystyle\int_{-\infty}^{\infty} f(x, y)dy.$

Proof. We only need to show that the right-hand side of (3.4.19) satisfies equation (3.3.1). We have

(3.4.20) $\displaystyle\int_{x_1}^{x_2} \left[\int_{-\infty}^{\infty} f(x, y)dy \right] dx = P(x_1 \leq X \leq x_2, -\infty < Y < \infty)$ by (3.4.1)

$= P(x_1 \leq X \leq x_2)$ by (3.4.18).   ◻

3.4.3 Conditional Density

We shall extend the notion of conditional density in Definitions 3.3.2 and 3.3.3 to the case of bivariate random variables. We shall consider first the situation where the conditioning event has a positive probability and second the situation where the conditioning event has zero probability. Under the first situation we shall define both the joint conditional density and the conditional density involving only one of the variables. A generalization of Definition 3.3.3 is straightforward:

DEFINITION 3.4.2 Let (X, Y) have the joint density $f(x, y)$ and let S be a subset of the plane such that $P[(X, Y) \in S] > 0$. Then the *conditional density* of (X, Y) given $(X, Y) \in S$, denoted by $f(x, y \mid S)$, is defined by

$$(3.4.21) \quad f(x, y \mid S) = \frac{f(x, y)}{P[(X, Y) \in S]} \quad \text{for } (x, y) \in S,$$

$$= 0 \qquad \text{otherwise.}$$

We are also interested in defining the conditional density for one of the variables above, say, X, given a conditioning event involving both X and Y. Formally, it can be obtained by integrating $f(x, y \mid S)$ with respect to y. We shall explicitly define it for the case that S has the form of Figure 3.3.

DEFINITION 3.4.3 Let (X, Y) have the joint density $f(x, y)$ and let S be a subset of the plane which has a shape as in Figure 3.3. We assume that $P[(X, Y) \in S] > 0$. Then the conditional density of X given $(X, Y) \in S$, denoted by $f(x \mid S)$, is defined by

$$(3.4.22) \quad f(x \mid S) = \frac{\int_{h(x)}^{g(x)} f(x, y) dy}{P[(X, Y) \in S]} \quad \text{for } a \leq x \leq b,$$

$$= 0 \qquad \text{otherwise.}$$

For an application of this definition, see Example 3.4.8.

It may be instructive to write down the formula (3.4.22) explicitly for a simple case where $a = -\infty$, $b = \infty$, $h(x) = y_1$, and $g(x) = y_2$ in Figure 3.3. Since in this case the subset S can be characterized as $y_1 \leq Y \leq y_2$, we have

$$(3.4.23) \qquad f(x \mid y_1 \leq Y \leq y_2) = \frac{\displaystyle\int_{y_1}^{y_2} f(x, y)dy}{\displaystyle\int_{-\infty}^{\infty}\int_{y_1}^{y_2} f(x, y)dy dx}.$$

The reasonableness of Definition 3.4.3 can be verified by noting that when (3.4.23) is integrated over an arbitrary interval $[x_1, x_2]$, it yields the conditional probability $P(x_1 \leq X \leq x_2 \mid y_1 \leq Y \leq y_2)$.

Next we shall seek to define the conditional probability when the conditioning event has zero probability. We shall confine our attention to the case where the conditioning event S represents a line on the (x, y) plane: that is to say, $S = \{(x, y) \mid y = y_1 + cx\}$, where y_1 and c are arbitrary constants.

We begin with the definition of the conditional probability $P(x_1 \leq X \leq x_2 \mid Y = y_1 + cX)$ and then seek to obtain the function of x that yields this probability when it is integrated over the interval $[x_1, x_2]$. Note that this conditional probability cannot be subjected to Theorem 2.4.1, since $P(Y = y_1 + cX) = 0$.

DEFINITION 3.4.4 The conditional probability that X falls into $[x_1, x_2]$ given $Y = y_1 + cX$ is defined by

$$(3.4.24) \qquad P(x_1 \leq X \leq x_2 \mid Y = y_1 + cX)$$

$$= \lim_{y_2 \to y_1} P(x_1 \leq X \leq x_2 \mid y_1 + cX \leq Y \leq y_2 + cX),$$

where $y_1 < y_2$.

Next we have

DEFINITION 3.4.5 The conditional density of X given $Y = y_1 + cX$, denoted by $f(x \mid Y = y_1 + cX)$, if it exists, is defined to be a function that satisfies

$$(3.4.25) \qquad P(x_1 \leq X \leq x_2 \mid Y = y_1 + cX) = \int_{x_1}^{x_2} f(x \mid Y = y_1 + cX)dx,$$

for all x_1, x_2 satisfying $x_1 \leq x_2$.

Now we can prove

THEOREM 3.4.2 The conditional density $f(x \mid Y = y_1 + cX)$ exists and is given by

(3.4.26) $\qquad f(x \mid Y = y_1 + cX) = \dfrac{f(x, y_1 + cx)}{\displaystyle\int_{-\infty}^{\infty} f(x, y_1 + cx)dx}$,

provided the denominator is positive.

Proof. We have

(3.4.27) $\qquad \displaystyle\lim_{y_2 \to y_1} P(x_1 \le X \le x_2 \mid y_1 + cX \le Y \le y_2 + cX)$

$$= \lim_{y_2 \to y_1} \frac{\displaystyle\int_{x_1}^{x_2}\int_{y_1+cx}^{y_2+cx} f(x, y)dy\,dx}{\displaystyle\int_{-\infty}^{\infty}\int_{y_1+cx}^{y_2+cx} f(x, y)dy\,dx} \quad \text{by Theorem 2.4.1}$$

$$= \frac{\displaystyle\int_{x_1}^{x_2} f(x, y_1 + cx)dx}{\displaystyle\int_{-\infty}^{\infty} f(x, y_1 + cx)dx} \quad \text{by the mean value theorem of integration.}$$

Therefore the theorem follows from (3.4.24), (3.4.25), and (3.4.27). ❑

For an application of Theorem 3.4.2, see Example 3.4.9. An alternative way to derive the conditional density (3.4.26) is as follows. By putting $a = -\infty$, $b = \infty$, $h(x) = y_1 + cx$, and $g(x) = y_2 + cx$ in Figure 3.3, we have from (3.4.22)

(3.4.28) $\qquad f(x \mid y_1 + cX \le Y \le y_2 + cX) = \dfrac{\displaystyle\int_{y_1+cx}^{y_2+cx} f(x, y)dy}{\displaystyle\int_{-\infty}^{\infty}\int_{y_1+cx}^{y_2+cx} f(x, y)dy\,dx}$.

Then the formula (3.4.26) can be obtained by defining

(3.4.29) $\qquad f(x \mid Y = y_1 + cX) = \displaystyle\lim_{y_2 \to y_1} f(x \mid y_1 + cX \le Y \le y_2 + cX)$.

A special case of Theorem 3.4.2 where $c = 0$ is important enough to write as a separate theorem:

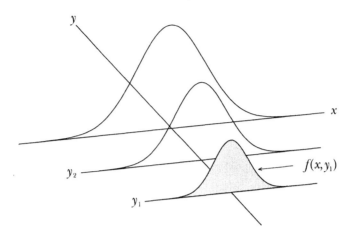

FIGURE 3.6 Joint density and marginal density

THEOREM 3.4.3 The conditional density of X given $Y = y_1$, denoted by $f(x \mid y_1)$, is given by

$$(3.4.30) \quad f(x \mid y_1) = \frac{f(x, y_1)}{f(y_1)},$$

provided that $f(y_1) > 0$.

Figure 3.6 describes the joint density and the marginal density appearing in the right-hand side of (3.4.30). The area of the shaded region represents $f(y_1)$.

3.4.4 Independence

Finally, we shall define the notion of independence between two continuous random variables.

DEFINITION 3.4.6 Continuous random variables X and Y are said to be independent if $f(x, y) = f(x)f(y)$ for all x and y.

This definition can be shown to be equivalent to stating

$$P(x_1 \le X \le x_2, y_1 \le Y \le y_2) = P(x_1 \le X \le x_2)P(y_1 \le Y \le y_2)$$

for all x_1, x_2, y_1, y_2 such that $x_1 \leq x_2$, $y_1 \leq y_2$. Thus stated, its connection to Definition 3.2.3, which defined independence for a pair of discrete random variables, is more apparent.

Definition 3.4.6 implies that in order to check the independence between a pair of continuous random variables, we should obtain the marginal densities and check whether their product equals the joint density. This may be a time-consuming process. The following theorem, stated without proof, provides a quicker method for determining independence.

THEOREM 3.4.4 Let S be a subset of the plane such that $f(x, y) > 0$ over S and $f(x, y) = 0$ outside S. Then X and Y are independent if and only if S is a rectangle (allowing $-\infty$ or ∞ to be an end point) with sides parallel to the axes and $f(x, y) = g(x)h(y)$ over S, where $g(x)$ and $h(y)$ are some functions of x and y, respectively. Note that if $g(x) = cf(x)$ for some c, $h(y) = c^{-1}f(y)$.

As examples of using Theorem 3.4.4, consider Examples 3.4.1 and 3.4.4. In Example 3.4.1, X and Y are independent because S is a rectangle and $xye^{-(x+y)} = xe^{-x} \cdot ye^{-y}$ over S. In Example 3.4.4, X and Y are not independent because S is a triangle, as shown in Figure 3.5, even though the joint density $24xy$ factors out as the product of a function of x alone and that of y alone over S. One can ascertain this fact by noting that $f(\frac{1}{2}, \frac{3}{4}) = 0$ since the point $(\frac{1}{2}, \frac{3}{4})$ is outside of the triangle whereas both $f(x = \frac{1}{2})$ and $f(y = \frac{3}{4})$ are clearly nonzero.

The next definition generalizes Definition 3.4.6 in the same way that Definition 3.2.5 generalizes 3.2.3.

DEFINITION 3.4.7 A finite set of continuous random variables X, Y, Z, . . . are said to be mutually independent if

$$f(x, y, z, \ldots) = f(x)f(y)f(z) \ldots .$$

(We have never defined a multivariate joint density $f(x, y, z, \ldots)$, but the reader should be able to generalize Definition 3.4.1 to a multivariate case.)

3.4.5 Examples

We shall give examples involving marginal density, conditional density, and independence.

EXAMPLE 3.4.5 Suppose $f(x, y) = (\frac{3}{2})(x^2 + y^2)$ for $0 < x < 1, 0 < y <$ 1 and $= 0$ otherwise. Calculate $P(0 < X < 0.5 \mid 0 < Y < 0.5)$ and $P(0 < X < 0.5 \mid Y = 0.5)$ and determine if X and Y are independent.
 We have

(3.4.31) $P(0 < X < 0.5 \mid 0 < Y < 0.5) = \dfrac{P(0 < X < 0.5,\, 0 < Y < 0.5)}{P(0 < Y < 0.5)}.$

By a simple double integration it is easy to determine that the numerator is equal to $\frac{1}{16}$. To obtain the denominator, we must first obtain the marginal density $f(y)$. By Theorem 3.4.1 we have

(3.4.32) $f(y) = \dfrac{3}{2} \displaystyle\int_0^1 (x^2 + y^2)\, dx = \dfrac{1}{2} + \dfrac{3}{2} y^2.$

Therefore

(3.4.33) $P(0 < Y < 0.5) = \displaystyle\int_0^{0.5} \left(\dfrac{1}{2} + \dfrac{3}{2} y^2 \right) dy = \dfrac{5}{16}.$

Therefore $P(0 < X < 0.5 \mid 0 < Y < 0.5) = \frac{1}{5}$.
 To calculate $P(0 < X < 0.5 \mid Y = 0.5)$, we must first obtain the conditional density $f(x \mid y)$. By Theorem 3.4.3,

(3.4.34) $f(x \mid y) = \dfrac{f(x, y)}{f(y)} = \dfrac{\dfrac{3}{2}(x^2 + y^2)}{\dfrac{1}{2} + \dfrac{3}{2} y^2}.$

Putting $y = 0.5$ in (3.4.34), we have

(3.4.35) $f(x \mid Y = 0.5) = \dfrac{3}{7} + \dfrac{12}{7} x^2.$

Therefore

(3.4.36) $P(0 < X < 0.5 \mid Y = 0.5) = \displaystyle\int_0^{0.5} \left(\dfrac{3}{7} + \dfrac{12}{7} x^2 \right) dx = \dfrac{2}{7}.$

 That X and Y are not independent is immediately known because $f(x, y)$ cannot be expressed as the product of a function of x alone and a function of y alone. We can ascertain this fact by showing that

(3.4.37) $\dfrac{3}{2}(x^2 + y^2) \neq \left(\dfrac{1}{2} + \dfrac{3}{2} x^2 \right)\left(\dfrac{1}{2} + \dfrac{3}{2} y^2 \right).$

EXAMPLE 3.4.6 Let $f(x, y)$ be the same as in Example 3.4.4. That is, $f(x, y) = 24xy$ for $0 < x < 1$ and $0 < y < 1 - x$ and $= 0$ otherwise. Calculate $P(0 < Y < \frac{3}{4} \mid X = \frac{1}{2})$.

We have

$$(3.4.38) \qquad f(x) = 24 \int_0^{1-x} xy \, dy = 12x(1 - x)^2, \qquad 0 < x < 1.$$

Therefore

$$(3.4.39) \qquad f(y \mid x) = \frac{f(x, y)}{f(x)} = \frac{2y}{(1 - x)^2}, \qquad \text{for } 0 < x < 1, \quad 0 < y < 1 - x,$$

$$= 0 \qquad \qquad \text{otherwise.}$$

Therefore

$$(3.4.40) \qquad P\left(0 < Y < \frac{3}{4} \mid X = \frac{1}{2}\right) = \int_0^{3/4} f\left(y \mid x = \frac{1}{2}\right) dy = \int_0^{1/2} 8y \, dy = 1.$$

Note that in (3.4.40) the range of the first integral is from 0 to $\frac{3}{4}$, whereas the range of the second integral is from 0 to $\frac{1}{2}$. This is because $f(y \mid x = \frac{1}{2}) = 8y$ only for $0 < y < \frac{1}{2}$ and $f(y \mid x = \frac{1}{2}) = 0$ for $\frac{1}{2} < y$, as can be seen either from (3.4.39) or from Figure 3.5. Such an observation is very important in solving this kind of problem, and diagrams such as Figure 3.5 are very useful in this regard.

EXAMPLE 3.4.7 Suppose $f(x, y) = \frac{1}{2}$ over the rectangle determined by the four corner points $(1, 0)$, $(0, 1)$, $(-1, 0)$, and $(0, -1)$ and $= 0$ otherwise. Calculate marginal density $f(y)$.

We should calculate $f(y)$ separately for $y \geq 0$ and $y < 0$ because the range of integration with respect to x differs in two cases. We have

$$(3.4.41) \qquad f(y) = \int_{-\infty}^{\infty} f(x, y) dx = \int_{y-1}^{1-y} \frac{1}{2} \, dx = 1 - y \quad \text{if } 0 \leq y \leq 1$$

and

$$(3.4.42) \qquad f(y) = \int_{-\infty}^{\infty} f(x, y) dx = \int_{-1-y}^{1+y} \frac{1}{2} \, dx = 1 + y \quad \text{if } -1 \leq y < 0.$$

Note that in (3.4.41), for example, $f(x, y)$ is integrated with respect to x from $-\infty$ to ∞ but $\frac{1}{2}$ is integrated from $y - 1$ to $1 - y$, since $f(x, y) = \frac{1}{2}$

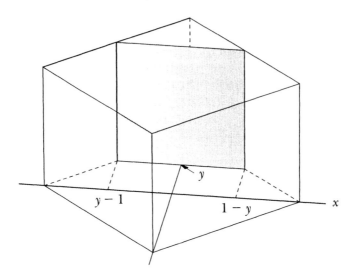

FIGURE 3.7   Marginal density

if x is within the interval $(y - 1, 1 - y)$ and $= 0$ if x is outside the interval. Figure 3.7 describes (3.4.41) as the area of the shaded region.

EXAMPLE 3.4.8   Suppose $f(x, y) = 1$ for $0 \leq x \leq 1$ and $0 \leq y \leq 1$ and $= 0$ otherwise. Obtain $f(x \mid X < Y)$.

    This example is an application of Definition 3.4.3. Put $a = 0$, $b = 1$, $h(x) = x$, and $g(x) = 1$ in Figure 3.3. Then from (3.4.22) we have

$$(3.4.43) \quad f(x \mid X < Y) = \frac{\displaystyle\int_x^1 dy}{\displaystyle\int_0^1 \int_x^1 dy\,dx} = 2(1 - x) \quad \text{for } 0 \leq x \leq 1,$$

$$= 0 \qquad \text{otherwise.}$$

EXAMPLE 3.4.9   Assume $f(x, y) = 1$ for $0 < x < 1$, $0 < y < 1$ and $= 0$ otherwise. Obtain the conditional density $f(x \mid Y = 0.5 + X)$.

    This example is an application of Theorem 3.4.2. The answer is immediately obtained by putting $y_1 = \frac{1}{2}$, $c = 1$ in (3.4.26) and noting that the range of X given $Y = \frac{1}{2} + X$ is the interval $(0, \frac{1}{2})$. Thus

(3.4.44) $f\left(x \mid Y = \dfrac{1}{2} + X\right) = 2, \quad \text{for } 0 < x < \dfrac{1}{2},$

$$= 0 \quad \text{otherwise.}$$

3.5 DISTRIBUTION FUNCTION

As we have seen so far, a discrete random variable is characterized by specifying the probability with which the random variable takes each single value, but this cannot be done for a continuous random variable. Conversely, a continuous random variable has a density function but a discrete random variable does not. This dichotomy can sometimes be a source of inconvenience, and in certain situations it is better to treat all the random variables in a unified way. This can be done by using a cumulative distribution function (or, more simply, a distribution function), which can be defined for any random variable.

DEFINITION 3.5.1 The *(cumulative) distribution function* of a random variable X, denoted by $F(\cdot)$, is defined by

(3.5.1) $F(x) = P(X < x)$ for every real x.

From the definition and the axioms of probability it follows directly that F is a monotonically nondecreasing function, is continuous from the left, $F(-\infty) = 0$, and $F(\infty) = 1$. Some textbooks define the distribution function as $F(x) = P(X \le x)$. Then the distribution function can be shown to be continuous from the right.

Let X be a finite discrete random variable such that $P(X = x_i) = p_i$, $i = 1, 2, \ldots, n$. Then its distribution is a step function with a jump of length p_i at x_i as shown in Figure 3.8. At each point of jump, the value of the distribution function is at the solid point instead of the empty point, indicating the fact that the function is continuous from the left.

The distribution function of a continuous random variable X with density function $f(\cdot)$ is given by

(3.5.2) $F(x) = \displaystyle\int_{-\infty}^{x} f(t)dt.$

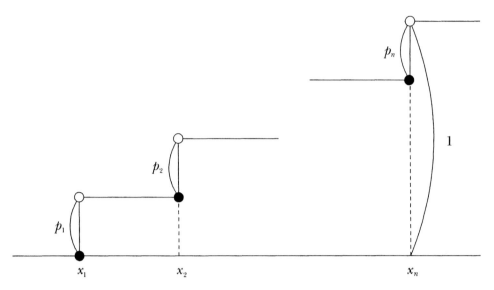

FIGURE 3.8   Distribution function of a discrete random variable

From (3.5.2) we can deduce that the density function is the derivative of the distribution function and that the distribution function of a continuous random variable is continuous everywhere.

The probability that a random variable falls into a closed interval can be easily evaluated if the distribution function is known, because of the following relationship:

$$(3.5.3) \qquad P(x_1 \le X \le x_2) = P(x_1 \le X < x_2) + P(X = x_2)$$

$$= P(X < x_2) - P(X < x_1) + P(X = x_2)$$

$$= F(x_2) - F(x_1) + P(X = x_2).$$

If X is a continuous random variable, $P(X = x_2) = 0$; hence it may be omitted from the terms in (3.5.3).

The following two examples show how to obtain the distribution function using the relationship (3.5.2), when the density function is given.

EXAMPLE 3.5.1   Suppose

$$(3.5.4) \qquad f(x) = \frac{1}{2} e^{-x/2} \quad \text{for } x > 0,$$

$$= 0 \qquad \text{otherwise.}$$

Then $F(x) = 0$ if $x \leq 0$. For $x > 0$ we have

$$(3.5.5) \qquad F(x) = \int_{-\infty}^{x} f(t)dt = \int_{-\infty}^{0} f(t)dt + \int_{0}^{x} f(t)dt$$

$$= 0 + \frac{1}{2}\int_{0}^{x} e^{-t/2}dt = [e^{-t/2}]_{0}^{x} = 1 - e^{-x/2}.$$

EXAMPLE 3.5.2 Suppose

$$(3.5.6) \qquad f(x) = 2(1 - x) \quad \text{for } 0 < x < 1,$$

$$= 0 \qquad\qquad \text{otherwise.}$$

Clearly, $F(x) = 0$ for $x \leq 0$ and $F(x) = 1$ for $x \geq 1$. For $0 < x < 1$ we have

$$(3.5.7) \qquad F(x) = \int_{-\infty}^{x} f(t)dt = \int_{-\infty}^{0} f(t)dt + \int_{0}^{x} f(t)dt$$

$$= 0 + 2\int_{0}^{x}(1 - t)\,dt = 2\left[t - \frac{t^2}{2}\right]_{0}^{x} = 2x - x^2.$$

Example 3.5.3 gives the distribution function of a mixture of a discrete and a continuous random variable.

EXAMPLE 3.5.3 Consider

$$(3.5.8) \qquad F(x) = 0, \qquad x \leq 0,$$

$$= 0.5, \qquad 0 < x \leq 0.5,$$

$$= x, \qquad 0.5 < x \leq 1,$$

$$= 1, \qquad x > 1.$$

This function is graphed in Figure 3.9. The random variable in question takes the value 0 with probability $\frac{1}{2}$ and takes a continuum of values between $\frac{1}{2}$ and 1 according to the uniform density over the interval with height 1.

A mixture random variable is quite common in economic applications. For example, the amount of money a randomly chosen person spends on the purchase of a new car in a given year is such a random variable because we can reasonably assume that it is equal to 0 with a positive probability and yet takes a continuum of values over an interval.

We have defined pairwise independence (Definitions 3.2.3 and 3.4.6)

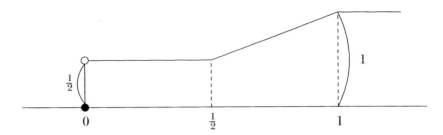

FIGURE 3.9   Distribution function of a mixture random variable

and mutual independence (Definitions 3.2.5 and 3.4.7) first for discrete random variables and then for continuous random variables. Here we shall give the definition of mutual independence that is valid for any sort of random variable: discrete or continuous or otherwise. We shall not give the definition of pairwise independence, because it is merely a special case of mutual independence. As a preliminary we need to define the multivariate distribution function $F(x_1, x_2, \ldots, x_n)$ for n random variables X_1, $X_2, \ldots, X_n$ by $F(x_1, x_2, \ldots, x_n) = P(X_1 < x_1, X_2 < x_2, \ldots, X_n < x_n)$.

DEFINITION 3.5.2   Random variables $X_1, X_2, \ldots, X_n$ are said to be mutually independent if for any points $x_1, x_2, \ldots, x_n$,

(3.5.9) $F(x_1, x_2, \ldots, x_n) = F(x_1)F(x_2) \ldots F(x_n).$

Equation (3.5.9) is equivalent to saying

(3.5.10) $P(X_1 \in S_1, X_2 \in S_2, \ldots, X_n \in S_n)$

$= P(X_1 \in S_1)P(X_2 \in S_2) \cdots P(X_n \in S_n)$

for any subsets of the real line $S_1, S_2, \ldots, S_n$ for which the probabilities in (3.5.10) make sense. Written thus, its connection to Definition 2.4.3 concerning the mutual independence of events is more apparent. Definitions 3.2.5 and 3.4.7 can be derived as theorems from Definition 3.5.2.

We still need a few more definitions of independence, all of which pertain to general random variables.

DEFINITION 3.5.3   An infinite set of random variables are mutually independent if any finite subset of them are mutually independent.

DEFINITION 3.5.4 Bivariate random variables (X_1, Y_1), (X_2, Y_2), . . . , (X_n, Y_n) are mutually independent if for any points x_1, x_2, . . . , x_n and y_1, y_2, . . . , y_n,

$$(3.5.11) \quad F(x_1, y_1, x_2, y_2, \ldots, x_n, y_n) = F(x_1, y_1)F(x_2, y_2) \cdots F(x_n, y_n).$$

Note that in Definition 3.5.4 nothing is said about the independence or nonindependence of X_i and Y_i. Definition 3.5.4 can be straightforwardly generalized to trivariate random variables and so on or even to the case where groups (terms inside parentheses) contain varying numbers of random variables. We shall not state such generalizations here. Note also that Definition 3.5.4 can be straightforwardly generalized to the case of an infinite sequence of bivariate random variables.

Finally, we state without proof:

THEOREM 3.5.1 Let ϕ and ψ be arbitrary functions. If a finite set of random variables $X, Y, Z, \ldots$ are independent of another finite set of random variables $U, V, W, \ldots$, then $\phi(X, Y, Z, \ldots)$ is independent of $\psi(U, V, W, \ldots)$.

Just as we have defined conditional probability and conditional density, we can define the conditional distribution function.

DEFINITION 3.5.5 Let X and Y be random variables and let S be a subset of the (x, y) plane. Then the *conditional distribution function* of X given S, denoted by $F(x \mid S)$, is defined by

$$(3.5.12) \quad F(x \mid S) = P(X < x \mid (X, Y) \in S).$$

Note that the conditional density $f(x \mid S)$ defined in Definition 3.4.3 may be derived by differentiating (3.5.12) with respect to x.

3.6 CHANGE OF VARIABLES

In this section we shall primarily study how to derive the probability distribution of a random variable Y from that of another random variable X when Y is given as a function, say $\phi(X)$, of X. The problem is simple if X and Y are discrete, as we saw in Section 3.2.1; here we shall assume that they are continuous.

We shall initially deal with monotonic functions (that is, either strictly increasing or decreasing) and later consider other cases. We shall first prove a theorem formally and then illustrate it by a diagram.

THEOREM 3.6.1   Let $f(x)$ be the density of X and let $Y = \phi(X)$, where ϕ is a monotonic differentiable function. Then the density $g(y)$ of Y is given by

$$(3.6.1) \qquad g(y) = f[\phi^{-1}(y)] \cdot \left| \frac{d\phi^{-1}}{dy} \right|,$$

where ϕ^{-1} is the inverse function of ϕ. (Do not mistake it for 1 over ϕ.)

Proof. We have

$$(3.6.2) \qquad P(Y < y) = P[\phi(X) < y].$$

Suppose ϕ is increasing. Then we have from (3.6.2)

$$(3.6.3) \qquad P(Y < y) = P[X < \phi^{-1}(y)].$$

Denote the distribution functions of Y and X by $G(\cdot)$ and $F(\cdot)$, respectively. Then (3.6.3) can be written as

$$(3.6.4) \qquad G(y) = F[\phi^{-1}(y)].$$

Differentiating both sides of (3.6.4) with respect to y, we obtain

$$(3.6.5) \qquad g(y) = f[\phi^{-1}(y)] \cdot \frac{d\phi^{-1}}{dy}.$$

Next, suppose ϕ is decreasing. Then we have from (3.6.2)

$$(3.6.6) \qquad P(Y < y) = P[X > \phi^{-1}(y)],$$

which can be rewritten as

$$(3.6.7) \qquad G(y) = 1 - F[\phi^{-1}(y)].$$

Differentiating both sides of (3.6.7), we obtain

$$(3.6.8) \qquad g(y) = -f[\phi^{-1}(y)] \frac{d\phi^{-1}}{dy}.$$

The theorem follows from (3.6.5) and (3.6.8). ❑

The term in absolute value on the right-hand side of (3.6.1) is called the *Jacobian of transformation.*

Since $d\phi^{-1}/dy = (d\phi/dx)^{-1}$, we can write (3.6.1) as

$$(3.6.9) \qquad g(y) = \frac{f(x)}{|dy/dx|} \quad \text{(or, mnemonically, } g(y)|dy| = f(x)|dx|),$$

which is a more convenient formula than (3.6.1) in most cases. However, since the right-hand side of (3.6.9) is still given as a function of x, one must replace x with $\phi^{-1}(y)$ to obtain the final answer.

EXAMPLE 3.6.1 Suppose $f(x) = 1$ for $0 < x < 1$ and $= 0$ otherwise. Assuming $Y = X^2$, obtain the density $g(y)$ of Y.

Since $dy/dx = 2x$, we have by (3.6.9)

$$(3.6.10) \qquad g(y) = \frac{1}{2x}, \qquad 0 < x < 1.$$

But, since $x = \sqrt{y}$, we have from (3.6.10)

$$(3.6.11) \qquad g(y) = \frac{1}{2\sqrt{y}}, \qquad 0 < y < 1.$$

It is a good idea to check for the accuracy of the result by examining that the obtained function is indeed a density. The test will be passed in this case, because (3.6.11) is clearly nonnegative and we have

$$(3.6.12) \qquad \int_0^1 \frac{1}{2\sqrt{y}}\, dy = \left[\sqrt{y}\right]_0^1 = 1.$$

The same result can be obtained by using the distribution function and without using Theorem 3.6.1, as follows. We have

$$(3.6.13) \qquad G(y) = P(Y < y) = P(X^2 < y) = P(X < \sqrt{y})$$

$$= \int_0^{\sqrt{y}} f(x)dx = \int_0^{\sqrt{y}} dx = \sqrt{y}.$$

Therefore, differentiating (3.6.13) with respect to y, we obtain

$$(3.6.14) \qquad g(y) = \frac{1}{2\sqrt{y}}.$$

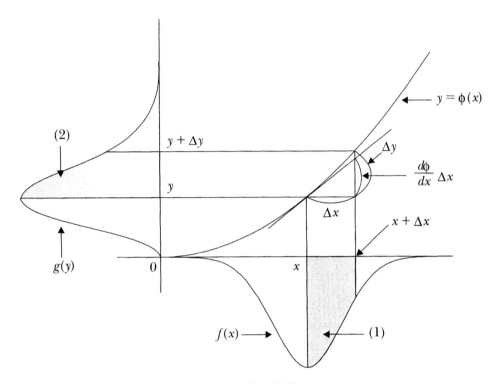

FIGURE 3.10   Change of variables: one-to-one case

This latter method is more lengthy, as it does not utilize the power of Theorem 3.6.1. It has the advantage, however, of being more fundamental.

Figure 3.10 illustrates the result of Theorem 3.6.1. Since Y lies between y and $y + \Delta y$ if and only if X lies between x and $x + \Delta x$, shaded regions (1) and (2) must have the same area. If Δx is small then Δy is also small, and the area of (1) is approximately $f(x)\Delta x$ and the area of (2) is approximately $g(y)\Delta y$. Therefore we have approximately

$$(3.6.15) \qquad g(y)\Delta y \cong f(x)\Delta x.$$

But if Δx is small, we also have approximately

$$(3.6.16) \qquad \Delta y = \frac{d\phi}{dx}\Delta x.$$

From (3.6.15) and (3.6.16) we have

$$(3.6.17) \qquad g(y) \cong \frac{f(x)}{d\phi/dx}\,.$$

Since we can make Δx arbitrarily small, (3.6.17) in fact holds exactly. In this example we have considered an increasing function. It is clear that we would need the absolute value of $d\phi/dx$ if we were to consider a decreasing function instead.

In the case of a nonmonotonic function, the formula of Theorem 3.6.1 will not work, but we can get the correct result if we understand the process by which the formula is derived, either through the formal approach, using the distribution function, or through the graphic approach.

EXAMPLE 3.6.2 Given $f(x) = \frac{1}{2}$, $-1 < x < 1$, and

$$Y = X \quad \text{if } X \geq 0,$$

$$= X^2 \quad \text{if } X < 0,$$

find $g(y)$.

We shall first employ a graphic approach. In Figure 3.11 we must have area (3) = area (1) + area (2). Therefore

$$(3.6.18) \qquad g(y)\Delta y \cong f(x_1)\Delta x_1 + f(x_2)\Delta x_2 = \frac{1}{2}\Delta x_1 + \frac{1}{2}\Delta x_2 .$$

Therefore

$$(3.6.19) \qquad g(y) = \frac{1}{2} - \frac{1}{2}\frac{1}{2x_2} = \frac{1}{2} + \frac{1}{4\sqrt{y}}, \qquad 0 < y < 1.$$

Figure 3.11 is helpful even in a formal approach. We have

$$(3.6.20) \qquad P(Y < y) = P(x_2 < X < x_1)$$

$$= P(-\sqrt{y} < X < y)$$

$$= P(X < y) - P(X < -\sqrt{y}).$$

Therefore

$$(3.6.21) \qquad G(y) = F(y) - F(-\sqrt{y}).$$

Differentiating (3.6.21) with respect to y, we get

$$(3.6.22) \qquad g(y) = f(y) + f(-\sqrt{y})\frac{1}{2\sqrt{y}} = \frac{1}{2} + \frac{1}{4\sqrt{y}}, \qquad 0 < y < 1.$$

The result of Example 3.6.2 can be generalized and stated formally as follows.

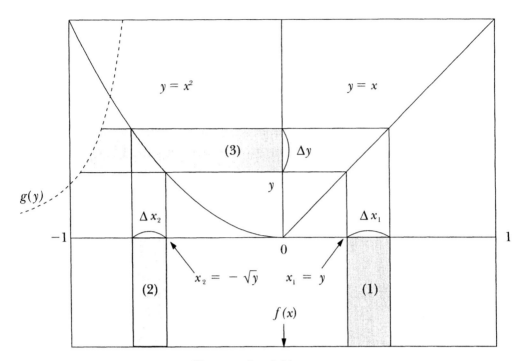

FIGURE 3.11   Change of variables: non-one-to-one case

THEOREM 3.6.2   Suppose the inverse of $y = \phi(x)$ is multivalued and can be written as

(3.6.23) $x_i = \psi_i(y), \quad i = 1, 2, \ldots, n_y.$

Note that n_y indicates the possibility that the number of values of x varies with y. Then the density $g(\cdot)$ of Y is given by

(3.6.24) $g(y) = \displaystyle\sum_{i=1}^{n_y} \frac{f[\psi_i(y)]}{|\phi'[\psi_i(y)]|} ,$

where $f(\cdot)$ is the density of X and ϕ' is the derivative of ϕ.

So far we have studied the transformation of one random variable into another. In the next three examples we shall show how to obtain the density of a random variable which is a function of two other random variables. We shall always use the method in which the distribution function is obtained first and then the density is obtained by differentiation. Later in this section we shall discuss an alternative method, called the

Jacobian method, which is a generalization of Theorem 3.6.1; but the present method is more fundamental and will work even when the Jacobian method fails.

EXAMPLE 3.6.3 Assume $f(x, y) = 1$ for $0 < x < 1, 0 < y < 1$ and $= 0$ otherwise. Calculate the density function $g(z)$ of $Z = \max(X, Y)$.

For any z, the event $(Z \le z)$ is equivalent to the event $(X \le z, Y \le z)$; hence, the probability of the two events is the same. Since X and Y are independent, we have

$$(3.6.25) \quad P(Z \le z) = P(X \le z) P(Y \le z)$$

$$= z^2, \quad 0 < z < 1.$$

Since the density $g(z)$ is the derivative of the distribution function, we conclude that $g(z) = 2z, 0 < z < 1$.

EXAMPLE 3.6.4 Let X and Y have the joint density $f(x, y) = 1$ for $0 < x < 1$ and $0 < y < 1$. Obtain the density of Z defined by $Z = Y/X$.

See Figure 3.12. Let $F(\cdot)$ be the distribution function of Z. Then

$$(3.6.26) \quad F(z) = P(Y/X < z) = P(Y < zX)$$

$$= \text{area A} = \frac{z}{2} \quad \text{for } 0 < z < 1,$$

$$= 1 - \text{area B} = 1 - \frac{1}{2z} \quad \text{for } z \ge 1.$$

Differentiating (3.6.26) with respect to z, we get

$$(3.6.27) \quad f(z) = \frac{1}{2} \quad \text{for } 0 < z < 1,$$

$$= \frac{1}{2z^2} \quad \text{for } z \ge 1.$$

EXAMPLE 3.6.5 Assume again $f(x, y) = 1$ for $0 < x < 1, 0 < y < 1$ and $= 0$ otherwise. Obtain the conditional density $f(x \mid Y = 0.5 + X)$.

This problem was solved earlier, in Example 3.4.9, but here we shall present an alternative solution using the distribution function. The present solution is more complicated but serves as an exercise. Define $Z = Y - X - 0.5$. Then we have

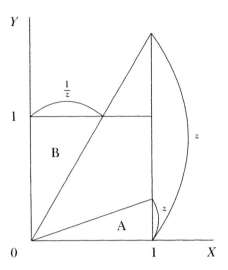

FIGURE 3.12   Illustration for Example 3.6.4

(3.6.28) $F(z \mid x) = P(Z < z \mid X = x) = P(Y < z + x + 0.5)$

$$= z + x + 0.5, \quad -0.5 - x < z < 0.5 - x.$$

Therefore

(3.6.29) $f(z \mid x) = 1, \quad -0.5 - x < z < 0.5 - x, \quad 0 < x < 1.$

Therefore, from (3.6.29) and the marginal density of X,

(3.6.30) $f(x, z) = 1, \quad -0.5 - x < z < 0.5 - x, \quad 0 < x < 1.$

The domain of the joint density $f(x, z)$ is indicated by the shaded region in Figure 3.13. From (3.6.30) we get

(3.6.31) $f(z) = \int_0^{(1/2)-z} dx = \dfrac{1}{2} - z, \quad -\dfrac{1}{2} < z < \dfrac{1}{2}$

$$= \int_{-(1/2)-z}^1 dx = \dfrac{3}{2} + z, \quad -\dfrac{3}{2} < z < -\dfrac{1}{2}.$$

Therefore, from (3.6.30) and (3.6.31), we finally get

(3.6.32) $f(x \mid Y = 0.5 + X) = f(x \mid Z = 0) = 2$ for $0 < x < 0.5,$

$$= 0 \qquad\qquad \text{otherwise.}$$

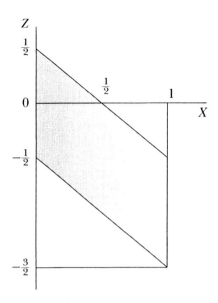

FIGURE 3.13   Domain of a joint density

Theorem 3.6.3 generalizes Theorem 3.6.1 to a linear transformation of a bivariate random variable into another.

THEOREM 3.6.3   Let $f(x_1, x_2)$ be the joint density of a bivariate random variable (X_1, X_2) and let (Y_1, Y_2) be defined by a linear transformation

(3.6.33) $Y_1 = a_{11}X_1 + a_{12}X_2$

$Y_2 = a_{21}X_1 + a_{22}X_2.$

Suppose $a_{11}a_{22} - a_{12}a_{21} \neq 0$ so that (3.6.33) can be solved for X_1 and X_2 as

(3.6.34) $X_1 = b_{11}Y_1 + b_{12}Y_2$

$X_2 = b_{21}Y_1 + b_{22}Y_2.$

Then the joint density $g(y_1, y_2)$ of (Y_1, Y_2) is given by

(3.6.35) $g(y_1, y_2) = \dfrac{f(b_{11}y_1 + b_{12}y_2, b_{21}y_1 + b_{22}y_2)}{|a_{11}a_{22} - a_{12}a_{21}|},$

where the *support* of g, that is, the range of (y_1, y_2) over which g is positive, must be appropriately determined.

The absolute value $|a_{11}a_{22} - a_{12}a_{21}|$ appearing on the right-hand side of (3.6.35) is called the *Jacobian of transformation*. That this is needed can be best understood by the following geometric consideration. Consider a small rectangle on the X_1–X_2 plane, where the coordinates of its four corners—counterclockwise starting from the southwest corner—are given by (X_1, X_2), $(X_1 + \Delta X_1, X_2)$, $(X_1 + \Delta X_1, X_2 + \Delta X_2)$, and $(X_1, X_2 + \Delta X_2)$. The linear mapping (3.6.33) maps this rectangle to a parallelogram on the Y_1–Y_2 plane, whose coordinates are given by $(a_{11}X_1 + a_{12}X_2, a_{21}X_1 + a_{22}X_2)$, $(a_{11}X_1 + a_{12}X_2 + a_{11}\Delta X_1, a_{21}X_1 + a_{22}X_2 + a_{21}\Delta X_1)$, $(a_{11}X_1 + a_{12}X_2 + a_{11}\Delta X_1 + a_{12}\Delta X_2, a_{21}X_1 + a_{22}X_2 + a_{21}\Delta X_1 + a_{22}\Delta X_2)$, and $(a_{11}X_1 + a_{12}X_2 + a_{12}\Delta X_2, a_{21}X_1 + a_{22}X_2 + a_{22}\Delta X_2)$. The area of the rectangle is $\Delta X_1 \Delta X_2$, and if we suppose for simplicity that all the a's are positive and that $a_{11}a_{22} - a_{12}a_{21} > 0$, then the area of the parallelogram must be $(a_{11}a_{22} - a_{12}a_{21})\Delta X_1 \Delta X_2$.

Chapter 11 shows that $a_{11}a_{22} - a_{12}a_{21}$ is the determinant of the 2×2 matrix

$$\begin{bmatrix} a_{11} & a_{12} \\ a_{21} & a_{22} \end{bmatrix}.$$

By using matrix notation, Theorem 3.6.3 can be generalized to a linear transformation of a general n-variate random variable into another.

EXAMPLE 3.6.6 Suppose $f(x_1, x_2) = 4x_1x_2$ for $0 \leq x_1 \leq 1$ and $0 \leq x_2 \leq 1$. If

$$(3.6.36) \qquad Y_1 = X_1 + 2X_2$$

$$Y_2 = X_1 - X_2,$$

what is the joint density of (Y_1, Y_2)?

Solving (3.6.36) for X_1 and X_2, we obtain

$$(3.6.37) \qquad X_1 = \frac{1}{3} Y_1 + \frac{2}{3} Y_2$$

$$X_2 = \frac{1}{3} Y_1 - \frac{1}{3} Y_2 .$$

Inserting the appropriate numbers into (3.6.35), we immediately obtain

$$(3.6.38) \qquad g(y_1, y_2) = \frac{4}{27} (y_1 + 2y_2)(y_1 - y_2).$$

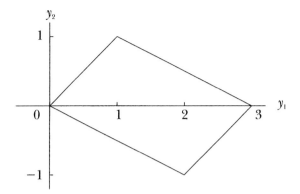

FIGURE 3.14   Illustration for Example 3.6.6

Next we derive the support of g. Since $0 \leq x_1 \leq 1$ and $0 \leq x_2 \leq 1$, we have from (3.6.37)

(3.6.39) $$0 \leq \frac{1}{3} Y_1 + \frac{2}{3} Y_2 \leq 1$$

$$0 \leq \frac{1}{3} Y_1 - \frac{1}{3} Y_2 \leq 1.$$

Thus the support of g is given as the inside of the parallelogram in Figure 3.14.

3.7 JOINT DISTRIBUTION OF DISCRETE AND CONTINUOUS RANDOM VARIABLES

In Section 3.2 we studied the joint distribution of discrete random variables and in Section 3.4 we studied the joint distribution of continuous random variables. In some applications we need to understand the characteristics of the joint distribution of a discrete and a continuous random variable.

Let X be a continuous random variable with density $f(x)$ and let Y be a discrete random variable taking values y_i, $i = 1, 2, \ldots, n$, with probabilities $P(y_i)$. If we assume that X and Y are related to each other, the best way to characterize the relationship seems to be to specify either the conditional density $f(x \mid y_i)$ or the conditional probability $P(y_i \mid x)$. In this section we ask two questions: (1) How are the four quantities $f(x)$, $P(y_i)$, $f(x \mid y_i)$, and $P(y_i \mid x)$ related to one another? (2) Is there a bivariate function $\psi(x, y_i)$ such that $P(a \leq X \leq b, Y \in S) = \int_a^b \Sigma_{i \in I} \psi(x, y_i) dx$, where I is a subset of integers $(1, 2, \ldots, n)$ and $S = \{y_i \mid i \in I\}$?

Note that, like any other conditional density defined in Sections 3.3 and 3.4, $f(x \mid y_i)$ must satisfy

(3.7.1) $$\int_a^b f(x \mid y_i) dx = P(a \leq X \leq b \mid Y = y_i)$$

for any $a \leq b$.

Since the conditional probability $P(y_i \mid x)$ involves the conditioning event that happens with zero probability, we need to define it as the limit of $P(y_i \mid x \leq X \leq x + \epsilon)$ as ϵ goes to zero. Thus we have

(3.7.2) $$P(y_i \mid x) = \lim_{\epsilon \to 0} P(Y = y_i \mid x \leq X \leq x + \epsilon)$$

$$= \lim_{\epsilon \to 0} \frac{P(Y = y_i, x \leq X \leq x + \epsilon)}{P(x \leq X \leq x + \epsilon)} \qquad \text{by Theorem 2.4.1}$$

$$= \lim_{\epsilon \to 0} \frac{P(x \leq X \leq x + \epsilon \mid Y = y_i) P(Y = y_i)}{P(x \leq X \leq x + \epsilon)} \qquad \begin{array}{l}\text{by Theorem}\\ \text{2.4.1}\end{array}$$

$$= \lim_{\epsilon \to 0} \frac{\int_x^{x+\epsilon} f(t \mid y_i) dt \cdot P(Y = y_i)}{\int_x^{x+\epsilon} f(t) dt} \qquad \text{by (3.7.1)}$$

$$= \frac{f(x \mid y_i) P(y_i)}{f(x)} \qquad \text{by the mean value theorem,}$$

which provides the answer to the first question.

Next consider

(3.7.3) $$\int_a^b \sum_{i \in I} f(x \mid y_i) P(y_i) dx$$

$$= \sum_{i \in I} P(a \leq X \leq b \mid Y = y_i) P(Y = y_i) \quad \text{by (3.7.1)}$$

$$= \sum_{i \in I} P(a \leq X \leq b, Y = y_i) \qquad \text{by Theorem 2.4.1}$$

$$= P(a \leq X \leq b, Y \in S) \qquad \text{by probability axiom (3),}$$

where $S = \{y_i \mid i \in I\}$. Thus $f(x \mid y_i)P(y_i)$ plays the role of the bivariate function $\psi(x, y_i)$ defined in the second question. Hence, by (3.7.2), so does $P(y_i \mid x)f(x)$.

EXERCISES

1. (Section 3.2.3)
   Let X, Y, and Z be binary random variables each taking two values, 1 or 0. Specify a joint distribution in such a way that the three variables are pairwise independent but not mutually independent.

2. (Section 3.4.3)
   Given the density $f(x, y) = 2(x + y)$, $0 < x < 1$, $0 < y < x$, calcluate
   (a) $P(X < 0.5, Y < 0.5)$.
   (b) $P(X < 0.5)$.
   (c) $P(Y < 0.5)$.

3. (Section 3.4.3)
   Let X be the midterm score of a student and Y be his final exam score. The score is scaled to range between 0 and 1, and grade A is given to a score between 0.8 and 1. Suppose the density of X is given by

   $$f(x) = 1, \quad 0 < x < 1$$

   and the conditional density of Y given X is given by

   $$f(y \mid x) = 2xy + 2(1 - x)(1 - y), \quad 0 < x < 1, \ 0 < y < 1.$$

   What is the probability that he will get an A on the final if he got an A on the midterm?

4. (Section 3.4.3)
   Let the joint density of (X, Y) be given by

   $$f(x, y) = 2, \quad 0 < x < 1, \ 0 < y < 1 - x.$$

   (a) Calculate marginal density $f(x)$.
   (b) Calculate $P(0 < Y < \frac{3}{4} \mid X = 0.5)$.

5. (Section 3.6)
   Given $f(x) = \exp(-x)$, $x > 0$, find the density of the variable
   (a) $Y = 2X + 1$.
   (b) $Y = X^2$.

(c) $Y = 1/X$.

(d) $Y = \log X$. (The symbol log refers to natural logarithm through-out.)

6. (Section 3.6)

Let X have density $f(x) = 0.5$ for $-1 < x < 1$. Define Y by

$$Y = X + 1 \quad \text{if } 0 < X < 1$$
$$= -2X \quad \text{if } -1 < X < 0.$$

Obtain the density of Y.

7. (Section 3.6)

Assuming $f(x, y) = 1, 0 < x < 1, 0 < y < 1$, obtain the density of $Z = X - Y$.

8. (Section 3.6)

Suppose that U and V are independent with density $f(t) = \exp(-t)$, $t > 0$. Find the conditional density of X given Y if $X = U$ and $Y = U + V$.

4 | MOMENTS

4.1 EXPECTED VALUE

We shall define the expected value of a random variable, first, for a discrete random variable in Definition 4.1.1 and, second, for a continuous random variable in Definition 4.1.2.

DEFINITION 4.1.1 Let X be a discrete random variable taking the value x_i with probability $P(x_i)$, $i = 1, 2, \ldots$. Then the *expected value* (*expectation* or *mean*) of X, denoted by EX, is defined to be $EX = \sum_{i=1}^{\infty} x_i P(x_i)$ if the series converges absolutely. We can write $EX = \sum_{+} x_i P(x_i) + \sum_{-} x_i P(x_i)$, where in the first summation we sum for i such that $x_i > 0$ and in the second summation we sum for i such that $x_i < 0$. If $\sum_{+} x_i P(x_i) = \infty$ and $\sum_{-} x_i P(x_i) = -\infty$, we say EX does not exist. If $\sum_{+} = \infty$ and $\sum_{-}$ is finite, then we say $EX = \infty$. If $\sum_{-} = -\infty$ and $\sum_{+}$ is finite, then we say $EX = -\infty$.

The expected value has an important practical meaning. If X is the payoff of a gamble (that is, if you gain x_i dollars with probability $P(x_i)$), the expected value signifies the amount you can expect to gain on the average. For example, if a fair coin is tossed and we gain one dollar when a head comes up and nothing when a tail comes up, the expected value of this gamble is 50 cents. It means that if we repeat this gamble many times we will gain 50 cents on the average. We can formalize this statement as follows. Let X_i be the payoff of a particular gamble made for the ith time. Then the average gain from repeating this gamble n times is $n^{-1}\sum_{i=1}^{n} X_i$, and it converges to EX in probability. This is a consequence of

Theorem 6.2.1. For the exact definition of convergence in probability, see Definition 6.1.2.

The quantity $n^{-1}\Sigma_{i=1}^{n}X_i$ is called the *sample mean.* (More exactly, it is the sample mean based on a sample of size n.) EX is sometimes called the *population mean* so that it may be distinguished from the sample mean. We shall learn in Chapter 7 that the sample mean is a good estimator of the population mean.

Coming back to the aforementioned gamble that pays one dollar when a head comes up, we may say that the fair price of the gamble is 50 cents. This does not mean, however, that everybody should pay exactly 50 cents to play. How much this gamble is worth depends upon the subjective evaluation of the risk involved. A risk taker may be willing to pay as much as 90 cents to gamble, whereas a risk averter may pay only 10 cents. The decision to gamble for c cents or not can be thought of as choosing between two random variables X_1 and X_2, where X_1 takes value 1 with probability $\frac{1}{2}$ and 0 with probability $\frac{1}{2}$ and X_2 takes value c with probability 1. More generally, decision making under uncertainty always means choosing one out of a set of random variables $X(d)$ that vary as d varies within the decision set D. Here $X(d)$ is the random gain (in dollars) that results from choosing a decision d.

Choosing the value of d that maximizes $EX(d)$ may not necessarily be a reasonable decision strategy. To illustrate this point, consider the following example. A coin is tossed repeatedly until a head comes up, and 2^i dollars are paid if a head comes up for the first time in the ith toss. The payoff of this gamble is represented by the random variable X that takes the value 2^i with probability 2^{-i}. Hence, by Definition 4.1.1, $EX = \infty$. Obviously, however, nobody would pay ∞ dollars for this gamble. This example is called the "St. Petersburg Paradox," because the Swiss mathematician Daniel Bernoulli wrote about it while visiting St. Petersburg Academy.

One way to resolve this paradox is to note that what one should maximize is not EX itself but, rather, $EU(X)$, where U denotes the utility function. If, for example, the utility function is logarithmic, the real worth of the St. Petersburg gamble is merely $E \log X = \log 2 \cdot \Sigma_{i=1}^{\infty} i (\frac{1}{2})^i = \log 4$, the utility of gaining four dollars for certainty. By changing the utility function, one can represent various degrees of risk-averseness. A good, simple exposition of this and related topics can be found in Arrow (1965).

Not all the decision strategies can be regarded as the maximization of

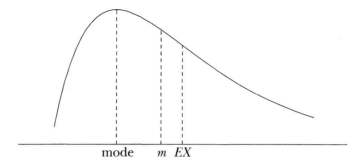

mode m EX

FIGURE 4.1   A positively skewed density

$EU(X)$ for some U, however. For example, an extremely risk-averse person may choose the d that maximizes $\min X(d)$, where $\min X$ means the minimum possible value X can take. Such a person will not undertake the St. Petersburg gamble for any price higher than two dollars. Such a strategy is called the *minimax strategy*, because it means minimizing the maximum loss (loss may be defined as negative gain). We can think of many other strategies which may be regarded as reasonable by certain people in certain situations.

DEFINITION 4.1.2   Let X be a continuous random variable with density $f(x)$. Then, the *expected value* of X, denoted by EX, is defined to be $EX = \int_{-\infty}^{\infty} xf(x)dx$ if the integral is absolutely convergent. If $\int_{0}^{\infty} xf(x)dx = \infty$ and $\int_{-\infty}^{0} xf(x)dx = -\infty$, we say the expected value does not exist. If $\int_{0}^{\infty} xf(x)dx = \infty$ and $\int_{-\infty}^{0} xf(x)dx$ is finite, we write $EX = \infty$. If $\int_{-\infty}^{0} xf(x)dx = -\infty$ and $\int_{0}^{\infty} xf(x)dx$ is finite, we write $EX = -\infty$.

Besides having an important practical meaning as the fair price of a gamble, the expected value is a very important characteristic of a probability distribution, being a measure of its central location. The other important measures of central location are mode and median. The *mode* is a value of x for which $f(x)$ is the maximum, and the *median m* is defined by the equation $P(X \le m) = \frac{1}{2}$. If the density function $f(x)$ is bell-shaped and symmetric around $x = \mu$, then $\mu = EX = m = \text{mode}(X)$. If the density is positively skewed as in Figure 4.1, then mode $(X) < m < EX$. The three measures of central location are computed in the following examples.

EXAMPLE 4.1.1 $f(x) = 2x^{-3}$ for $x > 1$. Then $EX = \int_1^\infty 2x^{-2}dx = 2$. The median m must satisfy $\frac{1}{2} = \int_1^m 2x^{-3}dx = -m^{-2} + 1$. Therefore $m = \sqrt{2}$. The mode is clearly 1.

EXAMPLE 4.1.2 $f(x) = x^{-2}$ for $x > 1$. Then $EX = \int_1^\infty x^{-1}dx = \infty$. Since $\frac{1}{2} = \int_1^m x^{-2}dx = -m^{-1} + 1$, we have $m = 2$. The mode is again 1. Note that the density of Example 4.1.2 has a fatter tail (that is, the density converges more slowly to 0 in the tail) than that of Example 4.1.1, which has pushed both the mean and the median to the right, affecting the mean much more than the median.

Theorems 4.1.1 and 4.1.2 show a simple way to calculate the expected value of a function of a random variable.

THEOREM 4.1.1 Let X be a discrete random variable taking value x_i with probability $P(x_i)$, $i = 1, 2, \ldots$, and let $\phi(\cdot)$ be an arbitrary function. Then

$$(4.1.1) \qquad E\phi(X) = \sum_{i=1}^\infty \phi(x_i)P(x_i).$$

Proof. Define $Y = \phi(X)$. Then Y takes value $\phi(x_i)$ with probability $P(x_i)$. Therefore (4.1.1) follows from Definition 4.1.1. ❏

THEOREM 4.1.2 Let X be a continuous random variable with density $f(x)$ and let $\phi(\cdot)$ be a function for which the integral below can be defined. Then

$$(4.1.2) \qquad E\phi(X) = \int_{-\infty}^\infty \phi(x)f(x)dx.$$

We shall not prove this theorem, because the proof involves a level of analysis more advanced than that of this book. If $\phi(\cdot)$ is continuous, differentiable, and monotonic, then the proof is an easy consequence of approximation (3.6.15). Let $Y = \phi(X)$ and denote the density of Y by $g(y)$. Then we have

$$(4.1.3) \qquad EY = \int_{-\infty}^\infty yg(y)dy = \lim \Sigma yg(y)\Delta y = \lim \Sigma \phi(x)f(x)\Delta x$$

$$= \int_{-\infty}^\infty \phi(x)f(x)dx.$$

Theorem 4.1.1 can be easily generalized to the case of a random variable obtained as a function of two other random variables.

THEOREM 4.1.3 Let (X, Y) be a bivariate discrete random variable taking value (x_i, y_j) with probability $P(x_i, y_j)$, $i, j = 1, 2, \ldots$, and let $\phi(\cdot, \cdot)$ be an arbitrary function. Then

$$(4.1.4) \qquad E\phi(X, Y) = \sum_{i=1}^{\infty} \sum_{j=1}^{\infty} \phi(x_i, y_j)P(x_i, y_j).$$

The following is a similar generalization of Theorem 4.1.2, which we state without proof.

THEOREM 4.1.4 Let (X, Y) be a bivariate continuous random variable with joint density function $f(x, y)$, and let $\phi(\cdot, \cdot)$ be an arbitrary function. Then

$$(4.1.5) \qquad E\phi(X, Y) = \int_{-\infty}^{\infty} \int_{-\infty}^{\infty} \phi(x, y)f(x, y)dxdy.$$

Note that given $f(x, y)$, $E\phi(X)$ can be computed either directly from (4.1.5) above or by first obtaining the marginal density $f(x)$ by Theorem 3.4.1 and then using Theorem 4.1.2. The same value is obtained by either procedure.

The following three theorems characterize the properties of operator E. Although we have defined the expected value so far only for a discrete or a continuous random variable, the following theorems are true for any random variable, provided that the expected values exist.

THEOREM 4.1.5 If α is a constant, $E\alpha = \alpha$.

THEOREM 4.1.6 If X and Y are random variables and α and β are constants, $E(\alpha X + \beta Y) = \alpha EX + \beta EY$.

THEOREM 4.1.7 If X and Y are independent random variables, $EXY = EXEY$.

The proof of Theorem 4.1.5 is trivial. The proofs of Theorems 4.1.6 and 4.1.7 when (X, Y) is either discrete or continuous follow easily from Definitions 4.1.1 and 4.1.2 and Theorems 4.1.3 and 4.1.4.

Theorem 4.1.7 is very useful. For example, let X and Y denote the face numbers showing in two dice rolled independently. Then, since $EX = EY = 7/2$, we have $EXY = 49/4$ by Theorem 4.1.7. Calculating EXY directly from Definition 4.1.3 without using this theorem would be quite time-consuming.

Theorems 4.1.6 and 4.1.7 may be used to evaluate the expected value of a mixture random variable which is partly discrete and partly continuous. Let X be a discrete random variable taking value x_i with probability $P(x_i)$, $i = 1, 2, \ldots$. Let Y be a continuous random variable with density $f(y)$. Let W be a binary random variable taking two values, 1 and 0, with probability p and $1 - p$, respectively, and, furthermore, assume that W is independent of either X or Y. Define a new random variable $Z = WX + (1 - W)Y$. Another way to define Z is to say that Z is equal to X with probability p and equal to Y with probability $1 - p$. A random variable such as Z is called a *mixture random variable*. Using Theorems 4.1.6 and 4.1.7, we have $EZ = EWEX + E(1 - W)EY$. But since $EW = p$ from Definition 4.1.1, we get $EZ = pEX + (1 - p)EY$. We shall write a generalization of this result as a theorem.

THEOREM 4.1.8 Let X be a mixture random variable taking discrete value x_i, $i = 1, 2, \ldots, n$, with probability p_i and a continuum of values in interval $[a, b]$ according to density $f(x)$: that is, if $[a, b] \supset [x_1, x_2]$, $P(x_1 \leq X \leq x_2) = \int_{x_1}^{x_2} f(x)dx$. Then $EX = \sum_{i=1}^{n} x_i p_i + \int_a^b xf(x)dx$. (Note that we must have $\sum_{i=1}^{n} p_i + \int_a^b f(x)dx = 1$.)

The following example from economics indicates another way in which a mixture random variable may be generated and its mean calculated.

EXAMPLE 4.1.3 Suppose that in a given year an individual buys a car if and only if his annual income is greater than 10 (ten thousand dollars) and that if he does buy a car, the one he buys costs one-fifth of his income. Assuming that his income is a continuous random variable with uniform density defined over the interval $[5, 15]$, compute the expected amount of money he spends on a car.

Let X be his income and let Y be his expenditure on a car. Then Y is related to X by

(4.1.6) $Y = 0$ if $5 \leq X < 10$,

$\qquad\qquad = \dfrac{X}{5}$ if $10 \leq X \leq 15$.

Clearly, Y is a mixture random variable that takes 0 with probability $\frac{1}{2}$ and a continuum of values in the interval $[2, 3]$ according to the density $f(y) = \frac{1}{2}$. Therefore, by Theorem 4.1.8, we have

(4.1.7) $EY = 0 \cdot \dfrac{1}{2} + \dfrac{1}{2} \displaystyle\int_2^3 y\,dy = \dfrac{5}{4}$.

Alternatively, EY may be obtained directly from Theorem 4.1.2 by taking ϕ to be a function defined in (4.1.6). Thus

(4.1.8) $EY = \displaystyle\int_{-\infty}^{\infty} \phi(x)f(x)dx = \dfrac{1}{10} \int_5^{15} \phi(x)dx$

$\qquad\qquad = \dfrac{1}{10} \left[\displaystyle\int_5^{10} \phi(x)dx + \int_{10}^{15} \phi(x)dx \right]$

$\qquad\qquad = \dfrac{1}{10} \left[0 + \displaystyle\int_{10}^{15} \dfrac{x}{5}\, dx \right] = \dfrac{5}{4}$.

4.2 HIGHER MOMENTS

As noted in Section 4.1, the expected value, or the mean, is a measure of the central location of the probability distribution of a random variable. Although it is probably the single most important measure of the characteristics of a probability distribution, it alone cannot capture all of the characteristics. For example, in the coin-tossing gamble of the previous section, suppose one must choose between two random variables, X_1 and X_2, when X_1 is 1 or 0 with probability 0.5 for each value and X_2 is 0.5 with probability 1. Though the two random variables have the same mean, they are obviously very different.

The characteristics of the probability distribution of random variable X can be represented by a sequence of moments defined either as

(4.2.1) kth moment around zero $= EX^k$

or

(4.2.2) kth moment around mean $= E(X - EX)^k$.

Knowing all the moments (either around zero or around the mean) for $k = 1, 2, \ldots$, is equivalent to knowing the probability distribution completely. The expected value (or the mean) is the first moment around zero. Since either x^k or $(x - EX)^k$ is clearly a continuous function of x, moments can be evaluated using the formulae in Theorems 4.1.1 and 4.1.2.

As we defined sample mean in the previous section, we can similarly define the *sample kth moment around zero*. Let $X_1, X_2, \ldots, X_n$ be mutually independent and identically distributed as X. Then, $n^{-1}\Sigma_{i=1}^{n}X_i^k$ is the sample kth moment around zero based on a sample of size n. Like the sample mean, the sample kth moment converges to the population kth moment in probability, as will be shown in Chapter 6.

Next to the mean, by far the most important moment is the second moment around the mean, which is called the *variance*. Denoting the variance of X by VX, we have

DEFINITION 4.2.1

$$VX = E(X - EX)^2$$
$$= EX^2 - (EX)^2.$$

The second equality in this definition can be easily proved by expanding the squared term in the above and using Theorem 4.1.6. It gives a more convenient formula than the first. It says that the variance is the mean of the square minus the square of the mean. The square root of the variance is called the *standard deviation* and is denoted by σ. (Therefore variance is sometimes denoted by σ^2 instead of V.) From the definition it is clear that $VX \geq 0$ for any random variable and that $VX = 0$ if and only if $X = EX$ with probability 1.

The variance measures the degree of dispersion of a probability distribution. In the example of the coin-tossing gamble we have $VX_1 = \frac{1}{4}$ and $VX_2 = 0$. (As can be deduced from the definition, the variance of any constant is 0.) The following three examples indicate that the variance is an effective measure of dispersion.

EXAMPLE 4.2.1

$$X = \alpha \quad \text{with probability } \frac{1}{2}$$
$$= -\alpha \quad \text{with probability } \frac{1}{2}$$
$$VX = EX^2 = \alpha^2.$$

EXAMPLE 4.2.2 X has density $f(x) = 1/(2\alpha)$, $-\alpha < x < \alpha$.

$$VX = EX^2 = \frac{1}{2\alpha} \int_{-\alpha}^{\alpha} x^2 dx = \frac{1}{2\alpha} \left[\frac{x^3}{3} \right]_{-\alpha}^{\alpha} = \frac{\alpha^2}{3} .$$

EXAMPLE 4.2.3 (same as Example 4.1.1). X has density $f(x) = 2x^{-3}$, $1 < x$.

$$EX^2 = 2 \int_1^{\infty} x^{-1} dx = 2[\log x]_1^{\infty}.$$

$$\therefore VX = \infty.$$

Note that we previously obtained $EX = 2$, which shows that the variance is more strongly affected by the fat tail.

Examples 4.2.4 and 4.2.5 illustrate the use of the second formula of Definition 4.2.1 for computing the variance.

EXAMPLE 4.2.4 A die is loaded so that the probability of a given face turning up is proportional to the number on that face. Calculate the mean and variance for X, the face number showing.

We have, by Definition 4.1.1,

$$(4.2.3) \qquad EX = \frac{1}{21} (1 + 4 + 9 + 16 + 25 + 36) = \frac{13}{3} .$$

Next, using Theorem 4.1.1,

$$(4.2.4) \qquad EX^2 = \frac{1}{21} (1 + 8 + 27 + 64 + 125 + 216) = 21.$$

Therefore, by Definition 4.2.1,

$$(4.2.5) \qquad VX = 21 - \frac{169}{9} = \frac{20}{9} .$$

EXAMPLE 4.2.5 X has density $f(x) = 2(1 - x)$ for $0 < x < 1$ and $= 0$ otherwise. Compute VX.

By Definition 4.1.2 we have

$$(4.2.6) \qquad EX = 2 \int_0^1 (x - x^2) dx = \frac{1}{3} .$$

By Theorem 4.1.2 we have

$$(4.2.7) \qquad EX^2 = 2 \int_0^1 (x^2 - x^3)dx = \frac{1}{6}.$$

Therefore, by Definition 4.2.1,

$$(4.2.8) \qquad VX = \frac{1}{6} - \frac{1}{9} = \frac{1}{18}.$$

The following useful theorem is an easy consequence of the definition of the variance.

THEOREM 4.2.1 If α and β are constants, we have

$$V(\alpha X + \beta) = \alpha^2 VX.$$

Note that Theorem 4.2.1 shows that adding a constant to a random variable does not change its variance. This makes intuitive sense because adding a constant changes only the central location of the probability distribution and not its dispersion, of which the variance is a measure.

We shall seldom need to know any other moment, but we mention the third moment around the mean. It is 0 if the probability distribution is symmetric around the mean, positive if it is positively skewed as in Figure 4.1, and negative if it is negatively skewed as the mirror image of Figure 4.1 would be.

4.3 COVARIANCE AND CORRELATION

Covariance, denoted by $\text{Cov}(X, Y)$ or σ_{XY}, is a measure of the relationship between two random variables X and Y and is defined by

DEFINITION 4.3.1 $\text{Cov}(X, Y) = E[(X - EX)(Y - EY)] = EXY - EXEY.$

The second equality follows from expanding $(X - EX)(Y - EY)$ as the sum of four terms and then applying Theorem 4.1.6. Note that because of Theorem 4.1.6 the covariance can be also written as $E[(X - EX)Y]$ or $E[(Y - EY)X]$.

Let (X_1, Y_1), (X_2, Y_2), . . . , (X_n, Y_n) be mutually independent in the sense of Definition 3.5.4 and identically distributed as (X, Y). Then we define the *sample covariance* by $n^{-1}\Sigma_{i=1}^n (X_i - \bar{X})(Y_i - \bar{Y})$, where $\bar{X}$ and $\bar{Y}$ are the sample means of X and Y, respectively. Using the results of Chapter

6, we can show that the sample covariance converges to the population covariance in probability.

It is apparent from the definition that $\text{Cov} > 0$ if $X - EX$ and $Y - EY$ tend to have the same sign and that $\text{Cov} < 0$ if they tend to have the opposite signs, which is illustrated by

EXAMPLE 4.3.1

$$
\begin{aligned}
(X, Y) &= (1, 1) && \text{with probability } \alpha/2, \\
&= (-1, -1) && \text{with probability } \alpha/2, \\
&= (1, -1) && \text{with probability } (1 - \alpha)/2, \\
&= (-1, 1) && \text{with probability } (1 - \alpha)/2.
\end{aligned}
$$

Since $EX = EY = 0$,

$$\text{Cov}(X, Y) = EXY = \alpha - (1 - \alpha) = 2\alpha - 1.$$

Note that in this example $\text{Cov} = 0$ if $\alpha = \frac{1}{2}$, which is the case of independence between X and Y. More generally, we have

THEOREM 4.3.1 If X and Y are independent, $\text{Cov}(X, Y) = 0$ provided that VX and VY exist.

The proof follows immediately from the second formula of Definition 4.3.1 and Theorem 4.1.7. The next example shows that the converse of Theorem 4.3.1 is not necessarily true.

EXAMPLE 4.3.2 Let the joint probability distribution of (X, Y) be given by

X \ Y	-1	0	1
1	$\frac{1}{6}$	$\frac{1}{12}$	$\frac{1}{6}$
0	$\frac{1}{12}$	0	$\frac{1}{12}$
-1	$\frac{1}{6}$	$\frac{1}{12}$	$\frac{1}{6}$

Clearly, X and Y are not independent by Theorem 3.2.1, but we have $\text{Cov}(X, Y) = EXY = 0$.

Examples 4.3.3 and 4.3.4 illustrate the use of the second formula of Definition 4.3.1 for computing the covariance.

EXAMPLE 4.3.3 Let the joint probability distribution of (X, Y) be given by

X \ Y	-1	0	
1	$\frac{1}{4}$	$\frac{1}{4}$	$\frac{1}{2}$
0	$\frac{1}{8}$	$\frac{3}{8}$	$\frac{1}{2}$
	$\frac{3}{8}$	$\frac{5}{8}$	

where the marginal probabilities are also shown. We have $EX = \frac{1}{2}$, $EY = \frac{3}{8}$, and $EXY = \frac{1}{4}$. Therefore, by Definition 4.3.1, $\text{Cov}(X, Y) = \frac{1}{4} - \frac{3}{16} = \frac{1}{16}$.

EXAMPLE 4.3.4 Let the joint density be

$$f(x, y) = x + y, \quad \text{for } 0 < x < 1 \quad \text{and} \quad 0 < y < 1,$$

$$= 0 \qquad \text{otherwise.}$$

Calculate $\text{Cov}(X, Y)$.

We have

$$f(x) = \int_0^1 (x + y)dy = x + \frac{1}{2}$$

$$\therefore EX = \int_0^1 \left(x^2 + \frac{x}{2} \right)dx = \frac{7}{12}$$

$$\therefore EY = \frac{7}{12} \quad \text{by symmetry}$$

$$EXY = \int_0^1 \int_0^1 (x^2y + y^2x)dxdy = 2 \int_0^1 x^2dx \int_0^1 ydy = \frac{1}{3}$$

$$\therefore \text{Cov}(X, Y) = \frac{1}{3} - \frac{49}{144} = -\frac{1}{144} \quad \text{by Definition 4.3.1.}$$

Theorem 4.3.2 gives a useful formula for computing the variance of the sum or the difference of two random variables.

THEOREM 4.3.2 $V(X \pm Y) = VX + VY \pm 2 \, \text{Cov}(X, Y)$.

The proof follows immediately from the definitions of variance and covariance.

Combining Theorems 4.3.1 and 4.3.2, we can easily show that the variance of the sum of independent random variables is equal to the sum of the variances, which we state as

THEOREM 4.3.3 Let $X_i, i = 1, 2, \ldots, n$, be pairwise independent. Then

$$V\left(\sum_{i=1}^{n} X_i\right) = \sum_{i=1}^{n} VX_i.$$

It is clear from Theorem 4.3.2 that the conclusion of Theorem 4.3.3 holds if we merely assume $\text{Cov}(X_i, X_j) = 0$ for every pair such that $i \neq j$. As an application of Theorem 4.3.3, consider

EXAMPLE 4.3.5 There are five stocks, each of which sells for $100 per share and has the same expected annual return per share, μ, and the same variance of return, σ^2. Assume that the returns from the five stocks are pairwise independent. (a) If you buy ten shares of one stock, what will be the mean and variance of the annual return on your portfolio? (b) What if you buy two shares of each stock?

Let X_i be the return per share from the ith stock. Then, (a) $E(10X_i) = 10\mu$ by Theorem 4.1.6, and $V(10X_i) = 100\sigma^2$ by Theorem 4.2.1. (b) $E(2 \, \Sigma_{i=1}^{5} X_i) = 10\mu$ by Theorem 4.1.6, and $V(2\Sigma_{i=1}^{5} X_i) = 20\sigma^2$ by Theorem 4.2.1 and Theorem 4.3.3.

A weakness of covariance as a measure of relationship is that it depends on the units with which X and Y are measured. For example, Cov(Income, Consumption) is larger if both variables are measured in cents than in dollars. This weakness is remedied by considering *correlation (coefficient)*, defined by

DEFINITION 4.3.2

$$\text{Correlation}(X, Y) = \frac{\text{Cov}(X, Y)}{\sigma_X \cdot \sigma_Y}.$$

Correlation is often denoted by ρ_{XY} or simply ρ. It is easy to prove

THEOREM 4.3.4 If α and β are nonzero constants,

$$\text{Correlation}(\alpha X, \beta Y) = \text{Correlation}(X, Y).$$

We also have

THEOREM 4.3.5 $|\rho| \leq 1$.

Proof. Since the expected value of a nonnegative random variable is nonnegative, we have

(4.3.1) $E[(X - EX) - \lambda(Y - EY)]^2 \geq 0$ for any λ.

Expanding the squared term, we have

(4.3.2) $VX + \lambda^2 VY - 2\lambda \text{ Cov} \geq 0$ for any λ.

In particular, putting $\lambda = \text{Cov}/VY$ into the left-hand side of (4.3.2), we obtain the *Cauchy-Schwartz inequality*

(4.3.3) $VX - \dfrac{\text{Cov}^2}{VY} \geq 0.$

The theorem follows immediately from (4.3.3). ❏

If $\rho = 0$, we say X and Y are uncorrelated. If $\rho > 0$ ($\rho < 0$), we say X and Y are positively (negatively) correlated.

We next consider the problem of finding the best predictor of one random variable, Y, among all the possible linear functions of another random variable, X. This problem has a bearing on the correlation coefficient because the proportion of the variance of Y that is explained by the best linear predictor based on X turns out to be equal to the square of the correlation coefficient between Y and X, as we shall see below.

We shall interpret the word *best* in the sense of minimizing the mean squared error of prediction. The problem can be mathematically formulated as

(4.3.4)   Minimize $E(Y - \alpha - \beta X)^2$ with respect to α and β.

We shall solve this problem by calculus. Expanding the squared term, we can write the minimand, denoted by S, as

(4.3.5) $S = EY^2 + \alpha^2 + \beta^2 EX^2 - 2\alpha EY - 2\beta EXY + 2\alpha\beta EX.$

Equating the derivatives to zero, we obtain

(4.3.6) $\dfrac{\partial S}{\partial \alpha} = 2\alpha - 2EY + 2\beta EX = 0$

and

(4.3.7) $\dfrac{\partial S}{\partial \beta} = 2\beta EX^2 - 2EXY + 2\alpha EX = 0.$

Solving (4.3.6) and (4.3.7) simultaneously for α and β and denoting the optimal values by α^* and β^*, we get

(4.3.8) $\beta^* = \dfrac{\mathrm{Cov}(X, Y)}{VX}$

and

(4.3.9) $\alpha^* = EY - \dfrac{\mathrm{Cov}(X, Y)}{VX} EX.$

Thus we have proved

THEOREM 4.3.6 The *best linear predictor* (or more exactly, the minimum mean-squared-error linear predictor) of Y based on X is given by $\alpha^* + \beta^* X$, where α^* and β^* are defined by (4.3.8) and (4.3.9).

Next we shall ask what proportion of VY is explained by $\alpha^* + \beta^* X$ and what proportion is left unexplained. Define $\hat{Y} = \alpha^* + \beta^* X$ and $U = Y - \hat{Y}$. The latter will be called either the *prediction error* or the *residual*. We have

(4.3.10) $V\hat{Y} = (\beta^*)^2 VX$ by Theorem 4.2.1

$$= \frac{\text{Cov}(X, Y)^2}{VX} \quad \text{by (4.3.8)}$$

$$= \rho^2 VY \qquad \text{by Definition 4.3.2.}$$

We have

(4.3.11) $VU = V(Y - \alpha^* - \beta^* X)$

$$= VY + (\beta^*)^2 VX - 2\beta^* \text{Cov}(X, Y) \quad \text{by Theorem 4.3.2}$$

$$= VY - \frac{\text{Cov}(X, Y)^2}{VX} \qquad\qquad \text{by (4.3.8)}$$

$$= (1 - \rho^2)VY \qquad\qquad\qquad \text{by Definition 4.3.2.}$$

We call VU the *mean squared prediction error* of the best linear predictor. We also have

(4.3.12) $\text{Cov}(\hat{Y}, U) = \text{Cov}(\hat{Y}, Y - \hat{Y})$

$$= \text{Cov}(\hat{Y}, Y) - V\hat{Y} \qquad \text{by Definition 4.3.1}$$

$$= \beta^* \text{Cov}(X, Y) - V\hat{Y} \quad \text{by Definition 4.3.1}$$

$$= 0 \qquad\qquad\qquad\qquad \text{by (4.3.8) and (4.3.10).}$$

Combining (4.3.10), (4.3.11), and (4.3.12), we can say that any random variable Y can be written as the sum of the two parts—the part which is expressed as a linear function of another random variable X (namely, $\hat{Y}$) and the part which is uncorrelated with X (namely, U); a ρ^2 proportion of the variance of Y is attributable to the first part and a $1 - \rho^2$ proportion to the second part. This result suggests that the correlation coefficient is a measure of the degree of a linear relationship between a pair of random variables.

   As a further illustration of the point that ρ is a measure of linear dependence, consider Example 4.3.1 again. Since $VX = VY = 1$ in that example, $\rho = 2\alpha - 1$. When $\alpha = 1$, there is an exact linear relationship between X and Y with a positive slope. When $\alpha = 0$, there is an exact linear relationship with a negative slope. When $\alpha = \frac{1}{2}$, the degree of linear dependence is at the minimum.

A nonlinear dependence may imply a very small value of ρ. Suppose that there is an exact nonlinear relationship between X and Y defined by $Y = X^2$, and also suppose that X has a symmetric density around $EX = 0$. Then $\text{Cov}(X, Y) = EXY = EX^3 = 0$. Therefore $\rho = 0$. This may be thought of as another example where no correlation does not imply independence. In the next section we shall obtain the best predictor and compare it with the best linear predictor.

4.4 CONDITIONAL MEAN AND VARIANCE

In Chapters 2 and 3 we noted that conditional probability and conditional density satisfy all the requirements for probability and density. Therefore, we can define the conditional mean in a way similar to that of Definitions 4.1.1 and 4.1.2, using the conditional probability defined in Section 3.2.2 and the various types of conditional densities defined in Section 3.3.2 and 3.4.3. Here we shall give two definitions: one for the discrete bivariate random variables and the other concerning the conditional density given in Theorem 3.4.3.

DEFINITION 4.4.1 Let (X, Y) be a bivariate discrete random variable taking values (x_i, y_j), $i, j = 1, 2, \ldots$. Let $P(y_j | X)$ be the conditional probability of $Y = y_j$ given X. Let $\phi(\cdot, \cdot)$ be an arbitrary function. Then the *conditional mean* of $\phi(X, Y)$ given X, denoted by $E[\phi(X, Y) | X]$ or by $E_{Y|X}\phi(X, Y)$, is defined by

$$(4.4.1) \qquad E_{Y|X}\phi(X, Y) = \sum_{j=1}^{\infty} \phi(X, y_j)P(y_j | X).$$

DEFINITION 4.4.2 Let (X, Y) be a bivariate continuous random variable with conditional density $f(y | x)$. Let $\phi(\cdot, \cdot)$ be an arbitrary function. Then the *conditional mean* of $\phi(X, Y)$ given X is defined by

$$(4.4.2) \qquad E_{Y|X}\phi(X, Y) = \int_{-\infty}^{\infty} \phi(X, y)f(y | X)dy.$$

The conditional mean $E_{Y|X}\phi(X, Y)$ is a function only of X. It may be evaluated at a particular value that X assumes, or it may be regarded as a random variable, being a function of the random variable X. If we treat it as a random variable, we can take a further expectation of it using the probability distribution of X. The following theorem shows what happens.

THEOREM 4.4.1 (law of iterated means) $E\phi(X, Y) = E_X E_{Y|X}\phi(X, Y)$. (The symbol E_X indicates that the expectation is taken treating X as a random variable.)

Proof. We shall prove it only for the case of continuous random variables; the proof is easier for the case of discrete random variables.

$$(4.4.3) \qquad E\phi(X, Y) = \int_{-\infty}^{\infty} \int_{-\infty}^{\infty} \phi(x, y) f(x, y) dx dy.$$

$$= \int_{-\infty}^{\infty} \int_{-\infty}^{\infty} \phi(x, y) f(y \mid x) f(x) dx dy.$$

$$= \int_{-\infty}^{\infty} \left[\int_{-\infty}^{\infty} \phi(x, y) f(y \mid x) dy \right] f(x) dx.$$

$$= E_X E_{Y|X}\phi(X, Y). \quad \square$$

The following theorem is sometimes useful in computing variance. It says that the variance is equal to the mean of the conditional variance plus the variance of the conditional mean.

THEOREM 4.4.2

$$(4.4.4) \qquad V\phi(X, Y) = E_X V_{Y|X}\phi(X, Y) + V_X E_{Y|X}\phi(X, Y).$$

Proof. Since

$$(4.4.5) \qquad V_{Y|X}\phi = E_{Y|X}\phi^2 - (E_{Y|X}\phi)^2,$$

we have

$$(4.4.6) \qquad E_X V_{Y|X}\phi = E\phi^2 - E_X(E_{Y|X}\phi)^2.$$

But we have

$$(4.4.7) \qquad V_X E_{Y|X}\phi = E_X(E_{Y|X}\phi)^2 - (E\phi)^2.$$

Therefore, by adding both sides of (4.4.6) and (4.4.7),

$$(4.4.8) \qquad E_X V_{Y|X}\phi + V_X E_{Y|X}\phi = E\phi^2 - (E\phi)^2 = V\phi. \quad \square$$

The following examples show the advantage of using the right-hand side of (4.4.3) and (4.4.4) in computing the unconditional mean and variance.

EXAMPLE 4.4.1 Suppose $f(x) = 1$ for $0 < x < 1$ and $= 0$ otherwise and $f(y \mid x) = x^{-1}$ for $0 < y < x$ and $= 0$ otherwise. Calculate EY.

This problem may be solved in two ways. First, use Theorem 4.4.1:

$$E(Y \mid x) = \int_0^x \frac{y}{x} \, dy = \frac{x}{2}.$$

$$E_X E(Y \mid X) = E_X \left(\frac{X}{2} \right) = \frac{1}{4}.$$

Second, use Definition 4.1.2:

$$f(x, y) = f(y \mid x)f(x) = \frac{1}{x}, \qquad 0 < x < 1, \quad 0 < y < x.$$

$$f(y) = \int_y^1 \frac{1}{x} \, dx = \log y, \qquad 0 < y < 1.$$

$$EY = \int_0^1 (-y \log y) dy = -\left[\frac{1}{2} y^2 \log y - \frac{1}{4} y^2 \right]_0^1 = \frac{1}{4}.$$

EXAMPLE 4.4.2 The marginal density of X is given by $f(x) = 1, 0 < x < 1$. The conditional probability of Y given X is given by

$$P(Y = 1 \mid X = x) = x.$$
$$P(Y = 0 \mid X = x) = 1 - x.$$

Find EY and VY.

$$EY = E_X E_{Y|X} Y = E_X X = \frac{1}{2}.$$

$$VY = V_X E_{Y|X} Y + E_X V_{Y|X} Y$$

$$= V_X X + E_X (X - X^2)$$

$$= E_X X - (E_X X)^2 = \frac{1}{4}.$$

The result obtained in Example 4.4.2 can be alternatively obtained using the result of Section 3.7, as follows. We have

(4.4.9) $P(Y = 1) = P(Y = 1, 0 < X < 1)$

$$= P(0 < X < 1 \mid Y = 1)P(Y = 1)$$

$$= \int_0^1 f(x \mid Y = 1)P(Y = 1)dx$$

$$= \int_0^1 P(Y = 1 \mid x)f(x)dx \quad \text{by (3.7.2)}$$

$$= \int_0^1 xdx$$

$$= \frac{1}{2}.$$

Therefore the mean and variance of Y can be shown to be the same as obtained above, using the definition of the mean and the variance of a discrete random variable which takes on either 1 or 0.

In the previous section we solved the problem of optimally predicting Y by a linear function of X. Here we shall consider the problem of optimally predicting Y by a general function of X. The problem can be mathematically formulated as

(4.4.10)   Minimize $E[Y - \phi(X)]^2$ with respect to ϕ.

Despite the apparent complexity of the problem, there is a simple solution. We have

(4.4.11) $E[Y - \phi(X)]^2 = E\{[Y - E(Y \mid X)] + [E(Y \mid X) - \phi(X)]\}^2$

$$= E[Y - E(Y \mid X)]^2 + E[E(Y \mid X) - \phi(X)]^2,$$

where the cross-product has dropped out because

$$E_{Y \mid X}\{[Y - E(Y \mid X)][E(Y \mid X) - \phi(X)]\} = 0.$$

Therefore (4.4.11) is clearly minimized by choosing $\phi(X) = E(Y \mid X)$. Thus we have proved

THEOREM 4.4.3 The *best predictor* (or more exactly, the minimum mean-squared-error predictor) of Y based on X is given by $E(Y \mid X)$.

In the next example we shall compare the best predictor with the best linear predictor.

EXAMPLE 4.4.3   A fair die is rolled. Let Y be the face number showing. Define X by the rule

$$X = Y \quad \text{if } Y \text{ is even,}$$

$$= 0 \quad \text{if } Y \text{ is odd.}$$

Find the best predictor and the best linear predictor of Y based on X.
The following table gives $E(Y \mid X)$.

X	0	2	4	6
$E(Y \mid X)$	3	2	4	6

To compute the best linear predictor, we must first compute the moments that appear on the right-hand sides of (4.3.8) and (4.3.9): $EY = 7/2$, $EX = 2$, $EX^2 = EXY = 28/3$, $EY^2 = 91/6$, $VX = 16/3$, $VY = 35/12$, Cov $= 7/3$. Therefore

$$\alpha^* = 21/8, \qquad \beta^* = 7/16.$$

Put $\hat{Y} = (21/8) + (7/16)X$. Thus we have

X	0	2	4	6
$\hat{Y}$	2.625	3.5	4.375	5.25

where the values taken by Y and X are indicated by empty circles in Figure 4.2.

We shall compute the mean squared error of prediction for each predictor:

$$E(Y - \hat{Y})^2 = VY - \text{Cov}^2/VX = 35/12 - 49/48$$

$$= 91/48 \cong 1.9.$$

$$E[Y - E(Y \mid X)]^2 = (1/6) \cdot 4 + (1/6) \cdot 4 = 4/3 \cong 1.3.$$

EXAMPLE 4.4.4   Let the joint probability distribution of X and Y be given as follows: $P(X = 1, Y = 1) \equiv P_{11} = 0.3$, $P(X = 1, Y = 0) \equiv P_{10} = 0.2$, $P(X = 0, Y = 1) \equiv P_{01} = 0.2$, $P(X = 0, Y = 0) \equiv P_{00} = 0.3$. Obtain the

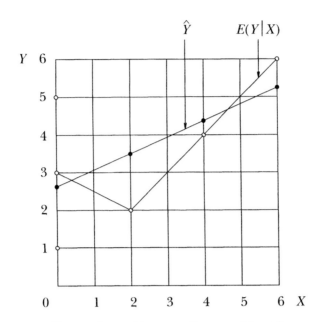

FIGURE 4.2   Comparison of best predictor and best linear predictor

best predictor and the best linear predictor of Y as functions of X and calculate the mean squared prediction error of each predictor.

We have

$$E(Y \mid X = 1) = P_{11}/(P_{11} + P_{10})$$

and

$$E(Y \mid X = 0) = P_{01}/(P_{01} + P_{00}).$$

Both equations can be combined into one as

(4.4.12) $E(Y \mid X) = [P_{11}/(P_{11} + P_{10})]X + [P_{01}/(P_{01} + P_{00})](1 - X),$

which is a linear function of X. This result shows that the best predictor is identical with the best linear predictor, but as an illustration we shall obtain two predictors separately.

Best predictor. From (4.4.12) we readily obtain $E(Y \mid X) = 0.4 + 0.2X$. Its mean squared prediction error (MSPE) can be calculated as follows:

(4.4.13) $MSPE = E[Y - E(Y \mid X)]^2$

$$= E_X E_{Y \mid X} [Y^2 + E(Y \mid X)^2 - 2YE(Y \mid X)]$$

$$= EY^2 - E_X[E(Y \mid X)^2]$$

$$= 0.5 - 0.26 = 0.24.$$

Best linear predictor. The moments of X and Y can be calculated as follows: $EX = EY = 0.5$, $VX = VY = 0.25$, and $\text{Cov}(X, Y) = 0.05$. Inserting these values into equations (4.3.8) and (4.3.9) yields $\beta^* = 0.2$ and $\alpha^* = 0.4$. From (4.3.11) we obtain

(4.4.14) $MSPE = VY - \dfrac{\text{Cov}(X, Y)^2}{VX} = 0.24.$

EXERCISES

1. (Section 4.1)
   A station is served by two independent bus lines going to the same destination. In the first line buses come at a regular interval of five minutes, and in the second line ten minutes. You get on the first bus that comes. What is the expected waiting time?

2. (Section 4.2)
   Let the probability distribution of (X, Y) be given by

X \ Y	1	2
1	$\frac{1}{8}$	$\frac{2}{8}$
2	$\frac{2}{8}$	$\frac{3}{8}$

   Find $V(X \mid Y)$.

3. (Section 4.2)
   Let X be the number of tosses required until a head comes up. Compute EX and VX assuming the probability of heads is equal to p.

4. (Section 4.2)
   Let the density of X be given by

$$f(x) = x \qquad \text{for } 0 < x < 1,$$
$$= 2 - x \quad \text{for } 1 < x < 2,$$
$$= 0 \qquad \text{otherwise.}$$

Calculate VX.

5. (Section 4.3)

Let the probability distribution of (X, Y) be given by

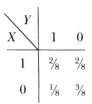

(a) Show that $X + Y$ and $X - (20/19)Y$ are uncorrelated.

(b) Are $X + Y$ and $X - (20/19)Y$ independent?

6. (Section 4.3)

Let (X, Y) have joint density $f(x, y) = x + y$ for $0 < x < 1$ and $0 < y < 1$. Compute $\mathrm{Cov}(X, Y)$.

7. (Section 4.3)

Let (X, Y) have joint density $f(x, y) = 2$ for $0 < x < 1$ and $0 < y < x$. Compute VX and $\mathrm{Cov}(X, Y)$.

8. (Section 4.3)

Let $EX = EY = 0$, $VX = VY = 2$, and $\mathrm{Cov}(X, Y) = 1$. Determine α and β so that $V(\alpha X + \beta Y) = 1$ and $\mathrm{Cov}(\alpha X + \beta Y, X) = 0$.

9. (Section 4.3)

Suppose X and Y are independent with $EX = 1, VX = 1, EY = 2$, and $VY = 1$. Define $Z = X + Y$ and $W = XY$. Calculate $\mathrm{Cov}(Z, W)$.

10. (Section 4.4)

Let X, Y, and Z be random variables, each of which takes only two values: 1 and 0. Given $P(X = 1) = 0.5$, $P(Y = 1 \mid X = 1) = 0.6$, $P(Y = 1 \mid X = 0) = 0.4$, $P(Z = 1 \mid Y = 1) = 0.7$, $P(Z = 1 \mid Y = 0) = 0.3$, find EZ and $E(Z \mid X = 1)$. Assume that the probability distribution of Y depends only on X and that of Z only on Y.

11. (Section 4.4)

    Let $X = 1$ with probability p and 0 with probability $1 - p$. Let the conditional density of Y given $X = 1$ be uniform over $0 < y < 1$ and given $X = 0$ be uniform over $0 < y < 2$. Obtain $\text{Cov}(X, Y)$.

12. (Section 4.4)

    Let $f(x, y) = 1$ for $0 < x < 1$ and $0 < y < 1$. Obtain $E(X \mid X < Y)$.

13. (Section 4.4)

    With the same density as in Exercise 6, obtain $E(X \mid Y = X + 0.5)$.

14. (Section 4.4–Prediction)

    Let the joint probability distribution of X and Y be given by

X \ Y	2	1	0
2	0.2	0.1	0
1	0.1	0.2	0.1
0	0	0.1	0.2

    Obtain the best predictor and the best linear predictor of Y as functions of X and calculate the mean squared prediction error for each predictor.

15. (Section 4.4–Prediction)

    Suppose $EX = EY = 0$, $VX = VY = 1$, and $\text{Cov}(X, Y) = 0.5$. If we define $Z = X + Y$, find the best linear predictor of Y based on Z.

16. (Section 4.4–Prediction)

    Give an example in which X can be used to predict Y perfectly, but Y is of no value in predicting X. Supply your own definition of the phrase "no value in predicting X."

17. (Section 4.4–Prediction)

    Let X be uniformly distributed over $[0, 1]$ and for some c in $(0, 1)$ define

    $$Y = 1 \quad \text{if } X \geq c,$$
    $$= 0 \quad \text{if } X < c.$$

Find the best predictor of X given Y, denoted $\hat{X}$ and compare the variances $V(X)$ and $V(U)$, where $U = X - \hat{X}$.

18. (Section 4.4–Prediction)

    Suppose U and V are independent with *exponential distribution* with parameter λ. (T is exponentially distributed with parameter λ if its density is given by $\lambda \exp(-\lambda t)$ for $t > 0$.) Define $X = U + V$ and $Y = UV$. Find the best predictor and the best linear predictor of Y given X.

19. (Section 4.4–Prediction)

    Suppose that X and Y are independent, each distributed as $B(1, p)$. (See Section 5.1 for the definition.) Find the best predictor and the best linear predictor of $X + Y$ given $X - Y$. Compute their respective mean squared prediction errors and directly compare them.

5 | BINOMIAL AND NORMAL RANDOM VARIABLES

5.1 BINOMIAL RANDOM VARIABLES

Let X be the number of successes in n independent trials of some experiment whose outcome is "success" or "failure" when the probability of success in each trial is p. Such a random variable often appears in practice (for example, the number of heads in n tosses) and is called a *binomial random variable*. More formally we state

DEFINITION 5.1.1 Let $\{Y_i\}$, $i = 1, 2, \ldots, n$, be mutually independent with the probability distribution given by

$$(5.1.1) \qquad Y_i = 1 \quad \text{with probability } p$$

$$= 0 \quad \text{with probability } 1 - p \equiv q.$$

Then the random variable X defined by

$$(5.1.2) \qquad X = \sum_{i=1}^{n} Y_i$$

is called a *binomial* random variable. Symbolically we write $X \sim B(n, p)$.

Note that Y_i defined in (5.1.1) is distributed as $B(1, p)$, which is called a *binary* or *Bernoulli* random variable.

THEOREM 5.1.1 For the binomial random variable X we have

$$(5.1.3) \qquad P(X = k) = C_k^n p^k q^{n-k},$$

(5.1.4) $EX = np,$

and

(5.1.5) $VX = npq.$

Proof. The probability that the first k trials are successes and the remaining $n - k$ trials are failures is equal to $p^k q^{n-k}$. Since k successes can occur in any of C_k^n combinations with an equal probability, we must multiply the above probability by C_k^n to give formula (5.1.3). Using (5.1.2), the mean and variance of X can be obtained by the following steps:

(5.1.6) $EY_i = p$ for every i

(5.1.7) $EY_i^2 = p$ for every i

(5.1.8) $VY_i = p - p^2 = pq$ for every i

(5.1.9) $EX = \sum_{i=1}^{n} EY_i = np$ by Theorem 4.1.6

(5.1.10) $VX = \sum_{i=1}^{n} VY_i = npq$ by Theorem 4.3.3.   ☐

Note that the above derivation of the mean and variance is much simpler than the direct derivation using (5.1.3). For example, in the direct derivation we must compute

$$EX = \sum_{k=1}^{n} k C_k^n p^k q^{n-k}.$$

EXAMPLE 5.1.1   Let X be the number of heads in five tosses of a fair coin. Obtain the probability distribution of X and calculate EX and VX.

In this example we have $n = 5$ and $p = 0.5$. Therefore by (5.1.3) we have

(5.1.11) $P(X = k) = C_k^5 \left(\dfrac{1}{2}\right)^k \left(\dfrac{1}{2}\right)^{5-k} = \dfrac{C_k^5}{32}.$

Evaluating (5.1.11) for each k, we have

(5.1.12) $P(X = 0) = P(X = 5) = 0.03125$

$$P(X = 1) = P(X = 4) = 0.15625$$

$$P(X = 2) = P(X = 3) = 0.3125.$$

Using (5.1.4) and (5.1.5), we have $EX = 2.5$ and $VX = 1.25$.

5.2 NORMAL RANDOM VARIABLES

The normal distribution is by far the most important continuous distribution used in statistics. Many reasons for its importance will become apparent as we study its properties below. We should mention that the binomial random variable X defined in Definition 5.1.1 is approximately normally distributed when n is large. This is a special case of the so-called central limit theorem, which we shall discuss in Chapter 6. Examples of the normal approximation of binomial are given in Section 6.3.

DEFINITION 5.2.1 The *normal density* is given by

$$(5.2.1) \qquad f(x) = \frac{1}{\sqrt{2\pi}\,\sigma} \exp\left[-\frac{1}{2}\left(\frac{x-\mu}{\sigma}\right)^2\right], \qquad -\infty < x < \infty, \quad \sigma > 0.$$

When X has the above density, we write symbolically $X \sim N(\mu, \sigma^2)$.

We can verify $\int_{-\infty}^{\infty} f(x)dx = 1$ for all μ and all positive σ by a rather complicated procedure using polar coordinates. See, for example, Hoel (1984, p. 78). The direct evaluation of a general integral $\int_a^b f(x)dx$ is difficult because the normal density does not have an indefinite integral. Such an integral may be approximately evaluated from a normal probability table or by a computer program based on a numerical method, however.

The normal density is completely characterized by two parameters, μ and σ. We have

THEOREM 5.2.1 Let X be $N(\mu, \sigma^2)$. Then $EX = \mu$ and $VX = \sigma^2$.

Proof. We have

$$(5.2.2) \qquad EX = \int_{-\infty}^{\infty} \frac{1}{\sqrt{2\pi}\,\sigma}\, x \exp\left[-\frac{1}{2}\left(\frac{x-\mu}{\sigma}\right)^2\right]dx$$

$$= \int_{-\infty}^{\infty} \frac{1}{\sqrt{2\pi}} (\sigma z + \mu) \exp(-z^2/2) dz \quad \text{by putting } z = \frac{x - \mu}{\sigma}$$

$$= \frac{\sigma}{\sqrt{2\pi}} \int_{-\infty}^{\infty} z \exp(-z^2/2) dz + \mu \int_{-\infty}^{\infty} \frac{1}{\sqrt{2\pi}} \exp(-z^2/2) dz.$$

But we have

(5.2.3) $$\int_{-\infty}^{\infty} z \exp(-z^2/2) dz = -[\exp(-z^2/2)]_{-\infty}^{\infty} = 0$$

and

(5.2.4) $$\int_{-\infty}^{\infty} \frac{1}{\sqrt{2\pi}} \exp(-z^2/2) dz = 1,$$

because the integrand in (5.2.4) is the density of $N(0, 1)$. Therefore, from (5.2.2), (5.2.3), and (5.2.4), we have $EX = \mu$. Next we have

(5.2.5) $$VX = \frac{1}{\sqrt{2\pi}\,\sigma} \int_{-\infty}^{\infty} (x - \mu)^2 \exp\left[-\frac{1}{2} \left(\frac{x - \mu}{\sigma} \right)^2 \right] dx$$

$$= \frac{\sigma^2}{\sqrt{2\pi}} \int_{-\infty}^{\infty} z^2 \exp(-z^2/2) dz \quad \text{by putting } z = \frac{x - \mu}{\sigma}$$

$$= -\frac{\sigma^2}{\sqrt{2\pi}} [z \exp(-z^2/2)]_{-\infty}^{\infty} + \sigma^2 \int_{-\infty}^{\infty} \frac{1}{\sqrt{2\pi}} \exp(-z^2/2) dz$$

using integration by parts

$$= \sigma^2. \quad \square$$

From (5.2.1) it is clear that $f(x)$ is symmetric and bell-shaped around μ. $EX = \mu$ follows directly from this fact. To study the effect of σ on the shape of $f(x)$, observe

(5.2.6) $$f(\mu) = \frac{1}{\sqrt{2\pi}\,\sigma},$$

which shows that the larger σ is, the flatter $f(x)$ is.

Theorem 5.2.2 shows an important property of a normal random variable: a linear function of a normal random variable is again normal.

THEOREM 5.2.2 Let X be $N(\mu, \sigma^2)$ and let $Y = \alpha + \beta X$. Then we have $Y \sim N(\alpha + \beta\mu, \beta^2\sigma^2)$.

Proof. Using Theorem 3.6.1, the density $g(y)$ of Y is given by

$$(5.2.7) \qquad g(y) = \frac{1}{\sqrt{2\pi}\,|\beta|\sigma} \exp\left[-\frac{1}{2\beta^2}\left(\frac{y - \alpha - \beta\mu}{\sigma}\right)^2\right].$$

Therefore, by Definition 5.2.1, $Y \sim N(\alpha + \beta\mu, \beta^2\sigma^2)$. ❑

A useful corollary of Theorem 5.2.2 is that if X is $N(\mu, \sigma^2)$, then $Z \equiv (X - \mu)/\sigma$ is $N(0, 1)$, which is called the *standard normal* random variable. We will often need to evaluate the probability $P(x_1 < X < x_2)$ when X is $N(\mu, \sigma^2)$. Defining Z in the above way, we have

$$(5.2.8) \qquad P(x_1 < X < x_2) = P\left(\frac{x_1 - \mu}{\sigma} < Z < \frac{x_2 - \mu}{\sigma}\right).$$

The right-hand side of (5.2.8) can be evaluated from the probability table of the standard normal distribution.

EXAMPLE 5.2.1 Assuming $X \sim N(10, 4)$, calculate $P(4 < X < 8)$.

$$(5.2.9) \qquad P(4 < X < 8) = P\left(\frac{4 - 10}{2} < \frac{X - 10}{2} < \frac{8 - 10}{2}\right)$$

$$= P(-3 < Z < -1) \quad \text{where } Z \sim N(0, 1)$$

$$= P(Z < -1) - P(Z < -3)$$

$$= 0.1587 - 0.0013$$

from the standard normal table

$$= 0.1574.$$

Sometimes the problem specifies a probability and asks one to determine the variance, as in the following example.

EXAMPLE 5.2.2 Assume that the life in hours of a light bulb is normally distributed with mean 100. If it is required that the life should exceed 80 with at least 0.9 probability, what is the largest value that σ can have?

Let X be the life of a light bulb. Then $X \sim N(100, \sigma^2)$. We must determine σ^2 so as to satisfy

(5.2.10) $P(X > 80) > 0.9$.

Defining $Z = (X - 100)/\sigma$, (5.2.10) is equivalent to

(5.2.11) $P\left(Z > \dfrac{-20}{\sigma}\right) > 0.9$.

From the standard normal table we see that

(5.2.12) $P(Z > -1.28) = 0.8997$.

From (5.2.11) and (5.2.12) we conclude that we must have $\sigma \leq 15.6$.

5.3 BIVARIATE NORMAL RANDOM VARIABLES

DEFINITION 5.3.1 The *bivariate normal density* is defined by

$$(5.3.1) \quad f(x, y) = \frac{1}{2\pi\sigma_X\sigma_Y\sqrt{1 - \rho^2}} \exp\left\{ -\frac{1}{2(1 - \rho^2)} \left[\left(\frac{x - \mu_X}{\sigma_X}\right)^2 \right. \right.$$

$$\left. \left. + \left(\frac{y - \mu_Y}{\sigma_Y}\right)^2 - 2\rho\left(\frac{x - \mu_X}{\sigma_X}\right)\left(\frac{y - \mu_Y}{\sigma_Y}\right) \right] \right\}.$$

THEOREM 5.3.1 Let (X, Y) have the density (5.3.1). Then the marginal densities $f(x)$ and $f(y)$ and the conditional densities $f(y \mid x)$ and $f(x \mid y)$ are univariate normal densities, and we have $EX = \mu_X$, $VX = \sigma_X^2$, $EY = \mu_Y$, $VY = \sigma_Y^2$, Correlation$(X, Y) = \rho$, and finally

$$(5.3.2) \quad E(Y \mid X) = \mu_Y + \rho\frac{\sigma_Y}{\sigma_X}(X - \mu_X), \qquad V(Y \mid X) = \sigma_Y^2(1 - \rho^2).$$

Proof. The joint density $f(x, y)$ can be rewritten as

$$(5.3.3) \quad f(x, y) = \frac{1}{\sqrt{2\pi}\,\sigma_Y\sqrt{1 - \rho^2}}$$

$$\cdot \exp\left\{ -\frac{1}{2\sigma_Y^2(1 - \rho^2)} \left[y - \mu_Y - \rho\frac{\sigma_Y}{\sigma_X}(x - \mu_X) \right]^2 \right\}$$

$$\cdot \frac{1}{\sqrt{2\pi}\,\sigma_X} \exp\left[-\frac{1}{2\sigma_X^2}(x - \mu_X)^2\right]$$

$$\equiv f_2 \cdot f_1,$$

where f_1 is the density of $N(\mu_X, \sigma_X^2)$ and f_2 is the density of $N[\mu_Y + \rho\sigma_Y\sigma_X^{-1}(x - \mu_X), \sigma_Y^2(1 - \rho^2)]$. All the assertions of the theorem follow from (5.3.3) without much difficulty. We have

$$(5.3.4) \qquad f(x) = \int_{-\infty}^{\infty} f_2 f_1 \, dy$$

$$= f_1 \int_{-\infty}^{\infty} f_2 dy \quad \text{because } f_1 \text{ does not depend on } y$$

$$= f_1 \qquad\qquad \text{because } f_2 \text{ is a normal density.}$$

Therefore we immediately see $X \sim N(\mu_X, \sigma_X^2)$. By symmetry we have $Y \sim N(\mu_Y, \sigma_Y^2)$. Next we have

$$(5.3.5) \qquad f(y \mid x) = \frac{f(x, y)}{f(x)} = \frac{f_2 f_1}{f_1} = f_2.$$

Therefore we can conclude that the conditional distribution of Y given $X = x$ is $N[\mu_Y + \rho\sigma_Y\sigma_X^{-1}(x - \mu_X), \sigma_Y^2(1 - \rho^2)]$. All that is left to show is that Correlation$(X, Y) = \rho$. We have by Theorem 4.4.1

$$(5.3.6) \qquad EXY = E_X E(XY \mid X) = E_X[XE(Y \mid X)]$$

$$= E_X[X\mu_Y + \rho\sigma_Y\sigma_X^{-1}X(X - \mu_X)]$$

$$= \mu_X\mu_Y + \rho\sigma_Y\sigma_X.$$

Therefore Cov$(X, Y) = \rho\sigma_Y\sigma_X$; hence Correlation$(X, Y) = \rho$. ❑

In the above discussion we have given the bivariate normal density (5.3.1) as a definition and then derived its various properties in Theorem 5.3.1. We can also prove that (5.3.1) is indeed the only function of x and y that possesses these properties. The next theorem shows a very important property of the bivariate normal distribution.

THEOREM 5.3.2 If X and Y are bivariate normal and α and β are constants, then $\alpha X + \beta Y$ is normal.

Proof. Because of Theorem 5.2.2, we need to prove the theorem only for the case that $\beta = 1$. Define $W = \alpha X + Y$. Then we have

$$(5.3.7) \qquad P(W < t) = \int_{-\infty}^{\infty} \int_{-\infty}^{t-\alpha x} f(x, y)\,dy\,dx$$

$$= \int_{-\infty}^{\infty} \left[\int_{-\infty}^{t-\alpha x} f(y \mid x)\,dy \right] f(x)\,dx.$$

Differentiating both sides of (5.3.7) with respect to t and denoting the density of W by $g(\cdot)$, we have

$$(5.3.8) \qquad g(t) = \int_{-\infty}^{\infty} f(t - \alpha x \mid x) f(x)\,dx$$

$$= \int_{-\infty}^{\infty} \frac{1}{\sqrt{2\pi}\,\sigma_Y \sqrt{1 - \rho^2}} \exp\left\{ -\frac{1}{2\sigma_Y^2(1 - \rho^2)} \right.$$

$$\left. \left[t - \alpha\mu_X - \mu_Y - \left(\rho\frac{\sigma_Y}{\sigma_X} + \alpha \right)(x - \mu_X) \right]^2 \right\}$$

$$\cdot \frac{1}{\sqrt{2\pi}\,\sigma_X} \exp\left[-\frac{1}{2\sigma_X^2}(x - \mu_X)^2 \right] dx.$$

If we define $(\sigma_Y^*)^2 = \alpha^2\sigma_X^2 + \sigma_Y^2 + 2\alpha\rho\sigma_X\sigma_Y$ and $\rho^* = (\rho\sigma_Y + \alpha\sigma_X)/\sigma_Y^*$, we can rewrite (5.3.8) as

$$(5.3.9) \qquad g(t) = \int_{-\infty}^{\infty} \frac{1}{\sqrt{2\pi}\,\sigma_Y^* \sqrt{1 - (\rho^*)^2}} \exp\left\{ -\frac{1}{2(\sigma_Y^*)^2[1 - (\rho^*)^2]} \right.$$

$$\left. \left[t - \alpha\mu_X - \mu_Y - \rho^*\frac{\sigma_Y^*}{\sigma_X}(x - \mu_X) \right]^2 \right\}$$

$$\cdot \frac{1}{\sqrt{2\pi}\,\sigma_X} \exp\left[-\frac{1}{2\sigma_X^2}(x - \mu_X)^2 \right] dx$$

$$\equiv \int_{-\infty}^{\infty} f_3 f_1\,dx.$$

But clearly f_3 is the density of $N[\alpha\mu_X + \mu_Y + \rho^*(\sigma_Y^*/\sigma_X)(x - \mu_X),$ $(\sigma_Y^*)^2(1 - \rho^{*2})]$ and f_1 is that of $N(\mu_X, \sigma_X^2)$, as before. We conclude, therefore, using Theorem 5.3.1 and equation (5.3.1), that $g(t)$ is a normal density. ❑

It is important to note that the conclusion of Theorem 5.3.2 does not necessarily follow if we merely assume that each of X and Y is univariately normal. See Ferguson (1967, p. 111) for an example of a pair of univariate normal random variables which are jointly not normal.

By applying Theorem 5.3.2 repeatedly, we can easily prove that a linear combination of n-variate normal random variables is normal. In particular, we have

THEOREM 5.3.3 Let $\{X_i\}$, $i = 1, 2, \ldots, n$, be pairwise independent and identically distributed as $N(\mu, \sigma^2)$. Then $\bar{X} \equiv (1/n)\Sigma_{i=1}^{n}X_i$ is $N(\mu, \sigma^2/n)$.

The following is another important property of the bivariate normal distribution.

THEOREM 5.3.4 If X and Y are bivariate normal and $\text{Cov}(X, Y) = 0$, then X and Y are independent.

Proof. If we put $\rho = 0$ in (5.3.1), we immediately see that $f(x, y) = f(x)f(y)$. Therefore X and Y are independent by Definition 3.4.6. ❑

Note that the expression for $E(Y \mid X)$ obtained in (5.3.2) is precisely the best linear predictor of Y based on X, which was obtained in Theorem 4.3.6. Since we showed in Theorem 4.4.3 that $E(Y \mid X)$ is the best predictor of Y based on X, the best predictor and the best linear predictor coincide in the case of the normal distribution—another interesting feature of normality.

In the preceding discussion we proved (5.3.2) before we proved Theorems 5.3.2 and 5.3.4. It may be worthwhile to point out that (5.3.2) follows readily from Theorems 5.3.2 and 5.3.4 and equations (4.3.10), (4.3.11), and (4.3.12). Recall that these three equations imply that for any pair of random variables X and Y there exists a random variable Z such that

$$(5.3.10) \quad Y = \mu_Y + \rho \frac{\sigma_Y}{\sigma_X}(X - \mu_X) + \sigma_Y Z,$$

$EZ = 0$, $VZ = 1 - \rho^2$, and $\text{Cov}(X, Z) = 0$. If, in addition, X and Y are bivariate normal, Z is also normal because of Theorem 5.3.2. Therefore Z and X are independent because of Theorem 5.3.4, which implies that

$E(Z \mid X) = EZ = 0$ and $V(Z \mid X) = VZ = 1 - \rho^2$. Therefore, taking the conditional mean and variance of both sides of (5.3.10), we arrive at (5.3.2).

Conversely, however, the linearity of $E(Y \mid X)$ does not imply the joint normality of X and Y, as Example 4.4.4 shows. Examples 4.4.1 and 4.4.2 also indicate the same point. The following two examples are applications of Theorems 5.3.1 and 5.3.3, respectively.

EXAMPLE 5.3.1   Suppose X and Y are distributed jointly normal with $EX = 1$, $EY = 2$, $VX = VY = \frac{1}{3}$, and the correlation coefficient $\rho = \frac{1}{2}$. Calculate $P(2.2 < Y < 3.2 \mid X = 3)$.

Using (5.3.2) we have

$$E(Y \mid X) = 2 + \frac{1}{2}(X - 1)$$

$$E(Y \mid X = 3) = 3$$

$$V(Y \mid X) = \frac{1}{3}\left(1 - \frac{1}{4}\right) = \frac{1}{4}.$$

Therefore, Y given $X = 3$ is $N(3, \frac{1}{4})$. Defining $Z \sim N(0, 1)$, we have

$$P(2.2 < Y < 3.2 \mid X = 3) = P(-1.6 < Z < 0.4)$$

$$= P(Z < 0.4) - P(Z < -1.6)$$

$$= 0.6554 - 0.0548 = 0.6006.$$

EXAMPLE 5.3.2   If you wish to estimate the mean of a normal population whose variance is 9, how large a sample should you take so that the probability is at least 0.8 that your estimate will not be in error by more than 0.5?

Put $X_i \sim N(\mu, 9)$. Then, by Theorem 5.3.3,

$$\bar{X}_n = \frac{1}{n}\sum_{i=1}^{n} X_i \sim N\left(\mu, \frac{9}{n}\right).$$

We want to choose n so that

$$P(|\bar{X}_n - \mu| < 0.5) > 0.8.$$

Defining the standard normal $Z \equiv \sqrt{n}\,(\bar{X}_n - \mu)/3$, the inequality above is equivalent to

$$P\left(|Z| < \frac{0.5\sqrt{n}}{3}\right) > 0.8,$$

which implies $n > 59.13$. Therefore, the answer is 60.

5.4 MULTIVARIATE NORMAL RANDOM VARIABLES

In this section we present results on multivariate normal variables in matrix notation. The student unfamiliar with matrix analysis should read Chapter 11 before this section. The results of this section will not be used directly until Section 9.7 and Chapters 12 and 13.

Let $\mathbf{x}$ be an n-dimensional column vector with $E\mathbf{x} = \boldsymbol{\mu}$ and $V\mathbf{x} = \boldsymbol{\Sigma}$. (Throughout this section, a matrix is denoted by a boldface capital letter and a vector by a boldface lowercase letter.) We write their elements explicitly as follows:

$$\mathbf{x} = \begin{bmatrix} x_1 \\ x_2 \\ \cdot \\ \cdot \\ \cdot \\ x_n \end{bmatrix}, \quad \boldsymbol{\mu} = \begin{bmatrix} \mu_1 \\ \mu_2 \\ \cdot \\ \cdot \\ \cdot \\ \mu_n \end{bmatrix}, \quad \boldsymbol{\Sigma} = \begin{bmatrix} \sigma_{11} & \sigma_{12} & \cdot & \cdot & \cdot & \sigma_{1n} \\ \sigma_{21} & \sigma_{22} & \cdot & \cdot & \cdot & \sigma_{2n} \\ \cdot & \cdot & & & & \\ \cdot & \cdot & & & & \\ \cdot & \cdot & & & & \\ \sigma_{n1} & \sigma_{n2} & \cdot & \cdot & \cdot & \sigma_{nn} \end{bmatrix}.$$

Note that $\sigma_{ij} = \mathrm{Cov}(x_i, x_j)$, $i, j = 1, 2, \ldots, n$, and, in particular, $\sigma_{ii} = Vx_i$, $i = 1, 2, \ldots, n$. We sometimes write σ_i^2 for σ_{ii}.

DEFINITION 5.4.1   We say $\mathbf{x}$ is *multivariate normal* with mean $\boldsymbol{\mu}$ and variance-covariance matrix $\boldsymbol{\Sigma}$, denoted $N(\boldsymbol{\mu}, \boldsymbol{\Sigma})$, if its density is given by

$$(5.4.1) \qquad f(\mathbf{x}) = (2\pi)^{-n/2}|\boldsymbol{\Sigma}|^{-1/2}\exp\left[-\frac{1}{2}(\mathbf{x} - \boldsymbol{\mu})'\boldsymbol{\Sigma}^{-1}(\mathbf{x} - \boldsymbol{\mu})\right].$$

The reader should verify that in the case of $n = 2$, the above density is reduced to the bivariate density (5.3.1).

Now we state without proof generalizations of Theorems 5.3.1, 5.3.2, and 5.3.4.

THEOREM 5.4.1 Let $x \sim N(\mu, \Sigma)$ and partition $x' = (y', z')$, where y is h-dimensional and z is k-dimensional such that $h + k = n$. Partition Σ conformably as

$$\Sigma = \begin{bmatrix} \Sigma_{11} & \Sigma_{12} \\ \Sigma_{21} & \Sigma_{22} \end{bmatrix},$$

where $\Sigma_{11} = Vy \equiv E[(y - Ey)(y - Ey)']$, $\Sigma_{22} = Vz \equiv E[(z - Ez)(z - Ez)']$, $\Sigma_{12} = E[(y - Ey)(z - Ez)']$, and $\Sigma_{21} = (\Sigma_{12})'$. Then any subvector of x, such as y or z, is multivariate normal, and the conditional distribution of y given z (similarly for z given y) is multivariate normal with

$$E(y \mid z) = Ey + \Sigma_{12}(\Sigma_{22})^{-1}(z - Ez)$$

and

$$V(y \mid z) = \Sigma_{11} - \Sigma_{12}(\Sigma_{22})^{-1}\Sigma_{21}.$$

THEOREM 5.4.2 Let $x \sim N(\mu, \Sigma)$ and let A be an $m \times n$ matrix of constants such that $m \le n$ and the rows of A are linearly independent. Then $Ax \sim N(A\mu, A\Sigma A')$.

THEOREM 5.4.3 Suppose $x \sim N(\mu, \Sigma)$ and let y and z be defined as in Theorem 5.4.1. If $\Sigma_{12} = 0$, y and z are independent. That is to say, $f(x) = f(y)f(z)$, where $f(y)$ and $f(z)$ are the multivariate densities of y and z, respectively.

EXERCISES

1. (Section 5.1)
   Five fair dice are rolled once. Let X be the number of aces that turn up. Compute EX, VX, and $P(X \ge 4)$.

2. (Section 5.2)
   Suppose X, Y, and W are mutually independent and distributed as $X \sim N(1, 4)$, $Y \sim N(2, 9)$, $W \sim B(1, 0.5)$. Calculate $P(U < 5)$ where $U = WX + (1 - W)Y$.

3. (Section 5.2)
   Let $X = S$ and $Y = T + TS^2$, where S and T are independent and distributed as $N(0, 1)$ and $N(1, 1)$, respectively. Find the best predic-

tor and the best linear predictor of Y given X and calculate their respective mean squared prediction errors.

4. (Section 5.3)

   Suppose U and V are independent and each is distributed as $N(0, 1)$. Define X and Y by

   $$Y = X - 1 - U,$$

   $$X = 2Y - 3 - V.$$

   Obtain $E(Y \mid X)$ and $V(Y \mid X)$.

5. (Section 5.3)

   Let (X_i, Y_i) be i.i.d. (independent and identically distributed) drawings from bivariate normal random variables with $EX = 1$, $EY = 2$, $VX = 4$, $VY = 9$, and $\mathrm{Cov}(X, Y) = 2.75$. Define $\bar{X} = \Sigma_{i=1}^{36} X_i / 36$ and $\bar{Y} = \Sigma_{i=1}^{36} Y_i / 36$. Calculate $P(\bar{Y} > 3 - 2\bar{X})$.

6. (Section 5.3)

   Suppose $(X, Y) \sim BN(0, 0, 1, 1, \rho)$, meaning that X and Y are bivariate normal with zero means and unit variances and correlation ρ. Find the best predictor and the best linear predictor of Y^2 given X and find their respective mean squared prediction errors.

6 | LARGE SAMPLE THEORY

We have already alluded to results in large sample theory without stating them in exact terms. In Chapter 1 we mentioned that the empirical frequency r/n, where r is the number of heads in n tosses of a coin, converges to the probability of heads; in Chapter 4, that a sample mean converges to the population mean; and in Chapter 5, that the binomial variable is approximately distributed as a normal variable. The first two are examples of a law of large numbers, and the third, an example of a central limit theorem. In this chapter we shall make the notions of these convergences more precise. Most of the theorems will be stated without proofs. For the proofs the reader should consult, for example, Rao (1973), Chung (1974), Serfling (1980), or Amemiya (1985).

6.1 MODES OF CONVERGENCE

Let us first review the definition of the convergence of a sequence of real numbers.

DEFINITION 6.1.1 A sequence of real numbers $\{\alpha_n\}$, $n = 1, 2, \ldots$, is said to converge to a real number α if for any $\epsilon > 0$ there exists an integer N such that for all $n > N$ we have

$$(6.1.1) \qquad |\alpha_n - \alpha| < \epsilon.$$

We write $\alpha_n \to \alpha$ as $n \to \infty$ or $\lim_{n \to \infty} \alpha_n = \alpha$ ($n \to \infty$ will be omitted if it is obvious from the context).

Now we want to generalize Definition 6.1.1 to a sequence of random variables. If α_n were a random variable, we could not have (6.1.1) exactly, because it would be sometimes true and sometimes false. We could only talk about the probability of (6.1.1) being true. This suggests that we should modify the definition in such a way that the conclusion states that (6.1.1) holds with a probability approaching 1 as n goes to infinity. Thus we have

DEFINITION 6.1.2 (convergence in probability). A sequence of random variables $\{X_n\}$, $n = 1, 2, \ldots$, is said to converge to a random variable X *in probability* if for any $\epsilon > 0$ and $\delta > 0$ there exists an integer N such that for all $n > N$ we have $P(|X_n - X| < \epsilon) > 1 - \delta$. We write $X_n \xrightarrow{P} X$ as $n \to \infty$ or $\text{plim}_{n \to \infty} X_n = X$. The last equality reads "the *probability limit* of X_n is X." (Alternatively, the if clause may be paraphrased as follows: if $\lim P(|X_n - X| < \epsilon) = 1$ for any $\epsilon > 0$.)

Unlike the case of the convergence of a sequence of constants, for which only one mode of convergence is sufficient, we need two other modes of convergence, *convergence in mean square* and *convergence in distribution*, for a sequence of random variables. There is still another mode of convergence, *almost sure convergence*, but we will not use it here. A definition can be found in any of the aforementioned books.

DEFINITION 6.1.3 (convergence in mean square) A sequence $\{X_n\}$ is said to *converge* to X *in mean square* if $\lim_{n \to \infty} E(X_n - X)^2 = 0$. We write $X_n \xrightarrow{M} X$.

DEFINITION 6.1.4 (convergence in distribution) A sequence $\{X_n\}$ is said to *converge* to X *in distribution* if the distribution function F_n of X_n converges to the distribution function F of X at every continuity point of F. We write $X_n \xrightarrow{d} X$, and we call F the *limit distribution* of $\{X_n\}$. If $\{X_n\}$ and $\{Y_n\}$ have the same limit distribution, we write $X_n \overset{\text{LD}}{=} Y_n$.

The following two theorems state that convergence in mean square implies convergence in probability, which, in turn, implies convergence in distribution.

THEOREM 6.1.1 (Chebyshev) $X_n \overset{M}{\to} X \Rightarrow X_n \overset{P}{\to} X$.

THEOREM 6.1.2 $X_n \overset{P}{\to} X \Rightarrow X_n \overset{d}{\to} X$.

Theorem 6.1.1 is deduced from the following inequality due to Chebyshev, which is useful on its own:

$$(6.1.2) \qquad P[g(X_n) \ge \epsilon^2] \le \frac{Eg(X_n)}{\epsilon^2},$$

where $g(\cdot)$ is any nonnegative continuous function. To prove Theorem 6.1.1, take $g(x)$ to be x^2 and take X_n of (6.1.2) to be $X_n - X$. Chebyshev's inequality follows from the simple result:

$$(6.1.3) \qquad Eg(X_n) = \int_{-\infty}^{\infty} g(x)f_n(x)dx \ge \epsilon^2 \int_S f_n(x)dx,$$

where $f_n(x)$ is the density function of X_n and $S = \{x \mid g(x) \ge \epsilon^2\}$. Here we have assumed the existence of the density for simplicity, but inequality (6.1.2) is true for any sequence of random variables, provided that $Eg(X_n)$ exists. The following two theorems are very useful in proving the convergence of a sequence of functions of random variables.

THEOREM 6.1.3   Let $\mathbf{X}_n$ be a vector of random variables with a fixed finite number of elements. Let g be a function continuous at a constant vector point $\boldsymbol{\alpha}$. Then $\mathbf{X}_n \overset{P}{\to} \boldsymbol{\alpha} \Rightarrow g(\mathbf{X}_n) \overset{P}{\to} g(\boldsymbol{\alpha})$.

THEOREM 6.1.4 (Slutsky)   If $X_n \overset{d}{\to} X$ and $Y_n \overset{P}{\to} \alpha$, then

(i) $X_n + Y_n \overset{d}{\to} X + \alpha$,

(ii) $X_n Y_n \overset{d}{\to} \alpha X$,

(iii) $(X_n / Y_n) \overset{d}{\to} X/\alpha$, provided $\alpha \ne 0$.

We state without proof the following generalization of the Slutsky theorem. Suppose that g is a continuous function except for finite discontinuities, plim $Y_{in} = \alpha_i$, $i = 1, 2, \ldots, J$, and $\{X_{in}\}$, $i = 1, 2, \ldots, K$, converge jointly to $\{X_i\}$ in distribution. Then the limit distribution of $g(X_{1n}, X_{2n}, \ldots, X_{Kn}, Y_{1n}, Y_{2n}, \ldots, Y_{Jn})$ is the same as the distribution of $g(X_1, X_2, \ldots, X_K, \alpha_1, \alpha_2, \ldots, \alpha_J)$. Here the joint convergence of $\{X_{in}\}$ to $\{X_i\}$ is an important necessary condition.

6.2 LAWS OF LARGE NUMBERS AND CENTRAL LIMIT THEOREMS

Given a sequence of random variables $\{X_i\}$, $i = 1, 2, \ldots$, define $\bar{X}_n = n^{-1}\Sigma_{i=1}^n X_i$. A *law of large numbers* (LLN) specifies the conditions under which $\bar{X}_n - E\bar{X}_n$ converges to 0 in probability. This law is sometimes referred to as a weak law of large numbers to distinguish it from a strong law of large numbers, which concerns the almost sure convergence. We do not use the strong law of convergence, however, and therefore the distinction is unnecessary here.

In many applications the simplest way to show $\bar{X}_n - E\bar{X}_n \overset{P}{\to} 0$ is to show $\bar{X}_n - E\bar{X}_n \overset{M}{\to} 0$ and then to apply Theorem 6.1.1 (Chebyshev). In certain situations it will be easier to apply

THEOREM 6.2.1 (Khinchine) Let $\{X_i\}$ be independent and identically distributed (i.i.d.) with $EX_i = \mu$. Then $\bar{X}_n \overset{P}{\to} \mu$.

Note that the conclusion of Theorem 6.2.1 can be obtained from a different set of assumptions on $\{X_i\}$ if we use Theorem 6.1.1 (Chebyshev). For example, if $\{X_i\}$ are uncorrelated with $EX_i = \mu$ and $VX_i = \sigma^2$, then $\bar{X}_n \overset{M}{\to} \mu$; therefore, by Theorem 6.1.1, $\bar{X}_n \overset{P}{\to} \mu$.

Now we ask the question, what is an approximate distribution of $\bar{X}_n$ when n is large? Suppose a law of large numbers holds for a sequence $\{X_i\}$ so that $\bar{X}_n - E\bar{X}_n \overset{P}{\to} 0$. It follows from Theorem 6.1.2 that $\bar{X}_n - E\bar{X}_n \overset{d}{\to} 0$. It is an uninteresting limit distribution, however, because it is degenerate. It is more meaningful to inquire into the limit distribution of $Z_n \equiv (V\bar{X}_n)^{-1/2}(\bar{X}_n - E\bar{X}_n)$. For if the limit distribution of Z_n exists, it should be nondegenerate, because $VZ_n = 1$ for all n. A central limit theorem (CLT) specifies the conditions under which Z_n converges in distribution to a standard normal random variable. We shall write $Z_n \to N(0, 1)$. More precisely, it means the following: if F_n is the distribution function of Z_n,

$$(6.2.1) \qquad \lim_{n\to\infty} F_n(z) = \int_{-\infty}^z \frac{1}{\sqrt{2\pi}} \exp(-x^2/2)dx.$$

We shall state two central limit theorems—Lindeberg-Lévy and Liapounov.

THEOREM 6.2.2 (Lindeberg-Lévy) Let $\{X_i\}$ be i.i.d. with $EX_i = \mu$ and $VX_i = \sigma^2$. Then $Z_n \to N(0, 1)$.

THEOREM 6.2.3 (Liapounov) Let $\{X_i\}$ be independent with $EX_i = \mu_i$, $VX_i = \sigma_i^2$, and $E(|X_i - \mu_i|^3) = m_{3i}$. If

$$\lim_{n \to \infty} \left(\sum_{i=1}^n \sigma_i^2 \right)^{-1/2} \left(\sum_{i=1}^n m_{3i} \right)^{1/3} = 0,$$

then $Z_n \to N(0, 1)$.

These two CLTs are complementary: the assumptions of one are more restrictive in some respects and less restrictive in other respects than those of the other. Both are special cases of the most general CLT, which is due to Lindeberg and Feller. We shall not use it in this book, however, because its condition is more difficult to verify.

In the terminology of Definition 6.1.4, central limit theorems provide conditions under which the limit distribution of $Z_n \equiv (V\bar{X}_n)^{-1/2}(\bar{X}_n - E\bar{X}_n)$ is $N(0, 1)$. We now introduce the term *asymptotic distribution*, which means the "approximate distribution when n is large." Given the mathematical result $Z_n \overset{d}{\to} N(0, 1)$, we shall make statements such as "the asymptotic distribution of Z_n is $N(0, 1)$" (written as $Z_n \overset{A}{\sim} N(0, 1)$) or "the asymptotic distribution of $\bar{X}_n$ is $N(E\bar{X}_n, V\bar{X}_n)$." This last statement may also be stated as "$\bar{X}_n$ is *asymptotically normal* with the *asymptotic mean* $E\bar{X}_n$ and the *asymptotic variance* $V\bar{X}_n$." These statements should be regarded merely as more intuitive paraphrases of the result $Z_n \overset{d}{\to} N(0, 1)$. Note that it would be meaningless to say that "the limit distribution of $\bar{X}_n$ is $N(E\bar{X}_n, V\bar{X}_n)$."

6.3 NORMAL APPROXIMATION OF BINOMIAL

Here we shall consider in detail the normal approximation of a binomial variable as an application of the Lindeberg-Lévy CLT (Theorem 6.2.2). In Definition 5.1.1 we defined a binomial variable X as a sum of i.i.d. Bernoulli variables $\{Y_i\}$: that is, $X = \Sigma_{i=1}^n Y_i$, where $Y_i = 1$ with probability p and $= 0$ with probability $q \equiv 1 - p$. Since $\{Y_i\}$ satisfy the conditions of the Lindeberg-Lévy CLT, with $EY_i = p$ and $VY_i = pq$, we can conclude

(6.3.1) $\dfrac{X/n - p}{\sqrt{pq/n}} \overset{d}{\to} N(0, 1).$

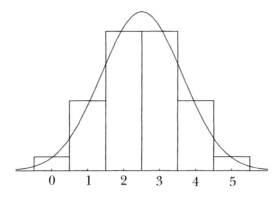

FIGURE 6.1   Normal approximation of $B(5,0.5)$

As we stated in the last paragraph of Section 6.2, we may replace $\xrightarrow{\text{d}}$ above by $\overset{\text{A}}{\sim}$. Or we may state alternatively that $X/n \overset{\text{A}}{\sim} N(p, pq/n)$ or that $X \overset{\text{A}}{\sim} (np, npq)$. We shall consider three examples of a normal approximation of a binomial.

EXAMPLE 6.3.1   Let X be as defined in Example 5.1.1. Since $EX = 2.5$ and $VX = 1.25$ in this case, we shall approximate binomial X by normal $X^* \sim N(2.5, 1.25)$. The density function $f(x)$ of $N(2.5, 1.25)$ is, after some rounding off,

$$(6.3.2) \qquad f(x) = \frac{1}{2.8} \exp[-(x - 2.5)^2/2.5].$$

Using (5.1.12) and (6.3.2), we draw the probability step function of binomial X and the density function of normal X^* in Figure 6.1. The figure suggests that $P(X = 1)$ should be approximated by $P(0.5 < X^* < 1.5)$, $P(X = 2)$ by $P(1.5 < X^* < 2.5)$, and so on. As for $P(X = 0)$, it may be approximated either by $P(X^* < 0.5)$ or $P(-0.5 < X^* < 0.5)$. The same is true of $P(X = 5)$. The former seems preferable, however, because it makes the sum of the approximate probabilities equal to unity. The true probabilities and their approximations are given in Table 6.1.

EXAMPLE 6.3.2   Change the above example to $p = 0.2$. Then $EX = 1$ and $VX = 0.8$. The results are summarized in Table 6.2 and Figure 6.2.

EXAMPLE 6.3.3   If 5% of the labor force is unemployed, what is the probability that one finds three or more unemployed workers among

TABLE 6.1 Normal approximation of $B(5, 0.5)$

X	Probability	Approximation
0 or 5	0.03125	0.0367
1 or 4	0.15625	0.1500
2 or 3	0.31250	0.3133

TABLE 6.2 Normal approximation of $B(5, 0.2)$

k	$P(X = k)$	Approximation
0	0.3277	0.2877
1	0.4096	0.4246
2	0.2048	0.2412
3	0.0512	0.0439
4	0.0064⎤	0.0026
5	0.0003⎦	

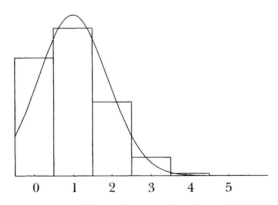

FIGURE 6.2 Normal approximation of $B(5,0.2)$

twelve randomly chosen workers? What if 50% of the labor force is unemployed?

Let X be the number of unemployed workers among twelve workers. Then $X \sim B(12, p)$, where we first assume $p = 0.05$. We first calculate the exact probability:

(6.3.3) $P(X \geq 3) = 1 - P(X = 0) - P(X = 1) - P(X = 2)$

$$= 1 - \left(\frac{19}{20}\right)^{12} - 12\left(\frac{1}{20}\right)\left(\frac{19}{20}\right)^{11} - 66\left(\frac{1}{20}\right)^2\left(\frac{19}{20}\right)^{10}$$

$$\cong 0.02.$$

Next, approximating X by $X^* \sim N(0.6, 0.57)$, we have

(6.3.4) $P(X \geq 3) \cong P(X^* > 2.5) = P\left(\dfrac{X^* - 0.6}{\sqrt{0.57}} > \dfrac{2.5 - 0.6}{\sqrt{0.57}}\right)$

$$= P(Z > 2.52) = 0.0059,$$

where Z is $N(0, 1)$. This is a poor approximation.

Next, put $p = 0.5$. Then the exact probability is given by

(6.3.5) $P(X \geq 3) = 1 - \left(\dfrac{1}{2}\right)^{12} - 12\left(\dfrac{1}{2}\right)^{12} - 66\left(\dfrac{1}{2}\right)^{12} = 0.9807,$

and the approximation using $X^* \sim N(6, 3)$ yields

(6.3.6) $P(X \geq 3) \cong P(X^* > 2.5) = P(Z > -2.02) = 0.9783,$

which is a good approximation.

6.4 EXAMPLES

We shall give further examples of applications of the convergence theorems of Section 6.1 and 6.2. There will be more applications in Chapter 7, as well.

EXAMPLE 6.4.1 Let $\{X_i\}$ be independent with $EX_i = \mu$, $VX_i = \sigma_i^2$. Under what conditions on σ_i^2 and $\{X_i\}$ does $\bar{X} \equiv \Sigma_{i=1}^n X_i/n$ converge to μ in probability?

We can answer this question by using either Theorem 6.1.1 (Chebyshev) or Theorem 6.2.1 (Khinchine). In the first case, note $E(\bar{X} - \mu)^2 = V\bar{X} = n^{-2}\Sigma_{i=1}^n\sigma_i^2$. The required condition, therefore, is that this last quantity should converge to 0 as n goes to infinity. In the second case, we should assume that $\{X_i\}$ are identically distributed in addition to being independent.

EXAMPLE 6.4.2 In Example 6.4.1, assume further that $E|X_i - \mu|^3 = m_3$. Under what conditions on σ_i^2 does $(\bar{X} - \mu)/\sqrt{V\bar{X}}$ converge to $N(0, 1)$?

The condition of Theorem 6.2.3 (Liapounov) in this case becomes

$$(m_3)^{1/3} \lim_{n\to\infty} n^{1/3} \left(\sum_{i=1}^n \sigma_i^2\right)^{-1/2} = 0.$$

A sufficient condition to ensure this is

$$\lim_{n\to\infty} n^{-2/3}\sum_{i=1}^n \sigma_i^2 = \infty.$$

EXAMPLE 6.4.3 Let $\{X_i\}$ be i.i.d. with a finite mean μ and a finite variance σ^2. Prove that the sample variance, defined as $S_X^2 \equiv n^{-1}\Sigma_{i=1}^n X_i^2 - \bar{X}^2$, converges to σ^2 in probability.

By Khinchine's LLN (Theorem 6.2.1) we have $\text{plim}_{n\to\infty} n^{-1}\Sigma_{i=1}^n X_i^2 = EX^2$ and $\text{plim}_{n\to\infty} \bar{X} = \mu$. Because S_X^2 is clearly a continuous function of $n^{-1}\Sigma_{i=1}^n X_i^2$ and $\bar{X}$, the desired result follows from Theorem 6.1.3.

EXAMPLE 6.4.4 Let $\{X_i\}$ be i.i.d. with $EX_i = \mu_X \neq 0$ and $VX_i = \sigma_X^2$ and let $\{Y_i\}$ be i.i.d. with $EY_i = \mu_Y$ and $VY_i = \sigma_Y^2$. Assume that $\{X_i\}$ and $\{Y_i\}$ are independent of each other. Obtain the asymptotic distribution of $\bar{Y}/\bar{X}$.

By Theorem 6.2.1 (Khinchine), $\bar{X} \xrightarrow{P} \mu_X$ and $\bar{Y} \xrightarrow{P} \mu_X$. Therefore, by Theorem 6.1.3, $\bar{Y}/\bar{X} \xrightarrow{P} \mu_Y/\mu_X$. The next step is to find an appropriate normalization of $(\bar{Y}/\bar{X} - \mu_Y/\mu_X)$ to make it converge to a proper random variable. For this purpose note the identity

$$(6.4.1) \qquad \frac{\bar{Y}}{\bar{X}} - \frac{\mu_Y}{\mu_X} = \frac{\mu_X(\bar{Y} - \mu_Y) - \mu_Y(\bar{X} - \mu_X)}{\bar{X}\mu_X}.$$

Then we can readily see that the numerator will converge to a normal variable with an appropriate normalization and the denominator will converge to $(\mu_X)^2$ in probability, so that we can use (iii) of Theorem 6.1.4 (Slutsky). Define $W_i = \mu_X Y_i - \mu_Y X_i$. Then $\{W_i\}$ satisfies the conditions of Theorem 6.2.2 (Lindeberg-Lévy). Therefore

$$(6.4.2) \qquad Z_n \equiv n^{-1/2}\sigma_W^{-1} \sum_{i=1}^{n} (W_i - EW_i) \to N(0, 1),$$

where $\sigma_W^2 = \mu_X^2\sigma_Y^2 + \mu_Y^2\sigma_X^2$. Using (iii) of Theorem 6.1.4 (Slutsky), we obtain from (6.4.1) and (6.4.2)

$$(6.4.3) \qquad \frac{\sqrt{n}}{\sigma_W}\left(\frac{\bar{Y}}{\bar{X}} - \frac{\mu_Y}{\mu_X}\right) = \frac{Z_n}{\bar{X}}\mu_X \to N(0, \mu_X^{-4}).$$

We therefore conclude

$$(6.4.4) \qquad \frac{\bar{Y}}{\bar{X}} \overset{A}{\sim} N\left(\frac{\mu_Y}{\mu_X}, \frac{\sigma_W^2}{n\mu_X^4}\right).$$

EXERCISES

1. (Section 6.1)
   Give an example of a sequence of random variables which converges to a constant in probability but not in mean square and an example of a sequence of random variables which converges in distribution but not in probability.

2. (Section 6.1)
   Prove that if a sequence of random variables converges to a constant in distribution, it converges to the same constant in probability.

3. (Section 6.2)
   Let $\{X_i, Y_i\}$, $i = 1, 2, \ldots, n$, be i.i.d. with the common mean $\mu > 0$ and common variance σ^2 and define $\bar{X} = n^{-1}\Sigma_{i=1}^{n}X_i$ and $\bar{Y} = n^{-1}\Sigma_{i=1}^{n}Y_i$. Assume that $\{X_i\}$ and $\{Y_i\}$ are independent. Assume also that $Y_i > 0$ for all i. Obtain the probability limit and the asymptotic distribution of $\bar{X} + \log \bar{Y}$. At each step of the derivation, indicate clearly which theorems of Chapter 6 are used.

4. (Section 6.3)
   It is known that 5% of a daily output of machines are defective. What is the probability that a sample of 10 contains 2 or more defective

machines? Solve this exercise both by using the binomial distribution and by using the normal approximation.

5. (Section 6.3)

There is a coin which produces heads with an unknown probability p. How many times should we throw this coin if the proportion of heads is to lie within 0.05 of p with probability at least 0.9?

6. (Section 6.4)

Let $\{X_i\}$ be as in Example 6.4.4. Obtain the asymptotic distribution of
(a) $\bar{X}^2$.
(b) $1/\bar{X}$.
(c) $\exp(\bar{X})$.

7. (Section 6.4)

Suppose X has a *Poisson distribution* $P(X = k) = (\lambda^k e^{-\lambda})/k!$ Derive the probability limit and the asymptotic distribution of the estimator

$$\hat{\lambda} = \frac{-1 + \sqrt{1 + 4Z_n}}{2},$$

based on a sample of size n, where $Z_n = n^{-1}\Sigma_{i=1}^n X_i^2$. Note that $EX = VX = \lambda$ and $V(X^2) = 4\lambda^3 + 6\lambda^2 + \lambda$.

8. (Section 6.4)

Let $\{X_i\}$ be independent with $EX = \mu$ and $VX = \sigma^2$. What more assumptions on $\{X_i\}$ are needed in order for $\hat{\sigma}^2 = \Sigma(X_i - \bar{X})^2/n$ to converge to σ^2 in probability? What more assumptions are needed for its asymptotic normality?

9. (Section 6.4)

Suppose $\{X_i\}$ are i.i.d. with $EX = 0$ and $VX = \sigma^2 < \infty$.
(a) Obtain

$$\text{plim}_{n\to\infty} n^{-1} \sum_{i=1}^n (X_i + X_{i+1}).$$

(b) Obtain the limit distribution of

$$n^{-1/2} \sum_{i=1}^n (X_i + X_{i+1}).$$

10. (Section 6.4)

Let $\{X_i, Y_i\}$ be i.i.d. with the means μ_X and μ_Y, the variances σ_X^2 and σ_Y^2, and the covariance σ_{XY}. Derive the asymptotic distribution of

$$\frac{\bar{X} - \bar{Y}}{\bar{X} + \bar{Y}}.$$

Explain carefully each step of the derivation and at each step indicate what convergence theorems you have used. If a theorem has a well-known name, you may simply refer to it. Otherwise, describe it.

11. (Section 6.4)

Suppose $X \sim N[\exp(\alpha\beta), 1]$ and $Y \sim N[\exp(\alpha), 1]$, independent of each other. Let $\{X_i, Y_i\}$, $i = 1, 2, \ldots, n$, be i.i.d. observations on (X, Y), and define $\bar{X} = n^{-1}\Sigma_{i=1}^n X_i$ and $\bar{Y} = n^{-1}\Sigma_{i=1}^n Y_i$. We are to estimate β by $\hat{\beta} = \log\bar{X}/\log\bar{Y}$. Prove the consistency of $\hat{\beta}$ (see Definition 7.2.5, p. 132) and derive its asymptotic distribution.

7 | POINT ESTIMATION

Chapters 7 and 8 are both concerned with estimation: Chapter 7 with point estimation and Chapter 8 with interval estimation. The goal of point estimation is to obtain a single-valued estimate of a parameter in question; the goal of interval estimation is to determine the degree of confidence we can attach to the statement that the true value of a parameter lies within a given interval. For example, suppose we want to estimate the probability (p) of heads on a given coin toss on the basis of five heads in ten tosses. Guessing p to be 0.5 is an act of point estimation. We can never be perfectly sure that the true value of p is 0.5, however. At most we can say that p lies within an interval, say, (0.3, 0.7), with a particular degree of confidence. This is an act of interval estimation.

In this chapter we discuss estimation from the standpoint of classical statistics. The Bayesian method, in which point estimation and interval estimation are more closely connected, will be discussed in Chapter 8.

7.1 WHAT IS AN ESTIMATOR?

In Chapter 1 we stated that statistics is the science of estimating the probability distribution of a random variable on the basis of repeated observations drawn from the same random variable. If we denote the random variable in question by X, the n repeated observations in mathematical terms mean a sequence of n mutually independent random variables $X_1, X_2, \ldots, X_n$, each of which has the same distribution as X. (We say that $\{X_i\}$ are i.i.d.)

For example, suppose we want to estimate the probability (p) of heads for a given coin. We can define $X = 1$ if a head appears and $= 0$ if a tail appears. Then X_i represents the outcome of the ith toss of the same coin. If X is the height of a male Stanford student, X_i is the height of the ith student randomly chosen.

We call the basic random variable X, whose probability distribution we wish to estimate, the *population,* and we call $(X_1, X_2, \ldots, X_n)$ a *sample* of size n. Note that $(X_1, X_2, \ldots, X_n)$ are random variables before we observe them. Once we observe them, they become a sequence of numbers, such as $(1, 1, 0, 0, 1, \ldots)$ or $(5.9, 6.2, 6.0, 5.8, \ldots)$. These observed values will be denoted by lowercase letters $(x_1, x_2, \ldots, x_n)$. They are also referred to by the same name, *sample.*

7.1.1 Sample Moments

In Chapter 4 we defined population moments of various kinds. Here we shall define the corresponding sample moments. Sample moments are "natural" estimators of the corresponding population moments. We define

Sample mean

$$\bar{X} \equiv \frac{1}{n} \sum_{i=1}^{n} X_i.$$

Sample variance

$$S_X^2 \equiv \frac{1}{n} \sum_{i=1}^{n} (X_i - \bar{X})^2 = \frac{1}{n} \sum_{i=1}^{n} X_i^2 - (\bar{X})^2.$$

Sample kth moment around zero

$$\frac{1}{n} \sum_{i=1}^{n} X_i^k.$$

Sample kth moment around the mean

$$\frac{1}{n} \sum_{i=1}^{n} (X_i - \bar{X})^k.$$

If (X_i, Y_i), $i = 1, 2, \ldots, n$, are mutually independent in the sense of Definition 3.5.4 and have the same distribution as (X, Y), we call $\{(X_i, Y_i)\}$ a bivariate sample of size n on a bivariate population (X, Y). We define

Sample covariance

$$\frac{1}{n} \sum_{i=1}^{n} (X_i - \bar{X})(Y_i - \bar{Y}) = \frac{1}{n} \sum_{i=1}^{n} X_i Y_i - \bar{X}\bar{Y}.$$

Sample correlation

$$\frac{\text{Sample Covariance}}{S_X S_Y}.$$

The observed values of the sample moments are also called by the same names. They are defined by replacing the capital letters in the definitions above by the corresponding lowercase letters. The observed values of the sample mean and the sample variance are denoted, respectively, by $\bar{x}$ and s_X^2.

The following way of representing the observed values of the sample moments is instructive. Let $(x_1, x_2, \ldots, x_n)$ be the observed values of a sample and define a discrete random variable X^* such that $P(X^* = x_i) = 1/n$, $i = 1, 2, \ldots, n$. We shall call X^* the *empirical image* of X and its probability distribution the *empirical distribution* of X. Note that X^* is always discrete, regardless of the type of X. Then the moments of X^* are the observed values of the sample moments of X.

We have mentioned that sample moments are "natural" estimators of population moments. Are they good estimators? This question cannot be answered precisely until we define the term "good" in Section 7.2. But let us concentrate on the sample mean and see what we can ascertain about its properties.

(1) Using Theorem 4.1.6, we know that $E\bar{X} = EX$, which means that the population mean is close to a "center" of the distribution of the sample mean.

(2) Suppose that $VX \equiv \sigma^2$ is finite. Then, using Theorem 4.3.3, we know that $V\bar{X} = \sigma^2/n$, which shows that the degree of dispersion of the distribution of the sample mean around the population mean is inversely proportional to the sample size n.

(3) Using Theorem 6.2.1 (Khinchine's law of large numbers), we know that $\mathrm{plim}_{n \to \infty} \bar{X} = EX$. If VX is finite, the same result also follows from (1) and (2) above because of Theorem 6.1.1 (Chebyshev).

On the basis of these results, we can say that the sample mean is a "good" estimator of the population mean, using the term "good" in its loose everyday meaning.

7.1.2 Estimators in General

We may sometimes want to estimate a parameter of a distribution other than a moment. An example is the probability (p_1) that the ace will turn up in a roll of a die. A "natural" estimator in this case is the ratio of the number of times the ace appears in n rolls to n—denote it by $\hat{p}_1$. In general, we estimate a parameter θ by some function of the sample. Mathematically we express it as

$$(7.1.1) \qquad \hat{\theta} = \phi(X_1, X_2, \ldots, X_n).$$

We call any function of a sample by the name *statistic*. Thus an *estimator* is a statistic used to estimate a parameter. Note that an estimator is a random variable. Its observed value is called an *estimate*.

The $\hat{p}_1$ just defined can be expressed as a function of the sample. Let X_i be the outcome of the ith roll of a die and define $Y_i = 1$ if $X_i = 1$ and $Y_i = 0$ otherwise. Then $\hat{p}_1 = (1/n)\Sigma_{i=1}^n Y_i$. Since Y_i is a function of X_i (that is, Y_i is uniquely determined when X_i is determined), $\hat{p}_1$ is a function of $X_1, X_2, \ldots, X_n$. In Section 7.3 we shall learn that $\hat{p}_1$ is a maximum likelihood estimator.

We stated above that the parameter p_i is not a moment. We shall show that it is in fact a function of moments. Consider the following six identities:

$$(7.1.2) \qquad EX^k = \sum_{j=1}^{6} j^k p_j, \qquad k = 0, 1, 2, \ldots, 5,$$

where $p_j = P(X = j), j = 1, 2, \ldots, 6$. When $k = 0$, (7.1.2) reduces to the identity which states that the sum of the probabilities is unity, and the remaining five identities for $k = 1, 2, \ldots, 5$ are the definitions of the first five moments around zero. We can solve these six equations for the six unknowns $\{p_j\}$ and express each p_j as a function of the five moments. If we replace these five moments with their corresponding sample moments, we obtain estimators of $\{p_j\}$. This method of obtaining estimators is known as the *method of moments*. Although, as in this case, the method of moments estimator sometimes coincides with the maximum likelihood estimator, it is in general not as good as the maximum likelihood estimator, because it does not use the information contained in the higher moments.

7.1.3 Nonparametric Estimation

In parametric estimation we can use two methods.

(1) *Distribution-specific method.* In the distribution-specific method, the distribution is assumed to belong to a class of functions that are characterized by a fixed and finite number of parameters—for example, normal—and these parameters are estimated.

(2) *Distribution-free method.* In the distribution-free method, the distribution is not specified and the first few moments are estimated.

In nonparametric estimation we attempt to estimate the probability distribution itself. The estimation of a probability distribution is simple for a discrete random variable taking a few number of values but poses problems for a continuous random variable. For example, suppose we want to estimate the density of the height of a Stanford male student, assuming that it is zero outside the interval [4, 7]. We must divide this interval into $3/d$ small intervals with length d and then estimate the ordinate of the density function over each of the small intervals by the number of students whose height falls into that interval divided by the sample size n. The difficulty of this approach is characterized by a dilemma: if d is large, the approximation of a density by a probability step function cannot be good, but if d is small, many intervals will contain only a small number of observations unless n is very large. Nonparametric estimation for a continuous random variable is therefore useful only when the sample size is very large. In this book we shall discuss only parametric estimation. The reader who wishes to study nonparametric density estimation should consult Silverman (1986).

7.2 PROPERTIES OF ESTIMATORS

7.2.1 Ranking Estimators

Inherent problems exist in ranking estimators, as illustrated by the following example.

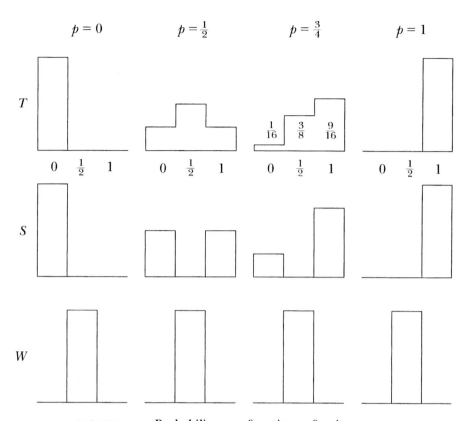

FIGURE 7.1   Probability step functions of estimators

EXAMPLE 7.2.1

Population: $X = 1$ with probability p,
$ = 0$ with probability $1 - p$.

Sample: (X_1, X_2).

Estimators: $T = (X_1 + X_2)/2$
$ S = X_1$
$ W = \frac{1}{2}$.

In Figure 7.1 we show the probability step functions of the three estimators for four different values of the parameter p.

This example shows two kinds of ambiguities which arise when we try to rank the three estimators.

(1) For a particular value of the parameter, say, $p = \frac{3}{4}$, it is not clear which of the three estimators is preferred.

(2) T dominates W for $p = 0$, but W dominates T for $p = \frac{1}{2}$.

These ambiguities are due to the inherent nature of the problem and should not be lightly dealt with. But because we usually must choose one estimator over the others, we shall have to find some way to get around the ambiguities.

7.2.2 Various Measures of Closeness

The ambiguity of the first kind is resolved once we decide on a measure of closeness between the estimator and the parameter. There are many reasonable measures of closeness, however, and it is not easy to choose a particular one. In this section we shall consider six measures of closeness and establish relationships among them. In the following discussion we shall denote two competing estimators by X and Y and the parameter by θ. Note that θ is always a fixed number in the present analysis. Each of the six statements below gives the condition under which estimator X is *preferred* to estimator Y. (We allow for the possibility of a tie. If X is preferred to Y and Y is not preferred to X, we say X is *strictly preferred* to Y.) Or, we might say, X is "better" than Y. Adopting a particular measure of closeness is thus equivalent to defining the term *better*. (The term *strictly better* is defined analogously.)

(1) $P(|X - \theta| \le |Y - \theta|) = 1$.

(2) $Eg(X - \theta) \le Eg(Y - \theta)$ for every continuous function $g(\cdot)$ which is nonincreasing for $x < 0$ and nondecreasing for $x > 0$.

(3) $Eg(|X - \theta|) \le Eg(|Y - \theta|)$ for every continuous and nondecreasing function g.

(4) $P(|X - \theta| > \epsilon) \le P(|Y - \theta| > \epsilon)$ for every ϵ.

(5) $E(X - \theta)^2 \le E(Y - \theta)^2$.

(6) $P(|X - \theta| < |Y - \theta|) \ge P(|X - \theta| > |Y - \theta|)$.

Criteria (1) through (5) are transitive; (6) is not. The reader should verify this. Criteria (3) and (4) are sometimes referred to as *universal dominance* and *stochastic dominance*, respectively; see Hwang (1985). The

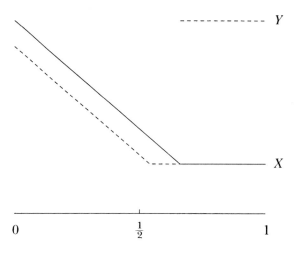

FIGURE 7.2   Illustration for Theorem 7.2.4

idea of stochastic dominance is also used in the finance literature; see, for example, Huang and Litzenberger (1988).

THEOREM 7.2.1 $(2) \Rightarrow (3)$ and $(3) \not\Rightarrow (2)$. (Obvious.)

THEOREM 7.2.2 $(3) \Rightarrow (5)$ and $(5) \not\Rightarrow (3)$. (Obvious.)

THEOREM 7.2.3 $(3) \Leftrightarrow (4)$.

Sketch of Proof. Define

$$h_\epsilon(z) = 1 \quad \text{if } |z| \geq \epsilon,$$
$$= 0 \quad \text{otherwise.}$$

Then $Eh_\epsilon(X - \theta) = P(|X - \theta| \geq \epsilon)$. Therefore, (4) is equivalent to stating that $Eh_\epsilon(X - \theta) \leq Eh_\epsilon(Y - \theta)$ for every ϵ. The theorem follows from the fact that a continuous function can be approximated to any desired degree of accuracy by a linear combination of step functions. (See Hwang, 1985, for a rigorous proof.) ❑

THEOREM 7.2.4   (4) ? (6), meaning that one does not imply the other.

Proof. Consider Figure 7.2. Here X (solid line) and Y (dashed line) are two random variables defined over the sample space $[0, 1]$. The probability distribution defined over the sample space is assumed to be such that the probability of any interval is equal to its length. We also assume that $\theta = 0$. Then, by our construction, X is strictly preferred to Y by criterion (4), whereas Y is strictly preferred to X by criterion (6). ❑

THEOREM 7.2.5   (1) $\Rightarrow$ (3) and (3) $\nRightarrow$ (1).

Proof.

(1) $\Rightarrow$ (3). Since g is nondecreasing, $|X - \theta| \le |Y - \theta| \Rightarrow g(|X - \theta|) \le g(|Y - \theta|)$. Thus, $1 = P(|X - \theta| \le |Y - \theta|) \le P[g(|X - \theta|) \le g(|Y - \theta|)]$. Therefore, $Eg(|X - \theta|) \le Eg(|Y - \theta|)$ for every continuous and nondecreasing function g.

(3) $\nRightarrow$ (1). Consider X and Y, defined in Figure 7.2. We have shown that X is preferred to Y by criterion (4). Therefore, X is preferred to Y by criterion (3) because of Theorem 7.2.3. But $P(|X - \theta| \le |Y - \theta|) = P(X < Y) < 1$. ❑

THEOREM 7.2.6   (1) $\Rightarrow$ (6) and (6) $\nRightarrow$ (1).

Proof.

(1) $\Rightarrow$ (6). The right-hand side of (6) is zero if (1) holds. Then (6) must hold.

(6) $\nRightarrow$ (1). Consider X and Y, defined in Figure 7.2. Clearly Y is preferred to X by criterion (6), but $P(|Y - \theta| \le |X - \theta|) = P(Y < X) < 1$.
❑

THEOREM 7.2.7   (1) ? (2).

Proof. Consider estimators S and T in Example 7.2.1 when $p = \frac{3}{4}$. Then T is preferred to S by criterion (1). Define a function g_0 in such a way that $g_0(-\frac{3}{4}) = g_0(-\frac{1}{4}) = 1$ and $g_0(\frac{1}{4}) = \frac{1}{2}$. Then T is not preferred to S by criterion (2), because $Eg_0(S - p) < Eg_0(T - p)$. This shows that (1) does not imply (2). Next, consider X and Y, defined in Figure 7.2. Since $X - \theta > 0$ and $Y - \theta > 0$ in this example, criteria (2) and (3) are equivalent. But, as we noted in the proof of Theorem 7.2.5, X is preferred to Y by criterion (3). Therefore X is preferred to Y by criterion (2). But clearly X is not preferred to Y by criterion (1). This shows that (2) does not imply (1). ❑

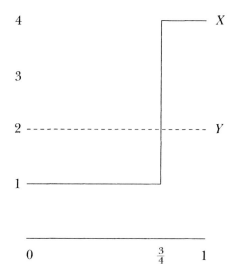

FIGURE 7.3   Illustration for Theorem 7.2.9

THEOREM 7.2.8   (2) ? (6).

Proof. Consider any pair of random variables X and Y such that $X - \theta$ > 0 and $Y - \theta > 0$. Then, as already noted, (2) and (3) are equivalent. But (3) and (4) are equivalent by Theorem 7.2.3, and (4) ? (6) by Theorem 7.2.4. ❑

THEOREM 7.2.9   (5) ? (6).

Proof. In Figure 7.3, X (solid line) and Y (dashed line) are defined over the same sample space as in Figure 7.2, and, as before, we assume that θ $= 0$. Then X is strictly preferred to Y by criterion (6). But $E(X - \theta)^2 = 4 + \frac{3}{4}$ and $E(Y - \theta)^2 = 4$; therefore Y is strictly preferred to X by criterion (5). ❑

The results obtained above are summarized in Figure 7.4. In the figure, an arrow indicates the direction of an implication, and a dashed line between a pair of criteria means that one does not imply the other.

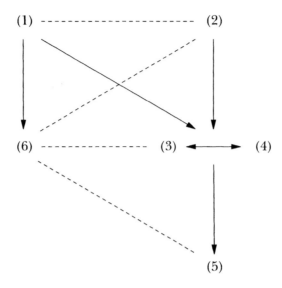

FIGURE 7.4   Relations among various criteria

7.2.3 Mean Squared Error

Although all the criteria defined in Section 7.2.2 are reasonable (except possibly criterion (6), because it is not transitive), and there is no a priori reason to prefer one over the others in every situation, statisticians have most frequently used criterion (5), known as the *mean squared error.* We shall follow this practice and define the term *better* in terms of this criterion throughout this book, unless otherwise noted.

If $\hat{\theta}$ is an estimator of θ, we call $E(\hat{\theta} - \theta)^2$ the *mean squared error* of the estimator. By adopting the mean squared error criterion, we have eliminated (though somewhat arbitrarily) the ambiguity of the first kind (see the end of Section 7.2.1). Now we can rank estimators according to this criterion though there may still be ties, for each value of the parameter. We can easily calculate the mean squared errors of the three estimators in Example 7.2.1: $E(T - \frac{3}{4})^2 = \frac{3}{32}$, $E(S - \frac{3}{4})^2 = \frac{3}{16}$, and $E(W - \frac{3}{4})^2 = \frac{1}{16}$. Therefore, for this value of the parameter p, W is the best estimator.

The ambiguity of the second kind remains, however, as we shall illustrate by referring again to Example 7.2.1. The mean squared errors of the three estimators as functions of p are obtained as

$$(7.2.1) \qquad E(T - p)^2 = \frac{1}{2} p(1 - p),$$

(7.2.2) $E(S - p)^2 = p(1 - p),$

(7.2.3) $E(W - p)^2 = \left(\dfrac{1}{2} - p\right)^2.$

They are drawn as three solid curves in Figure 7.5. (Ignore the dashed curve, for the moment.) It is evident from the figure that T clearly dominates S but that T and W cannot be unequivocally ranked, because T is better for some values of p and W is better for other values of p. When T dominates S as in this example, we say that T is *better* than S. This should be distinguished from the statement that T is better than S at a specific value of p. More formally, we state

DEFINITION 7.2.1 Let X and Y be two estimators of θ. We say X is *better* (or *more efficient*) than Y if $E(X - \theta)^2 \le E(Y - \theta)^2$ for all $\theta \in \Theta$ and $E(X - \theta)^2 < E(Y - \theta)^2$ for at least one value of θ in Θ. (Here Θ denotes the parameter space, the set of all the possible values the parameter can take. In Example 7.2.1, it is the closed interval $[0, 1]$.)

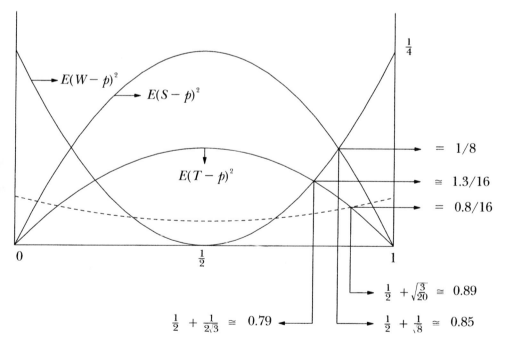

FIGURE 7.5   Mean squared errors of estimators in Example 7.2.1

When an estimator is dominated by another estimator, as in the case of S by T in the above example, we say that the estimator is *inadmissible*.

DEFINITION 7.2.2   Let $\hat{\theta}$ be an estimator of θ. We say that $\hat{\theta}$ is *inadmissible* if there is another estimator which is better in the sense of Definition 7.2.1. An estimator is *admissible* if it is not inadmissible.

Thus, in Example 7.2.1, S is inadmissible and T and W are admissible. We can ignore all the inadmissible estimators and pay attention only to the class of admissible estimators.

7.2.4   Strategies for Choosing an Estimator

How can we resolve the ambiguity of the second kind and choose between two admissible estimators, T and W, in Example 7.2.1?

Subjective strategy. One strategy is to compare the graphs of the mean squared errors for T and W in Figure 7.5 and to choose one after considering the a priori likely values of p. For example, suppose we believe a priori that any value of p is equally likely and express this situation by a uniform density over the interval $[0, 1]$. We would then choose the estimator which has the minimum area under the mean squared error function. In our example, T and W are equally good by this criterion. This strategy is highly subjective; therefore, it is usually not discussed in a textbook written in the framework of classical statistics. It is more in the spirit of Bayesian statistics, although, as we shall explain in Chapter 8, a Bayesian would proceed in an entirely different manner, rather than comparing the mean squared errors of estimators.

Minimax strategy. According to the minimax strategy, we choose the estimator for which the largest possible value of the mean squared error is the smallest. This strategy may be regarded as the most pessimistic and risk-averse approach. In our example, T is preferred to W by this strategy. We formally define

DEFINITION 7.2.3   Let $\hat{\theta}$ be an estimator of θ. It is a *minimax estimator* if, for any other estimator $\tilde{\theta}$, we have

$$\max_{\theta} E(\hat{\theta} - \theta)^2 \leq \max_{\theta} E(\tilde{\theta} - \theta)^2.$$

We see in Figure 7.5 that W does well for the values of p around $\frac{1}{2}$, whereas T does well for the values of p near 0 or 1. This suggests that we can perhaps combine the two estimators and produce an estimator which is better than either in some sense. One possible way to combine the two estimators is to define

$$(7.2.4) \qquad Z = \frac{X_1 + X_2 + 1}{4}.$$

The mean squared error of Z is computed to be

$$(7.2.5) \qquad E(Z - p)^2 = \frac{2p^2 - 2p + 1}{16}$$

and is graphed as the dashed curve in Figure 7.5. When we compare the three estimators T, W, and Z, we see that Z is chosen both by the subjective strategy with the uniform prior density for p and by the minimax strategy. In Chapter 8 we shall learn that Z is a Bayes estimator.

7.2.5 Best Linear Unbiased Estimator

Neither of the two strategies discussed in Section 7.2.4 is the primary strategy of classical statisticians, although the second is less objectionable to them. Their primary strategy is that of defining a certain class of estimators within which we can find the best estimator in the sense of Definition 7.2.1. For example, in Example 7.2.1, if we eliminate W and Z from our consideration, T is the best estimator within the class consisting of only T and S. A certain degree of arbitrariness is unavoidable in this strategy. One of the classes most commonly considered is that of linear unbiased estimators. We first define

DEFINITION 7.2.4 $\hat{\theta}$ is said to be an *unbiased* estimator of θ if $E\hat{\theta} = \theta$ for all $\theta \in \Theta$. We call $E\hat{\theta} - \theta$ *bias*.

Among the three estimators in Example 7.2.1, T and S are unbiased and W and Z are biased. Although unbiasedness is a desirable property of an estimator, it should not be regarded as an absolutely necessary condition. In many practical situations the statistician prefers a biased estimator with a small mean squared error to an unbiased estimator with a large mean squared error.

Theorem 7.2.10 gives a formula which relates the bias to the mean squared error. This formula is convenient when we calculate the mean squared error of an estimator.

THEOREM 7.2.10 The mean squared error is the sum of the variance and the bias squared. That is, for any estimator $\hat{\theta}$ of θ,

$$(7.2.6) \qquad E(\hat{\theta} - \theta)^2 = V\hat{\theta} + (E\hat{\theta} - \theta)^2.$$

Proof. It follows from the identity

$$(7.2.7) \qquad E(\hat{\theta} - \theta)^2 = E[(\hat{\theta} - E\hat{\theta}) + (E\hat{\theta} - \theta)]^2$$

$$= E(\hat{\theta} - E\hat{\theta})^2 + (E\hat{\theta} - \theta)^2.$$

Note that the second equality above holds because $E[(\hat{\theta} - E\hat{\theta})(E\hat{\theta} - \theta)] = (E\hat{\theta} - \theta)E(\hat{\theta} - E\hat{\theta}) = 0$. □

In the following example we shall generalize Example 7.2.1 to the case of a general sample of size n and compare the mean squared errors of the generalized versions of the estimators T and Z using Theorem 7.2.10.

EXAMPLE 7.2.2

Population: $X = 1$ with probability p,
                $= 0$ with probability $1 - p$.

Sample: $(X_1, X_2, \ldots, X_n)$.

Estimators: $T = \bar{X}$

$$Z = \frac{\sum_{i=1}^{n} X_i + 1}{n + 2}.$$

Since $ET = p$, we have

$$(7.2.8) \qquad \mathrm{MSE}(T) = VT = \frac{p(1 - p)}{n},$$

where MSE stands for mean squared error. We have

(7.2.9) $\text{Bias}(Z) = \dfrac{1 - 2p}{n + 2}$,

(7.2.10) $VZ = \dfrac{np(1 - p)}{(n + 2)^2}$.

Therefore, using Theorem 7.2.10, we obtain

(7.2.11) $\text{MSE}(Z) = \dfrac{(n - 4)p(1 - p) + 1}{(n + 2)^2}$.

From (7.2.8) and (7.2.11) we conclude that $\text{MSE}(Z) < \text{MSE}(T)$ if and only if

(7.2.12) $\dfrac{1}{2} - \dfrac{1}{2}\sqrt{\dfrac{n + 1}{2n + 1}} < p < \dfrac{1}{2} + \dfrac{1}{2}\sqrt{\dfrac{n + 1}{2n + 1}}$.

Since $(n + 1)/(2n + 1)$ is a decreasing function of n, $\text{MSE}(Z) < \text{MSE}(T)$ for every n if

$$\frac{1}{2} - \sqrt{\frac{1}{8}} \leq p \leq \frac{1}{2} + \sqrt{\frac{1}{8}} \quad \left(\sqrt{\frac{1}{8}} \cong 0.354\right).$$

As we stated in Section 7.1.1, the sample mean is generally an unbiased estimator of the population mean. The same cannot necessarily be said of all the other moments defined in that section. For example, the sample variance defined there is biased, as we show in (7.2.13). We have

(7.2.13) $E \displaystyle\sum_{i=1}^{n} (X_i - \bar{X})^2 = E \sum_{i=1}^{n} [(X_i - \mu) - (\bar{X} - \mu)]^2$

$\qquad\qquad = \displaystyle\sum_{i=1}^{n} E[(X_i - \mu)^2 + (\bar{X} - \mu)^2 - 2(X_i - \mu)(\bar{X} - \mu)]$

$\qquad\qquad = \displaystyle\sum_{i=1}^{n} \left(\sigma^2 + \dfrac{\sigma^2}{n} - 2\dfrac{\sigma^2}{n}\right)$

$\qquad\qquad = (n - 1)\sigma^2.$

Therefore $ES_X^2 = (n - 1)\sigma^2/n$. For this reason some authors define the sample variance by dividing the sum of squares by $n - 1$ instead of n to produce an unbiased estimator of the population variance.

The class of linear estimators consists of estimators which can be expressed as a linear function of the sample $(X_1, X_2, \ldots, X_n)$. All four estimators considered in Example 7.2.1 are linear estimators. This class is considered primarily for its mathematical convenience rather than for its practical usefulness. Despite the caveats we have expressed concerning unbiased estimators and linear estimators, the following theorem is one of the most important in mathematical statistics.

THEOREM 7.2.11 Let $\{X_i\}$, $i = 1, 2, \ldots, n$ be independent and have the common mean μ and variance σ^2. Consider the class of linear estimators of μ which can be written in the form $\Sigma_{i=1}^n a_i X_i$ and impose the unbiasedness condition

$$(7.2.14) \qquad E\sum_{i=1}^{n} a_i X_i = \mu.$$

Then

$$(7.2.15) \qquad V\bar{X} \le V\left(\sum_{i=1}^{n} a_i X_i\right) \quad \text{for all } \{a_i\} \text{ satisfying (7.2.14)}$$

and, moreover, the equality in (7.2.15) holds if and only if $a_i = 1/n$ for all i. (In words, the sample mean is the *best linear unbiased estimator*, or BLUE, of the population mean.)

   Proof. We have

$$(7.2.16) \qquad V\bar{X} = \frac{\sigma^2}{n},$$

and

$$(7.2.17) \qquad V\left(\sum_{i=1}^{n} a_i X_i\right) = \sigma^2 \sum_{i=1}^{n} a_i^2.$$

Now consider the identity

$$(7.2.18) \qquad \sum_{i=1}^{n}\left(a_i - \frac{1}{n}\right)^2 = \sum_{i=1}^{n} a_i^2 - \frac{2}{n}\sum_{i=1}^{n} a_i + \frac{1}{n}.$$

The unbiasedness condition (7.2.14) implies $\Sigma_{i=1}^n a_i = 1$. Therefore, noting that the left-hand side of (7.2.18) is the sum of squared terms and hence nonnegative, we obtain

(7.2.19) $\displaystyle\sum_{i=1}^{n} a_i^2 \geq \frac{1}{n}$.

The equality in (7.2.19) clearly holds if and only if $a_i = 1/n$. Therefore the theorem follows from (7.2.16), (7.2.17), and (7.2.19). ❑

(Note that we could define the class of linear estimators as $a_0 + \sum_{i=1}^{n} a_i X_i$ with a constant term. This would not change the theorem, because the unbiasedness condition (7.2.14) would ensure that $a_0 = 0$.) We now know that the dominance of T over S in Example 7.2.1 is merely a special case of this theorem.

From a purely mathematical standpoint, Theorem 7.2.11 provides the solution to minimizing $\sum_{i=1}^{n} a_i^2$ with respect to $\{a_i\}$ subject to condition $\sum_{i=1}^{n} a_i = 1$. We shall prove a slightly more general minimization problem, which has a wide applicability.

THEOREM 7.2.12   Consider the problem of minimizing $\sum_{i=1}^{n} a_i^2$ with respect to $\{a_i\}$ subject to the condition $\sum_{i=1}^{n} a_i b_i = 1$. The solution to this problem is given by

$$a_i = \frac{b_i}{\displaystyle\sum_{i=1}^{n} b_i^2}, \qquad i = 1, 2, \ldots, n.$$

Proof. Consider the identity

$$(7.2.20) \quad \sum_{i=1}^{n} \left(a_i - \frac{b_i}{\displaystyle\sum_{i=1}^{n} b_i^2} \right)^2 = \sum_{i=1}^{n} a_i^2 - 2 \frac{\displaystyle\sum_{i=1}^{n} a_i b_i}{\displaystyle\sum_{i=1}^{n} b_i^2} + \frac{1}{\displaystyle\sum_{i=1}^{n} b_i^2}$$

$$= \sum_{i=1}^{n} a_i^2 - \frac{1}{\displaystyle\sum_{i=1}^{n} b_i^2} ,$$

where we used the condition $\sum_{i=1}^{n} a_i b_i = 1$ to obtain the second equality. The theorem follows by noting that the left-hand side of the first equality of (7.2.20) is the sum of squares and hence nonnegative. ❑

(Theorem 7.2.11 follows from Theorem 7.2.12 by putting $b_i = 1$ for all i.) We shall give two examples of the application of Theorem 7.2.12.

EXAMPLE 7.2.3　Let X_i be the return per share of the ith stock, $i = 1, 2,$ $\ldots, n$, and let c_i be the number of shares of the ith stock to purchase. Put $EX_i = \mu_i$ and $VX_i = \sigma_i^2$. Determine c_i so as to minimize $V(\Sigma_{i=1}^n c_i X_i)$ subject to $M = \Sigma_{i=1}^n c_i \mu_i$, where M is a known constant. Assume that X_i are uncorrelated.

If we put $a_i = c_i \sigma_i$ and $b_i = \mu_i / (M\sigma_i)$, this problem is reduced to the minimization problem of Theorem 7.2.12. Therefore, the solution is

$$(7.2.21) \qquad c_i = M \left(\frac{\mu_i}{\sigma_i^2} \right) \Big/ \sum_{i=1}^n \left(\frac{\mu_i^2}{\sigma_i^2} \right), \qquad i = 1, 2, \ldots, n.$$

That is, c_i is proportional to μ_i / σ_i^2.

EXAMPLE 7.2.4　Let $\hat{\theta}_i$, $i = 1, 2, \ldots, n$, be unbiased estimators of θ with variances σ_i^2, $i = 1, 2, \ldots, n$. Choose $\{c_i\}$ so that $\Sigma_{i=1}^n c_i \hat{\theta}_i$ is unbiased and has a minimum variance. Assume that $\hat{\theta}_i$ are uncorrelated.

Since the unbiasedness condition is equivalent to the condition $\Sigma_{i=1}^n c_i = 1$, the problem is that of minimizing $\Sigma_{i=1}^n c_i^2 \sigma_i^2$ subject to $\Sigma_{i=1}^n c_i = 1$. Thus it is a special case of Example 7.2.3, where $\mu_i = 1$ and $M = 1$. Therefore the solution is $c_i = \sigma_i^{-2} / \Sigma_{i=1}^n \sigma_i^{-2}$.

Theorem 7.2.11 shows that the sample mean has a minimum variance (and hence minimum mean squared error) among all the linear unbiased estimators. We have already seen that a biased estimator, such as W and Z of Example 7.2.1, can have a smaller mean squared error than the sample mean for some values of the parameter. Example 7.2.5 provides a case in which the sample mean is dominated by an unbiased, nonlinear estimator.

EXAMPLE 7.2.5

Population: X has density $f(x) = \dfrac{1}{\theta}$　for $0 < x < \theta$,

$$= 0 \quad \text{otherwise.}$$

Sample: $(X_1, X_2, \ldots, X_n)$.

Parameter to estimate: $\mu \equiv \dfrac{\theta}{2}$.

Estimators: $\hat{\mu}_1 = \bar{X}$

$$\hat{\mu}_2 = \frac{n+1}{2n} Z, \quad \text{where} \quad Z = \max(X_1, X_2, \ldots, X_n).$$

An intuitive motivation for the second estimator is as follows: Since θ is the upper bound of X, we know that $Z \le \theta$ and Z approaches θ as n increases. Therefore it makes sense to multiply Z by a factor which is greater than 1 but decreases monotonically to 1 to estimate θ. More rigorously, we shall show in Example 7.4.5 that $\hat{\mu}_2$ is the bias-corrected maximum likelihood estimator.

We have $EX^2 = \theta^{-1}\int_0^\theta x^2 dx = \theta^2/3$. Therefore $VX = \theta^2/12$. Hence

$$(7.2.22) \qquad \text{MSE}(\hat{\mu}_1) = V\bar{X} = \frac{\theta^2}{12n}.$$

Let $G(z)$ and $g(z)$ be the distribution and density function of Z, respectively. Then we have for any $0 < z < \theta$,

$$(7.2.23) \qquad G(z) = P(Z < z) = P(X_1 < z)P(X_2 < z) \cdots P(X_n < z) = \frac{z^n}{\theta^n}.$$

Differentiating (7.2.23) with respect to z, we obtain

$$(7.2.24) \qquad g(z) = \frac{n}{\theta^n} z^{n-1}, \quad 0 < z < \theta.$$

Using (7.2.24), we can calculate

$$(7.2.25) \qquad EZ = \frac{n}{\theta^n} \int_0^\theta z^n dz = \frac{n}{n+1} \theta$$

and

$$(7.2.26) \qquad EZ^2 = \frac{n}{\theta^n} \int_0^\theta z^{n+1} dz = \frac{n}{n+2} \theta^2.$$

Therefore

$$(7.2.27) \qquad VZ = \frac{n}{n+2} \theta^2 - \frac{n^2}{(n+1)^2} \theta^2.$$

Since (7.2.25) shows that $\hat{\mu}_2$ is an unbiased estimator, we have, using (7.2.27),

$$(7.2.28) \qquad \text{MSE}(\hat{\mu}_2) = \left(\frac{n+1}{2n}\right)^2 VZ = \frac{\theta^2}{4n(n+2)}\,.$$

Comparing (7.2.22) and (7.2.27), we conclude that $\text{MSE}(\hat{\mu}_2) \le \text{MSE}(\hat{\mu}_1)$, with equality holding if and only if $n = 1$.

7.2.6 Asymptotic Properties

Thus far we have discussed only the finite sample properties of estimators. It is frequently difficult, however, to obtain the exact moments, let alone the exact distribution, of estimators. In such cases we must obtain an approximation of the distribution or the moments. *Asymptotic approximation* is obtained by considering the limit of the sample size going to infinity. In Chapter 6 we studied the techniques necessary for this most useful approximation.

One of the most important asymptotic properties of an estimator is consistency.

DEFINITION 7.2.5 We say $\hat{\theta}$ is a *consistent* estimator of θ if $\text{plim}_{n\to\infty} \hat{\theta} = \theta$. (See Definition 6.1.2.)

In Examples 6.4.1 and 6.4.3, we gave conditions under which the sample mean and the sample variance are consistent estimators of their respective population counterparts. We can also show that under reasonable assumptions, all the sample moments are consistent estimators of their population values.

Another desirable property of an estimator is asymptotic normality. (See Section 6.2.) In Example 6.4.2 we gave conditions under which the sample mean is asymptotically normal. Under reasonable assumptions all the moments can be shown to be asymptotically normal. We may even say that all the consistent estimators we are likely to encounter in practice are asymptotically normal. Consistent and asymptotically normal estimators can be ranked by Definition 7.2.1, using the asymptotic variance in lieu of the exact mean squared error. This defines the term *asymptotically better or asymptotically efficient*.

7.3 MAXIMUM LIKELIHOOD ESTIMATOR: DEFINITION AND COMPUTATION

7.3.1 Discrete Sample

Suppose we want to estimate the probability (p) that a head will appear for a particular coin; we toss it ten times and a head appears nine times. Call this event A. Then we suspect that the coin is loaded in favor of heads: in other words, we conclude that $p = \frac{1}{2}$ is not likely. If p were $\frac{1}{2}$, event A would be expected to occur only once in a hundred times, since we have $P(A \mid p = \frac{1}{2}) = C_9^{10}(\frac{1}{2})^{10} \cong 0.01$. In the same situation $p = \frac{3}{4}$ is more likely, because $P(A \mid p = \frac{3}{4}) = C_9^{10}(\frac{3}{4})^9(\frac{1}{4}) \cong 0.19$, and $p = \frac{9}{10}$ is even more likely, because $P(A \mid p = \frac{9}{10}) = C_9^{10}(\frac{9}{10})^9(\frac{1}{10}) \cong 0.39$. Thus it makes sense to call $P(A \mid p) = C_9^{10}p^9(1 - p)$ the *likelihood function* of p given event A. Note that it is the probability of event A given p, but we give it a different name when we regard it as a function of p. The *maximum likelihood estimator* of p is the value of p that maximizes $P(A \mid p)$, which in our example is equal to $\frac{9}{10}$. More generally, we state

DEFINITION 7.3.1 Let $(X_1, X_2, \ldots, X_n)$ be a random sample on a discrete population characterized by a vector of parameters $\boldsymbol{\theta} = (\theta_1, \theta_2, \ldots, \theta_K)$ and let x_i be the observed value of X_i. Then we call

$$L = \prod_{i=1}^n P(X_i = x_i \mid \boldsymbol{\theta})$$

the *likelihood function* of $\boldsymbol{\theta}$ given $(x_1, x_2, \ldots, x_n)$, and we call the value of $\boldsymbol{\theta}$ that maximizes L the *maximum likelihood estimator.*

Recall that the purpose of estimation is to pick a probability distribution among many (usually infinite) probability distributions that could have generated given observations. Maximum likelihood estimation means choosing that probability distribution under which the observed values could have occurred with the highest probability. It therefore makes good intuitive sense. In addition, we shall show in Section 7.4 that the maximum likelihood estimator has good asymptotic properties. The following two examples show how to derive the maximum likelihood estimator in the case of a discrete sample.

EXAMPLE 7.3.1 Suppose $X \sim B(n, p)$ and the observed value of X is k. The likelihood function of p is given by

(7.3.1) $L = C_k^n p^k (1 - p)^{n-k}.$

We shall maximize $\log L$ rather than L because it is simpler ("log" refers to natural logarithm throughout this book). Since log is a monotonically increasing function, the value of the maximum likelihood estimator is unchanged by this transformation. We have

(7.3.2) $\log L = \log C_k^n + k \log p + (n - k) \log(1 - p).$

Setting the derivative with respect to p equal to 0 yields

(7.3.3) $\dfrac{\partial \log L}{\partial p} = \dfrac{k}{p} - \dfrac{n - k}{1 - p} = 0.$

Solving (7.3.3) and denoting the maximum likelihood estimator by $\hat{p}$, we obtain

(7.3.4) $\hat{p} = \dfrac{k}{n}.$

To be complete, we should check to see that (7.3.4) gives a maximum rather than any other stationary point by showing that $\partial^2 \log L / \partial p^2$ evaluated at $p = k/n$ is negative.

This example arises if we want to estimate the probability of heads on the basis of the information that heads came up k times in n tosses. Suppose that we are given more complete information: whether each toss has resulted in a head or a tail. Define $X_i = 1$ if the ith toss shows a head and $= 0$ if it is a tail. Let x_i be the observed value of X_i, which is, of course, also 1 or 0. The likelihood function is given by

(7.3.5) $L = \displaystyle\prod_{i=1}^{n} p^{x_i} (1 - p)^{1-x_i}.$

Taking the logarithm, we have

(7.3.6) $\log L = \left(\displaystyle\sum_{i=1}^{n} x_i \right) \log p + \left(n - \displaystyle\sum_{i=1}^{n} x_i \right) \log(1 - p).$

But, since $k = \sum_{i=1}^{n} x_i$, (7.3.6) is the same as (7.3.2) aside from a constant term, which does not matter in the maximization. Therefore the maximum likelihood estimator is the same as before, meaning that the extra information is irrelevant in this case. In other words, as far as the estimation of p is concerned, what matters is the total number of heads and not the particular order in which heads and tails appear. A function of a sample, such as $\Sigma_{i=1}^{n} x_i$ in the present case, that contains all the necessary information about a parameter is called a *sufficient statistic*.

EXAMPLE 7.3.2 This is a generalization of Example 7.3.1. Let X_i, $i = 1$, $2, \ldots, n$, be a discrete random variable which takes K integer values 1, $2, \ldots, K$ with probabilities $p_1, p_2, \ldots, p_K$. This is called the *multinomial* distribution. (The subsequent argument is valid if X_i takes a finite number of distinct values, not necessarily integers.) Let n_j, $j = 1, 2, \ldots, K$, be the number of times we observe $X = j$. (Thus $\Sigma_{j=1}^{K} n_j = n$.) The likelihood function is given by

$$(7.3.7) \qquad L = c \prod_{j=1}^{K} p_j^{n_j},$$

where $c = n!/(n_1! n_2! \cdots n_K!)$. The log likelihood function is given by

$$(7.3.8) \qquad \log L = \log c + \sum_{j=1}^{K} n_j \log p_j.$$

Differentiate (7.3.8) with respect to $p_1, p_2, \ldots, p_{K-1}$, noting that $p_K = 1 - p_1 - p_2 - \ldots - p_{K-1}$, and set the derivatives equal to zero:

$$(7.3.9) \qquad \frac{\partial \log L}{\partial p_j} = \frac{n_j}{p_j} - \frac{n_K}{p_K} = 0, \qquad j = 1, 2, \ldots, K-1.$$

Adding the identity $n_K/p_K = n_K/p_K$ to the above, we can write the K equations as

$$(7.3.10) \qquad p_j = a n_j, \qquad j = 1, 2, \ldots, K,$$

where a is a constant which does not depend on j. Summing both sides of (7.3.10) with respect to j and noting that $\Sigma_{j=1}^{K} p_j = 1$ and $\Sigma_{j=1}^{K} n_j = n$ yields

$$(7.3.11) \qquad a = \frac{1}{n}.$$

Therefore, from (7.3.10) and (7.3.11) we obtain the maximum likelihood estimator

(7.3.12) $\hat{p}_j = \dfrac{n_j}{n}$, $j = 1, 2, \ldots, K$.

The die example of Section 7.1.2 is a special case of this example.

7.3.2 Continuous Sample

For the continuous case, the principle of the maximum likelihood estimator is essentially the same as for the discrete case, and we need to modify Definition 7.3.1 only slightly.

DEFINITION 7.3.2   Let $(X_1, X_2, \ldots, X_n)$ be a random sample on a continuous population with a density function $f(\cdot|\boldsymbol{\theta})$, where $\boldsymbol{\theta} = (\theta_1, \theta_2, \ldots, \theta_K)$, and let x_i be the observed value of X_i. Then we call $L = \Pi_{i=1}^n f(x_i \mid \boldsymbol{\theta})$ the *likelihood function* of $\boldsymbol{\theta}$ given $(x_1, x_2, \ldots, x_n)$ and the value of $\boldsymbol{\theta}$ that maximizes L, the *maximum likelihood estimator.*

EXAMPLE 7.3.3   Let $\{X_i\}$, $i = 1, 2, \ldots, n$, be a random sample on $N(\mu, \sigma^2)$ and let $\{x_i\}$ be their observed values. Then the likelihood function is given by

(7.3.13) $L = \displaystyle\prod_{i=1}^n \frac{1}{\sqrt{2\pi}\,\sigma} \exp\left[-\frac{1}{2\sigma^2} (x_i - \mu)^2 \right]$

so that

(7.3.14) $\log L = -\dfrac{n}{2} \log(2\pi) - \dfrac{n}{2} \log \sigma^2 - \dfrac{1}{2\sigma^2} \displaystyle\sum_{i=1}^n (x_i - \mu)^2.$

Equating the derivatives to zero, we obtain

(7.3.15) $\dfrac{\partial \log L}{\partial \mu} = \dfrac{1}{\sigma^2} \displaystyle\sum_{i=1}^n (x_i - \mu) = 0$

and

(7.3.16) $\dfrac{\partial \log L}{\partial \sigma^2} = -\dfrac{n}{2\sigma^2} + \dfrac{1}{2\sigma^4} \displaystyle\sum_{i=1}^n (x_i - \mu)^2 = 0.$

The maximum likelihood estimator of μ and σ^2, denoted as $\hat{\mu}$ and $\hat{\sigma}^2$, are obtained by solving (7.3.15) and (7.3.16). (Do they indeed give a maximum?) Therefore we have

(7.3.17) $\hat{\mu} = \dfrac{1}{n} \sum_{i=1}^{n} x_i = \bar{x}$

and

(7.3.18) $\hat{\sigma}^2 = \dfrac{1}{n} \sum_{i=1}^{n} (x_i - \bar{x})^2.$

They are the sample mean and the sample variance, respectively.

7.3.3 Computation

In all the examples of the maximum likelihood estimator in the preceding sections, it has been possible to solve the likelihood equation explicitly, equating the derivative of the log likelihood to zero, as in (7.3.3). The likelihood equation is often so highly nonlinear in the parameters, however, that it can be solved only by some method of iteration.

The most common method of iteration is the *Newton-Raphson method*, which can be used to maximize or minimize a general function, not just the likelihood function, and is based on a quadratic approximation of the maximand or minimand. Let $Q(\theta)$ be the function we want to maximize (or minimize). Its quadratic Taylor expansion around an initial value $\hat{\theta}_1$ is given by

(7.3.19) $Q(\theta) \cong Q(\hat{\theta}_1) + \dfrac{\partial Q}{\partial \theta}\bigg|_{\hat{\theta}_1} (\theta - \hat{\theta}_1) + \dfrac{1}{2} \dfrac{\partial^2 Q}{\partial \theta^2}\bigg|_{\hat{\theta}_1} (\theta - \hat{\theta}_1)^2,$

where the derivatives are evaluated at $\hat{\theta}_1$. The second-round estimator of the iteration, denoted $\hat{\theta}_2$, is the value of θ that maximizes the right-hand side of the above equation. Therefore,

(7.3.20) $\hat{\theta}_2 = \hat{\theta}_1 - \left(\dfrac{\partial Q}{\partial \theta}\bigg|_{\hat{\theta}_1} \bigg/ \dfrac{\partial^2 Q}{\partial \theta^2}\bigg|_{\hat{\theta}_1} \right).$

Next $\hat{\theta}_2$ can be used as the initial value to compute the third-round estimator, and the iteration should be repeated until it converges. Whether the iteration will converge to the global maximum, rather than some other stationary point, and, if it does, how fast it converges depend upon the shape of Q and the initial value. Various modifications have been proposed to improve the convergence.

7.4 MAXIMUM LIKELIHOOD ESTIMATOR: PROPERTIES

In Section 7.4.1 we show that the maximum likelihood estimator is the best unbiased estimator under certain conditions. We show this by means of the Cramér-Rao lower bound. In Sections 7.4.2 and 7.4.3 we show the consistency and the asymptotic normality of the maximum likelihood estimator under general conditions. In Section 7.4.3 we define the concept of asymptotic efficiency, which is closely related to the Cramér-Rao lower bound. In Section 7.4.4 examples are given. To avoid mathematical complexity, some results are given without full mathematical rigor. For a rigorous discussion, see Amemiya (1985).

7.4.1 Cramér-Rao Lower Bound

We shall derive a lower bound to the variance of an unbiased estimator and show that in certain cases the variance of the maximum likelihood estimator attains the lower bound.

THEOREM 7.4.1 (Cramér-Rao) Let $L(X_1, X_2, \ldots, X_n | \theta)$ be the likelihood function and let $\hat{\theta}(X_1, X_2, \ldots, X_n)$ be an unbiased estimator of θ. Then, under general conditions, we have

$$(7.4.1) \qquad V(\hat{\theta}) \geq -\frac{1}{E\dfrac{\partial^2 \log L}{\partial \theta^2}}.$$

The right-hand side is known as the *Cramér-Rao lower bound* (CRLB).

(In Section 7.3 the likelihood function was always evaluated at the observed values of the sample, because there we were only concerned with the definition and computation of the maximum likelihood estimator. In this section, however, where we are concerned with the properties of the maximum likelihood estimator, we need to evaluate the likelihood function at the random variables $X_1, X_2, \ldots, X_n$, which makes the likelihood function itself a random variable. Note that E, the expectation operation, is taken with respect to the random variables $X_1, X_2, \ldots, X_n$.)

Sketch of Proof. (A rigorous proof is obviously not possible, because the theorem uses the phrase "under general conditions.") Put $X = \hat{\theta}$ and $Y = \partial \log L/\partial\theta$ in Theorem 7.4.1. Then we have

$$(7.4.2) \qquad EY = E \frac{\partial \log L}{\partial\theta} = E \frac{1}{L} \frac{\partial L}{\partial\theta} = \int \frac{1}{L} \frac{\partial L}{\partial\theta} L d\mathbf{x}$$

$$= \int \frac{\partial L}{\partial\theta} d\mathbf{x} = \frac{\partial}{\partial\theta} \int L d\mathbf{x} = \frac{\partial 1}{\partial\theta} = 0,$$

where the integral is an n-tuple integral with respect to $x_1, x_2, \ldots, x_n$. We also have

$$(7.4.3) \qquad E \frac{\partial^2 \log L}{\partial\theta^2} = E \frac{\partial}{\partial\theta} \frac{\partial \log L}{\partial\theta} = E \frac{\partial}{\partial\theta} \left(\frac{1}{L} \frac{\partial L}{\partial\theta} \right)$$

$$= -E \frac{1}{L^2} \left(\frac{\partial L}{\partial\theta} \right)^2 + E \frac{1}{L} \frac{\partial^2 L}{\partial\theta^2}$$

$$= -E \frac{1}{L^2} \left(\frac{\partial L}{\partial\theta} \right)^2$$

$$= -E \left(\frac{\partial \log L}{\partial\theta} \right)^2,$$

where the fourth equality follows from noting that $E(1/L)(\partial^2 L/\partial\theta^2) = \int (\partial^2 L/\partial\theta^2) d\mathbf{x} = \partial^2/\partial\theta^2 (\int L d\mathbf{x}) = 0$. Therefore, from (7.4.2) and (7.4.3) we have

$$(7.4.4) \qquad VY = EY^2 = -E \frac{\partial^2 \log L}{\partial\theta^2}.$$

We also have

$$(7.4.5) \qquad \mathrm{Cov}(X, Y) = E\hat{\theta} \frac{\partial \log L}{\partial\theta} = \int \hat{\theta} \frac{1}{L} \frac{\partial L}{\partial\theta} L d\mathbf{x} = \frac{\partial}{\partial\theta} \int \hat{\theta} L d\mathbf{x}$$

$$= \frac{\partial}{\partial\theta} E\hat{\theta} = \frac{\partial\theta}{\partial\theta} = 1.$$

Therefore (7.4.1) follows from the Cauchy-Schwartz inequality (4.3.3). ∎

The unspecified general conditions, known as *regularity conditions,* are essentially the conditions on L which justify interchanging the derivative and the integration operations in (7.4.2), (7.4.3), and (7.4.5). If, for example, the support of L (the domain of L over which L is positive) depends on θ, the conditions are violated because the fifth equality of (7.4.2), the fourth equality of (7.4.3), and the third equality of (7.4.5) do not hold. We shall give two examples in which the maximum likelihood estimator attains the Cramér-Rao lower bound.

EXAMPLE 7.4.1 Let $X \sim B(n, p)$ as in Example 7.3.1. Differentiating (7.3.3) again with respect to p, we obtain

$$(7.4.6) \qquad \frac{\partial^2 \log L}{\partial p^2} = - \frac{X}{p^2} - \frac{n - X}{(1 - p)^2},$$

where we have substituted X for k because here we must treat L as a random variable. Therefore we obtain

$$(7.4.7) \qquad \text{CRLB} = \frac{p(1 - p)}{n}.$$

Since $V\hat{p} = p(1 - p)/n$ by (5.1.5), the maximum likelihood estimator $\hat{p}$ attains the Cramér-Rao lower bound and hence is the best unbiased estimator.

EXAMPLE 7.4.2 Let $\{X_i\}$ be as in Example 7.3.3 (normal density) except that we now assume σ^2 is known, so that μ is the only parameter to estimate. Differentiating (7.3.15) again with respect to μ, we obtain

$$(7.4.8) \qquad \frac{\partial^2 \log L}{\partial \mu^2} = - \frac{n}{\sigma^2}.$$

Therefore

$$(7.4.9) \qquad \text{CRLB} = \frac{\sigma^2}{n}.$$

But we have previously shown that $V(\bar{X}) = \sigma^2/n$. Therefore the maximum likelihood estimator attains the Cramér-Rao lower bound; in other words, $\bar{X}$ is the best unbiased estimator. It can be also shown that even if σ^2 is unknown and estimated, $\bar{X}$ is the best unbiased estimator.

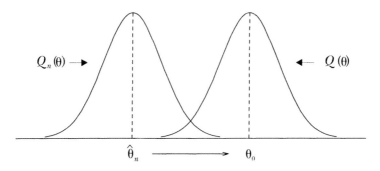

FIGURE 7.6 Convergence of log likelihood functions

7.4.2 Consistency

The maximum likelihood estimator can be shown to be consistent under general conditions. We shall only provide the essential ingredients of the proof. Suppose $\{X_i\}$ are i.i.d. with the density $f(x, \theta)$. The discrete case can be similarly analyzed. Define

$$(7.4.10) \qquad Q_n(\theta) \equiv \frac{1}{n} \log L_n(\theta) = \frac{1}{n} \sum_{i=1}^{n} \log f(X_i, \theta),$$

where a random variable X_i appears in the argument of f because we need to consider the property of the likelihood function as a random variable. To prove the consistency of the maximum likelihood estimator, we essentially need to show that $Q_n(\theta)$ converges in probability to a nonstochastic function of θ, denoted $Q(\theta)$, which attains the global maximum at the true value of θ, denoted θ_0. This is illustrated in Figure 7.6. Note that $Q_n(\theta)$ is maximized at $\hat{\theta}_n$, the maximum likelihood estimator. If $Q_n(\theta)$ converges to $Q(\theta)$, we should expect $\hat{\theta}_n$ to converge to θ_0. (In the present analysis it is essential to distinguish θ, the domain of the likelihood function, from θ_0, the true value. This was unnecessary in the analysis of the preceding section. Whenever L or its derivatives appeared in the equations, we implicitly assumed that they were evaluated at the true value of the parameter, unless it was noted otherwise.)

Next we shall show why we can expect $Q_n(\theta)$ to converge to $Q(\theta)$ and why we can expect $Q(\theta)$ to be maximized at θ_0. To answer the first question, note by (7.4.10) that $Q_n(\theta)$ is $(1/n)$ times the sum of i.i.d. random variables. Therefore we can apply Khinchine's LLN (Theorem 6.2.1), provided that $E \log f(X_i, \theta) < \infty$. Therefore $\operatorname{plim}_{n \to \infty} Q_n(\theta) = Q(\theta) \equiv E \log f(X_i, \theta)$.

To answer the second question, we need

THEOREM 7.4.2 (Jensen) Let X be a proper random variable (that is, it is not a constant) and let $g(\cdot)$ be a strictly concave function. That is to say, $g[\lambda a + (1 - \lambda)b] > \lambda g(a) + (1 - \lambda)g(b)$ for any $a < b$ and $0 < \lambda < 1$. Then

(7.4.11) $Eg(X) < g(EX)$.   *(Jensen's inequality)*

Taking g to be log and X to be $f(X, \theta)/f(X, \theta_0)$ in Theorem 7.4.2, we obtain

(7.4.12) $E \log \dfrac{f(X, \theta)}{f(X, \theta_0)} < \log E \dfrac{f(X, \theta)}{f(X, \theta_0)}$ if $\theta \neq \theta_0$.

But the right-hand side of the above inequality is equal to zero, because

(7.4.13) $E \dfrac{f(X, \theta)}{f(X, \theta_0)} = \displaystyle\int_{-\infty}^{\infty} \dfrac{f(x, \theta)}{f(x, \theta_0)} f(x, \theta_0)dx = \int_{-\infty}^{\infty} f(x, \theta)dx = 1.$

Therefore we obtain from (7.4.12) and (7.4.13)

(7.4.14) $E \log f(X, \theta) < E \log f(X, \theta_0)$ if $\theta \neq \theta_0$.

We have essentially proved the consistency of the *global maximum likelihood estimator*. To prove the consistency of a *local maximum likelihood estimator*, we should replace (7.4.14) by the statement that the derivative of $Q(\theta)$ is zero at θ_0. In other words, we should show

(7.4.15) $\dfrac{\partial}{\partial \theta} E \log L = 0.$

But assuming we can interchange the derivative and the expectation operation, this is precisely what we showed in (7.4.2). The reader should verify (7.4.2) or (7.4.15) in Examples 7.4.1 and 7.4.2.

7.4.3 Asymptotic Normality

THEOREM 7.4.3 Let the likelihood function be $L(X_1, X_2, \ldots, X_n \mid \theta)$. Then, under general conditions, the maximum likelihood estimator $\hat{\theta}$ is asymptotically distributed as

(7.4.16) $\qquad \hat{\theta} \overset{A}{\sim} N \left(\theta, -\left[E\, \dfrac{\partial^2 \log L}{\partial \theta^2} \right]^{-1} \right)$.

(Here we interpret the maximum likelihood estimator as a solution to the likelihood equation obtained by equating the derivative to zero, rather than the global maximum likelihood estimator. Since the asymptotic normality can be proved only for this local maximum likelihood estimator, henceforth this is always what we mean by the maximum likelihood estimator.)

Sketch of Proof. By definition, $\partial \log L / \partial \theta$ evaluated at $\hat{\theta}$ is zero. We expand it in a Taylor series around θ_0 to obtain

(7.4.17) $\qquad 0 = \dfrac{\partial \log L}{\partial \theta} \bigg|_{\hat{\theta}} = \dfrac{\partial \log L}{\partial \theta} \bigg|_{\theta_0} + \dfrac{\partial^2 \log L}{\partial \theta^2} \bigg|_{\theta^*} (\hat{\theta} - \theta_0),$

where θ^* lies between $\hat{\theta}$ and θ_0. Solving for $(\hat{\theta} - \theta_0)$, we obtain

(7.4.18) $\qquad \sqrt{n}\,(\hat{\theta} - \theta_0) = -\dfrac{1}{\sqrt{n}} \dfrac{\partial \log L}{\partial \theta} \bigg|_{\theta_0} \bigg/ \dfrac{1}{n} \dfrac{\partial^2 \log L}{\partial \theta^2} \bigg|_{\theta^*} .$

But we can show (see the paragraph following this proof) that

(7.4.19) $\qquad \dfrac{1}{\sqrt{n}} \dfrac{\partial \log L}{\partial \theta} \bigg|_{\theta_0} \overset{d}{\to} N\left(0, E\left[\dfrac{\partial \log f}{\partial \theta} \bigg|_{\theta_0} \right]^2 \right)$

and

(7.4.20) $\qquad \dfrac{1}{n} \dfrac{\partial^2 \log L}{\partial \theta^2} \bigg|_{\theta^*} \overset{P}{\to} E\, \dfrac{\partial^2 \log f}{\partial \theta^2} \bigg|_{\theta_0} ,$

where we have simply written f for $f(X_i)$. But we have (the derivatives being evaluated at θ_0 throughout)

(7.4.21) $\qquad E\, \dfrac{\partial^2 \log f}{\partial \theta^2} = -E\left[\dfrac{\partial \log f}{\partial \theta} \right]^2,$

as in (7.4.3). Therefore, by (iii) of Theorem 6.1.4 (Slutsky), we conclude

(7.4.22) $\qquad \sqrt{n}\,(\hat{\theta} - \theta_0) \overset{d}{\to} N\left(0, -\left[E\, \dfrac{\partial^2 \log f}{\partial \theta^2} \right]^{-1} \right) .$

We may paraphrase (7.4.22) as

$$(7.4.23) \qquad \hat{\theta} \overset{A}{\sim} N \left(\theta_0, \, - \left[nE \frac{\partial^2 \log f}{\partial \theta^2} \right]^{-1} \right).$$

Finally, the conclusion of the theorem follows from the identity

$$(7.4.24) \qquad nE \frac{\partial^2 \log f}{\partial \theta^2} = E \frac{\partial^2 \log L}{\partial \theta^2}. \qquad \square$$

The convergence result (7.4.19) follows from noting that

$$(7.4.25) \qquad \frac{1}{\sqrt{n}} \frac{\partial \log L}{\partial \theta} \bigg|_{\theta_0} = \frac{1}{\sqrt{n}} \sum_{i=1}^{n} \frac{\partial \log f(X_i)}{\partial \theta} \bigg|_{\theta_0}$$

and that the right-hand side satisfies the conditions for the Lindeberg-Lévy CLT (Theorem 6.2.2). Somewhat more loosely than the above, (7.4.20) follows from noting that

$$(7.4.26) \qquad \frac{1}{n} \frac{\partial^2 \log L}{\partial \theta^2} \bigg|_{\theta*} \cong \frac{1}{n} \sum_{i=1}^{n} \frac{\partial^2 \log f(X_i)}{\partial \theta^2} \bigg|_{\theta_0}$$

and that the right-hand side satisfies the conditions for Khinchine's LLN (Theorem 6.2.1).

A significant consequence of Theorem 7.4.3 is that the asymptotic variance of the maximum likelihood estimator is identical with the Cramér-Rao lower bound given in (7.4.1). This is almost like (but not quite the same as) saying that the maximum likelihood estimator has the smallest asymptotic variance among all the consistent estimators. Therefore we define

DEFINITION 7.4.1 A consistent estimator is said to be *asymptotically efficient* if its asymptotic distribution is given by (7.4.16).

Thus the maximum likelihood estimator is asymptotically efficient essentially by definition.

7.4.4 Examples

We shall give three examples to illustrate the properties of the maximum likelihood estimator and to compare it with the other estimators.

EXAMPLE 7.4.3 Let X have density $f(x) = (1 + \theta)x^\theta$, $\theta > -1$, $0 < x < 1$. Obtain the maximum likelihood estimator of $EX(\equiv \mu)$ based on n

observations $X_1, X_2, \ldots, X_n$ and compare its asymptotic variance with the variance of the sample mean $\bar{X}$.

We have

$$(7.4.27) \qquad \mu = (1 + \theta) \int_0^1 x^{\theta+1} dx = \frac{\theta + 1}{\theta + 2}.$$

Since (7.4.27) defines a one-to-one function and $\theta > -1$, we must have $0 < \mu < 1$. Solving (7.4.27) for θ, we have

$$(7.4.28) \qquad \theta = \frac{1 - 2\mu}{\mu - 1}.$$

The log likelihood function in terms of θ is given by

$$(7.4.29) \qquad \log L = n \log(1 + \theta) + \theta \sum_{i=1}^{n} \log x_i.$$

Inserting (7.4.28) into (7.4.29), we can express the log likelihood function in terms of μ as

$$(7.4.30) \qquad \log L = n \log \left(\frac{\mu}{1 - \mu} \right) + \frac{1 - 2\mu}{\mu - 1} \sum_{i=1}^{n} \log x_i.$$

Differentiating (7.4.30) with respect to μ yields

$$(7.4.31) \qquad \frac{\partial \log L}{\partial \mu} = \frac{n}{\mu(1 - \mu)} + \frac{1}{(1 - \mu)^2} \sum_{i=1}^{n} \log x_i.$$

Equating (7.4.31) to zero, we obtain the maximum likelihood estimator

$$(7.4.32) \qquad \hat{\mu} = \frac{n}{n - \sum_{i=1}^{n} \log x_i}.$$

Differentiating (7.4.31) again, we obtain

$$(7.4.33) \qquad \frac{\partial^2 \log L}{\partial \mu^2} = -\frac{(1 - 2\mu)n}{\mu^2(1 - \mu)^2} + \frac{2}{(1 - \mu)^3} \sum_{i=1}^{n} \log x_i.$$

Since we have, using integration by parts,

$$(7.4.34) \qquad E \log X = (1 + \theta) \int_0^1 (x^\theta \log x) dx = \frac{\mu - 1}{\mu},$$

we obtain from (7.4.33)

$$(7.4.35) \qquad -E \frac{\partial^2 \log L}{\partial \mu^2} = \frac{n}{\mu^2 (1 - \mu)^2}.$$

Therefore, by Theorem 7.4.3, the asymptotic variance of $\hat{\mu}$, denoted $AV(\hat{\mu})$, is given by

$$(7.4.36) \qquad AV(\hat{\mu}) = \frac{\mu^2 (1 - \mu)^2}{n}.$$

Next we obtain the variance of the sample mean. We have

$$(7.4.37) \qquad EX^2 = (1 + \theta) \int_0^1 x^{\theta+2} dx = \frac{\theta + 1}{\theta + 3} = \frac{\mu}{2 - \mu}.$$

Therefore

$$(7.4.38) \qquad VX = \frac{\mu}{2 - \mu} - \mu^2 = \frac{\mu(1 - \mu)^2}{2 - \mu}.$$

Hence

$$(7.4.39) \qquad V\bar{X} = \frac{\mu(1 - \mu)^2}{(2 - \mu)n}.$$

Finally, from (7.4.36) and (7.4.39), we conclude

$$(7.4.40) \qquad V\bar{X} - AV(\hat{\mu}) = \frac{\mu(1 - \mu)^4}{(2 - \mu)n} > 0 \quad \text{for } 0 < \mu < 1.$$

There are several points worth noting with regard to this example, which we state as remarks.

Remark 1. In this example, solving $\partial \log L / \partial \mu = 0$ for μ led to the closed-form solution (7.4.32), which expressed $\hat{\mu}$ as an explicit function of the sample, as in Examples 7.3.1, 7.3.2, and 7.3.3. This is not possible in many applications; in such cases the maximum likelihood estimator can be defined only implicitly by the likelihood equation, as pointed out in Section 7.3.3. Even then, however, the asymptotic variance can be obtained by the method presented here.

Remark 2. Since $\hat{\mu}$ in (7.4.32) is a nonlinear function of the sample, the exact mean and variance, let alone the exact distribution, of the estimator are difficult to find. That is why our asymptotic results are useful.

Remark 3. In a situation such as this example, where the maximum likelihood estimator is explicitly written as a function of the sample, the consistency can be directly shown by using the convergence theorems of Chapter 6, without appealing to the general result of Section 7.4.2. For this purpose rewrite (7.4.32) as

$$(7.4.41) \quad \hat{\mu} = \frac{1}{1 - \frac{1}{n} \sum_{i=1}^{n} \log X_i},$$

where X_i has been substituted for x_i because we must treat $\hat{\mu}$ as a random variable. But since $\{\log X_i\}$ are i.i.d. with mean $(\mu - 1)/\mu$ as given in (7.4.34), we have by Khinchine's LLN (Theorem 6.2.1)

$$(7.4.42) \quad \plim_{n \to \infty} \frac{1}{n} \sum_{i=1}^{n} \log X_i = \frac{\mu - 1}{\mu}.$$

Therefore the consistency of $\hat{\mu}$ follows from Theorem 6.1.3.

Remark 4. Similarly, we can derive the asymptotic normality directly without appealing to Theorem 7.4.3:

$$(7.4.43) \quad \sqrt{n} \, (\hat{\mu} - \mu) = \frac{\sqrt{n} \, \mu \left(\frac{1}{n} \sum_{i=1}^{n} \log X_i - \frac{\mu - 1}{\mu} \right)}{1 - \frac{1}{n} \sum_{i=1}^{n} \log X_i}$$

$$\overset{LD}{=} \mu^2 \sqrt{n} \left(\frac{1}{n} \sum_{i=1}^{n} \log X_i - \frac{\mu - 1}{\mu} \right)$$

$$\overset{d}{\to} \mu^2 N \left[0, \frac{(1 - \mu)^2}{\mu^2} \right]$$

$$= N[0, \mu^2 (1 - \mu)^2].$$

Therefore, we can state

$$(7.4.44) \quad \hat{\mu} \overset{A}{\sim} N \left[\mu, \frac{\mu^2 (1 - \mu)^2}{n} \right].$$

The second equality with LD in (7.4.43), as defined in Definition 6.1.4, means that both sides have the same limit distribution and is a consequence of (iii) of Theorem 6.1.4 (Slutsky). The convergence in distribution appearing next in (7.4.43) is a consequence of the Lindeberg-Lévy CLT (Theorem 6.2.2). Here we need the variance of $\log X$, which can be obtained as follows: By integration by parts,

$$(7.4.45) \qquad E(\log X)^2 = \frac{2(1 - \mu)^2}{\mu^2}.$$

Therefore

$$(7.4.46) \qquad V \log X = \frac{(1 - \mu)^2}{\mu^2}.$$

Remark 5. We first expressed the log likelihood function in terms of μ in (7.4.30) and found the value of μ that maximizes (7.4.30). We would get the same estimator if we maximized (7.4.29) with respect to θ and inserted the maximum likelihood estimator of θ into the last term of (7.4.27). More generally, if two parameters θ_1 and θ_2 are related by a one-to-one continuous function $\theta_1 = g(\theta_2)$, the respective maximum likelihood estimators are related by $\hat{\theta}_1 = g(\hat{\theta}_2)$.

EXAMPLE 7.4.4 Assuming $\sigma^2 = \mu^2$ in Example 7.3.3 (normal density), so that μ is the sole parameter of the distribution, obtain the maximum likelihood estimator of μ and directly prove its consistency. Assume that $\mu \neq 0$.

From (7.3.14) we have

$$(7.4.47) \qquad \log L = -\frac{n}{2} \log (2\pi) - \frac{n}{2} \log \mu^2 - \frac{1}{2\mu^2} \sum_{i=1}^{n} (x_i - \mu)^2$$

$$\equiv A + B + C,$$

where

$$(7.4.48) \qquad A = -\frac{n}{2} \log \mu^2 - \frac{\sum_{i=1}^{n} x_i^2}{2\mu^2},$$

$$(7.4.49) \qquad B = \frac{\sum_{i=1}^{n} x_i}{\mu},$$

and C is a constant term that does not depend on the parameter μ.

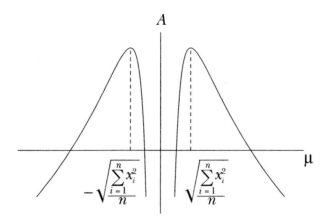

FIGURE 7.7 Illustration for function (7.4.48)

We shall study the shape of log L as a function of μ. The function A is an even function depicted in Figure 7.7. The shape of the function B depends on the sign of $\Sigma_{i=1}^{n} x_i$ and looks like Figure 7.8. From these two figures it is clear that log L is maximized at a positive value of μ when $\Sigma_{i=1}^{n} x_i > 0$ and at a negative value of μ when $\Sigma_{i=1}^{n} x_i < 0$.

Setting the derivative of (7.4.47) with respect to μ equal to zero yields

$$(7.4.50) \qquad \frac{\partial \log L}{\partial \mu} = -\frac{n}{\mu} + \frac{\displaystyle\sum_{i=1}^{n} (x_i - \mu)}{\mu^2} + \frac{\displaystyle\sum_{i=1}^{n} (x_i - \mu)^2}{\mu^3} = 0,$$

which can be written as

$$(7.4.51) \qquad n\mu^2 + \mu\sum_{i=1}^{n} x_i - \sum_{i=1}^{n} x_i^2 = 0.$$

There are two roots for the above, one positive, one negative, given by

$$(7.4.52) \qquad \hat{\mu} = \frac{1}{2}\left\{ - n^{-1}\sum_{i=1}^{n} x_i \pm \left[n^{-2}\left(\sum_{i=1}^{n} x_i\right)^2 + 4n^{-1}\sum_{i=1}^{n} x_i^2 \right]^{1/2} \right\}.$$

We know from the argument of the preceding paragraph that the positive root is the maximum likelihood estimator if $\Sigma_{i=1}^{n} x_i > 0$ and the negative root if $\Sigma_{i=1}^{n} x_i < 0$.

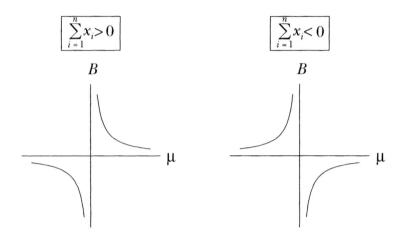

FIGURE 7.8   Illustration for function (7.4.49)

Next we shall directly prove the consistency of the maximum likelihood estimator in this example. We have, using Khinchine's LLN (Theorem 6.2.1),

$$(7.4.53) \qquad \operatorname*{plim}_{n\to\infty} \frac{\sum\limits_{i=1}^{n} x_i}{n} = \mu$$

and

$$(7.4.54) \qquad \operatorname*{plim}_{n\to\infty} \frac{\sum\limits_{i=1}^{n} x_i^2}{n} = 2\mu^2.$$

Therefore, by Theorem 6.1.3, we have

$$(7.4.55) \qquad \operatorname*{plim}_{n\to\infty} \hat{\mu} = \frac{1}{2}\left(-\mu \pm \sqrt{9\mu^2}\right) = \frac{1}{2}\left(-\mu \pm 3|\mu|\right)$$

$$= \begin{cases} \mu \\ -2\mu \end{cases} \quad \text{if } \mu > 0$$

$$= \begin{cases} -2\mu \\ \mu \end{cases} \quad \text{if } \mu < 0,$$

which shows that the positive root is consistent if $\mu > 0$ and the negative root is consistent if $\mu < 0$. But because of (7.4.53), the signs of $\Sigma_{i=1}^{n} x_i$ and

μ are the same with probability approaching one as n goes to infinity. Therefore the maximum likelihood estimator is consistent.

EXAMPLE 7.4.5 Let the model be the same as in Example 7.2.5. The likelihood function of the model is given by

$$(7.4.56) \qquad L = \frac{1}{\theta^n} \quad \text{for } \theta \geq z,$$

$$\qquad = 0 \quad \text{otherwise,}$$

where $z = \max(x_1, x_2, \ldots, x_n)$, the observed value of Z defined in Example 7.2.5. Clearly, therefore, the maximum likelihood estimator of θ is Z. Since $\mu = \theta/2$, the maximum likelihood estimator of μ is $Z/2$ because of remark 5 of Example 7.4.3. Thus we see that $\hat{\mu}_2$ defined in that example is the bias-corrected maximum likelihood estimator.

In this example, the support of the likelihood function depends on the unknown parameter θ and, therefore, the regularity conditions do not hold. Therefore the asymptotic distribution cannot be obtained by the standard procedure given in Section 7.4.3.

EXERCISES

1. (Section 7.1.2)
   Let X_i take three values 1, 2, and 3 with probabilities p_1, p_2, and p_3. Define $Y_{ji} = 1$ if $X_i = j$ and $Y_{ji} = 0$ if $X_i \neq j$, $j = 1, 2,$ and 3. Further define $\hat{p}_j = n^{-1} \sum_{i=1}^{n} Y_{ji}$, $j = 1, 2,$ and 3. Then show that $\hat{p}_j$ satisfies $n^{-1} \sum_{i=1}^{n} X_i^k = \sum_{j=1}^{3} j^k \hat{p}_j$, $k = 0, 1,$ and 2.

2. (Section 7.1.2)
   Let $X_1, \ldots, X_n$ be independent with exponential distribution with parameter λ.
   (a) Find a method of moments estimate of λ.
   (b) Find a method of moments estimate of λ different from the one in (a).

3. (Section 7.2.2)
   Suppose X_1 and X_2 are independent, each distributed as $U(0, \theta)$. Compare $\max(X_1, X_2)$ and $X_1 + X_2$ as two estimators of θ by criterion (6) in Section 7.2.2.

4. (Section 7.2.2)
   Show that criteria (1) through (5) are transitive, whereas (6) is not.

5. (Section 7.2.2)
   Let X_1 and X_2 be independent, each taking the value of 1 with probability p and 0 with probability $1 - p$. Let two estimators of p be defined by $T = (X_1 + X_2)/2$ and $S = X_1$. Show that $Eg(T - p) \leq Eg(S - p)$ for any convex function g and for any p. Note that a function $g(\cdot)$ is convex if for any $a < b$ and any $0 < \lambda < 1$, $\lambda g(a) + (1 - \lambda)g(b) \geq g[\lambda a + (1 - \lambda)b]$. (A more general theorem can be proved: in this model the sample mean is the best linear unbiased estimator of p in terms of an arbitrary convex loss function.)

6. (Section 7.2.3)
   Let X_1, X_2, and X_3 be independent binary random variables taking 1 with probability p and 0 with probability $1 - p$. Define two estimators $\hat{p}_1 = \bar{X}$ and $\hat{p}_2 = (\bar{X}/2) + (1/4)$, where $\bar{X} = (X_1 + X_2 + X_3)/3$. For what values of p is the mean squared error of $\hat{p}_2$ smaller than that of $\hat{p}_1$?

7. (Section 7.2.3)
   Let X_1 and X_2 be independent, and let each take 1 and 0 with probability p and $1 - p$. Define the following two estimators of $\theta = p(1 - p)$ based on X_1 and X_2.

   $$\hat{\theta}_1 = (X_1 + X_2 - 2X_1X_2)/2$$

   $$\hat{\theta}_2 = X_1(1 - X_2).$$

   Which estimator do you prefer? Why?

8. (Section 7.2.3)
   Let X_1, X_2, and X_3 be independently distributed as $B(1, p)$ and let two estimators of p be defined as follows:

   $$\hat{p}_1 = X_1(1 + X_2 - X_3)$$

   $$\hat{p}_2 = X_1 + X_2 - X_3.$$

   Obtain the mean squared errors of the two estimators. Can you say one estimator is better than the other?

9. (Section 7.2.5)

Suppose we define *better* in the following way: "Estimator X is *better* than Y in the estimation of θ if $P(|X - \theta| < \epsilon) \geq P(|Y - \theta| < \epsilon)$ for every $\epsilon > 0$ and $>$ for at least one value of ϵ." Consider the binary model: $P(X_i = 1) = p$ and $P(X_i = 0) = 1 - p$. Show that the sample mean $\bar{X}$ is *not* the best linear unbiased estimator. You may consider the special case where $n = 2$ and the true value of p is equal to $\frac{3}{4}$.

10. (Section 7.3.1)

Suppose we want to estimate the probability that Stanford will win a football game, denoted by p. Suppose the only information we have about p consists of the forecasts of n people published in the *Stanford Daily*. Assume that these forecasts are independent and that each forecast is accurate with a known probability π. If r of them say Stanford will win, how would you estimate p? Justify your choice of estimator.

11. (Section 7.3.1)

Suppose the probability distribution of X and Y is given as follows:

$$P(X = 1) = p, \qquad P(X = 0) = 1 - p, \qquad P(Y = 1) = \frac{1}{4},$$

$$P(Y = 0) = \frac{3}{4}, \quad \text{and } X \text{ and } Y \text{ are independent.}$$

Define $Z = X + Y$. Supposing that twenty i.i.d. observations on Z yield "$Z = 2$" four times, "$Z = 1$" eight times, and "$Z = 0$" eight times, compute the maximum likelihood estimator of p. Note that we observe neither X nor Y.

12. (Section 7.3.1)

A proportion μ of n jurors always acquit everyone, regardless of whether a defendant has committed a crime or not. The remaining $1 - \mu$ proportion of jurors acquit a defendant who has not committed a crime with probability 0.9 and acquit a criminal with probability 0.2. If it is known that the probability a defendant has committed a crime is 0.5, find the maximum likelihood estimator of μ when we observe that r jurors have acquitted the defendant. If $n = 5$ and $r = 3$, what is your maximum likelihood estimator of μ?

13. (Section 7.3.1)

Let $X \sim B(n, p)$. Find the maximum likelihood estimator of p based on a single observation on X, assuming you know a priori that $0 \leq p \leq 0.5$. Derive its variance for the case of $n = 3$.

14. (Section 7.3.1)
Suppose the probability distribution of X and Y is given as follows:

$$P(X_i = 1) = \alpha, \qquad P(X_i = 0) = 1 - \alpha,$$

$$P(Y_i = 1 \mid X_i = 1) = \tfrac{3}{4}, \qquad P(Y_i = 0 \mid X_i = 1) = \tfrac{1}{4},$$

$$P(Y_i = 1 \mid X_i = 0) = \tfrac{1}{2}, \qquad P(Y_i = 0 \mid X_i = 0) = \tfrac{1}{2}.$$

(a) Given i.i.d. sample $Y_1, Y_2, \ldots, Y_n$, find the maximum likelihood estimator of α.
(b) Find the exact mean and variance of the maximum likelihood estimator of α assuming that $n = 4$ and the true value of α is 1.

15. (Section 7.3.2)
Let $X_1, \ldots, X_n$ be a sample drawn from a uniform distribution $U[\theta - 0.5, \theta + 0.5]$. Find the maximum likelihood estimator of θ.

16. (Section 7.3.2)
Suppose that $X_i - \theta, i = 1, \ldots, n$, are i.i.d. with the common density $f(x) = (1/2)\exp(-|x|)$ (the *Laplace* or *double-exponential density*).
(a) Show that the maximum likelihood estimator of θ is the same as the least absolute deviations estimator that minimizes $\Sigma|X_i - \theta|$.
(b) Show that it is also equal to the median of $\{Y_i\}$.

17. (Section 7.3.2)
Let $X_1, \ldots, X_n$ be a sample from the *Cauchy distribution* with the density $f(x, \theta) = \{\pi[1 + (x - \theta)^2]\}^{-1}$.
(a) Show that if $n = 1$, the maximum likelihood estimator of θ is X_1.
(b) Show that if $n = 2$, the likelihood function has multiple maxima, and the maximum likelihood estimator is not unique.

18. (Section 7.3.2)
The density of X is given by

$$f(x) = 3/(4\theta) \quad \text{for } 0 \leq x \leq \theta,$$

$$= 1/(4\theta) \quad \text{for } \theta < x \leq 2\theta,$$

$$= 0 \qquad\qquad \text{otherwise.}$$

Assuming that a sample of size 4 from this distribution yielded observations 1, 2.5, 3.5, and 4, calculate the maximum likelihood estimator of θ.

19. (Section 7.3.2)
    Let the density function of X be given by

$$f(x) = 2x/\theta \qquad\qquad \text{for } 0 \le x \le \theta,$$
$$= 2(x - 1)/(\theta - 1) \quad \text{for } \theta < x \le 1,$$

where $0 < \theta < 1$. Supposing that two independent observations on X yield x_1 and x_2, derive the maximum likelihood estimator of θ. Assume $x_1 < x_2$.

20. (Section 7.3.2)
    Show that $\hat{\mu}$ and $\hat{\sigma}^2$ obtained by solving (7.3.15) and (7.3.16) indeed maximize log L given by (7.3.14).

21. (Section 7.3.3)
    Suppose that $X_1, \ldots, X_n$ are independent and that it is known that $(X_i)^\lambda - 10$ has a standard normal distribution, $i = 1, \ldots, n$. This is called the *Box-Cox transformation*. See Box and Cox (1964).
    (a) Derive the second-round estimator $\hat{\lambda}_2$ of the Newton-Raphson iteration (7.3.19), starting from an initial guess that $\hat{\lambda}_1 = 1$.
    (b) For the following data, compute $\hat{\lambda}_2$:

    96, 125, 146, 76, 114, 69, 130, 119, 85, 106.

22. (Section 7.4.1)
    Given $f(x) = \theta \exp(-\theta x)$, $x > 0$, $\theta > 0$,
    (a) Find the maximum likelihood estimator of θ.
    (b) Find the maximum likelihood estimator of EX.
    (c) Show that the maximum likelihood estimator of EX is best unbiased.

23. (Section 7.4.1)
    Suppose $X \sim N(\mu, 1)$ and $Y \sim N(2\mu, 1)$, independent of each other. Obtain the maximum likelihood estimator of μ based on N_X i.i.d. observations on X and N_Y i.i.d. observations on Y and show that it is best unbiased.

24. (Section 7.4.2)

   Let $\{X_{1i}\}$ and $\{X_{2i}\}$, $i = 1, 2, \ldots, n$, be independent of each other and across i, each distributed as $B(1, p)$. We are to observe $X_{1i} - X_{2i}$, $i = 1, 2, \ldots, n$. Find the maximum likelihood estimator of p assuming we know $0 < p \leq 0.5$. Prove its consistency.

25. (Section 7.4.3)

   Using a coin whose probability of a head, p, is unknown, we perform ten experiments. In each experiment we toss the coin until a head appears and record the number of tosses required. Suppose the experiments yielded the following sequence of numbers:

$$1, \; 3, \; 4, \; 1, \; 2, \; 2, \; 5, \; 1, \; 3, \; 3.$$

   Compute the maximum likelihood estimator of p and an estimate of its asymptotic variance.

26. (Section 7.4.3)

   Let $\{X_i\}$, $i = 1, 2, \ldots, n$, be a random sample on $N(\mu, \mu)$, where we assume $\mu > 0$. Obtain the maximum likelihood estimator of μ and prove its consistency. Also obtain its asymptotic variance and compare it with the variance of the sample mean.

27. (Section 7.4.3)

   Let $\{X_i\}$, $i = 1, 2, \ldots, 5$, be i.i.d. $N(\mu, 1)$ and let $\{Y_i\}$, $i = 1, 2, \ldots, 5$, be i.i.d. $N(\mu^2, 1)$. Assume that all the X's are independent of all the Y's. Suppose that the observed values of $\{X_i\}$ and $\{Y_i\}$ are $(-2, 0, 1, -3, -1)$ and $(1, 1, 0, 2, -1.5)$, respectively. Calculate the maximum likelihood estimator of μ and an estimate of its asymptotic variance.

28. (Section 7.4.3)

   It is known that in a certain criminal court those who have not committed a crime are always acquitted. It is also known that those who have committed a crime are acquitted with 0.2 probability and are convicted with 0.8 probability. If 30 people are acquitted among 100 people who are brought to the court, what is your estimate of the true proportion of people who have not committed a crime? Also obtain the estimate of the mean squared error of your estimator.

29. (Section 7.4.3)

Let X and Y be independent and distributed as $N(\mu, 1)$ and $N(0, \mu)$, respectively, where $\mu > 0$. Derive the asymptotic variance of the maximum likelihood estimator of μ based on a combined sample of $(X_1, X_2, \ldots, X_n)$ and $(Y_1, Y_2, \ldots, Y_n)$.

30. (Section 7.4.3)

Suppose that X has the *Hardy-Weinberg distribution*:

$$X = 1 \quad \text{with probability } \mu^2,$$

$$= 2 \quad \text{with probability } 2\mu(1 - \mu),$$

$$= 3 \quad \text{with probability } (1 - \mu)^2,$$

where $0 < \mu < 1$. Suppose we observe $X = 1$ three times, $X = 2$ four times, and $X = 3$ three times.

(a) Find the maximum likelihood estimate of μ.

(b) Obtain an estimate of the variance of the maximum likelihood estimator.

(c) Show that the maximum likelihood estimator attains the Cramér-Rao lower bound in this model.

31. (Section 7.4.3)

In the same model as in Exercise 30, let N_i be the number of times $X = i$ in N trials. Prove the consistency of $\hat{\mu}_1 = \sqrt{N_1/N}$ and of $\hat{\mu}_2 = 1 - \sqrt{N_3/N}$ and obtain their asymptotic distributions as N goes to infinity.

32. (Section 7.4.3)

Let $\{X_i\}$, $i = 1, 2, \ldots, n$, be i.i.d. with $P(X > t) = \exp(-\lambda t)$. Define $\theta = \exp(-\lambda)$. Find the maximum likelihood estimator of θ and its asymptotic variance.

33. (Section 7.4.3)

Suppose $f(x) = \theta/(1 + x)^{1+\theta}$, $0 < x < \infty$, $\theta > 0$. Find the maximum likelihood estimator of θ based on a sample of size n from f and obtain its asymptotic variance in two ways:

(a) Using an explicit formula for the maximum likelihood estimator.

(b) Using the Cramér-Rao lower bound.

Hint: $E \log (1 + X) = \theta^{-1}$, $V \log (1 + X) = \theta^{-2}$.

34. (Section 7.4.3)

    Suppose $f(x) = \theta^{-1} \exp(-x/\theta)$, $x \geq 0$, $\theta > 0$. Observe a sample of size n from f. Compare the asymptotic variances of the following two estimators of θ:

    (a) $\hat{\theta} = $ maximum likelihood estimator (derive it).

    (b) $\tilde{\theta} = \sqrt{\Sigma x_i^2 / 2n}$.

35. (Section 7.4.3)

    Suppose $f(x) = 1/(b - a)$ for $a < x < b$. Observe a sample of size n from f. Compare the asymptotic variances of the following two estimators of $\theta = b - a$:

    (a) $\hat{\theta} = $ maximum likelihood estimator (derive it).

    (b) $\tilde{\theta} = 2\sqrt{3\Sigma(x_i - \bar{x})^2/n}$.

36. (Section 7.4.3)

    Let the joint distribution of X and Y be given as follows:

$$P(X = 1) = \theta, \qquad P(X = 0) = 1 - \theta,$$

$$P(Y = 1 \mid X = 1) = \theta, \qquad P(Y = 0 \mid X = 1) = 1 - \theta,$$

$$P(Y = 1 \mid X = 0) = 0.5, \qquad P(Y = 0 \mid X = 0) = 0.5,$$

    where we assume $0.25 \leq \theta \leq 1$. Suppose we observe only Y and not X, and we see that $Y = 1$ happens N_1 times in N trials. Find an explicit formula for the maximum likelihood estimator of θ and derive its asymptotic distribution.

37. (Section 7.4.3)

    Suppose that $P(X = 1) = (1 - \theta)/3$, $P(X = 2) = (1 + \theta)/3$, and $P(X = 3) = \frac{1}{3}$. Suppose X is observed N times and let N_i be the number of times $X = i$. Define $\hat{\theta}_1 = 1 - (3N_1/N)$ and $\hat{\theta}_2 = (3N_2 / N) - 1$. Compute their variances. Derive the maximum likelihood estimator and compute its asymptotic variance.

38. (Section 7.4.3)

    A box contains cards on which are written consecutive whole numbers 1 through N, where N is unknown. We are to draw cards at random from the box with replacement. Let X_i denote the number obtained on the ith drawing.

    (a) Find EX_i and VX_i.

(b) Define estimator $\hat{N} = 2\bar{X} - 1$, where $\bar{X}$ is the average value of the K numbers drawn. Find $E\hat{N}$ and $V\hat{N}$.

(c) If five drawings produced numbers 411, 950, 273, 156, and 585, what is the numerical value of $\hat{N}$? Do you think $\hat{N}$ is a good estimator of $\hat{N}$? Why or why not?

39. (Section 7.4.3)

Verify (7.4.15) in Examples 7.4.1 and 7.4.2.

8 | INTERVAL ESTIMATION

8.1 INTRODUCTION

Obtaining an estimate of a parameter is not the final purpose of statistical inference. Because we can never be certain that the true value of the parameter is exactly equal to an estimate, we would like to know how close the true value is likely to be to an estimated value in addition to just obtaining the estimate. We would like to be able to make a statement such as "the true value is believed to lie within a certain interval with such and such *confidence*." This degree of confidence obviously depends on how good an estimator is. For example, suppose we want to know the true probability, p, of getting a head on a given coin, which may be biased in either direction. We toss it ten times and get five heads. Our point estimate using the sample mean is $\frac{1}{2}$, but we must still allow for the possibility that p may be, say, 0.6 or 0.4, although we are fairly certain that p will not be 0.9 or 0.1. If we toss the coin 100 times and get 50 heads, we will have more confidence that p is very close to $\frac{1}{2}$, because we will have, in effect, a better estimator.

More generally, suppose that $\hat{\theta}(X_1, X_2, \ldots, X_n)$ is a given estimator of a parameter θ based on the sample $X_1, X_2, \ldots, X_n$. The estimator $\hat{\theta}$ summarizes the information concerning θ contained in the sample. The better the estimator, the more fully it captures the relevant information contained in the sample. How should we express the information contained in $\hat{\theta}$ about θ in the most meaningful way? Writing down the observed value of $\hat{\theta}$ is not enough—this is the act of point estimation. More information is contained in $\hat{\theta}$: namely, the smaller the mean squared error of $\hat{\theta}$, the greater confidence we have that θ is close to the observed value of $\hat{\theta}$. Thus, given $\hat{\theta}$, we would like to know how much confidence we can have that θ lies in a given interval. This is an act of interval estimation and utilizes more information contained in $\hat{\theta}$.

Note that we have used the word *confidence* here and have deliberately avoided using the word *probability*. As discussed in Section 1.1, in classical statistics we use the word probability only when a probabilistic statement can be tested by repeated observations; therefore, we do not use it concerning parameters. The word confidence, however, has the same practical connotation as the word probability. In Section 8.3 we shall examine how the Bayesian statistician, who uses the word probability for any situation, carries out statistical inference. Although there are certain important differences, the classical and Bayesian methods of inference often lead to a conclusion that is essentially the same except for a difference in the choice of words. The classical statistician's use of the word confidence may be somewhat like letting probability in through the back door.

8.2 CONFIDENCE INTERVALS

We shall assume that confidence is a number between 0 and 1 and use it in statements such as "a parameter θ lies in the interval $[a, b]$ with 0.95 confidence," or, equivalently, "a 0.95 *confidence interval* for θ is $[a, b]$." A confidence interval is constructed using some estimator of the parameter in question. Although some textbooks define it in a more general way, we shall define a confidence interval mainly when the estimator used to construct it is either normal or asymptotically normal. This restriction is not a serious one, because most reasonable estimators are at least asymptotically normal. (An exception occurs in Example 8.2.5, where a chi-square distribution is used to construct a confidence interval concerning a variance.) The concept of confidence or confidence intervals can be best understood through examples.

EXAMPLE 8.2.1 Let X_i be distributed as $B(1, p)$, $i = 1, 2, \ldots, n$. Then $T \equiv \bar{X} \overset{A}{\sim} N[p, p(1 - p)/n]$. Therefore, we have

$$(8.2.1) \qquad \frac{T - p}{\sqrt{\dfrac{p(1 - p)}{n}}} \overset{A}{\sim} N(0, 1).$$

Let Z be $N(0, 1)$ and define

(8.2.2) $\gamma_k = P(|Z| < k)$.

Then we can evaluate the value of γ_k for various values of k from the standard normal table. From (8.2.1) we have approximately

(8.2.3) $P\left[\dfrac{|T - p|}{\sqrt{\dfrac{p(1 - p)}{n}}} < k\right] = \gamma_k$.

Suppose an observed value of T is t. Then we define *confidence* by

(8.2.4) $C\left[\dfrac{|t - p|}{\sqrt{\dfrac{p(1 - p)}{n}}} < k\right] = \gamma_k$,

which reads "the confidence that p lies in the interval defined by the inequality within the bracket is γ_k" or "the γ_k confidence interval of p is as indicated by the inequality within the bracket."

Definition (8.2.4) is motivated by the observation that the probability that T lies within a certain distance from p is equal to the confidence that p lies within the same distance from an observed value of T. Note that this definition establishes a kind of mutual relationship between the estimator and the parameter in the sense that if the estimator as a random variable is close to the parameter with a large probability, we have a proportionately large confidence that the parameter is close to the observed value of the estimator. Equation (8.2.3) may be equivalently written as

(8.2.5) $P\left[\left(1 + \dfrac{k^2}{n}\right)p^2 - \left(2T + \dfrac{k^2}{n}\right)p + T^2 < 0\right] = \gamma_k$,

which may be further rewritten as

(8.2.6) $P[h_1(T) < p < h_2(T)] = \gamma_k$,

where

(8.2.7) $h_1, h_2 = \dfrac{2T + \dfrac{k^2}{n} \pm \sqrt{\left(2T + \dfrac{k^2}{n}\right)^2 - 4\left(1 + \dfrac{k^2}{n}\right)T^2}}{2\left(1 + \dfrac{k^2}{n}\right)}$.

Similarly, (8.2.4) can be written as

(8.2.8) $C[h_1(t) < p < h_2(t)] = \gamma_k.$

The probabilistic statement (8.2.6) is a legitimate one, because it concerns a random variable T. It states that a random interval $[h_1(T), h_2(T)]$ contains p with probability γ_k. Definition (8.2.8) is appealing as it equates the probability that a random interval contains p to the confidence that an observed value of the random interval contains p.

Let us construct a 95% confidence interval of p, assuming $n = 10$ and $t = 0.5$. Then, since $\gamma_k = 0.95$ when $k = 1.96$, we have from (8.2.8)

(8.2.9) $C(0.2366 < p < 0.7634) = 0.95.$

If $n = 100$ and $t = 0.5$, we have

(8.2.10) $C(0.4038 < p < 0.5962) = 0.95.$

Thus a 95% confidence interval keeps getting shorter as n increases—a reasonable result.

Next we want to study how confidence intervals change as k changes for fixed values of n and t. For this purpose, consider $n(t - p)^2/p(1 - p)$ as a function of p for fixed values of n and t. It is easy to see that this function shoots up to infinity near $p = 0$ and 1, attains the minimum value of 0 at $p = t$, and is decreasing in the interval $(0, t)$ and increasing in $(t, 1)$. This function is graphed in Figure 8.1. We have also drawn horizontal lines whose ordinates are equal to k^2 and k^{*2}. Thus the intervals (a, b) and (a^*, b^*) correspond to the γ_k and γ_{k*} confidence intervals, respectively. By definition, confidence clearly satisfies probability axioms (1) and (2) if in (2) we interpret the sample space as the parameter space, which in this example is the interval $[0, 1]$. Moreover, Figure 8.1 shows that if interval I_1 contains interval I_2, we have $C(I_1) \geq C(I_2)$. This suggests that we may extend the definition of confidence to a larger class of sets than in (8.2.4), so that confidence satisfies probability axiom (3) as well. For example, (8.2.4) defines $C(a < p < b) = \gamma_k$, and $C(a^* < p < b^*) = \gamma_{k*}$, and we may further define $C[(a < p < a^*) \cup (b^* < p < b)] = \gamma_k - \gamma_{k*}$.

Confidence is not as useful as probability, however, because there are many important sets for which confidence cannot be defined, even after such an extension. For example, $C(a < p < a^*)$ cannot be uniquely determined from definition (8.2.4). This is definitely a shortcoming of the confidence approach. In Bayesian statistics we would be able to treat p as a random variable and hence construct its density function. Then we could

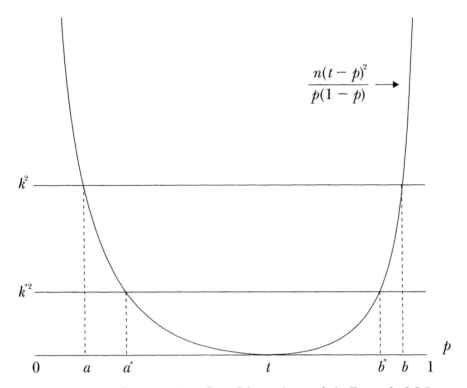

$$\frac{n(t - p)^2}{p(1 - p)} \longrightarrow$$

k^2

k^{*2}

$0 \qquad a \qquad a^* \qquad\qquad t \qquad\qquad b^* \; b \;\; 1$

p

FIGURE 8.1   Construction of confidence intervals in Example 8.2.1

calculate the probability that p lies in a given interval simply as the area under the density function over that interval. This is not possible in the confidence approach, shown above. In other words, there is no unique function ("confidence density," so to speak) such that the area under the curve over an interval gives the confidence of the interval as defined in (8.2.4). For, given one such function, we can construct another by raising the portion of the function over $(0, t)$ and lowering the portion over $(t, 1)$ by the right amount.

EXAMPLE 8.2.2   Let $X_i \sim N(\mu, \sigma^2)$, $i = 1, 2, \ldots, n$, where μ is unknown and σ^2 is known. We have $T \equiv \bar{X} \sim N(\mu, \sigma^2/n)$. Define

(8.2.11) $P\left(\dfrac{|T - \mu|}{\sqrt{\dfrac{\sigma^2}{n}}} < k\right) = \gamma_k.$

Therefore, given $T = t$, we define confidence

$$(8.2.12) \quad C\left(\frac{|t - \mu|}{\sqrt{\frac{\sigma^2}{n}}} < k\right) = \gamma_k.$$

Thus the greater the probability that T lies within a certain distance from μ, the greater the confidence that μ lies within the same distance from t. Note that (8.2.12) defines confidence only for intervals with the center at t. We may be tempted to define $N(t, \sigma^2/n)$ as a confidence density for μ, but this is one among infinite functions for which the area under the curve gives the confidence defined in (8.2.12). For example, the function obtained by eliminating the left half of the normal density $N(t, \sigma^2/n)$ and doubling the right half will also serve as a confidence density.

Suppose that the height of the Stanford male student is distributed as $N(\mu, 0.04)$ and that the average height of ten students is observed to be 6 (in feet). We can construct a 95% confidence interval by putting $t = 6$, $\sigma^2 = 0.04$, $n = 10$, and $k = 1.96$ in (8.2.12) as

$$(8.2.13) \quad C\left(|6 - \mu| < \frac{0.2}{\sqrt{10}} \cdot 1.96\right) = 0.95.$$

Therefore the interval is $(5.88 < \mu < 6.12)$.

EXAMPLE 8.2.3 Suppose that $X_i \sim N(\mu, \sigma^2)$, $i = 1, 2, \ldots, n$, with both μ and σ^2 unknown. Let $T \equiv \bar{X}$ be the estimator of μ and let $S^2 = n^{-1}\sum_{i=1}^{n}(X_i - \bar{X})^2$ be the estimator of σ^2. Then the probability distribution of $t_{n-1} = S^{-1}(T - \mu)\sqrt{n - 1}$ is known and has been tabulated. It depends only on n and is called the *Student's t distribution* with $n - 1$ *degrees of freedom*. See Theorem 5 of the Appendix for its derivation. Its density is symmetric around 0 and approaches that of $N(0, 1)$ as n goes to infinity. Define

$$(8.2.14) \quad \gamma_k = P(|t_{n-1}| < k),$$

where γ_k for various values of k can be computed or read from the Student's t table. Then we have

$$(8.2.15) \quad P\left(\frac{|T - \mu|\sqrt{n - 1}}{S} < k\right) = \gamma_k.$$

Given $T = t$, $S = s$, we define confidence by

(8.2.16) $\quad C\left(\dfrac{|t - \mu|\sqrt{n - 1}}{s} < k\right) = \gamma_k$.

Consider the same data on Stanford students used in Example 8.2.2, but assume that σ^2 is unknown and estimated by S^2, which is observed to be 0.04. Putting $t = 6$ and $s = 0.2$ in (8.2.16), we get

(8.2.17) $\quad C\left(\dfrac{|6 - \mu| \cdot 3}{0.2} < 2.262\right) = 0.95$.

Therefore the 95% confidence interval of μ is $(5.85 < \mu < 6.15)$. Note that this interval is slightly larger than the one obtained in the previous example. The larger interval seems reasonable, because in the present example we have less precise information.

EXAMPLE 8.2.4   Let $X_i \sim N(\mu_X, \sigma^2)$, $i = 1, \ldots, n_X$, let $Y_i \sim N(\mu_Y, \sigma^2)$, $i = 1, \ldots, n_Y$, and assume that $\{X_i\}$ are independent of $\{Y_i\}$. Then, as shown in Theorem 6 of the Appendix,

(8.2.18) $\quad \dfrac{(\bar{X} - \bar{Y}) - (\mu_X - \mu_Y)}{\sqrt{n_X S_X^2 + n_Y S_Y^2}} \sqrt{\dfrac{n_X n_Y (n_X + n_Y - 2)}{n_X + n_Y}} \sim t_{n_X + n_Y - 2}$.

Thus, given the observed values $\bar{x}$, $\bar{y}$, s_X^2, and s_Y^2, we can define the γ_k confidence interval for $\mu_X - \mu_Y$ by

(8.2.19) $\quad C\left[\dfrac{|(\bar{x} - \bar{y}) - (\mu_X - \mu_Y)|}{\sqrt{n_X s_X^2 + n_Y s_Y^2}} \sqrt{\dfrac{n_X n_Y (n_X + n_Y - 2)}{n_X + n_Y}} < k\right] = \gamma_k$,

where $\gamma_k = P(|t_{n_X + n_Y - 2}| < k)$. The assumption that X and Y have the same variance is crucial, because otherwise (8.2.18) does not follow from equation (11) of the Appendix. See Section 10.3.1 for a method which can be used in the case of $\sigma_X^2 \neq \sigma_Y^2$.

As an application of the formula (8.2.19), consider constructing a 0.95 confidence interval for the true difference between the average lengths of unemployment spells for female and male workers, given that a random sample of 35 unemployment spells of female workers lasted 42 days on the average with a standard deviation of 2.5 days, and that a random sample of 40 unemployment spells of male workers lasted 40 days on the average with a standard deviation of 2 days. Since $P(|t_{73}| < 2) \cong 0.95$, inserting $k = 2$, $\bar{x} = 42$, $\bar{y} = 40$, $n_X = 35$, $n_Y = 40$, $s_X^2 = (2.5)^2$, and $s_Y^2 = 2^2$ into (8.2.19) yields

(8.2.20) $C(0.9456 < \mu_X - \mu_Y < 3.0544) = 0.95$.

EXAMPLE 8.2.5 Let $X_i \sim N(\mu, \sigma^2)$, $i = 1, 2, \ldots, n$, with both μ and σ^2 unknown, as in Example 8.2.3. This time we want to define a confidence interval on σ^2. It is natural to use the sample variance defined by $S^2 = n^{-1}\Sigma_{i=1}^{n}(X_i - \bar{X})^2$. Using it, we would like to define a confidence interval of the form

(8.2.21) $a + bS^2 < \sigma^2 < c + dS^2$,

where we can get varying intervals by varying a, b, c, and d. A crucial question is, then, can we calculate the probability of the event (8.2.21) for various values of a, b, c, and d? We reverse the procedure and start out with a statistic of which we know the distribution and see if we can form an interval like that in (8.2.21). We begin by observing $nS^2/\sigma^2 \sim \chi_{n-1}^2$, given in Theorem 3 of the Appendix, and proceed as follows:

(8.2.22) $P\left(k_1 < \dfrac{nS^2}{\sigma^2} < k_2\right) = P\left(\dfrac{1}{k_2} < \dfrac{\sigma^2}{nS^2} < \dfrac{1}{k_1}\right) = P\left(\dfrac{nS^2}{k_2} < \sigma^2 < \dfrac{nS^2}{k_1}\right).$

Therefore, given the observed value s^2 of S^2, a γ-confidence interval is defined by

(8.2.23) $\dfrac{ns^2}{k_2} < \sigma^2 < \dfrac{ns^2}{k_1}$,

where k_1 and k_2 are chosen so as to satisfy

(8.2.24) $P(k_1 < \chi_{n-1}^2 < k_2) = \gamma$.

This example differs from the examples we have considered so far in that (8.2.24) does not determine k_1 and k_2 uniquely. In practice it is customary to determine these two values so as to satisfy

(8.2.25) $P(\chi_{n-1}^2 < k_1) = P(\chi_{n-1}^2 > k_2) = \dfrac{1 - \gamma}{2}$.

Given γ, k_1 and k_2 can be computed or read from the table of *chi-square distribution*.

As an application of the formula (8.2.23), consider constructing a 95% confidence interval for the true variance σ^2 of the height of the Stanford male student, given that the sample variance computed from a random sample of 100 students gave 36 inches. Assume that the height is normally distributed. Inserting $n = 100$, $s^2 = 36$, $k_1 = 74.22$, and $k_2 = 129.56$ into (8.2.23) yields the confidence interval $(27.79, 48.50)$.

EXAMPLE 8.2.6 Besides the preceding five examples, there are many situations where T, as estimator of θ, is either normal or asymptotically normal. If, moreover, the variance of T is consistently estimated by some estimator V, we may define confidence approximately by

$$(8.2.26) \qquad C\left(\frac{|t - \theta|}{\sqrt{v}} < k\right) = P(|Z| < k),$$

where Z is $N(0, 1)$ and t and v are the observed values of T and V, respectively. If the situations of Examples 8.2.1, 8.2.3, 8.2.4, or 8.2.5 actually occur, it is better to define confidence by the method given under the respective examples, even though we can also use the approximate method proposed in this example.

As an application of the formula (8.2.26), consider the same data given at the end of Example 8.2.5. Then, by Theorem 4 of the Appendix,

$$(8.2.27) \qquad S^2 \overset{A}{\sim} N(\sigma^2, \sigma^4/50).$$

Estimating the asymptotic variance $\sigma^4/50$ by $36^2/50$ and using (8.2.26), we obtain an alternative confidence interval, $(26.02, 45.98)$, which does not differ greatly from the one obtained by the more exact method in Example 8.2.5.

8.3 BAYESIAN METHOD

We have stated earlier that the goal of statistical inference is not merely to obtain an estimator but to be able to say, using the estimator, where the true value of the parameter is likely to lie. This is accomplished by constructing confidence intervals, but a shortcoming of this method is that confidence can be defined only for a certain restricted sets of intervals. In the Bayesian method this problem is alleviated, because in it we can treat a parameter as a random variable and therefore define a probability distribution for it. If the parameter space is continuous, as is usually the case, we can define a density function over the parameter space and thereby consider the probability that a parameter lies in any given interval. This probability distribution, called the *posterior distribution*, defined over the parameter space, embodies all the information an investigator can obtain from the sample as well as from the a priori information. It is derived by Bayes' theorem, which was proved in Theorem 2.4.2. We shall subsequently show examples of the posterior distribution and how to derive it. Note that in classical statistics an estimator is defined first and then confidence intervals are constructed using the estimator, whereas in the Bayesian statistics the posterior distribution is obtained directly from the sample without defining any estimator. After the posterior distribution has been obtained, we can define estimators using the posterior distribution if we wish, as will be shown below. The two methods are thus opposite in this respect. For more discussion of the Bayesian method, see DeGroot (1970) and Zellner (1971).

EXAMPLE 8.3.1 Suppose there is a sack containing a mixture of red marbles and white marbles. The fraction of the marbles that are red is known to be either $p = \frac{1}{3}$ or $p = \frac{1}{2}$. We are to guess the value of p after taking a sample of five drawings (replacing each marble drawn before drawing another). The Bayesian expresses the subjective a priori belief about the value of p, which he has before he draws any marble, in the form of what is called the *prior distribution*. Suppose he believes that $p = \frac{1}{3}$ is as three times as likely as $p = \frac{1}{2}$, so that his prior distribution is

(8.3.1) $P(p = \frac{1}{3}) = \frac{3}{4}$

$P(p = \frac{1}{2}) = \frac{1}{4}.$

Suppose he obtains three red marbles and two white marbles in five drawings. Then the posterior distribution of p given the sample, denoted by A, is calculated via Bayes' theorem as follows:

$$(8.3.2) \quad P\left(p = \frac{1}{3} \mid A\right) = \frac{P\left(A \mid p = \frac{1}{3}\right)P\left(p = \frac{1}{3}\right)}{P\left(A \mid p = \frac{1}{3}\right)P\left(p = \frac{1}{3}\right) + P\left(A \mid p = \frac{1}{2}\right)P\left(p = \frac{1}{2}\right)}$$

$$= \frac{C_3^5\left(\frac{1}{3}\right)^3\left(\frac{2}{3}\right)^2\frac{3}{4}}{C_3^5\left(\frac{1}{3}\right)^3\left(\frac{2}{3}\right)^2\frac{3}{4} + C_3^5\left(\frac{1}{2}\right)^3\left(\frac{1}{2}\right)^2\frac{1}{4}}$$

$$\cong 0.61$$

$$P\left(p = \frac{1}{2} \mid A\right) \cong 0.39.$$

This calculation shows how the prior information embodied in (8.3.1) has been modified by the sample. It indicates a higher value of p than the Bayesian's a priori beliefs: it has yielded the posterior distribution (8.3.2), which assigns a larger probability to the event $p = \frac{1}{2}$.

Suppose we change the question slightly as follows. There are four sacks containing red marbles and white marbles. One of them contains an equal number of red and white marbles and three of them contain twice as many white marbles as red marbles. We are to pick one of the four sacks at random and draw five marbles. If three red and two white marbles are drawn, what is the probability that the sack with the equal number of red and white marbles was picked? Answering this question using Bayes' theorem, we obtain 0.39 as before. The reader should recognize the subtle difference between this and the previous question. In the wording of the present question, the event ($p = \frac{1}{2}$) means the event that we pick the sack that contains the equal number of red marbles and white marbles. Since this is a repeatable event, the classical statistician can talk meaningfully about the probability of this event. In contrast, in the previous question, there is only one sack; hence, the classical statistician must view the event ($p = \frac{1}{2}$) as a statement which is either true or false and cannot assign a probability to it. The Bayesian, however, is free to assign a probability to it, because probability to him merely represents the degree of uncertainty. The prior probability in the previous question is purely subjective, whereas

TABLE 8.1   Loss matrix in estimation

	State of Nature	
Decision	$p = \frac{1}{3}$	$p = \frac{1}{2}$
$p = \frac{1}{3}$	0	γ_2
$p = \frac{1}{2}$	γ_1	0

the corresponding probability in the present question has an objective basis.

Given the posterior distribution (8.3.2), the Bayesian may or may not wish to pick either $p = \frac{1}{3}$ or $p = \frac{1}{2}$ as his point estimate. If he simply wanted to know the truth of the situation, (8.3.2) would be sufficient, because it contains all he could possibly know about the situation. If he wanted to make a point estimate, he would consider the loss he would incur in making a wrong decision, as given in Table 8.1. For example, if he chooses $p = \frac{1}{3}$ when $p = \frac{1}{2}$ is in fact true, he incurs a loss γ_2. Thus the Bayesian regards the act of choosing a point estimate as a game played against nature. He chooses the decision for which the expected loss is the smallest, where the expectation is calculated using the posterior distribution. In the present example, therefore, he chooses $p = \frac{1}{3}$ as his point estimate if

(8.3.3) $0.39\gamma_2 < 0.61\gamma_1.$

For simplicity, let us assume $\gamma_1 = \gamma_2$. In this case the Bayesian's point estimate will be $p = \frac{1}{3}$. This estimate is different from the maximum likelihood estimate obtained by the classical statistician under the same circumstances. The difference occurs because the classical statistician obtains information only from the sample, which indicates a greater likelihood that $p = \frac{1}{2}$ than $p = \frac{1}{3}$, whereas the Bayesian allows his conclusion to be influenced by a strong prior belief indicating a greater probability that $p = \frac{1}{3}$. If the Bayesian's prior distribution assigned equal probability to $p = \frac{1}{3}$ and $p = \frac{1}{2}$ instead of (8.3.1), then his estimate would be the same as the maximum likelihood estimate.

What if we drew five red marbles and two white marbles, instead? Denoting this event by B, the posterior distribution now becomes

$$(8.3.4) \qquad P\left(p = \frac{1}{3} \,\middle|\, B\right) = \frac{21 \cdot \dfrac{4}{3^7} \cdot \dfrac{3}{4}}{21 \cdot \dfrac{4}{3^7} \cdot \dfrac{3}{4} + 21 \cdot \dfrac{1}{2^7} \cdot \dfrac{1}{4}} \cong 0.41$$

$$P\left(p = \frac{1}{2} \,\middle|\, B\right) \cong 0.59.$$

In this case the Bayesian would also pick $p = \frac{1}{2}$ as his estimate, assuming $\gamma_1 = \gamma_2$ as before, because the information contained in the sample has now dominated his a priori information.

EXAMPLE 8.3.2 Let X be distributed as $B(n, p)$. In Example 8.3.1, for the purpose of illustration, we assumed that p could take only two values. It is more realistic to assume that p can take any real number between 0 and 1. Suppose we a priori think any value of p between 0 and 1 is equally likely. This situation can be expressed by the *prior density*

$$(8.3.5) \qquad f(p) = 1, \quad 0 < p < 1.$$

Suppose the observed value of X is k and we want to derive the *posterior density* of p, that is, the conditional density of p given $X = k$. Using the result of Section 3.7, we can write Bayes' formula in this example as

$$(8.3.6) \qquad f(p \,|\, X = k) = \frac{P(X = k \,|\, p)f(p)}{\displaystyle\int_0^1 P(X = k \,|\, p)f(p)dp},$$

where the denominator is the marginal probability that $X = k$. Therefore we have

$$(8.3.7) \qquad f(p \,|\, X = k) = \frac{p^k(1 - p)^{n-k}}{\displaystyle\int_0^1 p^k(1 - p)^{n-k}dp}$$

$$= \frac{(n + 1)! \, p^k(1 - p)^{n-k}}{k!(n - k)!},$$

where the second equality above follows from the identity

$$(8.3.8) \qquad \int_0^1 y^n(1 - y)^m dy = \frac{n! \, m!}{(1 + n + m)!} \quad \text{for nonnegative integers } n \text{ and } m.$$

Using (8.3.7), the Bayesian can evaluate the probability that p falls into any given interval. We shall assume that $n = 10$ and $k = 5$ in the model of Example 8.2.1 and compare the Bayesian posterior probability with the confidence obtained there. In (8.2.9) we obtained the 95% confidence interval as $(0.2366 < p < 0.7634)$. We have from (8.3.7)

$$(8.3.9) \qquad P(0.2366 < p < 0.7634) = 2772 \int_{0.2366}^{0.7634} p^5 (1 - p)^5 dp$$

$$= 2772 \left[\frac{1}{6} p^6 - \frac{5}{7} p^7 + \frac{5}{4} p^8 - \frac{10}{9} p^9 + \frac{1}{2} p^{10} - \frac{1}{11} p^{11} \right]_{0.2366}^{0.7634}$$

$$= 0.947.$$

From (8.2.8) we can calculate the 80% confidence interval

$$(8.3.10) \qquad C(0.3124 < p < 0.6876) = 0.8.$$

We have from (8.3.7)

$$(8.3.11) \qquad P(0.3124 < p < 0.6876) = 0.8138.$$

These calculations show that the Bayesian inference based on the uniform prior density leads to results similar to those obtained in classical inference.

We shall now consider the general problem of choosing a point estimate of a parameter θ given its posterior density, say, $f_1(\theta)$. This problem is a generalization of the game against nature considered earlier. Let $\hat{\theta}$ be the estimate and assume that the loss of making a wrong estimate is given by

$$(8.3.12) \qquad \text{Loss} = (\hat{\theta} - \theta)^2.$$

Then the Bayesian chooses $\hat{\theta}$ so as to minimize

$$(8.3.13) \qquad E(\hat{\theta} - \theta)^2 = \int_{-\infty}^{\infty} (\hat{\theta} - \theta)^2 f_1(\theta) d\theta.$$

Note that the expectation is taken with respect to θ in the above equation, since θ is the random variable and $\hat{\theta}$ is the control variable. Equating the derivative of (8.3.13) with respect to $\hat{\theta}$ to 0, we obtain

$$(8.3.14) \qquad 2 \int_{-\infty}^{\infty} (\hat{\theta} - \theta) f_1(\theta) d\theta = 0.$$

Note that in obtaining (8.3.14) we have assumed that it is permissible to differentiate the integrand in (8.3.13). Therefore we finally obtain

$$(8.3.15) \quad \hat{\theta} = \int_{-\infty}^{\infty} \theta f_1(\theta) d\theta.$$

We call this the *Bayes estimator* (or, more precisely, the Bayes estimator under the *squared error loss*). In words, the Bayes estimator is the expected value of θ where the expectation is taken with respect to its posterior distribution.

Let us apply the result (8.3.15) to our example by putting $\theta = p$ and $f_1(p) = f(p \mid X = k)$ in (8.3.7). Using the formula (8.3.8) again, we obtain

$$(8.3.16) \quad \hat{p} = \frac{(n+1)!}{k!(n-k)!} \int_0^1 p^{k+1}(1-p)^{n-k} dp = \frac{k+1}{n+2}.$$

This is exactly the estimator Z that was defined in Example 7.2.2 and found to have a smaller mean squared error than the maximum likelihood estimator k/n over a relatively wide range of the parameter value. It gives a more reasonable estimate of p than the maximum likelihood estimator when n is small. For example, if a head comes up in a single toss ($k = 1$, $n = 1$), the Bayesian estimate $p = \frac{2}{3}$ seems more reasonable than the maximum likelihood estimate, $p = 1$. As n approaches infinity, however, both estimators converge to the true value of p in probability.

As this example shows, the Bayesian method is sometimes a useful tool of analysis even for the classical statistician, because it can give her an estimator which may prove to be desirable by her own standard. Nothing prevents the classical statistician from using an estimator derived following the Bayesian principle, as long as the estimator is judged to be a good one by the standard of classical statistics.

Note that if the prior density is uniform, as in (8.3.5), the posterior density is proportional to the likelihood function, as we can see from (8.3.7). In this case the difference between the maximum likelihood estimator and the Bayes estimator can be characterized by saying that the former chooses the maximum of the posterior density, whereas the latter chooses its average. Classical statistics may therefore be criticized, from the Bayesian point of view, for ignoring the shape of the posterior density except for the location of its maximum. Although the classical statistician uses an intuitive word, "likelihood," she is not willing to make full use of its implication. The *likelihood principle*, an intermediate step between classical and Bayesian principles, was proposed by Birnbaum (1962).

EXAMPLE 8.3.3 Let $\{X_i\}$ be independent and identically distributed as $N(\mu, \sigma^2)$, $i = 1, 2, \ldots, n$, where σ^2 is assumed known. Let x_i be the observed value of X_i. Then the likelihood function of μ given the vector $\mathbf{x} = (x_1, x_2, \ldots, x_n)$ is given by

$$(8.3.17) \quad f(\mathbf{x} \mid \mu) = \left(\frac{1}{\sqrt{2\pi}\,\sigma}\right)^n \exp\left[-\frac{1}{2\sigma^2} \sum_{i=1}^{n} (x_i - \mu)^2\right].$$

Suppose the prior density of μ is $N(\mu_0, \lambda^2)$; that is,

$$(8.3.18) \quad f(\mu) = \frac{1}{\sqrt{2\pi}\,\lambda} \exp\left[-\frac{1}{2\lambda^2} (\mu - \mu_0)^2\right].$$

Then the posterior density of μ given $\mathbf{x}$ is by the Bayes rule

$$(8.3.19) \quad f(\mu \mid \mathbf{x}) = \frac{f(\mathbf{x} \mid \mu)f(\mu)}{\displaystyle\int_{-\infty}^{\infty} f(\mathbf{x} \mid \mu)f(\mu)\,d\mu}$$

$$= c_1 \exp\left[-\frac{1}{2\sigma^2} \sum_{i=1}^{n} (x_i - \mu)^2\right] \exp\left[-\frac{1}{2\lambda^2} (\mu_0 - \mu_0)^2\right],$$

where c_1 is chosen to satisfy $\int_{-\infty}^{\infty} f(\mu \mid \mathbf{x})\,d\mu = 1$. We shall write the exponent part successively as

$$(8.3.20) \quad -\frac{1}{2\sigma^2} \sum_{i=1}^{n} (x_i - \mu)^2 - \frac{1}{2\lambda^2} (\mu - \mu_0)^2$$

$$= -\frac{1}{2} \frac{n\lambda^2 + \sigma^2}{\sigma^2\lambda^2}\left[\mu^2 - \frac{2\lambda^2\Sigma x_i + 2\sigma^2\mu_0}{n\lambda^2 + \sigma^2}\,\mu + \frac{\lambda^2\Sigma x_i^2 + \sigma^2\mu_0^2}{n\lambda^2 + \sigma^2}\right]$$

$$= -\frac{1}{2} \frac{n\lambda^2 + \sigma^2}{\sigma^2\lambda^2}\left[\left(\mu - \frac{\lambda^2\Sigma x_i + \sigma^2\mu_0}{n\lambda^2 + \sigma^2}\right)^2 - \left(\frac{\lambda^2\Sigma x_i + \sigma^2\mu_0}{n\lambda^2 + \sigma^2}\right)^2\right.$$

$$\left. + \frac{\lambda^2\Sigma x_i^2 + \sigma^2\mu_0^2}{n\lambda^2 + \sigma^2}\right].$$

Therefore we have

$$(8.3.21) \quad f(\mu \mid \mathbf{x}) = c_2 \exp\left[- \frac{n\lambda^2 + \sigma^2}{2\sigma^2\lambda^2} \left(\mu - \frac{\lambda^2\Sigma x_i + \sigma^2\mu_0}{n\lambda^2 + \sigma^2} \right)^2 \right],$$

where $c_2 = (1/\sqrt{2\pi})(\sqrt{n\lambda^2 + \sigma^2}/\sigma\lambda)$ in order for $f(\mu \mid \mathbf{x})$ to be a density. Therefore we conclude that the posterior distribution of μ given $\mathbf{x}$ is

$$(8.3.22) \quad \mu \mid \mathbf{x} \sim N\left(\frac{\lambda^2\bar{x} + \dfrac{\sigma^2}{n}\mu_0}{\lambda^2 + \dfrac{\sigma^2}{n}}, \frac{\dfrac{\sigma^2}{n}\lambda^2}{\lambda^2 + \dfrac{\sigma^2}{n}} \right).$$

$E(\mu \mid \mathbf{x})$ in the above formula is suggestive, as it is the optimally weighted average of $\bar{x}$ and μ_0. (Cf. Example 7.2.4.) As we let λ approach infinity in (8.3.22), the prior distribution approaches that which represents total prior ignorance. Then (8.3.22) becomes

$$(8.3.23) \quad \mu \mid \mathbf{x} \sim N\left(\bar{x}, \frac{\sigma^2}{n} \right).$$

Note that (8.3.23) is what we mentioned as one possible confidence density in Example 8.2.2. The probability calculated by (8.3.23) coincides with the confidence given by (8.2.12) whenever the latter is defined.

Note that the right-hand side of (8.3.22) depends on the sample $\mathbf{x}$ only through $\bar{x}$. This result is a consequence of the fact that $\bar{x}$ is a sufficient statistic for the estimation of μ. (Cf. Example 7.3.1.) Since we have $\bar{X} \sim N(\mu, n^{-1}\sigma^2)$, we have

$$(8.3.24) \quad f(\bar{x} \mid \mu) = \frac{\sqrt{n}}{\sqrt{2\pi}\sigma} \exp\left[- \frac{n}{2\sigma^2}(\bar{x} - \mu)^2 \right].$$

Using (8.3.24), we could have obtained a result identical to (8.3.21) by calculating

$$(8.3.25) \quad f(\mu \mid \bar{x}) = \frac{f(\bar{x} \mid \mu)f(\mu)}{\displaystyle\int_{-\infty}^{\infty} f(\bar{x} \mid \mu)f(\mu)d\mu}.$$

EXAMPLE 8.3.4 Let X be uniformly distributed over the interval $(\theta, 10.5)$. Assuming that the prior density of θ is given by

$$f(\theta) = 5 \quad \text{for } 9.5 < \theta < 9.7,$$

$$= 0 \quad \text{otherwise},$$

calculate the posterior density of θ given that an observation of X is 10. We have

(8.3.26) $\quad f(\theta \mid x = 10) = \dfrac{f(x = 10 \mid \theta)f(\theta)}{\displaystyle\int_{9.5}^{9.7} f(x = 10 \mid \theta)f(\theta)d\theta}$

$$= \frac{\dfrac{5}{10.5 - \theta}}{\displaystyle\int_{9.5}^{9.7} \frac{5}{10.5 - \theta}\,d\theta}$$

$$= -\frac{1}{(\log 0.8)(10.5 - \theta)}$$

$$\cong \frac{4.48}{10.5 - \theta} \quad \text{for } 9.5 < \theta < 9.7.$$

One weakness of Bayesian statistics is the possibility that a prior distribution, which is the product of a researcher's subjective judgment, might unduly influence statistical inference. The classical school, in fact, was developed by R. A. Fisher and his followers in an effort to establish statistics as an objective science. This weakness could be eliminated if statisticians could agree upon a reasonable prior distribution which represents total prior ignorance (such as the one considered in Examples 8.3.2 and 8.3.3) in every case. This, however, is not always possible. We might think that a uniform density over the whole parameter domain is the right prior that represents total ignorance, but this is not necessarily so. For example, if parameters θ and μ are related by $\theta = \mu^{-1}$, a uniform prior over μ,

$$f(\mu) = 1, \quad \text{for } 1 < \mu < 2,$$

$$= 0 \quad \text{otherwise},$$

implies a nonuniform prior over θ:

$$f(\theta) = \theta^{-2}, \quad \text{for} \quad 1/2 < \theta < 1,$$

$$= 0 \quad \text{otherwise}.$$

Table 8.2 summarizes the advantages and disadvantages of Bayesian school vis-à-vis classical statistics.

TABLE 8.2 Comparison of Bayesian and classical schools

Bayesian school	Classical school
*Can make exact inference using posterior distribution.	Use confidence intervals as substitute.
*Bayes estimator is good, even by classical standard.	If sample size is large, maximum likelihood estimator is just as good.
Bayes inference may be robust against misspecification of distribution.	*Can use good estimator such as sample mean without assuming any distribution.
Use prior distribution that represents total ignorance.	*Objective inference.
*No need to obtain distribution of estimator.	*No need to calculate complicated integrals.

Note: Asterisk indicates school's advantage.

EXERCISES

1. (Section 8.2)
   Suppose you have a coin for which the probability of a head is the unknown parameter p. How many times should you toss the coin in order that the 95% confidence interval for p is less than or equal to 0.5 in length?

2. (Section 8.2)
   The heights (in feet) of five randomly chosen male Stanford students were 6.3, 6.1, 5.7, 5.8, and 6.2. Find a 90% confidence interval for the mean height, assuming the height is normally distributed.

3. (Section 8.2)

   Suppose $X_i \sim N(\theta, \theta^2)$, $i = 1, 2, \ldots, 100$. Obtain an 80% confidence interval for θ assuming $\bar{x} = 10$.

4. (Section 8.2)

   A particular drug was given to a group of 100 patients (Group 1), and no drug was given to another group of 100 patients (Group 2). Assuming that 60 patients of Group 1 and 50 patients of Group 2 recovered, construct an 80% confidence interval on the difference of the mean rates of recovery of the two groups ($\mu_1 - \mu_2$).

5. (Section 8.2)

   If 50 students in an econometrics class took on the average 35 minutes to solve an exam problem with a variance of 10 minutes, construct a 90% confidence interval for the true standard deviation of the time it takes students to solve the given problem. Answer using both exact and asymptotic methods.

6. (Section 8.3)

   Let X_1 and X_2 be independent and let each be $B(1, p)$. Let the prior probabilities of p be given by $P(p = \frac{1}{2}) = 0.5$ and $P(p = \frac{3}{4}) = 0.5$. Calculate the posterior probabilities $P_1(p) = P(p \mid X_1 = 1)$ and $P_2(p) = P(p \mid X_1 = 1, X_2 = 1)$. Also calculate $P(p \mid X_2 = 1)$ using $P_1(p)$ as the prior probabilities. Compare it with $P_2(p)$.

7. (Section 8.3)

   A Bayesian is to estimate the probability of a head, p, of a particular coin. If her prior density is $f(p) = 6p(1 - p)$, $0 \le p \le 1$, and two heads appear in two tosses, what is her estimate of p?

8. (Section 8.3)

   Suppose the density of X is given by

   $$f(x \mid \theta) = 1/\theta \quad \text{for } 0 \le x \le \theta,$$
   $$= 0 \quad \text{otherwise,}$$

   and the prior density of θ is given by

   $$f(\theta) = 1/\theta^2 \quad \text{for } \theta \ge 1,$$
   $$= 0 \quad \text{otherwise.}$$

Obtain the Bayes estimate of θ, assuming that the observed value of X is 2.

9. (Section 8.3)

Suppose that a head comes up in one toss of a coin. If your prior probability distribution of the probability of a head, p, is given by $P(p = \frac{1}{2}) = \frac{1}{3}$, $P(p = \frac{3}{4}) = \frac{1}{3}$, and $P(p = \frac{4}{5}) = \frac{1}{3}$ and your loss function is given by $|p - \hat{p}|$, what is your estimate $\hat{p}$? What if your prior density of p is given by $f(p) = 1$ for $0 \le p \le 1$?

10. (Section 8.3)

Let $X \sim B(1, p)$ and the prior density of p is given by $f(p) = 1$ for $0 \le p \le 1$. Suppose the loss function $L(\cdot)$ is given by

$$L(e) = -2e \quad \text{if } -1 \le e \le 0,$$

$$= e \qquad \text{if } 0 \le e \le 1,$$

where $e = \hat{p} - p$. Obtain the Bayes estimate of p, given $X = 1$.

11. (Section 8.3)

In the preceding exercise, change the loss function to $L(e) = |e|$. Obtain the Bayes estimate of p, given $X = 1$.

12. (Section 8.3)

Suppose the density of X is given by

$$f(x \mid \theta) = \theta + 2(1 - \theta)x \quad \text{for } 0 \le x \le 1$$

$$= 0 \qquad\qquad \text{otherwise,}$$

where we assume $0 \le \theta \le 2$. Suppose we want to estimate θ on the basis of one observation on X.

(a) Find the maximum likelihood estimator of θ and obtain its exact mean squared error.

(b) Find the Bayes estimator of θ using the uniform prior density of θ given by

$$f(\theta) = 0.5 \quad \text{for } 0 \le \theta \le 2,$$

$$= 0 \quad \text{otherwise.}$$

Obtain its exact mean squared error.

13. (Section 8.3)
    Let $\{X_i\}$ be i.i.d. with the density

    $$f(x\,|\,\theta) = 1/\theta, \quad 0 \le x \le \theta, \quad 1 \le \theta,$$

    and define $\{Y_i\}$ by

    $$Y_i = 1 \quad \text{if } X_i \ge 1,$$
    $$ = 0 \quad \text{if } X_i < 1.$$

    Suppose we observe $\{Y_i\}$, $i = 1$ and 2, and find $Y_1 = 1$ and $Y_2 = 0$.
    We do not observe $\{X_i\}$.
    (a) Find the maximum likelihood estimator of θ.
    (b) Assuming the prior density of θ is $f(\theta) = \theta^{-2}$ for $\theta \ge 1$, find the
    Bayes estimate of θ.

14. (Section 8.3)
    The density of X, given an unknown parameter $\lambda \in [0, 1]$, is given
    by

    $$f(x\,|\,\lambda) = \lambda f_1(x) + (1 - \lambda)f_2(x),$$

    where $f_1(\cdot)$ and $f_2(\cdot)$ are known density functions. Derive the maxi-
    mum likelihood estimator of λ based on one observation on X.
    Assuming the prior density of λ is uniform over the interval $[0, 1]$,
    derive the Bayes estimator of λ based on one observation on X.

15. (Section 8.3)
    Let the density function of X be given by

    $$f(x) = 2x/\theta \qquad\qquad \text{for } 0 \le x \le \theta,$$
    $$ = 2(x - 1)/(\theta - 1) \quad \text{for } \theta < x \le 1,$$

    where $0 < \theta < 1$. Assuming the prior density $f(\theta) = 6\theta(1 - \theta)$, derive
    the Bayes estimator of θ based on a single observation of X.

16. (Section 8.3)
    We have a coin for which the probability of a head is p. In the
    experiment of tossing the coin until a head appears, we observe that
    a head appears in the kth toss. Assuming the uniform prior density,
    find the Bayes estimator of p.

9 | TESTS OF HYPOTHESES

9.1 INTRODUCTION

There are two kinds of hypotheses: one concerns the form of a probability distribution, and the other concerns the parameters of a probability distribution when its form is known. The hypothesis that a sample follows the normal distribution rather than some other distribution is an example of the first, and the hypothesis that the mean of a normally distributed sample is equal to a certain value is an example of the second. Throughout this chapter we shall deal with tests of hypotheses of the second kind only.

The purpose of estimation is to consider the whole parameter space and guess what values of the parameter are more likely than others. In hypothesis testing we pay special attention to a particular set of values of the parameter space and decide if that set is likely or not, compared with some other set.

In hypothesis tests we choose between two competing hypotheses: the *null hypothesis,* denoted H_0, and the *alternative hypothesis,* denoted H_1. We make the decision on the basis of the sample $(X_1, X_2, \ldots, X_n)$, denoted simply as **X**. Thus **X** is an *n*-variate random variable taking values in E_n, *n*-dimensional Euclidean space. Then a test of the hypothesis H_0 mathematically means determining a subset R of E_n such that we reject H_0 (and therefore accept H_1) if $\mathbf{X} \in R$, and we accept H_0 (and therefore reject H_1) if $\mathbf{X} \in \bar{R}$, the complement of R in E_n. The set R is called the *region of rejection* or the *critical region* of the test. Thus the question of hypothesis testing mathematically concerns how we determine the critical region.

As we shall show in Section 9.3, a test of a hypothesis is often based on the value of a real function of the sample (a statistic). If $T(\mathbf{X})$ is such a statistic, the critical region is a subset R of the real line such that we reject H_0 if $T(\mathbf{X}) \in R$. In Chapter 7 we called a statistic used to estimate a parameter an *estimator*. A statistic which is used to test a hypothesis is called a *test statistic*. In the general discussion that follows, we shall treat a critical region as a subset of E_n, because the event $T(\mathbf{X}) \in R$ can always be regarded as defining a subset of the space of $\mathbf{X}$.

A hypothesis may be either simple or composite.

DEFINITION 9.1.1 A hypothesis is called *simple* if it specifies the values of all the parameters of a probability distribution. Otherwise, it is called *composite*.

For example, the assumption that $p = \frac{1}{2}$ in the binomial distribution is a simple hypothesis and the assumption that $p > \frac{1}{2}$ is a composite hypothesis. Specifying the mean of a normal distribution is a composite hypothesis if its variance is unspecified.

In Sections 9.2 and 9.3 we shall assume that both the null and the alternative hypotheses are simple. Sections 9.4 and 9.5 will deal with the case where one or both of the two competing hypotheses may be composite. In practice, the most interesting case is testing a composite hypothesis against a composite hypothesis. Most textbooks, however, devote the greatest amount of space to the study of the simple against simple case. There are two reasons: one is that we can learn about a more complicated realistic case by studying a simpler case; the other is that the classical theory of hypothesis testing is woefully inadequate for the realistic case.

9.2 TYPE I AND TYPE II ERRORS

The question of how to determine the critical region ideally should depend on the cost of making a wrong decision. In this regard it is useful to define the following two types of error.

DEFINITION 9.2.1 A *Type I error* is the error of rejecting H_0 when it is true. A *Type II error* is the error of accepting H_0 when it is false (that is, when H_1 is true).

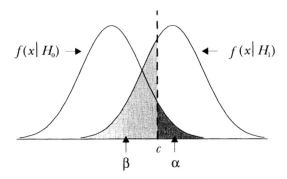

$f(x|H_0) \rightarrow$ $\leftarrow f(x|H_1)$

c

β α

FIGURE 9.1   Relationship between α and β

The probabilities of the two types of error are crucial in the choice of a critical region. We denote the probability of Type I error by α and that of Type II error by β. Therefore we can write mathematically

(9.2.1) $\alpha = P(\mathbf{X} \in R \mid H_0)$

and

(9.2.2) $\beta = P(\mathbf{X} \in \bar{R} \mid H_1)$.

The probability of Type I error is also called the *size* of a test.

Sometimes it is useful to consider a test which chooses two critical regions, say, R_1 and R_2, with probabilities δ and $1 - \delta$ respectively, where δ is chosen a priori. Such a test can be performed if a researcher has a coin whose probability of a head is δ, and she decides in advance that she will choose R_1 if a toss of the coin yields a head and R_2 otherwise. Such a test is called a *randomized test*. If the probabilities of the two types of error for R_1 and R_2 are (α_1, β_1) and (α_2, β_2), respectively, the probabilities of the two types of error for the randomized test, denoted as (α, β), are given by

(9.2.3) $\alpha = \delta\alpha_1 + (1 - \delta)\alpha_2$ and $\beta = \delta\beta_1 + (1 - \delta)\beta_2$.

We call the values of (α, β) the *characteristics* of the test.

We want to use a test for which both α and β are as small as possible. Making α small tends to make β large and vice versa, however, as illustrated in Figure 9.1. In the figure the densities of X under the null and the alternative hypotheses are $f(x \mid H_0)$ and $f(x \mid H_1)$, respectively. If we consider only the critical regions of the form $R = \{x \mid x > c\}$, α and β are represented by the areas of the shaded regions. An optimal test, therefore, should ideally be devised by considering the relative costs of the two types of error. For example, if Type I error is much more costly than Type II error, we should devise a test so as to make α small even though it would imply a large value for β. Even if we do not know the relative costs of the two types of error, this much is certain: given two tests with the same value of α, we should choose the one with the smaller value of β. Thus we define

DEFINITION 9.2.2 Let (α_1, β_1) and (α_2, β_2) be the characteristics of two tests. The first test is *better* (or *more powerful*) than the second test if $\alpha_1 \leq \alpha_2$ and $\beta_1 \leq \beta_2$ with a strict inequality holding for at least one of the $\leq$.

If we cannot determine that one test is better than another by Definition 9.2.2, we must consider the relative costs of the two types of errors. Classical statisticians usually fail to do this, because a consideration of the costs tends to bring in a subjective element. In Section 9.3 we shall show how the Bayesian statistician determines the best test by explicit consideration of the costs, or the so-called *loss function*. Definition 9.2.2 is useful to the extent that we can eliminate from consideration any test which is "worse" than another test. The remaining tests that we need to consider are termed *admissible tests*.

DEFINITION 9.2.3 A test is called *inadmissible* if there exists another test which is better in the sense of Definition 9.2.2. Otherwise it is called *admissible*.

The following examples will illustrate the relationship between α and β as well as the notion of admissible tests.

EXAMPLE 9.2.1 Let X be distributed as $B(2, p)$, and suppose we are to test H_0: $p = \frac{1}{2}$ against H_1: $p = \frac{3}{4}$ on the basis of one observation on X. Construct all possible nonrandomized tests for this problem and calculate the values of α and β for each test.

Table 9.1 describes the characteristics of all the nonrandomized tests. Figure 9.2 plots the characteristics of the eight tests on the α, β plane. Any point on the line segments connecting (1)–(4)–(7)–(8) except the end points themselves represents the characteristics of an admissible ran-

TABLE 9.1 Two types of errors in a binomial example

Test	R	$\bar{R}$	$\alpha = P(R \mid H_0)$	$\beta = P(\bar{R} \mid H_1)$
(1)	$\varnothing$	0,1,2	0	1
(2)	0	1,2	$\frac{1}{4}$	$\frac{15}{16}$
(3)	1	0,2	$\frac{1}{2}$	$\frac{5}{8}$
(4)	2	0,1	$\frac{1}{4}$	$\frac{7}{16}$
(5)	0,1	2	$\frac{3}{4}$	$\frac{9}{16}$
(6)	0,2	1	$\frac{1}{2}$	$\frac{3}{8}$
(7)	1,2	0	$\frac{3}{4}$	$\frac{1}{16}$
(8)	0,1,2	$\varnothing$	1	0

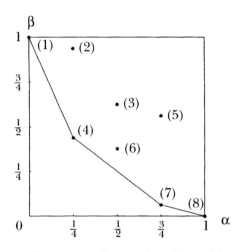

FIGURE 9.2 Two types of errors in a binomial example

domized test. It is clear that the set of tests whose characteristics lie on the line segments constitutes the set of all the admissible tests. Tests (2), (3), and (5) are all dominated by (4) in the sense of Definition 9.2.2. Although test (6) is not dominated by any other nonrandomized test, it is inadmissible because it is dominated by some randomized tests based on (4) and (7). For example, the randomized test that chooses the critical regions of tests (4) and (7) with the equal probability of $\frac{1}{2}$ has the characteristics $\alpha = \frac{1}{2}$ and $\beta = \frac{1}{4}$ and therefore dominates (6). Such a randomized test can be performed by choosing H_0 if $X = 0$, choosing H_1

if $X = 2$, and, if $X = 1$, flipping a coin and choosing H_0 if it is a head and H_1 otherwise.

In Definition 9.2.2 we defined the *more powerful* of two tests. When we consider a specific problem such as Example 9.2.1 where all the possible tests are enumerated, it is natural to talk about the *most powerful* test. In the two definitions that follow, the reader should carefully distinguish two terms, *size* and *level*. In stating these definitions we identify a test with a critical region, but the definitions apply to a randomized test as well.

DEFINITION 9.2.4 R is the *most powerful test of size* α if $\alpha(R) = \alpha$ and for any test R_1 of size α, $\beta(R) \leq \beta(R_1)$. (It may not be unique.)

DEFINITION 9.2.5 R is the *most powerful test of level* α if $\alpha(R) \leq \alpha$ and for any test R_1 of level α (that is, such that $\alpha(R_1) \leq \alpha$), $\beta(R) \leq \beta(R_1)$.

We shall illustrate the two terms using Example 9.2.1. We can state:

The most powerful test of size $\frac{1}{4}$ is (4).

The most powerful nonrandomized test of level $\frac{3}{8}$ is (4).

The most powerful randomized test of size $\frac{3}{8}$ is $\frac{3}{4} \cdot (4) + \frac{1}{4} \cdot (7)$.

Note that if we are allowed randomization, we do not need to use the word *level*.

EXAMPLE 9.2.2   Let X have the density

(9.2.4) $f(x) = 1 - \theta + x$ for $\theta - 1 \leq x < \theta$,

$\qquad\qquad = 1 + \theta - x$ for $\theta \leq x \leq \theta + 1$,

$\qquad\qquad = 0$ otherwise.

We are to test H_0: $\theta = 0$ against H_1: $\theta = 1$ on the basis of a single observation on X. Represent graphically the characteristics of all the admissible tests.

The densities of X under the two hypotheses, denoted by $f_0(x)$ and $f_1(x)$, are graphed in Figure 9.3. Intuitively it is obvious that the critical region of an admissible nonrandomized test is a half-line of the form $[t, \infty)$ where $0 \leq t \leq 1$. In Figure 9.3, α is represented by the area of the

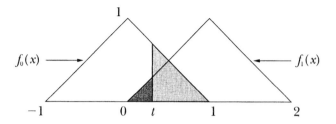

FIGURE 9.3   Densities under two hypotheses

lightly shaded triangle and β by the area of the darker triangle. Therefore, algebraically,

(9.2.5) $\alpha = \dfrac{1}{2}(1 - t)^2$

$$\beta = \frac{1}{2}t^2, \quad 0 \le t \le 1.$$

Eliminating t from (9.2.5) yields

(9.2.6) $\beta = \dfrac{1}{2}(1 - \sqrt{2\alpha})^2, \quad 0 \le \alpha \le \dfrac{1}{2}.$

Equation (9.2.6) is graphed in Figure 9.4. Every point on the curve represents the characteristics of an admissible nonrandomized test. Because of the convexity of the curve, no randomized test can be admissible in this situation.

A more general result concerning the set of admissible characteristics is given in the following theorem, which we state without proof.

THEOREM 9.2.1   The set of admissible characteristics plotted on the α, β plane is a continuous, monotonically decreasing, convex function which starts at a point within $[0, 1]$ on the β axis and ends at a point within $[0, 1]$ on the α axis.

9.3 NEYMAN-PEARSON LEMMA

In this section we study the Bayesian strategy of choosing an optimal test among all the admissible tests and a practical method which enables us to find a best test of a given size. The latter is due to Neyman and Pearson

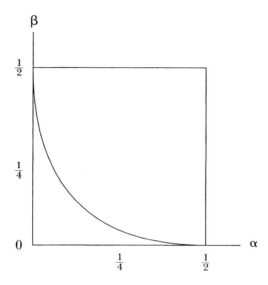

FIGURE 9.4   A set of admissible characteristics

and is stated in the lemma that bears their names. A Bayesian interpretation of the Neyman-Pearson lemma will be pedagogically useful here.

We first consider how the Bayesian would solve the problem of hypothesis testing. For her it is a matter of choosing between H_0 and H_1 given the *posterior probabilities* $P(H_0 \mid \mathbf{x})$ and $P(H_1 \mid \mathbf{x})$ where $\mathbf{x}$ is the observed value of $\mathbf{X}$. Suppose the loss of making a wrong decision is as given in Table 9.2. For example, if we choose H_0 when H_1 is in fact true, we incur a loss γ_2.

Assuming that the Bayesian chooses the decision for which the expected loss is smaller, where the expectation is taken with respect to the posterior distribution, her solution is given by the rule

(9.3.1)   Reject H_0 if $\gamma_1 P(H_0 \mid \mathbf{x}) < \gamma_2 P(H_1 \mid \mathbf{x})$.

In other words, her critical region, R_0, is given by

(9.3.2) $R_0 = \{\mathbf{x} \mid \gamma_1 P(H_0 \mid \mathbf{x}) < \gamma_2 P(H_1 \mid \mathbf{x})\}$.

Alternatively, the Bayesian problem may be formulated as that of determining a critical region R in the domain of $\mathbf{X}$ so as to

(9.3.3)   Minimize $\phi(R) \equiv \gamma_1 P(H_0 \mid \mathbf{X} \in R) P(\mathbf{X} \in R)$

$$+ \gamma_2 P(H_1 \mid \mathbf{X} \in \bar{R}) P(\mathbf{X} \in \bar{R}).$$

TABLE 9.2 Loss matrix in hypothesis testing

	State of Nature	
Decision	H_0	H_1
H_0	0	γ_2
H_1	γ_1	0

We shall show that R_0 as defined by (9.3.2) is indeed the solution of (9.3.3). Let R_1 be some other set in the domain of **X**. Then we have

$$(9.3.4) \qquad \phi(R_0) = \gamma_1 P(H_0 \mid R_0 \cap R_1) P(R_0 \cap R_1)$$
$$+ \gamma_1 P(H_0 \mid R_0 \cap \bar{R}_1) P(R_0 \cap \bar{R}_1)$$
$$+ \gamma_2 P(H_1 \mid \bar{R}_0 \cap R_1) P(\bar{R}_0 \cap R_1)$$
$$+ \gamma_2 P(H_1 \mid \bar{R}_0 \cap \bar{R}_1) P(\bar{R}_0 \cap \bar{R}_1)$$

and

$$(9.3.5) \qquad \phi(R_1) = \gamma_1 P(H_0 \mid R_1 \cap R_0) P(R_1 \cap R_0)$$
$$+ \gamma_1 P(H_0 \mid R_1 \cap \bar{R}_0) P(R_1 \cap \bar{R}_0)$$
$$+ \gamma_2 P(H_1 \mid \bar{R}_1 \cap R_0) P(\bar{R}_1 \cap R_0)$$
$$+ \gamma_2 P(H_1 \mid \bar{R}_1 \cap \bar{R}_0) P(\bar{R}_1 \cap \bar{R}_0).$$

Compare the terms on the right-hand side of (9.3.4) with those on the right-hand side of (9.3.5). The first and fourth terms are identical. The second and the third terms of (9.3.4) are smaller than the third and the second terms of (9.3.5), respectively, because of the definition of R_0 given in (9.3.2). Therefore we have

$$(9.3.6) \qquad \phi(R_0) < \phi(R_1).$$

We can rewrite $\phi(R)$ as

$$(9.3.7) \qquad \phi(R) = \gamma_1 P(H_0) P(R \mid H_0) + \gamma_2 P(H_1) P(\bar{R} \mid H_1)$$
$$\equiv \eta_0 \alpha(R) + \eta_1 \beta(R),$$

where $\eta_0 = \gamma_1 P(H_0)$, $\eta_1 = \gamma_2 P(H_1)$, and $P(H_0)$ and $P(H_1)$ are the *prior probabilities* for the two hypotheses. When the minimand is written in the form of (9.3.7), it becomes clear that the Bayesian optimal test R_0 is determined at the point where the curve of the admissible characteristics on the α, β plane, such as those drawn in Figures 9.2 and 9.4, touches the line that lies closest to the origin among all the straight lines with the slope equal to $-\eta_0/\eta_1$. If the curve is differentiable as in Figure 9.4, the point of the characteristics of the Bayesian optimal test is the point of tangency between the curve of admissible characteristics and the straight line with slope $-\eta_0/\eta_1$.

The classical statistician does not wish to specify the losses γ_1 and γ_2 or the prior probabilities $P(H_0)$ and $P(H_1)$; hence he does not wish to specify the ratio η_0/η_1, without which the minimization of (9.3.7) cannot be carried out. The best he can do, therefore, is to obtain the set of admissible tests. This attitude of the classical statistician is analogous to that of the economist who obtains the *Pareto optimality* condition without specifying the weights on two people's utilities in the social welfare function.

By virtue of Theorem 9.2.1, which shows the convexity of the curve of admissible characteristics, the above analysis implies that every admissible test is the Bayesian optimal test corresponding to some value of the ratio η_0/η_1. This fact is the basis of the Neyman-Pearson lemma. Let $L(\mathbf{x})$ be the joint density or probability of $\mathbf{X}$ depending on whether $\mathbf{X}$ is continuous or discrete. Multiply both sides of the inequality in (9.3.2) by $L(\mathbf{x})$ and replace $P(H_i \mid \mathbf{x})L(\mathbf{x})$ with $L(\mathbf{x} \mid H_i)P(H_i)$, $i = 0, 1$. Then the Bayesian optimal test R_0 can be written as

$$(9.3.8) \qquad R_0 = \left\{ \mathbf{x} \mid \frac{L(\mathbf{x} \mid H_1)}{L(\mathbf{x} \mid H_0)} > \frac{\eta_0}{\eta_1} \right\}.$$

Thus we have proved

THEOREM 9.3.1 (Neyman-Pearson lemma)   In testing H_0: $\theta = \theta_0$ against H_1: $\theta = \theta_1$, the best critical region of size α is given by

$$(9.3.9) \qquad R = \left\{ \mathbf{x} \mid \frac{L(\mathbf{x} \mid \theta_1)}{L(\mathbf{x} \mid \theta_0)} > c \right\},$$

where L is the likelihood function and c (the *critical value*) is determined so as to satisfy

$$(9.3.10) \qquad P(R \mid \theta_0) = \alpha,$$

provided that such c exists. (Here, as well as in the following analysis, θ may be a vector.)

The last clause in the theorem is necessary because, for example, in Example 9.2.1 the Neyman-Pearson test consists of (1), (4), (7), and (8), and there is no c that satisfies (9.3.10) for $\alpha = \frac{1}{2}$.

THEOREM 9.3.2 The Bayes test is admissible.

Proof. Let R_0 be as defined in (9.3.2). Then, by (9.3.7),

$$(9.3.11) \qquad \eta_0 \alpha(R_0) + \eta_1 \beta(R_0) \leq \eta_0 \alpha(R) + \eta_1 \beta(R).$$

Therefore, it is not possible to have $\alpha(R) \leq \alpha(R_0)$ and $\beta(R) \leq \beta(R_0)$ with a strict inequality in at least one. $\square$

The Neyman-Pearson test is admissible because it is a Bayes test.

The choice of α is in principle left to the researcher, who should determine it based on subjective evaluation of the relative costs of the two types of error. There is a tendency, however, for the classical statistician automatically to choose $\alpha = 0.05$ or 0.01. A small value is often selected because of the classical statistician's reluctance to abandon the null hypothesis until the evidence of the sample becomes overwhelming. We shall consider a few examples of application of Theorem 9.3.1.

EXAMPLE 9.3.1 Let X be distributed as $B(n, p)$ and let x be its observed value. The best critical region for testing H_0: $p = p_0$ against H_1: $p = p_1$ is, from (9.3.9),

$$(9.3.12) \qquad \frac{p_1^x(1 - p_1)^{n-x}}{p_0^x(1 - p_0)^{n-x}} > c \quad \text{for some } c.$$

Taking the logarithm of both sides of (9.3.12) and collecting terms, we get

$$(9.3.13) \qquad x\left(\log \frac{p_1}{p_0} - \log \frac{1 - p_1}{1 - p_0}\right) > \log c - n \log \frac{1 - p_1}{1 - p_0}.$$

Suppose $p_1 > p_0$. Then the term inside the parentheses on the left-hand side of (9.3.13) is positive. Therefore the best critical region of size α is defined by

$$(9.3.14) \qquad x > d, \quad \text{where } d \text{ is determined by } P(X > d \mid H_0) = \alpha.$$

If $p_1 < p_0$, the inequality in (9.3.14) is reversed. The result is consistent with our intuition.

EXAMPLE 9.3.2 Let X_i be distributed as $N(\mu, \sigma^2)$, $i = 1, 2, \ldots, n$, where σ^2 is assumed known. Let x_i be the observed value of X_i. The best critical region for testing H_0: $\mu = \mu_0$ against H_1: $\mu = \mu_1$ is, from (9.3.9),

$$(9.3.15) \qquad \frac{\exp\left[-\dfrac{1}{2\sigma^2}\Sigma(x_i - \mu_1)^2\right]}{\exp\left[-\dfrac{1}{2\sigma^2}\Sigma(x_i - \mu_0)^2\right]} > c \quad \text{for some } c.$$

Taking the logarithm of both sides of (9.3.15) and collecting terms, we obtain

$$(9.3.16) \qquad (\mu_1 - \mu_0)\sum_{i=1}^{n} x_i > \sigma^2 \log c + \frac{n}{2}(\mu_1^2 - \mu_0^2).$$

Therefore if $\mu_1 > \mu_0$, the best critical region of size α is of the form

$$(9.3.17) \qquad \bar{x} > d, \quad \text{where } d \text{ is determined by } P(\bar{X} > d \mid H_0) = \alpha.$$

If $\mu_1 < \mu_0$, the inequality in (9.3.17) is reversed. This result is also consistent with our intuition.

In both examples the critical region is reduced to a subset of the domain of a univariate statistic (which in both cases is a sufficient statistic). There are often situations where a univariate statistic is used to test a hypothesis about a parameter. As stated in Section 9.1, such a statistic is called a *test statistic*. Common sense tells us that the better the estimator we use as a test statistic, the better the test becomes. Therefore, even in situations where the Neyman-Pearson lemma does not indicate the best test of a given size α, we should do well if we used the best available estimator of a parameter as a test statistic to test a hypothesis concerning the parameter. Given a test statistic, it is often possible to find a reasonable critical region on an intuitive ground. Intuition, however, does not always work, as the following counterexample shows.

EXAMPLE 9.3.3 Let the density of X be given by

$$(9.3.18) \qquad f(x, \theta) = \frac{1}{2(1 + x - \theta)^2} \quad \text{if } x \geq \theta,$$

$$= \frac{1}{2(1 - x + \theta)^2} \quad \text{if } x < \theta.$$

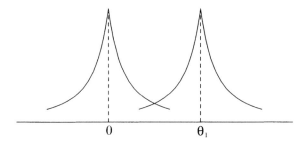

FIGURE 9.5   Densities in a counterintuitive case

Find the Neyman-Pearson test of H_0: $\theta = 0$ against H_1: $\theta = \theta_1 > 0$. The densities under H_0 and H_1 are shown in Figure 9.5. We have

$$(9.3.19) \quad \frac{L(H_1)}{L(H_0)} = \frac{(1-x)^2}{(1-x+\theta_1)^2} \quad \text{if } x < 0,$$

$$= \frac{(1+x)^2}{(1-x+\theta_1)^2} \quad \text{if } 0 \le x \le \theta_1,$$

$$= \frac{(1+x)^2}{(1+x-\theta_1)^2} \quad \text{if } x > \theta_1.$$

The Neyman-Pearson critical region, denoted R, is identified in Figure 9.6. The shape of the function (9.3.19) changes with θ_1. In the figure it is drawn assuming $\theta_1 = 1$.

9.4   SIMPLE AGAINST COMPOSITE

We have so far considered only situations in which both the null and the alternative hypotheses are simple in the sense of Definition 9.1.1. Now we shall turn to the case where the null hypothesis is simple and the alternative hypothesis is composite.

We can mathematically express the present case as testing H_0: $\theta = \theta_0$ against H_1: $\theta \in \Theta_1$, where Θ_1 is a subset of the parameter space. If Θ_1 consists of a single element, it is reduced to the simple hypothesis considered in the previous sections. Definition 9.2.4 defined the concept of the most powerful test of size α in the case of testing a simple against a simple

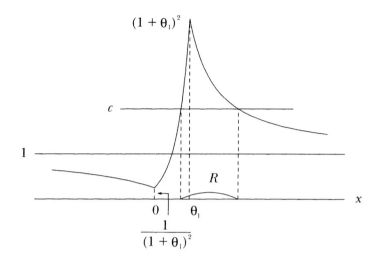

FIGURE 9.6 The Neyman-Pearson critical region
in a counterintuitive case

hypothesis. In the present case we need to modify it, because here the β value (the probability of accepting H_0 when H_1 is true) is not uniquely determined if Θ_1 contains more than one element. In this regard it is useful to consider the concept of the *power function*.

DEFINITION 9.4.1 If the distribution of the sample **X** depends on a vector of parameters θ, we define the *power function* of the test based on the critical region R by

(9.4.1) $\quad Q(\theta) = P(\mathbf{X} \in R \mid \theta).$

Using the idea of the power function, we can rank tests of a simple null hypothesis against a composite alternative hypothesis by the following definition.

DEFINITION 9.4.2 Let $Q_1(\theta)$ and $Q_2(\theta)$ be the power functions of two tests respectively. Then we say that the first test is *uniformly better* (or *uniformly more powerful*) than the second test in testing $H_0: \theta = \theta_0$ against $H_1: \theta \in \Theta_1$ if $Q_1(\theta_0) = Q_2(\theta_0)$ and

(9.4.2) $\quad Q_1(\theta) \geq Q_2(\theta) \quad$ for all $\theta \in \Theta_1$

and

(9.4.3) $Q_1(\theta) > Q_2(\theta)$ for at least one $\theta \in \Theta_1$.

Note that $Q(\theta_0)$ is what we earlier called α, and if Θ_1 consists of a single element equal to θ_1, we have $Q(\theta_1) = 1 - \beta$.

The following is an example of the power function.

EXAMPLE 9.4.1 Let X have the density

$$f(x) = \frac{1}{\theta} \quad \text{for } 0 \le x \le \theta,$$

$$= 0 \quad \text{otherwise.}$$

We are to test H_0: $\theta = 1$ against H_1: $\theta > 1$ on the basis of one observation on X. Obtain and draw the power function of the test based on the critical region $R = [0.75, \infty)$.

By (9.4.1) we have

(9.4.4) $Q(\theta) = P(X \ge 0.75 \mid \theta) = 1 - \dfrac{0.75}{\theta}$.

Its graph is shown in Figure 9.7.

The following is a generalization of Definitions 9.2.4 and 9.2.5. This time we shall state it for *size* and indicate the necessary modification for *level* in parentheses.

DEFINITION 9.4.3 A test R is the *uniformly most powerful* (UMP) test of size (level) α for testing H_0: $\theta = \theta_0$ against H_1: $\theta \in \Theta_1$ if $P(R \mid \theta_0) = (\le)\ \alpha$ and for any other test R_1 such that $P(R_1 \mid \theta_0) = (\le)\ \alpha$, we have $P(R \mid \theta) \ge P(R_1 \mid \theta)$ *for any* $\theta \in \Theta_1$.

In the case where both the null and the alternative hypotheses are simple, the Neyman-Pearson lemma provides a practical way to find the most powerful test of a given size α. In the present case, where the alternative hypothesis is composite, the UMP test of a given size α may not always exist. The so-called *likelihood ratio test*, however, which may be thought of as a generalization of the Neyman-Pearson test, usually gives

FIGURE 9.7   Power function

the UMP test if a UMP test exists; even when it does not, the likelihood ratio test is known to have good asymptotic properties.

DEFINITION 9.4.4   Let $L(\mathbf{x} \mid \theta)$ be the likelihood function and let the null and alternative hypotheses be H_0: $\theta = \theta_0$ and H_1: $\theta \in \Theta_1$, where Θ_1 is a subset of the parameter space Θ. Then the *likelihood ratio test* of H_0 against H_1 is defined by the critical region

(9.4.5) $\Lambda \equiv \dfrac{L(\theta_0)}{\sup\limits_{\theta_0 \cup \theta_1} L(\theta)} < c,$

where c is chosen to satisfy $P(\Lambda < c \mid H_0) = \alpha$ for a certain specified value of α. Sup, standing for *supremum,* means the least upper bound and is equal to the maximum if the latter exists. Note that we have $0 \le \Lambda \le 1$ because the subset of the parameter space within which the supremum is taken contains θ_0.

Below we give several examples of the likelihood ratio test. In some of them the test is UMP, but in others it is not.

EXAMPLE 9.4.2   Let X be distributed as $B(n, p)$. We are to test H_0: $p = p_0$ against H_1: $p > p_0$, given the observation $X = x$. The likelihood function is $L(x, p) = C_x^n p^x (1 - p)^{n-x}$. If $x/n \le p_0$, clearly $\Lambda = 1$, which means that H_0 is accepted for any value of α less than 1. If $x/n > p_0$, $\max_{p \ge p_0} L(x, p)$ is attained at $p = x/n$. Therefore the critical region of the likelihood ratio test is given by

(9.4.6) $\Lambda = \dfrac{p_0^x (1 - p_0)^{n-x}}{\left(\dfrac{x}{n}\right)^x \left(1 - \dfrac{x}{n}\right)^{n-x}} < c$ for a certain c.

Taking the logarithm of both sides of (9.4.6) and dividing by $-n$, we obtain

(9.4.7) $t \log t + (1 - t) \log (1 - t) - t \log p_0 - (1 - t) \log (1 - p_0)$

$$> - \frac{\log c}{n},$$

where we have put $t = x/n$. Since it can be shown by differentiation that the left-hand side of (9.4.7) is an increasing function of t whenever $t > p_0$, it is equivalent to

(9.4.8) $\dfrac{x}{n} > d,$

where d should be determined so as to make the probability of event (9.4.8) under the null hypothesis (approximately) equal to α. (Note that c need not be determined.)

This test is UMP because it is the Neyman-Pearson test against any specific value of $p > p_0$ (see Example 9.3.1) and because the test defined by (9.4.8) does not depend on the value of p.

EXAMPLE 9.4.3   Let the sample be $X_i \sim N(\mu, \sigma^2)$, $i = 1, 2, \ldots , n$, where σ^2 is assumed known. Let x_i be the observed value of X_i. We are to test $H_0: \mu = \mu_0$ against $H_1: \mu > \mu_0$. The likelihood ratio test is to reject H_0 if

(9.4.9) $$\Lambda \equiv \frac{\exp\left[-\dfrac{1}{2\sigma^2} \sum_{i=1}^{n} (x_i - \mu_0)^2 \right]}{\sup\limits_{\mu \geq \mu_0} \exp\left[-\dfrac{1}{2\sigma^2} \sum_{i=1}^{n} (x_i - \mu)^2 \right]} < c.$$

If $\bar{x} \leq \mu_0$, then $\Lambda = 1$ because we can write $\Sigma (x_i - \mu)^2 = \Sigma (x_i - \bar{x})^2 + n(\mu - \bar{x})^2$; therefore, we accept H_0. So suppose $\bar{x} > \mu_0$. Then the denominator of Λ attains a maximum at $\mu = \bar{x}$. Therefore, we have

(9.4.10) $(\bar{x} - \mu_0)^2 > - \dfrac{2\sigma^2 \log c}{n}.$

Therefore, since $\bar{x} > \mu_0$, the likelihood ratio test in this case is characterized by the critical region

(9.4.11) $\bar{x} > d$, where d is determined by $P(\bar{X} > d \mid H_0) = \alpha$.

For the same reason as in the previous example, this test is UMP.

EXAMPLE 9.4.4 The assumptions are the same as those of Example 9.4.3 except that H_1: $\mu \neq \mu_0$. Then the denominator in (9.4.9) is maximized with respect to the freely varying μ, attaining its maximum at $\mu = \bar{x}$. Therefore we again obtain (9.4.10), but this time without the further constraint that $\bar{x} > \mu_0$. Therefore the critical region is

(9.4.12) $|\bar{x} - \mu_0| > d$,

$$\text{where } d \text{ is determined by } P(|\bar{X} - \mu_0| > d \mid H_0) = \alpha.$$

This test cannot be UMP, because it is not a Neyman-Pearson test against a specific value of μ.

Tests such as (9.4.8) and (9.4.11) are called *one-tail tests*, whereas tests such as (9.4.12) are called *two-tail tests*. In a two-tail test such as (9.4.12) we could perform the same test using a confidence interval, as discussed in Section 8.2. From Example 8.2.2 the $1 - \alpha$ confidence interval of μ is defined by $|\bar{x} - \mu| < d$, where d is the same as in (9.4.12). Therefore, H_0 should be rejected if and only if μ_0 lies outside the confidence interval.

EXAMPLE 9.4.5 Consider the model of Example 9.3.3 and test H_0: $\theta = 0$ against H_1: $\theta > 0$ on the basis of one observation x. If $x \leq 0$, then $\Lambda = 1$, so we accept H_0. Therefore assume $x > 0$. Then the numerator of Λ is equal to $1/[2(1 + x)^2]$ and the denominator is equal to $\frac{1}{2}$. Therefore the likelihood ratio test is to reject H_0 if $x > d$, where d is chosen appropriately. This test is not UMP because it is not a Neyman-Pearson test, which was obtained in Example 9.3.3. That the UMP test does not exist in this case can be seen more readily by noting that the Neyman-Pearson test in this example depends on a particular value of θ.

EXAMPLE 9.4.6 Suppose X has a uniform density over $[0, \theta]$, $0 < \theta \leq 1$. We are to test H_0: $\theta = \frac{1}{2}$ against H_1: $\theta \neq \frac{1}{2}$ on the basis of one observation

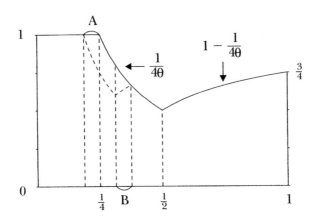

FIGURE 9.8   Power function of a likelihood ratio test

x. Derive the likelihood ratio test of size $\frac{1}{2}$, draw its power function, and show that it is UMP.

First, note that $\Lambda = 0$ for $x \in [0.5, 1]$; therefore, $[0.5, 1]$ should be part of the critical region. Next assume that $x \in [0, 0.5)$. Then we have

$$(9.4.13) \qquad \Lambda = \frac{2}{1/x} = 2x.$$

Therefore we reject H_0 if $2x < c$, where c should satisfy $P(2X < c \mid H_0) = \frac{1}{2}$. This implies that $c = \frac{1}{2}$. We conclude that the critical region is $[0, 0.25]$ $\cup$ $[0.5, 1]$. Its power function is depicted as a solid curve in Figure 9.8. To show that this is UMP, first note that $[0.5, 1]$ should be part of any reasonable critical region, because this portion does not affect the size and can only increase the power. Suppose the portion A of $[0, 0.25]$ is removed from the critical region and the portion B is added in such a way that the size remains the same. Then part of the power function shifts downward to the broken curve. This completes the proof.

In all the examples of the likelihood ratio test considered thus far, the exact probability of $\Lambda < c$ can be either calculated exactly or read from appropriate tables. There are cases, however, where $P(\Lambda < c)$ cannot be easily evaluated. In such a case the following theorem is useful.

THEOREM 9.4.1   Let Λ be the likelihood ratio test statistic defined in (9.4.5). Then, $-2 \log \Lambda$ is asymptotically distributed as chi-square with the degrees of freedom equal to the number of exact restrictions implied by

H_0. (For example, if there are r parameters and H_0 specifies the values of all of them, the degrees of freedom are r.)

9.5 COMPOSITE AGAINST COMPOSITE

In this section we consider testing a composite null hypothesis against a composite alternative hypothesis. As noted earlier, this situation is the most realistic. Let the null and alternative hypotheses be H_0: $\theta \in \Theta_0$ and H_1: $\theta \in \Theta_1$, where Θ_0 and Θ_1 are subsets of the parameter space Θ. Here we define the concept of the UMP test as follows:

DEFINITION 9.5.1 A test R is the uniformly most powerful test of size (level) α if $\sup_{\theta \in \Theta_0} P(R \mid \theta) = (\leq) \alpha$ and for any other test R_1 such that $\sup_{\theta \in \Theta_0} P(R_1 \mid \theta) = (\leq) \alpha$ we have $P(R \mid \theta) \geq P(R_1 \mid \theta)$ for any $\theta \in \Theta_1$.

For the present situation we define the likelihood ratio test as follows.

DEFINITION 9.5.2 Let $L(\mathbf{x} \mid \theta)$ be the likelihood function. Then the *likelihood ratio test* of H_0 against H_1 is defined by the critical region

$$(9.5.1) \qquad \Lambda \equiv \frac{\sup_{\Theta_0} L(\theta)}{\sup_{\Theta_0 \cup \Theta_1} L(\theta)} < c,$$

where c is chosen to satisfy $\sup_{\Theta_0} P(\Lambda < c \mid \theta) = \alpha$ for a certain specified value of α.

The following are examples of the likelihood ratio test.

EXAMPLE 9.5.1 Consider the same model as in Example 9.4.2, but here test H_0: $p \leq p_0$ against H_1: $p > p_0$. If $x/n \leq p_0$, $\Lambda = 1$; therefore, accept H_0. Henceforth suppose $x/n > p_0$. Since the numerator of the likelihood ratio attains its maximum at $p = p_0$, Λ is the same as in (9.4.6). Therefore the critical region is again given by (9.4.8). Next we must determine d so as to satisfy

$$(9.5.2) \qquad \sup_{p \leq p_0} P\left(\frac{X}{n} > d \mid p\right) = \alpha.$$

But since $P(X/n > d \mid p)$ can be shown to be a monotonically increasing function of p, we have

(9.5.3) $$\sup_{p \le p_0} P\left(\frac{X}{n} > d \mid p\right) = P\left(\frac{X}{n} > d \mid p_0\right).$$

Therefore the value of d is also the same as in Example 9.4.2.

This test is UMP. To see this, let R be the test defined above and let R_1 be some other test such that $\sup_{p \le p_0} P(R_1 \mid p) \le \alpha$. Then it follows that $P(R_1 \mid p_0) \le \alpha$. But since R is the UMP test of H_0: $p = p_0$ against H_1: $p > p_0$, we have $P(R_1 \mid p) \le P(R \mid p)$ for all $p > p_0$ by the result of Example 9.4.2.

EXAMPLE 9.5.2   Let the sample be $X_i \sim N(\mu, \sigma^2)$ with unknown σ^2, $i = 1, 2, \ldots, n$. We are to test H_0: $\mu = \mu_0$ and $0 < \sigma^2 < \infty$ against H_1: $\mu > \mu_0$ and $0 < \sigma^2 < \infty$.

Denoting (μ, σ^2) by θ, we have

(9.5.4) $$L(\theta) = (2\pi)^{-n/2}(\sigma^2)^{-n/2}\exp\left[-\frac{1}{2\sigma^2}\sum_{i=1}^{n}(x_i - \mu)^2\right].$$

Therefore

(9.5.5) $$\sup_{\Theta_0} L(\theta) = (2\pi)^{-n/2}(\bar{\sigma}^2)^{-n/2}\exp\left[-\frac{1}{2\bar{\sigma}^2}\sum_{i=1}^{n}(x_i - \mu_0)^2\right]$$

$$= (2\pi)^{-n/2}(\bar{\sigma}^2)^{-n/2}\exp\left[-\frac{n}{2}\right],$$

where $\bar{\sigma}^2 = n^{-1}\Sigma_{i=1}^{n}(x_i - \mu_0)^2$. If $x/n \le p_0$, $\Lambda = 1$; therefore, accept H_0. Henceforth suppose $x/n > p_0$. Then we have

(9.5.6) $$\sup_{\Theta_0 \cup \Theta_1} L(\theta) = (2\pi)^{-n/2}(\hat{\sigma}^2)^{-n/2}\exp\left[-\frac{n}{2}\right],$$

where $\hat{\sigma}^2 = n^{-1}\Sigma_{i=1}^{n}(x_i - \bar{x})^2$. Therefore the critical region is

(9.5.7) $(\bar{\sigma}^2/\hat{\sigma}^2)^{-n/2} < c$ for some c,

which can be equivalently written as

(9.5.8) $$\frac{\bar{x} - \mu_0}{\sqrt{(\bar{\sigma}^2/n)}} > k,$$

where $\hat{\sigma}^2$ is the unbiased estimator of σ^2 defined by $(n-1)^{-1}\Sigma_{i=1}^{n}(x_i - \bar{x})^2$. Since the left-hand side of (9.5.8) is distributed as Student's t with $n-1$ degrees of freedom, k can be computed or read from the appropriate table. Note that since $P(R \mid H_0)$ is uniquely determined in this example in spite of the composite null hypothesis, there is no need to compute the supremum.

If the alternative hypothesis specifies $\mu \neq \mu_0$, the critical region (9.5.8) should be modified by putting the absolute value sign around the left-hand side. In this case the same test can be performed using the confidence interval defined in Example 8.2.3.

In Section 9.3 we gave a Bayesian interpretation of the classical method for the case of testing a simple null hypothesis against a simple alternative hypothesis. Here we shall do the same for the composite against composite case, and we shall see that the classical theory of hypothesis testing becomes more problematic. Let us first see how the Bayesian would solve the problem of testing $H_0: \theta \leq \theta_0$ against $H_1: \theta > \theta_0$. Let $L_2(\theta)$ be the loss incurred by choosing H_0, and $L_1(\theta)$ by choosing H_1. Then the Bayesian rejects H_0 if

$$(9.5.9) \qquad \int_{-\infty}^{\infty} L_1(\theta) f(\theta \mid \mathbf{x}) d\theta < \int_{-\infty}^{\infty} L_2(\theta) f(\theta \mid \mathbf{x}) d\theta,$$

where $f(\theta \mid \mathbf{x})$ is the posterior density of θ. Suppose, for simplicity, that $L_1(\theta)$ and $L_2(\theta)$ are simple step functions defined by

$$(9.5.10) \qquad L_1(\theta) = 0 \quad \text{for } \theta > \theta_0$$
$$= \gamma_1 \quad \text{for } \theta \leq \theta_0$$

and

$$L_2(\theta) = 0 \quad \text{for } \theta < \theta_0$$
$$= \gamma_2 \quad \text{for } \theta \geq \theta_0.$$

In this case the losses are as given in Table 9.2; therefore (9.5.9), as can be seen in (9.3.8), is reduced to

$$(9.5.11) \qquad \frac{L(\mathbf{x} \mid H_1)}{L(\mathbf{x} \mid H_0)} > \frac{\eta_0}{\eta_1}.$$

Recall that (9.5.11) is the basis for interpreting the Neyman-Pearson test. Here, in addition to the problem of not being able to evaluate η_0/η_1, the classical statistician faces the additional problem of not being able to make sense of $L(\mathbf{x} \mid H_1)$ and $L(\mathbf{x} \mid H_0)$.

The likelihood ratio test is essentially equivalent to rejecting H_0 if

(9.5.12)
$$\frac{\sup_{\theta > \theta_0} L(\mathbf{x} \mid \theta)}{\sup_{\theta \leq \theta_0} L(\mathbf{x} \mid \theta)} > c.$$

A problem here is that the left-hand side of (9.5.12) may not be a good substitute for the left-hand side of (9.5.11).

Sometimes a statistical decision problem we face in practice need not and/or cannot be phrased as the problem of testing a hypothesis on a parameter. For example, consider the problem of deciding whether or not we should approve a certain drug on the basis of observing x cures in n independent trials. Let p be the probability of a cure when the drug is administered to a patient, and assume that the net benefit to society of approving the drug can be represented by a function $U(p)$, nondecreasing in p. According to the Bayesian principle, we should approve the drug if

(9.5.13)
$$\int_0^1 U(p)f(p \mid x)dp > 0,$$

where $f(p \mid x)$ is the posterior density of p given x. Note that in this decision problem, hypothesis testing on the parameter p is not explicitly considered. The decision rule (9.5.13) is essentially the same kind as (9.5.9), however.

Next we try to express (9.5.13) more explicitly as an inequality concerning x, assuming for simplicity that $f(p \mid x)$ is derived from a uniform prior density: that is, from (8.3.7),

(9.5.14) $f(p \mid x) = (n + 1)C_x^n p^x (1 - p)^{n-x}.$

Now suppose $y > x$. Then $f(p \mid x)$ and $f(p \mid y)$ cross only once, except possibly at $p = 0$ or 1. To see this, put $f(p \mid x) = f(p \mid y)$. If $p \neq 0$ or 1, this equality can be written as

(9.5.15)
$$\frac{C_x^n}{C_y^n}\left(\frac{1}{p} - 1\right)^{y-x} = 1.$$

The left-hand side of (9.5.15) is 0 if $p = 1$ and is monotonically increasing as p decreases to 0. Let p^* be the solution to (9.5.15) such that $p^* \neq 0$ or

1, and define $h(p) = f(p \mid y) - f(p \mid x)$ and $k(p) = f(p \mid x) - f(p \mid y)$. Then we have

$$(9.5.16) \qquad \frac{\int_{p*}^{1} U(p)h(p)dp}{\int_{p*}^{1} h(p)dp} > \frac{\int_{0}^{p*} U(p)k(p)dp}{\int_{0}^{p*} k(p)dp},$$

because the left-hand side is greater than $U(p^*)$, whereas the right-hand side is smaller than $U(p^*)$. But (9.5.16) is equivalent to

$$(9.5.17) \qquad \int_{0}^{1} U(p)f(p \mid y)dp > \int_{0}^{1} U(p)f(p \mid x)dp,$$

which establishes the result that the left-hand side of (9.5.13) is an increasing function in x. Therefore (9.5.13) is equivalent to

$$(9.5.18) \qquad x > c,$$

where c is determined by (9.5.13).

The classical statistician facing this decision problem will, first, paraphrase the problem into that of testing hypothesis $H_0: p \geq p_0$ versus $H_1: p < p_0$ for a certain constant p_0 and then use the likelihood ratio test. Her decision rule is of the same form as (9.5.18), except that she will determine c so as to conform to a preassigned size α. If the classical statistician were to approximate the Bayesian decision, she would have to engage in a rather intricate thought process in order to let her p_0 and α reflect the utility consideration.

9.6 EXAMPLES OF HYPOTHESIS TESTS

In the preceding sections we have studied the theory of hypothesis testing. In this section we shall apply it to various practical problems.

EXAMPLE 9.6.1 (mean of binomial)   It is expected that a particular coin is biased *in such a way that a head is more probable than a tail.* We toss this coin ten times and a head comes up eight times. Should we conclude that the coin is biased at the 5% significance level (more precisely, size)? What if the significance level is 10%?

From the wording of the question we know we must put

$$(9.6.1) \qquad H_0: p = \tfrac{1}{2} \quad \text{and} \quad H_1: p > \tfrac{1}{2}.$$

From Example 9.4.2, we know that we should use $X \sim B(10, p)$, the number of heads in ten tosses, as the test statistic, and the critical region should be of the form

(9.6.2) $R = \{c, c + 1, \ldots, 10\}$,

where c (the critical value) should be chosen to satisfy

(9.6.3) $P(X \in R \mid H_0) = \alpha$,

where α is the prescribed size. In this kind of question there is no need to determine c by solving (9.6.3) for a given value of α. In fact, in this particular question there is no value of c which exactly satisfies (9.6.3) for either $\alpha = 0.05$ or $\alpha = 0.1$. Instead we should calculate the probability that we will obtain the values of X greater than or equal to the observed value under the null hypothesis, called the *p-value*: that is,

(9.6.4) $P(X = 8 \text{ or } 9 \text{ or } 10 \mid p = \frac{1}{2}) = 45 \left(\frac{1}{2}\right)^{10} + 10 \left(\frac{1}{2}\right)^{10} + \left(\frac{1}{2}\right)^{10}$

$$\cong 0.055.$$

From (9.6.4) we conclude that H_0 should be accepted if $\alpha = 0.05$ and rejected if $\alpha = 0.1$.

We must determine whether to use a one-tail test or a two-tail test from the wording of the problem. This decision can sometimes be difficult. For example, what if the italicized phrase were removed from Example 9.6.1? Then the matter becomes somewhat ambiguous. If, instead of the italicized phrase, we were to add, "but the direction of bias is a priori unknown," a two-tail test would be indicated. Then we should calculate the *p*-value

(9.6.5) $P(X = 8 \text{ or } 9 \text{ or } 10 \text{ or } 0 \text{ or } 1 \text{ or } 2) = 0.11$,

which would imply a different conclusion from the previous one.

Another caveat: Sometimes a problem may not specify the size. In such a case we must provide our own. It is perfectly appropriate, however, to say "H_0 should be accepted if $\alpha < 0.055$ and rejected if $\alpha > 0.055$." This is another reason why it is wise to calculate the *p*-value, rather than determining the critical region for a given size.

EXAMPLE 9.6.2 (mean of normal, variance known)   Suppose the height of the Stanford male student is distributed as $N(\mu, \sigma^2)$, where σ^2 is known to be 0.16. We are to test H_0: $\mu = 5.8$ against H_1: $\mu = 6$. If the sample average of 10 students yields 6, should we accept H_0 at the 5% significance level? What if the significance level is 10%?

From Example 9.3.2, we know that the best test of a given size α should use $\bar{X}$ as the test statistic and its critical region should be given by

(9.6.6) $\bar{X} > c$, where c is determined by $P(\bar{X} > c \mid H_0) = \alpha$.

Since $\bar{X} \sim N(5.8, 0.016)$ under H_0, we have

(9.6.7) $P(\bar{X} > 6) = P(Z > 1.58) = 0.0571$,

where Z is $N(0, 1)$. From (9.6.7) we conclude that H_0 should be accepted if α is 5% and rejected if it is 10%. Note that, as before, determining the critical region by (9.6.6) and then checking if the observed value $\bar{x}$ falls into the region is equivalent to calculating the p-value $P(\bar{X} > \bar{x} \mid H_0)$ and then checking if it is smaller than α.

EXAMPLE 9.6.3 (mean of normal, variance unknown). Assume the same model as in Example 9.6.2, except that now σ^2 is unknown and we have the unbiased estimator of variance $\tilde{\sigma}^2 = 0.16$. We have under H_0

(9.6.8) $\dfrac{\sqrt{10}(\bar{X} - 5.8)}{\tilde{\sigma}} = t_9$, Student's t with 9 degrees of freedom.

Therefore, by Example 9.5.2, the critical region should be chosen as

(9.6.9) $\dfrac{\sqrt{10}(\bar{X} - 5.8)}{\tilde{\sigma}} > c$, where c is determined by $P(t_9 > c) = \alpha$.

We have

(9.6.10) $P\left[\dfrac{\sqrt{10}(\bar{X} - 5.8)}{\tilde{\sigma}} > \dfrac{\sqrt{10}(6 - 5.8)}{0.4}\right] = P(t_9 > 1.58) \cong 0.074$.

Therefore we conclude that H_0 should be accepted at the 5% significance level but rejected at 10%.

EXAMPLE 9.6.4 (difference of means of normal, variance known)
Suppose that in 1970 the average height of 25 Stanford male students was 6 feet with a standard deviation of 0.4 foot, while in 1990 the average

height of 30 students was 6.2 with a standard deviation of 0.3 foot. Should we conclude that the mean height of Stanford male students increased in this period? Assume that the sample standard deviation is equal to the population standard deviation.

Let Y_i and X_i be the height of the ith student in the 1970 sample and the 1990 sample, respectively. Define $\bar{Y} = (\Sigma_{i=1}^{25} Y_i)/25$ and $\bar{X} = (\Sigma_{i=1}^{30} X_i)/30$. Assuming the normality and independence of X_i and Y_i, we have

$$(9.6.11) \qquad \bar{X} - \bar{Y} \sim N\left[\mu_X - \mu_Y, \frac{(0.3)^2}{30} + \frac{(0.4)^2}{25}\right],$$

where μ_X, μ_Y are the unknown means of X_i and Y_i, respectively. Our hypotheses can be expressed as

$$(9.6.12) \qquad H_0: \mu_X - \mu_Y = 0 \quad \text{and} \quad H_1: \mu_X - \mu_Y > 0.$$

We have chosen H_1 as in (9.6.12) because it is believed that the height of young American males has been increasing during these years. Once we formulate the problem mathematically as (9.6.11) and (9.6.12), we realize that this example is actually of the same type as Example 9.6.2. Since we have under H_0

$$(9.6.13) \qquad P(\bar{X} - \bar{Y} > 0.2) = P(Z > 2.063) = 0.02,$$

we conclude that H_0 should be accepted if $\alpha < 0.02$ and rejected if $\alpha > 0.02$.

EXAMPLE 9.6.5 (differences of means of binomial)   In a poll 51 of 300 men favored a certain proposition, and 46 of 200 women favored it. Is there a real difference of opinion between men and women on this proposition?

Define $Y_i = 1$ if the ith man favors the proposition and $= 0$ otherwise. Similarly define $X_i = 1$ if the ith woman favors the proposition and $= 0$ otherwise. Define $p_Y = P(Y_i = 1)$ and $p_X = P(X_i = 1)$. If we define $\bar{Y} = (\Sigma_{i=1}^{300} Y_i)/300$ and $\bar{X} = (\Sigma_{i=1}^{200} X_i)/200$, we have asymptotically

$$(9.6.14) \qquad \bar{X} - \bar{Y} \overset{A}{\sim} N\left[p_X - p_Y, \frac{p_X(1 - p_X)}{200} + \frac{p_Y(1 - p_Y)}{300}\right],$$

where we have assumed the independence of X and Y. The competing hypotheses are

(9.6.15) H_0: $p_X - p_Y = 0$ and H_1: $p_X - p_Y \neq 0$.

Therefore this example essentially belongs to the same category as Example 9.6.4. The only difference is that in the present example the variance of the test statistic $\bar{X} - \bar{Y}$ under H_0 should be estimated in a special way. One way is to estimate p_X by $46/200$ and p_Y by $51/300$. But since $p_X = p_Y$ under H_0, we can get a better estimate of the common value by pooling the two samples to obtain $(46 + 51)/(200 + 300)$. Using the latter method, we have under H_0

(9.6.16) $\bar{X} - \bar{Y} \overset{A}{\sim} N(0, 0.0013)$.

Since we have under H_0

(9.6.17) $P\left(|\bar{X} - \bar{Y}| > \dfrac{46}{200} - \dfrac{51}{300}\right) \cong P(|Z| > 1.66) = 0.097$,

we conclude that H_0 should be accepted if $\alpha < 0.097$ and rejected if $\alpha > 0.097$.

EXAMPLE 9.6.6 (difference of means of normal, variance unknown)
This example is the same as Example 9.6.4 except that now we shall not assume that the sample standard deviation is equal to the population standard deviation. However, we shall assume $\sigma_X^2 = \sigma_Y^2$.

By Theorem 6 of the Appendix we have under H_0

(9.6.18) $\dfrac{\bar{X} - \bar{Y}}{\left(n_X S_X^2 + n_Y S_Y^2\right)^{1/2}} \left[\dfrac{n_X n_Y (n_X + n_Y - 2)}{n_X + n_Y}\right]^{1/2} \sim t_{n_X + n_Y - 2}.$

Inserting $n_X = 30$, $n_Y = 25$, $\bar{X} = 6.2$, $\bar{Y} = 6$, $S_X = 0.3$, and $S_Y = 0.4$ into (9.6.18) above, we calculate the observed value of the Student's t variable to be 2.077. We have

(9.6.19) $P(t_{53} > 2.077) = 0.021$.

Therefore we conclude that H_0 should be accepted if $\alpha < 0.021$ and rejected if $\alpha > 0.021$. In this particular example the use of the Student's t statistic has not changed the result of Example 9.6.4 very much.

EXAMPLE 9.6.7 (difference of variances) In using the Student's t test in Example 9.6.6, we need to assume $\sigma_X^2 = \sigma_X^2$. Therefore, it is wise to test this hypothesis. By Theorem 3 of the Appendix, we have

$$(9.6.20) \qquad \frac{n_X S_X^2}{\sigma_X^2} \sim \chi_{n_X-1}^2$$

and

$$(9.6.21) \qquad \frac{n_Y S_Y^2}{\sigma_Y^2} \sim \chi_{n_Y-1}^2.$$

Applying Definition 3 of the Appendix and (9.6.21), we have, under the null hypothesis $\sigma_X^2 = \sigma_Y^2$,

$$(9.6.22) \qquad \frac{(n_Y - 1)n_X S_X^2}{(n_X - 1)n_Y S_Y^2} \sim F(n_X - 1, n_Y - 1).$$

Inserting the same numerical values as in Example 9.6.6 into the left-hand side of (9.6.22) yields the value 0.559. But we have

$$(9.6.23) \qquad P[F(29, 24) < 0.559] = 0.068.$$

Since a two-tail test is appropriate here (that is, the alternative hypothesis is $\sigma_X^2 \neq \sigma_Y^2$), we conclude that H_0 should be accepted if $\alpha < 0.136$ and rejected if $\alpha > 0.136$.

9.7 TESTING ABOUT A VECTOR PARAMETER

Those who are not familiar with matrix analysis should study Chapter 11 before reading this section. The results of this chapter will not be needed to understand Chapter 10. Insofar as possible, we shall illustrate our results in the two-dimensional case.

We consider the problem of testing H_0: $\boldsymbol{\theta} = \boldsymbol{\theta}_0$ against H_1: $\boldsymbol{\theta} \neq \boldsymbol{\theta}_0$, where $\boldsymbol{\theta}$ is a K-dimensional vector of parameters. We are to use the test statistic $\hat{\boldsymbol{\theta}} \sim N(\boldsymbol{\theta}, \boldsymbol{\Sigma})$, where $\boldsymbol{\Sigma}$ is a $K \times K$ *variance-covariance matrix:* that is, $\boldsymbol{\Sigma} = E(\hat{\boldsymbol{\theta}} - \boldsymbol{\theta})(\hat{\boldsymbol{\theta}} - \boldsymbol{\theta})'$. (Throughout this section a matrix is denoted by a boldface capital letter and a vector by a boldface lower-case letter.) In

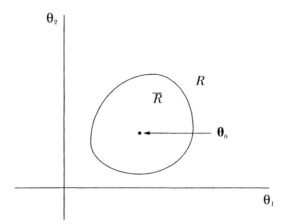

FIGURE 9.9   Critical region for testing about two parameters

Section 9.7.1 we consider the case where Σ is completely known, and in Section 9.7.2 the case where Σ is known only up to a scalar multiple.

9.7.1 Variance-Covariance Matrix Assumed Known

Consider the case of $K = 2$. We can write $\boldsymbol{\theta} = (\theta_1, \theta_2)'$ and $\boldsymbol{\theta}_0 = (\theta_{10}, \theta_{20})'$. It is intuitively reasonable that an optimal critical region should be outside some enclosure containing $\boldsymbol{\theta}_0$, as depicted in Figure 9.9. What should be the specific shape of the enclosure?

An obvious first choice would be a circle with $\boldsymbol{\theta}_0$ at its center. That would amount to the test:

$$(9.7.1) \qquad \text{Reject } H_0 \text{ if } (\hat{\theta}_1 - \theta_{10})^2 + (\hat{\theta}_2 - \theta_{20})^2 > c$$

for some c, where c is chosen so as to make the probability of Type I error equal to a given value α. An undesirable feature of this choice can be demonstrated as follows: Suppose $V\hat{\theta}_1$ is much larger than $V\hat{\theta}_2$. Then a large value of $|\hat{\theta}_2 - \theta_{20}|$ should be more cause for rejecting H_0 than an equally large value of $|\hat{\theta}_1 - \theta_{10}|$, for the latter could be a result of the large variability of $\hat{\theta}_1$ rather than the falseness of the null hypothesis.

This weakness is alleviated by the following strategy:

$$(9.7.2) \qquad \text{Reject } H_0 \text{ if } \frac{(\hat{\theta}_1 - \theta_{10})^2}{\sigma_1^2} + \frac{(\hat{\theta}_1 - \theta_{20})^2}{\sigma_2^2} > c,$$

where $\sigma_1^2 \equiv V\hat{\theta}_1$ and $\sigma_2^2 \equiv V\hat{\theta}_2$. Geometrically, the inequality in (9.7.2) represents the region outside an ellipse with $\boldsymbol{\theta}_0$ at its center, elongated horizontally. We should not be completely satisfied by this solution either, because the fact that this critical region does not depend on the covariance, $\sigma_{12} \equiv \text{Cov}(\hat{\theta}_1, \hat{\theta}_2)$, suggests its deficiency.

We shall now proceed on the intuitively reasonable premise that if $\sigma_1^2 = \sigma_2^2$ and $\sigma_{12} = 0$, the optimal test should be defined by (9.7.1). Suppose that $\boldsymbol{\Sigma}$ is a positive definite matrix, not necessarily diagonal nor identity. Then by Theorem 11.5.1 we can find a matrix $\mathbf{A}$ such that $\mathbf{A\Sigma A}' = \mathbf{I}$. By this transformation the original testing problem can be paraphrased as testing H_0: $\mathbf{A\theta} = \mathbf{A\theta}_0$ against $\mathbf{A\theta} \neq \mathbf{A\theta}_0$ using $\mathbf{A\hat{\theta}} \sim N(\mathbf{A\theta}_0, \mathbf{I})$ as the test statistic. Thus, by our premise, we should

(9.7.3)   Reject H_0 if $(\mathbf{A\hat{\theta}} - \mathbf{A\theta}_0)'(\mathbf{A\hat{\theta}} - \mathbf{A\theta}_0) > c$.

But $\mathbf{A\Sigma A}' = \mathbf{I}$ implies $\boldsymbol{\Sigma} = \mathbf{A}^{-1}(\mathbf{A}')^{-1}$, which implies $\boldsymbol{\Sigma}^{-1} = \mathbf{A}'\mathbf{A}$. Therefore, using

$$(\mathbf{A\hat{\theta}} - \mathbf{A\theta}_0)'(\mathbf{A\hat{\theta}} - \mathbf{A\theta}_0) = (\hat{\boldsymbol{\theta}} - \boldsymbol{\theta}_0)'\mathbf{A}'\mathbf{A}(\hat{\boldsymbol{\theta}} - \boldsymbol{\theta}_0)$$
$$= (\hat{\boldsymbol{\theta}} - \boldsymbol{\theta}_0)'\boldsymbol{\Sigma}^{-1}(\hat{\boldsymbol{\theta}} - \boldsymbol{\theta}_0),$$

(9.7.3) can be written as

(9.7.4)   Reject H_0 if $(\hat{\boldsymbol{\theta}} - \boldsymbol{\theta}_0)'\boldsymbol{\Sigma}^{-1}(\hat{\boldsymbol{\theta}} - \boldsymbol{\theta}_0) > c$.

In the two-dimensional case, where

$$\boldsymbol{\Sigma} = \begin{bmatrix} \sigma_1^2 & \sigma_{12} \\ \sigma_{12} & \sigma_2^2 \end{bmatrix},$$

(9.7.4) becomes

(9.7.5)   Reject H_0 if

$$\frac{\sigma_2^2(\hat{\theta}_1 - \theta_{10})^2 + \sigma_1^2(\hat{\theta}_2 - \theta_{20})^2 - 2\sigma_{12}(\hat{\theta}_1 - \theta_{10})(\hat{\theta}_2 - \theta_{20})}{\sigma_1^2\sigma_2^2 - \sigma_{12}^2} > c.$$

Note that (9.7.5) is reduced to (9.7.2) if $\sigma_{12} = 0$ and, further, to (9.7.1) if $\sigma_1^2 = \sigma_2^2$.

An additional justification of the test (9.7.4) is provided by the fact that it is a likelihood ratio test. To see this, note that by (5.4.1) and (9.4.5),

$$\Lambda = \frac{\exp\left[-\frac{1}{2}(\hat{\boldsymbol{\theta}} - \boldsymbol{\theta}_0)'\boldsymbol{\Sigma}^{-1}(\hat{\boldsymbol{\theta}} - \boldsymbol{\theta}_0)\right]}{\max_{\boldsymbol{\theta}} \exp\left[-\frac{1}{2}(\hat{\boldsymbol{\theta}} - \boldsymbol{\theta})'\boldsymbol{\Sigma}^{-1}(\hat{\boldsymbol{\theta}} - \boldsymbol{\theta})\right]}.$$

But the maximand in the denominator clearly attains its unique maximum at $\boldsymbol{\theta} = \hat{\boldsymbol{\theta}}$.

Another attractive feature of the test (9.7.4) is the fact that

(9.7.6) $(\hat{\boldsymbol{\theta}} - \boldsymbol{\theta}_0)'\boldsymbol{\Sigma}^{-1}(\hat{\boldsymbol{\theta}} - \boldsymbol{\theta}_0) \sim \chi_K^2$

under the null hypothesis, so that c can be computed to conform to a specified value of α. This result is a consequence of the following important theorem.

THEOREM 9.7.1 Suppose $\mathbf{x}$ is an n-vector distributed as $N(\boldsymbol{\mu}, \mathbf{A})$, where $\mathbf{A}$ is a positive definite matrix. Then $(\mathbf{x} - \boldsymbol{\mu})'\mathbf{A}^{-1}(\mathbf{x} - \boldsymbol{\mu}) \sim \chi_n^2$.

Proof. Let $\mathbf{H}$ be the orthogonal matrix which diagonalizes $\mathbf{A}$, that is,

$\mathbf{H}'\mathbf{A}\mathbf{H} = \Lambda,$

where Λ is the diagonal matrix of the characteristic roots of $\mathbf{A}$ (see Theorem 11.5.1). Following (11.5.4), define

$\mathbf{A}^{-1/2} = \mathbf{H}\Lambda^{-1/2}\mathbf{H}'$

where $\Lambda^{-1/2}$ is the diagonal matrix obtained by taking the $(-\frac{1}{2})$th power of each diagonal element of Λ. Then, we can easily show that

$\mathbf{A}^{-1/2}\mathbf{A}\,\mathbf{A}^{-1/2} = \mathbf{I}$ and $\mathbf{A}^{-1/2}\mathbf{A}^{-1/2} = \mathbf{A}^{-1}.$

Therefore, we obtain $\mathbf{A}^{-1/2}(\mathbf{x} - \boldsymbol{\mu}) \sim N(\mathbf{0}, \mathbf{I})$. By Definition 1 of the Appendix, $(\mathbf{x} - \boldsymbol{\mu})'\mathbf{A}^{-1/2}\mathbf{A}^{-1/2}(\mathbf{x} - \boldsymbol{\mu}) \sim \chi_n^2$. ❑

As an illustration of the above, consider a three-sided die (assume that such a die exists) which yields numbers 1, 2, and 3 with respective probabilities p_1, p_2, and p_3. We are to test the hypothesis that the die is not loaded versus the hypothesis that it is loaded on the basis of n independent rolls. That is,

(9.7.7)   Test $H_0: p_1 = p_2 = p_3 = \frac{1}{3}$ versus $H_1:$ not H_0.

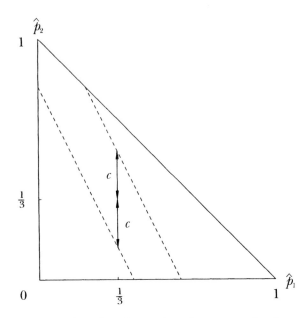

FIGURE 9.10   Critical region for testing the mean of a three-sided die

If we should be constrained to use any of the univariate testing methods expounded in the preceding sections, we would somehow have to reduce the problem to one with a single parameter, but that would not be entirely satisfactory, as we shall show below. Suppose, for example, we decide to test the hypothesis that the expected value of the outcome of the roll is consistent with that of an unloaded die; namely,

(9.7.8)   Test H_0: $p_1 + 2p_2 + 3p_3 = 2$ versus H_1: $p_1 + 2p_2 + 3p_3 \neq 2$.

Since $p_3 = 1 - p_1 - p_2$, the null hypothesis can be stated as $1 - 2p_1 - p_2 = 0$. If we define $\hat{p}_1$ and $\hat{p}_2$ as the relative frequencies of 1 and 2 in n rolls, a reasonable test would be to

(9.7.9)   Reject H_0 if $|1 - 2\hat{p}_1 - \hat{p}_2| > c$

for some c, which can be approximately determined from the standard normal table because of the asymptotic normality of $\hat{p}_1$ and $\hat{p}_2$. In Figure 9.10 the critical region of the test (9.7.9) is outside the parallel dashed lines and inside the triangle that defines the total feasible region. A weakness of the test (9.7.9) as a solution of the original testing problem

(9.7.7) is obvious: an outcome such as $\hat{p}_1 = 0$ and $\hat{p}_2 = 1$, which is extremely unlikely under the original null hypothesis, will lead to an acceptance by this test.

Now we apply the test (9.7.5) to the original problem (9.7.7). We have, under the null hypothesis,

$$(9.7.10) \qquad \begin{bmatrix} \hat{p}_1 \\ \hat{p}_2 \end{bmatrix} \overset{A}{\sim} N\left\{ \begin{bmatrix} \dfrac{1}{3} \\ \dfrac{1}{3} \end{bmatrix}, \dfrac{1}{9n} \begin{bmatrix} 2 & -1 \\ -1 & 2 \end{bmatrix} \right\}.$$

Therefore (9.7.5) becomes

(9.7.11)   Reject H_0

$$\text{if} \quad 6n\left[\left(\hat{p}_1 - \dfrac{1}{3} \right)^2 + \left(\hat{p}_2 - \dfrac{1}{3} \right)^2 + \left(\hat{p}_1 - \dfrac{1}{3} \right)\left(\hat{p}_2 - \dfrac{1}{3} \right) \right] > c.$$

The left-hand side of the above inequality is asymptotically distributed as χ_2^2 under the null hypothesis.

Since (9.7.10) holds only asymptotically, the test (9.7.11) is not identical with the likelihood ratio test. In such a case, (9.7.11) is called the *generalized Wald test*.

Next we derive the likelihood ratio test and compare it with the generalized Wald test. By Definition 9.4.4 the likelihood ratio test of the problem (9.7.7) is

$$(9.7.12) \qquad \Lambda = \dfrac{1}{3^n \hat{p}_1^{\,n_1} \hat{p}_2^{\,n_2} \hat{p}_3^{\,n_3}} < d,$$

where n_j is the number of times j appears in n rolls. In order to make use of Theorem 9.4.1 we transform the above inequality to

$$(9.7.13) \qquad -2 \log \Lambda = 2\,(n \log 3 + n_1 \log \hat{p}_1 + n_2 \log \hat{p}_2 + n_3 \log \hat{p}_3)$$
$$> -2 \log d.$$

Noting that $\hat{p}_j = n_j/n$ and defining $c = -2 \log d$, we can write (9.7.13) equivalently as

$$(9.7.14) \qquad 2n(\log 3 + \hat{p}_1 \log \hat{p}_1 + \hat{p}_2 \log \hat{p}_2 + \hat{p}_3 \log \hat{p}_3) > c.$$

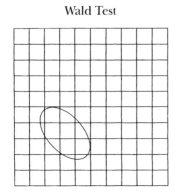
Wald Test

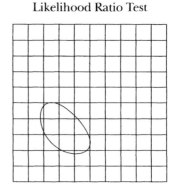
Likelihood Ratio Test

FIGURE 9.11   The 5% acceptance regions of the generalized Wald test and the likelihood ratio test

To show the approximate equality of the left-hand side of (9.7.11) and (9.7.14), use the Taylor expansion

$$x \log x \cong \frac{1}{3} \log \frac{1}{3} + \left(\log \frac{1}{3} + 1 \right) \left(x - \frac{1}{3} \right) + \frac{3}{2} \left(x - \frac{1}{3} \right)^2$$

and apply it to the three similar terms within the parentheses of the left-hand side of (9.7.14). Figure 9.11 describes the acceptance region of the two tests for the case of $n = 50$ and $c = 6$. Note that $P(\chi_2^2 > 6) \cong 0.05$.

9.7.2   Variance-Covariance Matrix Known up to a Scalar Multiple

There is no optimal solution to our problem if Σ is completely unknown. There is, however, sometimes a good solution if $\Sigma = \sigma^2 Q$, where Q is a known positive definite matrix and σ^2 is an unknown scalar parameter. In this case it seems intuitively reasonable to reject H_0 if

(9.7.15) $$\frac{(\hat{\theta} - \theta_0)' Q^{-1} (\hat{\theta} - \theta_0)}{\hat{\sigma}^2} > c,$$

where $\hat{\sigma}^2$ is some reasonable estimator of σ^2. For what kind of estimator can we compute the distribution of the statistic above, so that we can determine c so as to conform to a given size α?

One solution is presented below. We first note (9.7.6). If we are given a statistic W such that

(9.7.16) $\qquad \dfrac{W}{\sigma^2} \sim \chi_M^2,$

which is independent of χ_K^2 in (9.7.6), we obtain by Definition 3 of the Appendix

(9.7.17) $\qquad \dfrac{(\hat{\boldsymbol{\theta}} - \boldsymbol{\theta}_0)' \mathbf{Q}^{-1} (\hat{\boldsymbol{\theta}} - \boldsymbol{\theta}_0)/K}{W/M} \sim F(K, M).$

Therefore, defining $\hat{\sigma}^2 = W/M$ will enable us to determine c appropriately.

Assuming the availability of such W may seem arbitrary, so we shall give a couple of examples.

EXAMPLE 9.7.1 Suppose $X \sim N(\mu_X, \sigma^2)$ and $Y \sim N(\mu_Y, \sigma^2)$ are independent of each other. We are to test

$$H_0: \begin{bmatrix} \mu_X \\ \mu_Y \end{bmatrix} = \begin{bmatrix} \mu_{X0} \\ \mu_{Y0} \end{bmatrix} \text{ versus } H_1: \begin{bmatrix} \mu_X \\ \mu_Y \end{bmatrix} \neq \begin{bmatrix} \mu_{X0} \\ \mu_{Y0} \end{bmatrix}$$

on the basis of n_X and n_Y independent observations on X and Y, respectively. We assume that the common variance σ^2 is unknown. Suppose that $\bar{X} = n_X^{-1} \Sigma_{i=1}^{n_X} X_i$ and $\bar{Y} = n_Y^{-1} \Sigma_{i=1}^{n_Y} Y_i$. We have, from Definition 1 and Theorem 1 of the Appendix,

(9.7.18) $\qquad \dfrac{n_X(\bar{X} - \mu_{X0})^2 + n_Y(\bar{Y} - \mu_{Y0})^2}{\sigma^2} \sim \chi_2^2,$

and because of Theorems 1 and 3 of the Appendix,

(9.7.19) $\qquad \dfrac{\displaystyle\sum_{i=1}^{n_X} (X_i - \bar{X})^2 + \sum_{i=1}^{n_Y} (Y_i - \bar{Y})^2}{\sigma^2} \sim \chi_{n_X + n_Y - 2}^2.$

Therefore, by Definition 3 of the Appendix,

(9.7.20) $\qquad \dfrac{[n_X(\bar{X} - \mu_{X0})^2 + n_Y(\bar{Y} - \mu_{Y0})^2]/2}{\left[\displaystyle\sum_{i=1}^{n_X} (X_i - \bar{X})^2 + \sum_{i=1}^{n_Y} (Y_i - \bar{Y})^2\right]/(n_X + n_Y - 2)} \sim F(2, n_X + n_Y - 2).$

We should reject H_0 if the above statistic is larger than a certain value, which we can determine from (9.7.20) to conform to a preassigned size of the test.

EXAMPLE 9.7.2 Suppose that $X \sim N(\mu_X, \sigma^2)$, $Y \sim N(\mu_Y, \sigma^2)$, and $Z \sim N(\mu_Z, \sigma^2)$ are mutually independent. We are to test H_0: $\mu_X = \mu_Y = \mu_Z$ versus H_1: not H_0 on the basis of n_X, n_Y, and n_Z independent observations on X, Y, and Z, respectively. Let $\bar{X}$, $\bar{Y}$, and $\bar{Z}$ be the sample averages based on n_X, n_Y, and n_Z observations, respectively. Similarly, let S_X^2, S_Y^2, and S_Z^2 be the sample variances based on n_X, n_Y, and n_Z observations, respectively. Define $\lambda_1 = \mu_X - \mu_Y$, $\lambda_2 = \mu_X - \mu_Z$, $\hat{\lambda}_1 = \bar{X} - \bar{Y}$, and $\hat{\lambda}_2 = \bar{X} - \bar{Z}$. Then we have

$$(9.7.21) \qquad \begin{bmatrix} \hat{\lambda}_1 \\ \hat{\lambda}_2 \end{bmatrix} \sim N \left\{ \begin{bmatrix} \lambda_1 \\ \lambda_2 \end{bmatrix}, \sigma^2 \mathbf{Q} \right\},$$

where

$$\mathbf{Q} = \begin{bmatrix} \dfrac{1}{n_X} + \dfrac{1}{n_Y} & \dfrac{1}{n_X} \\ \dfrac{1}{n_X} & \dfrac{1}{n_X} + \dfrac{1}{n_Z} \end{bmatrix}$$

because of Theorem 9.7.1, we have under H_0,

$$(9.7.22) \qquad \frac{(\hat{\lambda}_1, \hat{\lambda}_2)\mathbf{Q}^{-1} \begin{bmatrix} \hat{\lambda}_1 \\ \hat{\lambda}_2 \end{bmatrix}}{\sigma^2} \sim \chi_2^2 .$$

But, by Theorems 1 and 3 of the Appendix,

$$(9.7.23) \qquad \frac{n_X S_X^2 + n_Y S_Y^2 + n_Z S_Z^2}{\sigma^2} \sim \chi_{n_X + n_Y + n_Z - 3}^2 .$$

Since the chi-square variables in (9.7.22) and (9.7.23) are independent, we have

$$(9.7.24) \qquad \frac{(\hat{\lambda}_1, \hat{\lambda}_2)\mathbf{Q}^{-1} \begin{bmatrix} \hat{\lambda}_1 \\ \hat{\lambda}_2 \end{bmatrix} / 2}{(n_X S_X^2 + n_Y S_Y^2 + n_Z S_Z^2)/(n_X + n_Y + n_Z - 3)} \sim F(2, n_X + n_Y + n_Z - 3).$$

EXERCISES

1. (Section 9.2)

   Given the density $f(x) = 1/\theta$, $0 < x < \theta$, and 0 elsewhere, we are to test the hypothesis H_0: $\theta = 2$ against H_1: $\theta = 3$ by means of a single observed value of X. Find a critical region of $\alpha = 0.5$ which minimizes β and compute the value of β. Is the region unique? If not, define the class of such regions.

2. (Section 9.2)

   Suppose that X has the following probability distribution:

   $X = 1$ with probability θ

        2   2θ

        3                                $1 - 3\theta$

   where $0 \le \theta \le 1/3$. We are to test H_0: $\theta = 0.2$ against H_1: $\theta = 0.25$ on the basis of one observation on X.

   (a) List all the nonrandomized admissible tests.

   (b) Find the most powerful nonrandomized test of size 0.4.

   (c) Find the most powerful randomized test of size 0.3.

3. (Section 9.3)

   An estimator T of a parameter μ is distributed as $N(\mu, 4)$, and we want to test H_0: $\mu = 25$ against H_1: $\mu = 30$. Assuming that the prior probabilities of H_0 and H_1 are equal and the costs of the Type I and II errors are equal, find the Bayesian optimal critical region.

4. (Section 9.3)

   Let $X \sim N(\mu, 16)$. We want to test H_0: $\mu = 2$ against H_1: $\mu = 3$ on the basis of four independent observations on X. Suppose the loss matrix is given by

Decision	True state H_0	H_1
H_0	0	1
H_1	e	0

   where e is Euler's e ($= 2.71 \ldots$). Assuming the prior probabilities $P(H_0) = P(H_1) = 0.5$, derive the Bayesian optimal critical region.

Calculate the probabilities of Type I and Type II errors for this critical region.

5. (Section 9.3)
Let $f(x) = \theta \exp(-\theta x)$, $x \geq 0$, $\theta > 0$. We want to test $H_0: \theta = 1$ against $H_1: \theta = 2$ on the basis of one observation on X. Derive:
(a) the Neyman-Pearson optimal critical region, assuming $\alpha = 0.05$;
(b) the Bayesian optimal critical region, assuming that $P(H_0) = P(H_1)$ and that the loss of Type I error is 2 and the loss of Type II error is 5.

6. (Section 9.3)
Supposing $f(x) = (1 + \theta)x^\theta$, $0 < x < 1$, $\theta > 0$, we are to test $H_0: \theta = \theta_0$ against $H_1: \theta = \theta_1 < \theta_0$. Find the Neyman-Pearson test based on a sample of size n. Indicate how to determine the critical region if the size of the test is α.

7. (Section 9.3)
Let X be the outcome of tossing a three-sided die with the numbers 1, 2, and 3 occurring with probabilities p_1, p_2, and p_3. Suppose that 100 independent tosses yielded N_1 ones, N_2 twos, and N_3 threes. Obtain a Neyman-Pearson test of $H_0: p_1 = p_2 = \frac{2}{5}$ against $H_1: p_1 = \frac{1}{2}$ and $p_2 = \frac{1}{5}$. Choose $\alpha = 0.05$. You may use the normal approximation.

8. (Section 9.3)
We wish to test the null hypothesis that a die is fair against the alternative hypothesis that each of numbers 1, 2, and 3 occurs with probability $\frac{1}{10}$, 4 and 5 each occurs with probability $\frac{1}{5}$, and 6 occurs with probability $\frac{3}{10}$.
(a) If number j appears N_j times, $j = 1, 2, \ldots, 6$, in N throws of the die, define the Neyman-Pearson test.
(b) If $N = 2$, obtain the most powerful test of size $\frac{1}{4}$ and compute its β value.
(c) If $N_1 = 16$, $N_2 = 13$, $N_3 = 14$, $N_4 = 22$, $N_5 = 17$, and $N_6 = 18$, should you reject the null hypothesis at the 5% significance level? What about at 10%? You may use the normal approximation.

9. (Section 9.4)
Given the density $f(x) = 1/\theta$, $0 < x < \theta$, and 0 elsewhere, we are to

test the hypothesis H_0: $\theta = 2$ against H_1: $\theta > 2$ by means of a single observed value of X. Consider the test which rejects H_0 if $X > c$. Determine c so that $\alpha = \frac{1}{4}$ and draw the graph of its power function.

10. (Section 9.4)

Let X be the number of trials needed before a success (with probability p) occurs. That is, $P(X = k) = p(1 - p)^{k-1}$, $k = 1, 2, \ldots$. Find the power function for testing H_0: $p = \frac{1}{4}$ if the critical region consists of the numbers $k = 1, 2, 3$. Compare it with the power function of the critical region consisting of the numbers $\{1, 2, 8, 9, \ldots\}$.

11. (Section 9.4)

Random variables X and Y have a joint density

$$f(x, y) = \theta^{-2}, \quad 0 \le x \le \theta, \ 0 \le y \le \theta, \ 0.1 \le \theta \le 1.$$

Find the uniformly most powerful test of the hypothesis $\theta = 1$ of size $\alpha = 0.01$ based on a single observation of X and Y. Derive its power function.

12. (Section 9.4)

Suppose that a bivariate random variable (X, Y) is uniformly distributed over the square defined by $\theta \le x, y \le 1$, where we assume $0 \le \theta < 1$. We are to test H_0: $\theta = 0.5$ against H_1: $\theta \ne 0.5$ on the basis of a single observation on (X, Y) with $\alpha = 0.25$.

(a) Derive the likelihood ratio test. If you cannot, define the best test you can think of and justify it from either intuitive or logical consideration.

(b) Obtain the power function of the likelihood ratio test (or your alternative test) and sketch its graph.

(c) Prove that the likelihood ratio test of the problem is the uniformly most powerful test of size 0.25.

13. (Section 9.4)

Suppose (X, Y) have density $f(x, y) = 1/(\mu\lambda)$, $0 \le x \le \mu$, $0 \le y \le \lambda$, $0 < \mu < \infty$, and $0 < \lambda < \infty$. We are to test H_0: $\mu = \lambda = 1$ versus H_1: not H_0 on the basis of one observation on (X, Y).

(a) Find the likelihood ratio test of size $0 < \alpha < 1$.

(b) Show that it is not the uniformly most powerful test of size α.

14. (Section 9.4)

The density of X is given by

$$f(x) = \theta(x - 0.5) + 1 \quad \text{for } -2 \le \theta \le 2 \text{ and } 0 \le x \le 1.$$

Obtain the likelihood ratio test of H_0: $\theta = 2$ against H_1: $\theta < 2$ on the basis of one observation of X at $\alpha = 0.05$. Show that this test is the uniformly most powerful test of size 0.05.

15. (Section 9.4)

The joint density of X and Y is given by

$$f(x, y) = 2\theta^{-2} \quad \text{for } x + y \le \theta, 0 \le x, 0 \le y,$$

$$= 0 \qquad \text{otherwise.}$$

We test H_0: $\theta = 0.5$ against H_1: $\theta \ne 0.5$, where we assume $0 < \theta \le 1$, on the basis of one observation on (X, Y).

(a) Derive the likelihood ratio test of size 0.25.

(b) Derive its power function and draw its graph.

(c) Show that it is the uniformly most powerful test of size 0.25.

16. (Section 9.5)

Let X be uniformly distributed over $[0, \theta]$. Assuming that the prior density of θ is uniform over $[1, 2]$, find the Bayes test of H_0: $\theta \in [1, 1.5]$ versus H_1: $\theta \in (1.5, 2]$ on the basis of one observation on X. Assume that the loss matrix is given by

| | True state | |
Decision	H_0	H_1
H_0	0	1
H_1	2	0

17. (Section 9.5)

Random variables X and Y have a joint density

$$f(x, y \mid \theta) = \theta^{-2} \quad \text{for } 0 \le x \le \theta, \ 0 \le y \le \theta, \ 0.1 \le \theta \le 1.$$

Find the Bayesian test of H_0: $\theta \ge \frac{1}{2}$ against H_1: $\theta < \frac{1}{2}$ based on a single observation of each of X and Y, assuming the prior density $f(\theta) = 1/0.9$ for $0.1 \le \theta \le 1$. Assume that the loss matrix is the same as in Exercise 16.

18. (Section 9.5)

Suppose that the density of X given θ is $f(x \mid \theta) = 2x/\theta^2$, $0 \le x \le \theta$, and the prior density of θ is $f(\theta) = 2\theta$, $0 < \theta < 1$. Suppose that we are given a single observation x of X.

(a) Derive the Bayes estimate of θ.

(b) Assuming that the costs of the Type I and II errors are the same, show how a Bayesian tests H_0: $\theta \le 0.5$ against H_1: $\theta > 0.5$.

19. (Section 9.5)

Let p be the probability that a patient having a particular disease is cured by a new drug. Suppose that the net social utility from a commercial production of the drug is given by

$$U(p) = -0.5 \qquad \text{for} \quad 0 \le p \le 0.5,$$

$$= 2(p - 0.5) \quad \text{for} \quad 0.5 < p \le 1.$$

Suppose that a prior density of p is uniform over the interval $[0, 1]$ and that x patients out of n randomly chosen homogeneous patients have been observed to be cured by the drug. Formulate a Bayesian decision rule regarding whether or not the drug should be approved. If $n = 2$, how large should x be for the drug to be approved?

20. (Section 9.6)

One hundred randomly selected people are polled on their preference between George Bush and Bill Clinton. How large a percentage point difference must be observed for you to be able to conclude that Clinton is ahead of Bush at the significance level of 5%?

21. (Section 9.6)

Thirty races are run, in which one runner is given a stimulant and another is not. If twenty races are won by the stimulated runner, should you decide that the stimulant has an effect at the 1% significance level? What about at 5%?

22. (Section 9.6)

Suppose you roll a die 100 times and the average number showing on the face turns out to be 4. Is it reasonable to conclude that the die is loaded? Why?

23. (Section 9.6)

We throw a die 20 times, 1 comes up four times and 2 comes up seven times. Let p_1 be the probability that 1 comes up and p_2 be the probability that 2 comes up. On the basis of our experiment, test the hypothesis $p_1 = p_2 = \frac{1}{6}$ against the negation of that hypothesis. Should we reject the hypothesis at 5%? What about at 10%?

24. (Section 9.6)
It is claimed that a new diet will reduce a person's weight by an average of 10 pounds in two weeks. The weights of seven women who followed the diet, recorded before and after the two-week period of dieting, are given in the accompanying table. Would you accept the claim made for the diet?

Participant	Weight before (lbs)	Weight after (lbs)
A	128	126
B	130	125
C	135	129
D	142	131
E	137	125
F	148	138
G	154	130

25. (Section 9.6)
The price of a certain food item was sampled in various stores in two cities, and the results were as given below. Test the hypothesis that there is no difference between the mean prices of the particular food item in the two cities using the 5% and 10% significance levels. Assume that the prices are normally distributed with the same variance (unknown) in each city.

	City A	City B
n	18	9
$\bar{x}$	10	9
$n^{-1}\Sigma(x_i - \bar{x})^2$	2	2

26. (Section 9.6)
The following data are from an experiment to study the effect of training on the duration of unemployment. Let X be the duration of

unemployment for those without training, and Y be the duration for those with training:

x	35	42	17	55	24
y	31	37	21	10	28

Assuming the two-sample normal model with equal variances, can we conclude that training has an effect at the 5% significance level? What about at 10%?

27. (Section 9.6)

The accompanying table shows the yields (tons per hectare) of a certain agricultural product in five experimental farms with and without an application of a certain fertilizer. Other things being equal, can we conclude that the fertilizer is effective at the 5% significance level? Is it at the 1% significance level? Assume that the yields are normally distributed.

Farm	Yield without fertilizer (tons)	Yield with fertilizer (tons)
A	5	7
B	6	8
C	7	7
D	8	10
E	9	10

28. (Section 9.6)

According to the *Stanford Observer* (October 1977), 1024 male students entered Stanford in the fall of 1972 and 885 graduated. Among the 1024 students were 84 athletes, of which 78 graduated. Would you conclude that the graduation record of athletes is superior to that of nonathletes at the 1% or 5% significance level?

29. (Section 9.6)

One pre-election poll, based on a sample of 5000 voters, showed Clinton ahead by 23 points, whereas another poll, based on a sample of 3000 voters, showed Clinton ahead by 20 points. Are the results significantly different at the 5% significance level? How about at 10%?

30. (Section 9.6)

    Using the data of Exercise 26 above, test the equality of the variances at the 10% significance level.

31. (Section 9.6)

    Using the data of Exercise 27 above, test the equality of the variances at the 10% significance level.

32. (Section 9.7)

    Test the hypothesis $\mu_1 = \mu_2 = \mu_3$ using the estimators $\hat{\mu}_1$, $\hat{\mu}_2$, and $\hat{\mu}_3$ having the joint distribution $\hat{\boldsymbol{\mu}} \sim N(\boldsymbol{\mu}, \mathbf{A})$, where $\hat{\boldsymbol{\mu}}' = (\hat{\mu}_1, \hat{\mu}_2, \hat{\mu}_3)$, $\boldsymbol{\mu}' = (\mu_1, \mu_2, \mu_3)$, and

$$\mathbf{A} = \begin{bmatrix} 2 & 1 & 1 \\ 1 & 2 & 0 \\ 1 & 0 & 1 \end{bmatrix}.$$

    Assume that the observed values of $\hat{\mu}_1$, $\hat{\mu}_2$, and $\hat{\mu}_3$ are 4, 2, and 1, respectively. Choose the 5% significance level.

33. (Section 9.7)

    There are three classes of five students each. The students all took the same test, and their test scores were as shown in the accompanying table. Assuming that the test scores are independently distributed as $N(\mu_i, \sigma^2)$ for class $i = 1, 2, 3$, test $H_0: \mu_1 = \mu_2 = \mu_3$ against H_1: not H_0. Choose the size of the test to be 1% and 5%.

	Score in	
Class 1	Class 2	Class 3
8.3	7.8	7.0
8.1	7.3	6.8
7.3	7.0	6.7
7.3	6.6	5.8
7.0	6.3	5.7

34. (Section 9.7)

    In Group 1, r_1 of n_1 students passed a test; in Group 2, r_2 of n_2 students passed the test. Students are homogeneous within each group. Let p_1 and p_2 be the probability that a student in Group 1 and in Group 2, respectively, passes the test. Assume that the test results across the students are independent. We are to test H_0: $p_1 = p_2 = 0.5$ against H_1: not H_0.

(a) Using the asymptotic normality of $\hat{p}_1 = r_1/n_1$ and $\hat{p}_2 = r_2/n_2$, derive the Wald test for the problem. Given $n_1 = 20$, $r_1 = 14$, $n_2 = 40$, and $r_2 = 16$, should you reject H_0 at $\alpha = 0.05$ or at $\alpha = 0.1$?

(b) Derive the likelihood ratio test for the problem. Use it to answer problem (a) above.

35. (Section 9.7)

In Exercise 25 above, add one more column as follows:

	City C
n	9
$\bar{x}$	8
$n^{-1}\Sigma(x_i - \bar{x})^2$	3

Test the hypothesis that the mean prices in the three cities are the same.

10 | BIVARIATE REGRESSION MODEL

10.1 INTRODUCTION

In Chapters 1 through 9 we studied statistical inference about the distribution of a single random variable on the basis of independent observations on the variable. Let $\{X_t\}$, $t = 1, 2, \ldots, T$, be a sequence of independent random variables with the same distribution F. Thus far we have considered statistical inference about F based on the observed values $\{x_t\}$ of $\{X_t\}$.

In Chapters 10, 12, and 13 we shall study statistical inference about the relationship among more than one random variable. In the present chapter we shall consider the relationship between two random variables, x and y. From now on we shall drop the convention of denoting a random variable by a capital letter and its observed value by a lowercase letter because of the need to denote a matrix by a capital letter. The reader should determine from the context whether a symbol denotes a random variable or its observed value.

By the inference about the relationship between two random variables x and y, we mean the inference about the joint distribution of x and y. Let us assume that x and y are continuous random variables with the joint density function $f(x, y)$. We make this assumption to simplify the following explanation, but it is not essential for the argument. The problem we want to examine is how to make an inference about $f(x, y)$ on the basis of independent observations $\{x_t\}$ and $\{y_t\}$, $t = 1, 2, \ldots, T$, on x and y. We call this bivariate (more generally, mutivariate) statistical analysis. Bivariate regression analysis is a branch of bivariate statistical analysis in which attention is focused on the conditional density of one variable given the other, say, $f(y \mid x)$. Since we can always write $f(x, y) = f(y \mid x)f(x)$, regression analysis implies that for the moment we ignore the estimation of $f(x)$.

Regression analysis is useful in situations where the value of one variable, y, is determined through a certain physical or behavioral process after the value of the other variable, x, is determined. A variable such as y is called a *dependent variable* or an *endogenous variable*, and a variable such as x is called an *independent variable*, an *exogenous variable*, or a *regressor.* For example, in a consumption function consumption is usually regarded as a dependent variable since it is assumed to depend on the value of income, whereas income is regarded as an independent variable since its value may safely be assumed to be determined independently of consumption. In situations where theory does not clearly designate which of the two variables should be the dependent variable or the independent variable, one can determine this question empirically. It is wise to choose as the independent variable the variable whose values are easier to predict.

Thus, we can state that the purpose of bivariate regression analysis is to make a statistical inference on the conditional density $f(y \mid x)$ based on independent observations of x and y. As in the single variate statistical inference, we may not always try to estimate the conditional density itself; instead, we often want to estimate only the first few moments of the density—notably, the mean and the variance. In this chapter we shall assume that the conditional mean is linear in x and the conditional variance is a constant independent of x.

We define the *bivariate linear regression* model as follows:

(10.1.1) $y_t = \alpha + \beta x_t + u_t, \quad t = 1, 2, \ldots, T,$

where $\{y_t\}$ are observable random variables, $\{x_t\}$ are known constants, and $\{u_t\}$ are unobservable random variables which are i.i.d. with $Eu_t = 0$ and $Vu_t = \sigma^2$. Here, α, β, and σ^2 are unknown parameters that we wish to estimate. We also assume that x_t is not equal to a constant for all t. The linear regression model with all the above assumptions is called the *classical regression model.*

Note that we assume $\{x_t\}$ to be known constants rather than random variables. This is equivalent to assuming that (10.1.1) specifies the mean and variance of the conditional distribution of y given x. We shall continue to call x_t the independent variable. At some points in the subsequent discussion, we shall need the additional assumption that $\{u_t\}$ are normally distributed. Then (10.1.1) specifies completely the conditional distribution of y given x.

The assumption that the conditional mean of y is linear in x is made for the sake of mathematical convenience. Given a joint distribution of x and y, $E(y \mid x)$ is, in general, nonlinear in x. Two notable exceptions are the cases where x and y are jointly normal and x is binary (that is, taking only two values), as we have seen in Chapters 4 and 5. However, the linearity assumption is not so stringent as it may seem, since if $E(y^* \mid x^*)$ is nonlinear in x^*, where y^* and x^* are the original variables (say, consumption and income), it is possible that $E(y \mid x)$ is linear in x after a suitable transformation—such as, for example, $y = \log y^*$ and $x = \log x^*$. The linearity assumption may be regarded simply as a starting point. In Section 13.4 we shall briefly discuss nonlinear regression models.

Our assumption concerning $\{u_t\}$ may also be regarded as a starting point. In Chapter 13 we shall also briefly discuss models in which $\{u_t\}$ are *serially correlated* (that is, $Eu_t u_s \neq 0$ even if $t \neq s$) or *heteroscedastic* (that is, Vu_t varies with t).

We have used the subscript t to denote a particular observation on each variable. If we are dealing with a time series of observations, t refers to the tth period (year, month, and so on). But in some applications t may represent the tth person, tth firm, tth nation, and the like. Data which are not time series are called *cross-section* data.

10.2 LEAST SQUARES ESTIMATORS

10.2.1 Definition

In this section we study the estimation of the parameters α, β, and σ^2 in the bivariate linear regression model (10.1.1). We first consider estimating α and β. The T observations on y and x can be plotted in a so-called scatter diagram, as in Figure 10.1. In that figure each dot represents a vector of observations on y and x. We have labeled one dot as the vector (y_t, x_t). We have also drawn a straight line through the scattered dots and labeled the point of intersection between the line and the dashed perpendicular line that goes through (y_t, x_t) as $(\hat{y}_t, x_t)$. Then the problem of estimating α and β can be geometrically interpreted as the problem of drawing a straight line such that its slope is an estimate of β and its intercept is an estimate of α.

Since $Eu_t = 0$, a reasonable person would draw a line somewhere

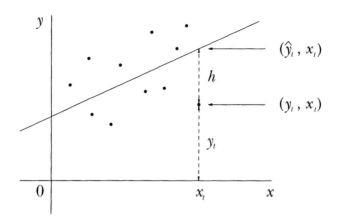

FIGURE 10.1   Scatter diagram

through a configuration of the scattered dots, but there are a multitude of ways to draw such a line. Gauss in a publication dated 1821 proposed the *least squares method* in which a line is drawn in such a way that the sum of squares of the vertical distances between the line and each dot is minimized. In Figure 10.1, the vertical distance between the line and the point (y_t, x_t) is indicated by h. Minimizing the sum of squares of distances in any other direction would result in a different line. Alternatively, we can draw a line so as to minimize the sum of absolute deviations, or the sum of the fourth power of the deviations, and so forth. Another simple method would be simply to connect the two dots signifying the largest and smallest values of x. We can go on forever defining different lines; how shall we choose one method?

The least squares method has proved to be by far the most popular method for estimating α, β, and σ^2 in the linear regression model because of its computational simplicity and certain other desirable properties, which we shall show below. Still, it should by no means be regarded as the best estimator in every situation. In the subsequent discussion the reader should pay special attention to the following question: In what sense and under what conditions is the least squares estimator the best estimator?

Algebraically, the *least squares (LS) estimators* of α and β, denoted by $\hat{\alpha}$ and $\hat{\beta}$, can be defined as the values of α and β which minimize the sum of squared residuals

$$(10.2.1) \quad S(\alpha, \beta) = \sum_{t=1}^{T} (y_t - \alpha - \beta x_t)^2.$$

Differentiating S with respect to α and β and equating the partial derivatives to 0, we obtain

$$(10.2.2) \qquad \frac{\partial S}{\partial \alpha} = -2\Sigma(y_t - \alpha - \beta x_t) = 0$$

and

$$(10.2.3) \qquad \frac{\partial S}{\partial \beta} = -2\Sigma(y_t - \alpha - \beta x_t)x_t = 0,$$

where Σ should be understood to mean $\Sigma_{t=1}^{T}$ unless otherwise noted. Solving (10.2.2) and (10.2.3) simultaneously for α and β yields the following solutions:

$$(10.2.4) \qquad \hat{\beta} = \frac{s_{xy}}{s_x^2},$$

$$(10.2.5) \qquad \hat{\alpha} = \bar{y} - \hat{\beta}\bar{x},$$

where we have defined $\bar{y} = T^{-1}\Sigma y_t$, $\bar{x} = T^{-1}\Sigma x_t$, $s_x^2 = T^{-1}\Sigma x_t^2 - \bar{x}^2$ and $s_{xy} = T^{-1}\Sigma x_t y_t - \bar{x}\bar{y}$. Note that $\bar{y}$ and $\bar{x}$ are sample means, s_x^2 is the sample variance of x, and s_{xy} is the sample covariance.

It is interesting to note that (10.2.4) and (10.2.5) can be obtained by substituting sample moments for the corresponding population moments in the formulae (4.3.8) and (4.3.9), which defined the best linear unbiased predictor. Thus the least squares estimates can be regarded as the natural estimates of the coefficients of the best linear predictor of y given x.

We define

$$(10.2.6) \qquad \hat{y}_t = \hat{\alpha} + \hat{\beta}x_t, \qquad t = 1, 2, \ldots, T,$$

and call it the *least squares predictor* of y_t. We define the error made by the least squares predictor as

$$(10.2.7) \qquad \hat{u}_t = y_t - \hat{y}_t, \qquad t = 1, 2, \ldots, T,$$

and call it the *least squares residual*. In Section 10.2.6 below we discuss the prediction of a "future" value of y; that is, y_t where t is not included in the sample period $(1, 2, \ldots, T)$.

So far we have treated α and β in a nonsymmetric way, regarding β as the slope coefficient on the only independent variable of the model, namely x_t, and calling α the intercept. But as long as we can regard $\{x_t\}$ as known constants, we can treat α and β on an equal basis by regarding α

as the coefficient on another sequence of known constants—namely, a sequence of T ones. We shall call this sequence of ones the *unity regressor.* This symmetric treatment is useful in understanding the mechanism of the least squares method.

Under this symmetric treatment we should call $\hat{y}_t$ as defined in (10.2.6) the least squares predictor of y_t based on the unity regressor and $\{x_t\}$. There is an important relationship between the error of the least squares prediction and the regressors: the sum of the product of the least squares residual and a regressor is zero. We shall call this fact the *orthogonality* between the least squares residual and a regressor. (See the general definition in Section 11.2.) Mathematically, we can express the orthogonality as

(10.2.8) $\Sigma \hat{u}_t = 0$

and

(10.2.9) $\Sigma \hat{u}_t x_t = 0.$

Note that (10.2.8) and (10.2.9) follow from (10.2.2) and (10.2.3), respectively.

We shall present a useful interpretation of the least squares estimators $\hat{\alpha}$ and $\hat{\beta}$ by means of the above-mentioned symmetric treatment. The least squares estimator $\hat{\beta}$ can be interpreted as measuring the effect of $\{x_t\}$ on $\{y_t\}$ after the effect of the unity regressor has been removed, and $\hat{\alpha}$ as measuring the effect of the unity regressor on $\{y_t\}$ after the effect of $\{x_t\}$ has been removed. The precise meaning of the statement above is as follows.

Define the least squares predictor of x_t based on the unit regressor as

(10.2.10) $\hat{x}_t = \hat{\gamma}, \quad t = 1, 2, \ldots, T,$

where $\hat{\gamma}$ is the value that minimizes $\Sigma(x_t - \gamma)^2$, that is, $\hat{\gamma} = \bar{x}$. In other words, we are predicting x_t by the sample mean. Define the error of the predictor as

(10.2.11) $x_t^* = x_t - \hat{x}_t, \quad t = 1, 2, \ldots, T,$

which is actually the deviation of x_t from the sample mean since $\hat{x}_t = \bar{x}$. Then $\hat{\beta}$, defined in (10.2.4), can be interpreted as the least squares estimator of the coefficient of the regression of y_t on x_t^* without the intercept: that is, $\hat{\beta}$ minimizes $\Sigma(y_t - \beta x_t^*)^2$. In this interpretation it is more natural to write $\hat{\beta}$ as

(10.2.12) $\hat{\beta} = \dfrac{\Sigma x_t^* y_t}{\Sigma(x_t^*)^2} .$

Reversing the roles of $\{x_t\}$ and the unity regressor, we define the least squares predictor of the unit regressor based on $\{x_t\}$ as

(10.2.13) $\hat{1}_t = \hat{\delta} x_t, \qquad t = 1, 2, \ldots, T,$

where $\hat{\delta}$ minimizes $\Sigma(1 - \delta x_t)^2$. Therefore

(10.2.14) $\hat{\delta} = \dfrac{\Sigma x_t}{\Sigma x_t^2} .$

We call $\hat{1}_t$ the predictor of 1 for the sake of symmetric treatment, even though there is of course no need to predict 1 in the usual sense. Then, if we define

(10.2.15) $1_t^* = 1 - \hat{1}_t,$

we can show that $\hat{\alpha}$, defined in (10.2.5), is the least squares estimator of the coefficient of the regression of y_t on 1_t^* without the intercept. In other words, $\hat{\alpha}$ minimizes $\Sigma(y_t - \alpha 1_t^*)^2$ so that

(10.2.16) $\hat{\alpha} = \dfrac{\Sigma 1_t^* y_t}{\Sigma(1_t^*)^2} .$

Note that this formula of $\hat{\alpha}$ has a form similar to $\hat{\beta}$ as given in (10.2.12).

The orthogonality between the least squares residual and a regressor is also true in the regression of $\{x_t\}$ on the unity regressor or in the regression of the unity regressor on $\{x_t\}$, as we can easily verify that

(10.2.17) $\Sigma x_t^* = 0$

and

(10.2.18) $\Sigma 1_t^* x_t = 0.$

10.2.2 Properties of $\hat{\alpha}$ and $\hat{\beta}$

First, we obtain the means and the variances of the least squares estimators $\hat{\alpha}$ and $\hat{\beta}$. For this purpose it is convenient to use the formulae (10.2.12) and (10.2.16) rather than (10.2.4) and (10.2.5).

Inserting (10.1.1) into (10.2.12) and using (10.2.17) yields

(10.2.19) $\hat{\beta} - \beta = \dfrac{\Sigma x_t^* u_t}{\Sigma (x_t^*)^2}$.

Since $Eu_t = 0$ and $\{x_t^*\}$ are constants by our assumptions, we have from (10.2.19) and Theorem 4.1.6,

(10.2.20) $E\hat{\beta} = \beta$.

In other words, $\hat{\beta}$ is an unbiased estimator of β. Similarly, inserting (10.1.1) into (10.2.16) and using (10.2.18) yields

(10.2.21) $\hat{\alpha} - \alpha = \dfrac{\Sigma 1_t^* u_t}{\Sigma (1_t^*)^2}$,

which implies

(10.2.22) $E\hat{\alpha} = \alpha$.

Using (10.2.19), the variance of $\hat{\beta}$ can be evaluated as follows:

(10.2.23) $V\hat{\beta} = \dfrac{1}{[\Sigma (x_t^*)^2]^2} V(\Sigma x_t^* u_t)$ by Theorem 4.2.1

$= \dfrac{\sigma^2}{[\Sigma (x_t^*)^2]^2} \Sigma (x_t^*)^2$ by Theorem 4.3.3

$= \dfrac{\sigma^2}{\Sigma (x_t^*)^2}$.

Similarly, we obtain from (10.2.21)

(10.2.24) $V\hat{\alpha} = \dfrac{\sigma^2}{\Sigma (1_t^*)^2}$.

How good are the least squares estimators? Before we compare them with other estimators, let us see what we can learn from the means and the variances obtained above. First, their unbiasedness is clearly a desirable property. Next, note that the denominator of the expression for $V\hat{\beta}$ given in (10.2.23) is equal to T times the sample variance of x_t. Therefore under reasonable circumstances we can expect $V\hat{\beta}$ to go to zero at about the same rate as the inverse of the sample size T. This is another desirable property. The variance of $\hat{\alpha}$ has a similar property. A problem arises if x_t

stays nearly constant for all t, for then both $\Sigma(x_t^*)^2$ and $\Sigma(1_t^*)^2$ are small. (Note that when we defined the bivariate regression model we excluded the possibility that x_t is a constant for all t, since in that case the least squares estimators cannot be defined.) Intuitively speaking, we cannot clearly distinguish the effects of $\{x_t\}$ and the unity regressor on $\{y_t\}$ when x_t is nearly constant. The problem of large variances caused by a closeness of regressors is called the problem of *multicollinearity*.

For the sake of completeness we shall derive the covariance between $\hat{\alpha}$ and $\hat{\beta}$, although its significance for the desirability of the estimators will not be discussed until Chapter 12.

$$(10.2.25) \quad \text{Cov}(\hat{\alpha}, \hat{\beta}) = \frac{E\Sigma x_t^* u_t \Sigma 1_t^* u_t}{\Sigma(x_t^*)^2 \Sigma(1_t^*)^2} = \frac{\sigma^2 \Sigma x_t^* 1_t^*}{\Sigma(x_t^*)^2 \Sigma(1_t^*)^2}.$$

Recall that in Chapter 7 we showed that we can define a variety of estimators with mean squared errors smaller than that of the sample mean for some values of the parameter to be estimated, but that the sample mean is best (in the sense of smallest mean squared error) among all the linear unbiased estimators. We can establish the same fact regarding the least squares estimators, which may be regarded as a natural generalization of the sample mean. (Note that the least squares estimator of the coefficient in the regression of $\{y_t\}$ on the unity regressor is precisely the sample mean of $\{y_t\}$.)

Let us consider the estimation of β. The class of linear estimators of β is defined by $\Sigma c_t y_t$ where $\{c_t\}$ are arbitrary constants. The class of linear unbiased estimators is defined by imposing the following condition on $\{c_t\}$:

$$(10.2.26) \quad E\Sigma c_t y_t = \beta \quad \text{for all } \alpha \text{ and } \beta.$$

Inserting (10.1.1) into the left-hand side of (10.2.26) and using $Eu_t = 0$, we see that the condition (10.2.26) is equivalent to the conditions

$$(10.2.27) \quad \Sigma c_t = 0 \quad \text{and}$$

$$(10.2.28) \quad \Sigma c_t x_t = 1.$$

From (10.2.12) we can easily verify that $\hat{\beta}$ is a member of the class of linear unbiased estimators. We have

$$(10.2.29) \quad V(\Sigma c_t y_t) = \sigma^2 \Sigma c_t^2.$$

Comparing (10.2.29) and (10.2.23), we note that proving that $\hat{\beta}$ is the *best linear unbiased estimator* (BLUE) of β is equivalent to proving

$$(10.2.30) \qquad \frac{1}{\Sigma(x_t^*)^2} \leq \Sigma c_t^2 \quad \text{for all } \{c_t\} \text{ satisfying (10.2.27) and (10.2.28).}$$

But (10.2.30) follows from the following identity similar to the one used in the proof of Theorem 7.2.12:

$$(10.2.31) \quad \Sigma\left[c_t - \frac{x_t^*}{\Sigma(x_t^*)^2} \right]^2 = \Sigma c_t^2 + \frac{1}{\Sigma(x_t^*)^2} - 2\frac{\Sigma c_t x_t^*}{\Sigma(x_t^*)^2}$$

$$= \Sigma c_t^2 - \frac{1}{\Sigma(x_t^*)^2},$$

since $\Sigma c_t x_t^* = 1$ using (10.2.27), (10.2.28), and (10.2.11). Note that (10.2.30) follows from (10.2.31) because the left-hand side of (10.2.31) is the sum of squared terms and hence is nonnegative. Equation (10.2.31) also shows that equality holds in (10.2.30) if and only if $c_t = x_t^*/\Sigma(x_t^*)^2$—in other words, the least squares estimator.

The proof of the best linear unbiasedness of $\hat{\alpha}$ is similar and therefore left as an exercise.

Actually, we can prove a stronger result. Consider the estimation of an arbitrary linear combination of the parameters $d_1\alpha + d_2\beta$. Then $d_1\hat{\alpha} + d_2\hat{\beta}$ is the best linear unbiased estimator of $d_1\alpha + d_2\beta$. The results obtained above can be derived as special cases of this general result by putting $d_1 = 0$ and $d_2 = 1$ for the estimation of β, and putting $d_1 = 1$ and $d_2 = 0$ for the estimation of α. Because the proof of this general result is lengthy, and inasmuch as we shall present a much simpler proof using matrix analysis in Chapter 12, we give only a partial proof here.

Again, we define the class of linear estimators of $d_1\alpha + d_2\beta$ by $\Sigma c_t y_t$. The unbiasedness condition implies

$$(10.2.32) \qquad \Sigma c_t = d_1$$

and

$$(10.2.33) \qquad \Sigma c_t x_t = d_2.$$

The variance of $\Sigma c_t y_t$ is again given by (10.2.29). Define

$$(10.2.34) \quad c_t^* = \frac{d_1 1_t^*}{\Sigma (1_t^*)^2} + \frac{d_2 x_t^*}{\Sigma (x_t^*)^2} .$$

Then the least squares estimator $d_1 \hat\alpha + d_2 \hat\beta$ can be written as $\Sigma c_t^* y_t$ and its variance is given by $\sigma^2 \Sigma (c_t^*)^2$. The best linear unbiasedness of the least squares estimator follows from the identity

$$\Sigma (c_t - c_t^*)^2 = \Sigma c_t^2 - \Sigma (c_t^*)^2.$$

We omit the proof of this identity, except to note that (10.2.32) and (10.2.33) imply $\Sigma c_t c_t^* = \Sigma (c_t^*)^2$.

It is well to remember at this point that we can construct many biased and/or nonlinear estimators which have smaller mean squared errors than the least squares estimators for certain values of the parameters. Moreover, in certain situations some of these estimators may be more desirable than the least squares. Also, we should note that the proof of the best linear unbiasedness of the least squares estimator depends on our assumption that $\{u_t\}$ are serially uncorrelated with a constant variance.

10.2.3 Estimation of σ^2

We shall now consider the estimation of σ^2. If $\{u_t\}$ were observable, the most natural estimator of σ^2 would be the sample variance $T^{-1} \Sigma u_t^2$. Since $\{u_t\}$ are not observable, we must first predict them by the least squares residuals $\{\hat u_t\}$ defined in (10.2.7). Then σ^2 can be estimated by

$$(10.2.35) \quad \hat\sigma^2 = \frac{1}{T} \Sigma \hat u_t^2,$$

which we shall call the least squares estimator of σ^2. Although the use of the term *least squares* here is not as compelling as in the case of $\hat\alpha$ and $\hat\beta$, we use it because it is an estimator based on the least squares residuals. Using $\hat\sigma^2$ we can estimate $V\hat\beta$ and $V\hat\alpha$ given in (10.2.23) and (10.2.24) by substituting $\hat\sigma^2$ for σ^2 in the respective formulae.

We shall evaluate $E\hat\sigma^2$. From (10.2.7) we can write

$$(10.2.36) \quad \hat u_t = u_t - (\hat\alpha - \alpha) - (\hat\beta - \beta) x_t.$$

Multiplying both sides of (10.2.36) by $\hat u_t$, summing over t, and using (10.2.8) and (10.2.9) yields

(10.2.37) $\Sigma \hat{u}_t^2 = \Sigma u_t \hat{u}_t,$

from which we obtain

(10.2.38) $\Sigma \hat{u}_t^2 = \Sigma u_t^2 - \Sigma(\hat{u}_t - u_t)^2.$

Using (10.2.36) and (10.2.38), we have

(10.2.39) $\Sigma(\hat{u}_t - u_t)^2 = \Sigma u_t(u_t - \hat{u}_t) = \dfrac{\Sigma u_t \Sigma 1_t^* u_t}{\Sigma(1_t^*)^2} + \dfrac{\Sigma x_t u_t \Sigma x_t^* u_t}{\Sigma(x_t^*)^2}.$

Taking the expectation of (10.2.39) yields

(10.2.40) $E\Sigma(\hat{u}_t - u_t)^2 = \sigma^2 \left[\dfrac{\Sigma 1_t^*}{\Sigma(1_t^*)^2} + \dfrac{\Sigma x_t^* x_t}{\Sigma(x_t^*)^2} \right].$

But multiplying both sides of (10.2.15) by 1_t^* and summing over t yields

(10.2.41) $\Sigma(1_t^*)^2 = \Sigma 1_t^*$

because of (10.2.18). Similarly, multiplying both sides of (10.2.11) by x_t^* and summing over t yields

(10.2.42) $\Sigma(x_t^*)^2 = \Sigma x_t^* x_t$

because of (10.2.17). Therefore, we obtain from (10.2.40), (10.2.41), and (10.2.42)

(10.2.43) $E\Sigma(\hat{u}_t - u_t)^2 = 2\sigma^2.$

Finally, from (10.2.38) and (10.2.43) we conclude that

(10.2.44) $E\Sigma \hat{u}_t^2 = (T - 2)\sigma^2.$

Equation (10.2.44) implies that $E\hat{\sigma}^2 = T^{-1}(T - 2)\sigma^2$ and hence $\hat{\sigma}^2$ is a biased estimator of σ^2, although the bias diminishes to zero as T goes to infinity. If we prefer an unbiased estimator, we can use the estimator defined by

(10.2.45) $\tilde{\sigma}^2 = \dfrac{\Sigma \hat{u}_t^2}{T - 2}.$

We shall not obtain the variance of $\hat{\sigma}^2$ here; in Section 10.3 we shall indicate the distribution of $\Sigma \hat{u}_t^2$, as well as its variance, assuming the normality of $\{u_t\}$.

One purpose of regression analysis is to explain the variation of $\{y_t\}$ by the variation of $\{x_t\}$. If $\{y_t\}$ are explained well by $\{x_t\}$, we say that the fit of the regression is good. The statistic $\hat{\sigma}^2$ may be regarded as a measure of the *goodness of fit*; the smaller the $\hat{\sigma}^2$, the better the fit. However, since $\hat{\sigma}^2$ depends on the unit of measurement of $\{y_t\}$, we shall use the measure of the goodness of fit known as *R square*, where

$$(10.2.46) \quad R^2 = 1 - \frac{\hat{\sigma}^2}{s_y^2}.$$

Here s_y^2 is the sample variance of $\{y_t\}$; namely, $s_y^2 = T^{-1}\Sigma(y_t - \bar{y})^2$. This statistic does not depend on the unit of measurement of either $\{y_t\}$ or $\{x_t\}$. Since

$$(10.2.47) \quad T\hat{\sigma}^2 = \min_{\alpha, \beta} \Sigma(y_t - \alpha - \beta x_t)^2$$

and

$$(10.2.48) \quad Ts_y^2 = \min_{\alpha} \Sigma(y_t - \alpha)^2,$$

we have $\hat{\sigma}^2 \leq s_y^2$; therefore, $0 \leq R^2 \leq 1$.

We can interpret R^2 defined in (10.2.46) as the square of the sample correlation between $\{y_t\}$ and $\{x_t\}$. From (10.2.5) and (10.2.7),

$$(10.2.49) \quad \hat{u}_t = y_t - \bar{y} - \hat{\beta}(x_t - \bar{x}).$$

Therefore, using (10.2.11), we have

$$(10.2.50) \quad \Sigma \hat{u}_t^2 = \Sigma(y_t - \bar{y})^2 + \hat{\beta}^2\Sigma(x_t^*)^2 - 2\hat{\beta}\Sigma x_t^* y_t.$$

Inserting (10.2.12) into the right-hand side of (10.2.50) yields

$$(10.2.51) \quad \Sigma \hat{u}_t^2 = \Sigma(y_t - \bar{y})^2 - \frac{(\Sigma x_t^* y_t)^2}{\Sigma(x_t^*)^2}.$$

Finally, from (10.2.46) and (10.2.51) we obtain

$$(10.2.52) \quad R^2 = \frac{(\Sigma x_t^* y_t)^2}{\Sigma(x_t^*)^2\Sigma(y_t - \bar{y})^2},$$

which is the square of the sample correlation coefficient between $\{y_t\}$ and $\{x_t\}$.

In practice we often face a situation in which we must decide whether $\{y_t\}$ are to be regressed on $\{x_t\}$ or on another independent sequence $\{s_t\}$. That is, we must choose between two regression equations

(10.2.53) $y_t = \alpha_1 + \beta_1 x_t + u_{1t}$

and

(10.2.54) $y_t = \alpha_2 + \beta_2 s_t + u_{2t}$.

This decision should be made on the basis of various considerations such as how accurate and plausible the estimates of regression coefficients are, how accurately the future values of the independent variables can be predicted, and so on. Other things being equal, it makes sense to choose the equation with the higher R^2. In Section 12.5, we shall discuss this issue further.

The statistic $\hat{\sigma}^2$ is merely one statistic derived from the least squares residual $\{\hat{u}_t\}$, from which one could derive more information. Since $\{\hat{u}_t\}$ are the predictors of $\{u_t\}$, they should behave much like $\{u_t\}$; it is usually a good idea for a researcher to plot $\{\hat{u}_t\}$ against time. A systematic pattern in that plot indicates that the assumptions of the model may be incorrect. Then we must respecify the model, perhaps by allowing serial correlation or heteroscedasticity in $\{u_t\}$, or by including other independent variables in the right-hand side of the regression equation.

10.2.4 Asymptotic Properties of Least Squares Estimators

In this section we prove the consistency and the asymptotic normality of the least squares estimators $\hat{\alpha}$ and $\hat{\beta}$ and the consistency of $\hat{\sigma}^2$ under suitable assumptions about the regressor $\{x_t\}$.

To prove the consistency of $\hat{\alpha}$ and $\hat{\beta}$, we use Theorem 6.1.1, which states that convergence in mean square implies consistency. Since both $\hat{\alpha}$ and $\hat{\beta}$ are unbiased estimators of the respective parameters, we need only show that the variances given in (10.2.23) and (10.2.24) converge to zero. Therefore, we conclude that $\hat{\alpha}$ and $\hat{\beta}$ are consistent if

(10.2.55) $\lim_{T \to \infty} \Sigma(1_t^*)^2 = \infty$

and

(10.2.56) $\lim_{T \to \infty} \Sigma(x_t^*)^2 = \infty.$

We shall rewrite these conditions in terms of the original variables $\{x_t\}$. Since $\Sigma(1_t^*)^2$ and $(\Sigma x_t^*)^2$ are the sums of squared prediction errors in predicting the unity regressor by $\{x_t\}$ and in predicting $\{x_t\}$ by the unity regressor, respectively, the condition that the two regressors are distinctly different in some sense is essential for (10.2.55) and (10.2.56) to hold. Given the sequences of constants $\{x_t\}$ and $\{z_t\}$, $t = 1, 2, \ldots, T$, we measure the degree of closeness of the two sequences by the index

(10.2.57) $\rho_T^2 = \dfrac{(\Sigma x_t z_t)^2}{\Sigma x_t^2 \Sigma z_t^2}.$

Then we have $0 \leq \rho_T^2 \leq 1$. To show $\rho_T^2 \leq 1$, consider the identity

(10.2.58) $\Sigma(x_t - \lambda z_t)^2 = \Sigma x_t^2 + \lambda^2 \Sigma z_t^2 - 2\lambda \Sigma x_t z_t.$

Since (10.2.58) holds for any λ, it holds in particular when

(10.2.59) $\lambda = \dfrac{\Sigma x_t z_t}{\Sigma z_t^2}.$

Inserting (10.2.59) into the right-hand side of (10.2.58) and noting that the left-hand side of (10.2.58) is the sum of nonnegative terms and hence is nonnegative, we obtain the *Cauchy-Schwartz inequality:*

(10.2.60) $\Sigma x_t^2 - \dfrac{(\Sigma x_t z_t)^2}{\Sigma z_t^2} \geq 0.$

(See Theorem 4.3.5 for another version of the Cauchy-Schwartz inequality.) The desired inequality $\rho_T^2 \leq 1$ follows from (10.2.60). Note that $\rho_T^2 = 1$ if and only if $x_t = z_t$ for all t and $\rho_T^2 = 0$ if and only if $\{x_t\}$ and $\{z_t\}$ are orthogonal (that is, $\Sigma x_t z_t = 0$).

Using the index (10.2.57) with $z_t = 1$, we can write

(10.2.61) $\rho_T^2 = \dfrac{(\Sigma x_t)^2}{T \Sigma x_t^2},$

(10.2.62) $\Sigma(1_t^*)^2 = (1 - \rho_T^2)T,$

and

(10.2.63) $\Sigma(x_t^*)^2 = (1 - \rho_T^2)\Sigma x_t^2.$

Finally, we state our result as

THEOREM 10.2.1 In the bivariate regression model (10.1.1), the least squares estimators $\hat{\alpha}$ and $\hat{\beta}$ are consistent if

(10.2.64) $\lim_{T \to \infty} \Sigma x_t^2 = \infty$

and

(10.2.65) $\lim_{T \to \infty} \rho_T^2 < 1.$

Note that when we defined the bivariate regression model in Section 10.1, we assumed $\rho_T \neq 1$. The assumption (10.2.65) states that $\rho_T \neq 1$ holds in the limit as well. The condition (10.2.64) is in general not restrictive. Examples of sequences that do not satisfy (10.2.64) are $x_t = t^{-2}$ and $x_t = 2^{-t}$, but we do not commonly encounter these sequences in practice.

Next we prove the consistency of $\hat{\sigma}^2$. From (10.2.38) we have

(10.2.66) $\hat{\sigma}^2 = \dfrac{\Sigma u_t^2}{T} - \dfrac{1}{T} \Sigma(\hat{u}_t - u_t)^2.$

Since $\{u_t^2\}$ are i.i.d. with mean σ^2, we have by the law of large numbers (Theorem 6.2.1)

(10.2.67) $\text{plim} \dfrac{\Sigma u_t^2}{T} = \sigma^2.$

Equation (10.2.43) and the Chebyshev's inequality (6.1.2) imply

(10.2.68) $\text{plim} \dfrac{1}{T} \Sigma(\hat{u}_t - u_t)^2 = 0.$

Therefore the consistency of $\hat{\sigma}^2$ follows from (10.2.66), (10.2.67), and (10.2.68) because of Theorem 6.1.3.

We shall prove the asymptotic normality of $\hat{\alpha}$ and $\hat{\beta}$. From (10.2.19) and (10.2.21) we note that both $\hat{\beta} - \beta$ and $\hat{\alpha} - \alpha$ can be written in expressions of the form

(10.2.69) $\dfrac{\Sigma z_t u_t}{\Sigma z_t^2},$

where $\{z_t\}$ is a certain sequence of constants. Since the variance of (10.2.69) goes to zero if Σz_t^2 goes to infinity, we transform (10.2.69) so that the transformed sequence has a constant variance for all T. This is accomplished by considering the sequence

$$(10.2.70) \quad \frac{\Sigma z_t u_t}{\sigma \sqrt{\Sigma z_t^2}},$$

since the variance of (10.2.70) is unity for all T. We need to obtain the conditions on $\{z_t\}$ such that the limit distribution of (10.2.70) is $N(0, 1)$. The answer is provided by the following theorem:

THEOREM 10.2.2 Let $\{u_t\}$ be i.i.d. with mean zero and a constant variance σ^2 as in the model (10.1.1). If

$$(10.2.71) \quad \lim_{T \to \infty} \frac{\max\limits_{1 \le t \le T} z_t^2}{\Sigma z_t^2} = 0,$$

then

$$(10.2.72) \quad \frac{\Sigma z_t u_t}{\sigma \sqrt{\Sigma z_t^2}} \to N(0, 1).$$

Note that if $z_t = 1$ for all t, (10.2.71) is clearly satisfied and this theorem is reduced to the Lindeberg-Lévy central limit theorem (Theorem 6.2.2). Accordingly, this theorem may be regarded as a generalization of the Lindeberg-Lévy theorem. It can be proved using the Lindeberg-Feller central limit theorem; see Amemiya (1985, p. 96).

We shall apply the result (10.2.72) to $\hat{\beta} - \beta$ and $\hat{\alpha} - \alpha$ by putting $z_t = x_t^*$ and $z_t = 1_t^*$ in turn. Using (10.2.63), we have

$$(10.2.73) \quad \frac{\max (x_t^*)^2}{\Sigma (x_t^*)^2} = \frac{\max (x_t - \bar{x})^2}{(1 - \rho_T^2)\Sigma x_t^2} \le \frac{4 \max x_t^2}{(1 - \rho_T^2)\Sigma x_t^2}.$$

Therefore $\{x_t^*\}$ satisfy the condition (10.2.71) if we assume (10.2.65) and

$$(10.2.74) \quad \lim_{T \to \infty} \frac{\max\limits_{1 \le t \le T} x_t^2}{\Sigma x_t^2} = 0.$$

Next, using (10.2.61) and (10.2.62), we have

(10.2.75)
$$\frac{\max(1_t^*)^2}{\Sigma(1_t^*)^2} = \frac{\max\left[1 + \left(\frac{\Sigma x_t}{\Sigma x_t^2}\right)^2 x_t^2 - 2\left(\frac{\Sigma x_t}{\Sigma x_t^2}\right)x_t\right]}{T(1 - \rho_T^2)}$$

$$\leq \frac{1}{T(1 - \rho_T^2)} + \frac{\rho_T^2}{(1 - \rho_T^2)}\frac{\max x_t^2}{\Sigma x_t^2}$$

$$+ \frac{2|\rho_T|}{\sqrt{T}(1 - \rho_T^2)}\left[\frac{\max x_t^2}{\Sigma x_t^2}\right]^{1/2}.$$

Therefore $\{1_t^*\}$ satisfy the condition (10.2.71) if we assume (10.2.65) and (10.2.74). Thus we have proved that Theorem 10.2.2 implies the following theorem:

THEOREM 10.2.3 In the bivariate regression model (10.1.1), assume further (10.2.65) and (10.2.74). Then we have

(10.2.76)
$$\frac{\sqrt{\Sigma(1_t^*)^2}}{\sigma}(\hat{\alpha} - \alpha) \to N(0, 1)$$

and

(10.2.77)
$$\frac{\sqrt{\Sigma(x_t^*)^2}}{\sigma}(\hat{\beta} - \beta) \to N(0, 1).$$

Using the terminology introduced in Section 6.2, we can say that $\hat{\alpha}$ and $\hat{\beta}$ are asymptotically normal with their respective means and variances. Note that the condition (10.2.74) is stronger than (10.2.64), which was required for the consistency proof; this is not surprising since the asymptotic normality is a stronger result than consistency. We should point out, however, that (10.2.74) is only mildly more restrictive than (10.2.64). In order to be convinced of this fact, the reader should try to construct a sequence which satisfies (10.2.64) but not (10.2.74).

The conclusion of Theorem 10.2.3 states that $\hat{\alpha}$ and $\hat{\beta}$ are asymptotically normal when each estimator is considered separately. The assumptions of that theorem are actually sufficient to prove the joint asymptotic normality of $\hat{\alpha}$ and $\hat{\beta}$; that is, the joint distribution of the random variables defined in (10.2.76) and (10.2.77) converges to a joint normal distribution with zero means, unit variances, and the covariance which is equal to the limit of the covariance. We shall state this result as a theorem in Chapter 12, where we discuss the general regression model in matrix notation.

10.2.5　Maximum Likelihood Estimators

In this section we show that if we assume the normality of $\{u_t\}$ in the model (10.1.1), the least squares estimators $\hat{\alpha}$, $\hat{\beta}$, and $\hat{\sigma}^2$ are also the maximum likelihood estimators.

The likelihood function of the parameters (that is, the joint density of $y_1, y_2, \ldots, y_T$) is given by

$$(10.2.78) \quad L = \prod_{t=1}^{T} \frac{1}{\sqrt{2\pi}\,\sigma} \exp\left[-\frac{1}{2\sigma^2}(y_t - \alpha - \beta x_t)^2\right]$$

$$= (2\pi\sigma^2)^{-T/2} \exp\left[-\frac{1}{2\sigma^2}\Sigma(y_t - \alpha - \beta x_t)^2\right].$$

Taking the natural logarithm of both sides of (10.2.78), we have

$$(10.2.79) \quad \log L = -\frac{T}{2}\log 2\pi - \frac{T}{2}\log \sigma^2 - \frac{1}{2\sigma^2}\Sigma(y_t - \alpha - \beta x_t)^2.$$

Since $\log L$ depends on α and β only via the last term of the right-hand side of (10.2.79), the maximum likelihood estimators of α and β are identical to the least squares estimators.

Inserting $\hat{\alpha}$ and $\hat{\beta}$ into the right-hand side of (10.2.79), we obtain the so-called *concentrated log-likelihood function,* which depends only on σ^2.

$$(10.2.80) \quad \log L^* = -\frac{T}{2}\log 2\pi - \frac{T}{2}\log \sigma^2 - \frac{1}{2\sigma^2}\Sigma\hat{u}_t^2.$$

Differentiating (10.2.80) with respect to σ^2 and equating the derivative to zero yields

$$(10.2.81) \quad \frac{d\log L^*}{d\sigma^2} = -\frac{T}{2\sigma^2} + \frac{1}{2\sigma^4}\Sigma\hat{u}_t^2 = 0.$$

Solving (10.2.81) for σ^2 yields the maximum likelihood estimator, which is identical to the least squares estimator $\hat{\sigma}^2$. These results constitute a generalization of the results in Example 7.3.3.

In Section 12.2.5 we shall show that the least squares estimators $\hat{\alpha}$ and $\hat{\beta}$ are best unbiased if $\{u_t\}$ are normal.

10.2.6 Prediction

The need to predict a value of the dependent variable outside the sample (a future value if we are dealing with time series) when the corresponding value of the independent variable is known arises frequently in practice. We add the following "prediction period" equation to the model (10.1.1):

(10.2.82) $y_p = \alpha + \beta x_p + u_p,$

where y_p and u_p are both unobservable, x_p is a known constant, and u_p is independent of $\{u_t\}$, $t = 1, 2, \ldots, T$, with $Eu_p = 0$ and $Vu_p = \sigma^2$. Note that the parameters α, β, and σ^2 are the same as in the model (10.1.1).

Consider the class of predictors of y_p which can be written in the form

(10.2.83) $\tilde{y}_p = \tilde{\alpha} + \tilde{\beta} x_p,$

where $\tilde{\alpha}$ and $\tilde{\beta}$ are arbitrary unbiased estimators of α and β, which are linear in $\{y_t\}$, $t = 1, 2, \ldots, T$. We call this the class of linear unbiased predictors of y_p. The mean squared prediction error of $\tilde{y}_p$ is given by

$$(10.2.84)\quad E(y_p - \tilde{y}_p)^2 = E\{u_p - [(\tilde{\alpha} + \tilde{\beta} x_p) - (\alpha + \beta x_p)]\}^2$$
$$= \sigma^2 + V(\tilde{\alpha} + \tilde{\beta} x_p),$$

where the second equality follows from the independence of u_p and $\{y_t\}$, $t = 1, 2, \ldots, T$.

The *least squares predictor* of y_p is given by

(10.2.85) $\hat{y}_p = \hat{\alpha} + \hat{\beta} x_p.$

It is clearly a member of the class defined in (10.2.83). Since $V(\hat{\alpha} + \hat{\beta} x_p) \leq V(\tilde{\alpha} + \tilde{\beta} x_p)$ because of the result of Section 10.2.2, we conclude that the least squares predictor is the *best linear unbiased predictor*. We have now reduced the problem of prediction to the problem of estimating a linear combination of α and β.

10.3 TESTS OF HYPOTHESES

10.3.1 Student's *t* Test

In Section 9.5 we showed that a hypothesis on the mean of a nomral i.i.d. sample with an unknown variance can be tested using the Student's t statistic. A similar test can be devised for testing hypotheses on α and β in the bivariate regession model. Throughout this section we assume that $\{u_t\}$ are normally distributed.

We shall consider the null hypothesis H_0: $\beta = \beta_0$, where β_0 is a known specified value. A hypothesis on α can be similarly dealt with. Since $\hat{\beta}$ is a good estimator of β, it is reasonable to expect that a test statistic which essentially depends on $\hat{\beta}$ is also a good one. A linear combination of normal random variables is normally distributed by Theorem 5.3.2, so we see from (10.2.19) that

$$(10.3.1) \qquad \frac{\sqrt{\Sigma(x_t^*)^2}}{\sigma} (\hat{\beta} - \beta_0) \sim N(0, 1)$$

under the null hypothesis H_0. Therefore, if σ^2 were known, the distribution of $\hat{\beta}$ would be completely specified and we could perform the standard normal test. If σ^2 is unknown, which is usually the case, we must use a Student's t test. From Definition 2 of the Appendix we know that in order to construct a Student's t statistic, we need a chi-square variable that is distributed independently of (10.3.1). In the next two paragraphs we show that $\sigma^{-2}\Sigma\hat{u}_t^2$ fits this specification.

We state without proof that

$$(10.3.2) \qquad \frac{\Sigma\hat{u}_t^2}{\sigma^2} \sim \chi_{T-2}^2 .$$

To prove (10.3.2) we must show that $\sigma^{-2}\Sigma\hat{u}_t^2$ can be written as a sum of the squares of $T - 2$ independent standard normal variables. We can do so by the method of induction, as in the proof of Theorem 3 of the Appendix. Since this proof is rather cumbersome, we shall postpone it until Chapter 12, where a simpler proof using matrix analysis is given.

We now prove that (10.3.1) and (10.3.2) are independent. Using (10.2.5) and (10.2.11), we have

$$(10.3.3) \qquad \hat{u}_t = u_t - \bar{u} - (\hat{\beta} - \beta)x_t^* .$$

Therefore, using (10.2.19), we obtain

$$(10.3.4) \qquad E(\hat{\beta} - \beta)\hat{u}_t = \sigma^2 \left[\frac{x_t^*}{\Sigma(x_t^*)^2} - \frac{\Sigma x_t^*}{T\Sigma(x_t^*)^2} - \frac{x_t^*}{\Sigma(x_t^*)^2} \right] = 0,$$

since $\Sigma x_t^* = 0$ by (10.2.17). Equation (10.3.4) shows that the covariance between $\hat{\beta}$ and $\hat{u}_t$ is zero; but since they are jointly normal, it implies their independence by Theorem 5.3.4. Therefore, (10.3.1) and (10.3.2) are independent by Theorem 3.5.1.

Using Definition 2 of the Appendix, we conclude that under H_0

$$(10.3.5) \qquad \frac{\sqrt{\Sigma(x_t^*)^2}}{\tilde{\sigma}} (\hat{\beta} - \beta_0) \sim t_{T-2} \text{ (Student's } t \text{ with } T - 2 \text{ degrees of freedom)}$$

where $\tilde{\sigma}^2$ is the unbiased estimator of σ^2 defined in (10.2.45). Note that the left-hand side of (10.3.5) is simply $\hat{\beta} - \beta_0$ divided by the square root of an unbiased estimate of its variance. We could use either a one-tail or a two-tail test, depending on the alternative hypothesis.

The test is not exact if $\{u_t\}$ are not normal. Because of the asymptotic normality given in (10.2.76), however, the test based on (10.3.5) is approximately correct for a large sample even if $\{u_t\}$ are not normal, provided that the assumptions for the asymptotic normality are satisfied.

A test on the null hypothesis $\alpha = \alpha_0$ can be performed using a similar result:

$$(10.3.6) \qquad \frac{\sqrt{\Sigma(1_t^*)^2}}{\tilde{\sigma}} (\hat{\alpha} - \alpha_0) \sim t_{T-2}.$$

10.3.2 Tests for Structural Change

Suppose we have two regression regimes

$$(10.3.7) \qquad y_{1t} = \alpha + \beta_1 x_{1t} + u_{1t}, \qquad t = 1, 2, \ldots, T_1$$

and

$$(10.3.8) \qquad y_{2t} = \alpha + \beta_2 x_{2t} + u_{2t}, \qquad t = 1, 2, \ldots, T_2,$$

where each equation satisfies the assumptions of the model (10.1.1). We denote $Vu_{1t} = \sigma_1^2$ and $Vu_{2t} = \sigma_2^2$. In addition, we assume that $\{u_{1t}\}$ and $\{u_{2t}\}$

are normally distributed and independent of each other. This two-regression model is useful to analyze the possible occurrence of a structural change from one period to another. For example, (10.3.7) may represent a relationship between y and x in the prewar period and (10.3.8) in the postwar period.

First, we study the test of the null hypothesis H_0: $\beta_1 = \beta_2$, assuming $\sigma_1^2 = \sigma_2^2$ under either the null or the alternative hypothesis. We can construct a Student's t statistic similar to the one defined in (10.3.5). Let $\hat{\beta}_1$ and $\hat{\beta}_2$ be the least squares estimators of β_1 and β_2 obtained from equations (10.3.7) and (10.3.8), respectively. Then, defining $x_{1t}^* = x_{1t} - \bar{x}_1$ and $x_{2t}^* = x_{2t} - \bar{x}_2$ as in (10.2.11), we have under H_0

$$(10.3.9) \qquad \left[\frac{\sigma_1^2}{\sum_{t=1}^{T_1} (x_{1t}^*)^2} + \frac{\sigma_2^2}{\sum_{t=1}^{T_2} (x_{2t}^*)^2} \right]^{-1/2} (\hat{\beta}_1 - \hat{\beta}_2) \sim N(0, 1).$$

Let $\{\hat{u}_{1t}\}$ and $\{\hat{u}_{2t}\}$ be the least squares residuals calculated from (10.3.7) and (10.3.8), respectively. Then (10.3.2) implies

$$(10.3.10) \qquad \frac{\sum_{t=1}^{T_1} \hat{u}_{1t}^2}{\sigma_1^2} \sim \chi_{T_1-2}^2$$

and

$$(10.3.11) \qquad \frac{\sum_{t=1}^{T_2} \hat{u}_{2t}^2}{\sigma_2^2} \sim \chi_{T_2-2}^2.$$

Therefore, by Theorem 1 of the Appendix, we have

$$(10.3.12) \qquad \frac{\sum_{t=1}^{T_1} \hat{u}_{1t}^2}{\sigma_1^2} + \frac{\sum_{t=1}^{T_2} \hat{u}_{2t}^2}{\sigma_2^2} \sim \chi_{T-4}^2,$$

where we have set $T_1 + T_2 = T$. Since (10.3.9) and (10.3.12) are independent, we have by Definition 2 of the Appendix

$$(10.3.13) \quad \frac{\sqrt{T-4}\,(\hat{\beta}_1 - \hat{\beta}_2)}{\left[\dfrac{\sigma_1^2}{\displaystyle\sum_{t=1}^{T_1}(x_{1t}^*)^2} + \dfrac{\sigma_2^2}{\displaystyle\sum_{t=1}^{T_2}(x_{2t}^*)^2}\right]^{1/2} \cdot \left[\dfrac{\displaystyle\sum_{t=1}^{T_1}\hat{u}_{1t}^2}{\sigma_1^2} + \dfrac{\displaystyle\sum_{t=1}^{T_2}\hat{u}_{2t}^2}{\sigma_2^2}\right]^{1/2}} \sim t_{T-4}.$$

Setting $\sigma_1^2 = \sigma_2^2$ in (10.3.13) simplifies it to

$$(10.3.14) \quad \frac{(\hat{\beta}_1 - \hat{\beta}_2)}{\left[\dfrac{\tilde{\sigma}^2}{\displaystyle\sum_{t=1}^{T_1}(x_{1t}^*)^2} + \dfrac{\tilde{\sigma}^2}{\displaystyle\sum_{t=1}^{T_2}(x_{2t}^*)^2}\right]^{1/2}} \sim t_{T-4},$$

where $\tilde{\sigma}^2 = (T-4)^{-1}(\Sigma_{t=1}^{T_1}\hat{u}_{1t}^2 + \Sigma_{t=1}^{T_2}\hat{u}_{2t}^2)$. The null hypothesis can be tested using (10.3.14) in either a one-tail or a two-tail test, depending on the alternative hypothesis.

Before discussing the difficult problem of testing $\beta_1 = \beta_2$ without assuming $\sigma_1^2 = \sigma_2^2$, let us consider testing the null hypothesis H_0: $\sigma_1^2 = \sigma_2^2$. A simple test of this hypothesis can be constructed by using the chi-square variables defined in (10.3.10) and (10.3.11). Since they are independent of each other because $\{u_{1t}\}$ and $\{u_{2t}\}$ are independent, we have by Definition 3 of the Appendix

$$(10.3.15) \quad \frac{\sigma_2^2(T_2 - 2)\displaystyle\sum_{t=1}^{T_1}\hat{u}_{1t}^2}{\sigma_1^2(T_1 - 2)\displaystyle\sum_{t=1}^{T_2}\hat{u}_{2t}^2} \sim F(T_1 - 2, T_2 - 2).$$

Note that σ_1^2 and σ_2^2 drop out of the formula above under the null hypothesis $\sigma_1^2 = \sigma_2^2$. A one-tail or a two-tail test should be used, depending on the alternative hypothesis.

Finally, we consider a test of the null hypothesis H_0: $\beta_1 = \beta_2$ without assuming $\sigma_1^2 = \sigma_2^2$. The difficulty of this situation arises from the fact that (10.3.14) cannot be derived from (10.3.13) without assuming $\sigma_1^2 = \sigma_2^2$. Several procedures are available to cope with this so-called *Behrens-Fisher problem,* but we shall present only one—the method proposed by Welch (1938). For other methods see Kendall and Stuart (1973).

Welch's method is based on the assumption that the following is approximately true when appropriate degrees of freedom, denoted ν, are chosen:

$$(10.3.16) \qquad \frac{(\hat{\beta}_1 - \hat{\beta}_2)}{\left[\dfrac{\tilde{\sigma}_1^2}{\sum\limits_{t=1}^{T_1} (x_{1t}^*)^2} + \dfrac{\tilde{\sigma}_2^2}{\sum\limits_{t=1}^{T_2} (x_{2t}^*)^2} \right]^{1/2}} \sim t_\nu ,$$

where $\tilde{\sigma}_1^2 = (T_1 - 2)^{-1} \Sigma_{t=1}^{T_1} \hat{u}_{1t}^2$ and $\tilde{\sigma}_2^2 = (T_2 - 2)^{-} \Sigma_{t=1}^{T_2} \hat{u}_{2t}^2$. The assumption that (10.3.16) is approximately true is equivalent to the assumption that $\nu\xi$, where ξ is defined by

$$(10.3.17) \qquad \xi = \left[\frac{\tilde{\sigma}_1^2}{\sum\limits_{t=1}^{T_1} (x_{1t}^*)^2} + \frac{\tilde{\sigma}_2^2}{\sum\limits_{t=1}^{T_2} (x_{2t}^*)^2} \right] \left[\frac{\sigma_1^2}{\sum\limits_{t=1}^{T_1} (x_{1t}^*)^2} + \frac{\sigma_2^2}{\sum\limits_{t=1}^{T_2} (x_{2t}^*)^2} \right]^{-1} ,$$

is approximately distributed as χ_ν^2 for an appropriately chosen value of ν. Then we can apply Definition 2 of the Appendix to (10.3.9) and (10.3.17) to obtain (10.3.16).

The remaining question, therefore, is how we should determine the degrees of freedom ν in such a way that $\nu\xi$ is approximately χ_ν^2. Since $E\xi = 1$ and since $E\chi_\nu^2 = \nu$ by Theorem 2 of the Appendix, we have $E\nu\xi = E\chi_\nu^2$. We now equate the variances of $\nu\xi$ and χ_ν^2:

$$(10.3.18) \qquad V\xi = \frac{\dfrac{2\sigma_1^4}{(T_1 - 2)\left[\sum\limits_{t=1}^{T_1} (x_{1t}^*)^2 \right]^2} + \dfrac{2\sigma_2^4}{(T_2 - 2)\left[\sum\limits_{t=1}^{T_2} (x_{2t}^*)^2 \right]^2}}{\left[\dfrac{\sigma_1^2}{\sum\limits_{t=1}^{T_1} (x_{1t}^*)^2} + \dfrac{\sigma_2^2}{\sum\limits_{t=1}^{T_2} (x_{2t}^*)^2} \right]^2} .$$

Since $V\chi_\nu^2 = 2\nu$ by Theorem 2 of the Appendix, we should determine ν by $\nu = 2(V\xi)^{-1}$. In practice, ν must be estimated by inserting $\tilde{\sigma}_1^2$ and

$\tilde{\sigma}_2^2$ into the right-hand side of (10.3.18) and then choosing the integer that most closely satisfies $v = 2(V\xi)^{-1}$.

EXERCISES

1. (Section 10.2.2)
   Following the proof of the best linear unbiasedness of $\hat{\beta}$, prove the same for $\hat{\alpha}$.

2. (Section 10.2.2)
   In the model (10.1.1) obtain the *constrained least squares estimator* of β, denoted by $\tilde{\beta}$, based on the assumption $\alpha = \beta$. That is to say, $\tilde{\beta}$ minimizes $\Sigma_{t=1}^{T}(y_t - \beta - \beta x_t)^2$. Derive its mean squared error without assuming that $\alpha = \beta$. Show that if in fact $\alpha = \beta$, the mean squared error of $\tilde{\beta}$ is smaller than that of the least squares estimator $\hat{\beta}$.

3. (Section 10.2.2)
   In the model (10.1.1) assume that $\alpha = 0$, $\beta = 1$, $T = 3$, and $x_t = t$ for $t = 1$, 2, and 3. Also assume that $\{u_t\}$, $t = 1$, 2, and 3, are i.i.d. with the distribution $P(u_t = 1) = P(u_t = -1) = 0.5$. Obtain the mean and mean squared error of the *reverse least squares estimator* (minimizing the sum of squares of the deviations in the direction of the x-axis) defined by $\hat{\beta}_R = \Sigma_{t=1}^{3} y_t^2 / \Sigma_{t=1}^{3} y_t x_t$ and compare them with those of the least squares estimator $\hat{\beta} = \Sigma_{t=1}^{3} y_t x_t / \Sigma_{t=1}^{3} x_t^2$. Create your own data by generating $\{u_t\}$ according to the above scheme and calculate $\hat{\beta}_R$ and $\hat{\beta}$ for $T = 25$ and $T = 50$.

4. (Section 10.2.4)
   Give an example of a sequence that satisfies (10.2.64) but not (10.2.74).

5. (Section 10.2.4)
   Suppose that $y_t = y_t^* + u_t$ and $x_t = x_t^* + v_t$, $t + 1$, 2, . . . , T, where $\{y_t^*\}$ and $\{x_t^*\}$ are unknown constants, $\{y_t\}$ and $\{x_t\}$ are observable random variables, and $\{u_t\}$ and $\{v_t\}$ are unobservable random variables. Assume (u_t, v_t) is a bivariate i.i.d. random variable with mean zero and variances σ_u^2 and σ_v^2 and covariance σ_{uv}. The problem is to estimate the unknown parameter β in the relationship $y_t^* = \beta x_t^*$, $t = 1$, 2, . . . , T, on the basis of observations $\{y_t\}$ and $\{x_t\}$. Obtain the probability limit

of $\hat{\beta} = \Sigma_{t=1}^T y_t x_t / \Sigma_{t=1}^T x_t^2$, assuming $\lim_{T \to \infty} T^{-1} \Sigma_{t=1}^T (x_t^*)^2 = c$. This is known as an *errors-in-variables model*.

6. (Section 10.2.4)

In the model of the preceding exercise, assume also that

$$\lim_{T \to \infty} T^{-1} \Sigma_{t=1}^T x_t^* = d \neq 0$$

and obtain the probability limit of

$$\tilde{\beta} = \sum_{t=1}^T y_t \Big/ \sum_{t=1}^T x_t.$$

7. (Section 10.2.4)

Consider a bivariate regression model $y_t = \alpha + \beta x_t + u_t$, $t = 1, 2, \ldots,$ T, where $\{x_t\}$ are known constants and $\{u_t\}$ are i.i.d. with $Eu_t = 0$ and $Vu_t = \sigma^2$. Arrange $\{x_t\}$ in ascending order and define $x_{(1)} \leq x_{(2)} \leq \ldots$ $\leq x_{(T)}$. Let S be $T/2$ if T is even and $(T+1)/2$ if T is odd. Also define

$$\bar{x}_1 = \frac{1}{S} \sum_{t=1}^S x_{(t)}, \quad \bar{x}_2 = \frac{1}{T-S} \sum_{t=S+1}^T x_{(t)},$$

$$\bar{y}_1 = \frac{1}{S} \sum_{t=1}^S y_{(t)}, \quad \bar{y}_2 = \frac{1}{T-S} \sum_{t=S+1}^T y_{(t)},$$

where we assume $\lim_{T \to \infty} \bar{x}_1 = c < \lim_{T \to \infty} \bar{x}_2 = d < \infty$. Prove the consistency of $\tilde{\beta}$ and $\tilde{\alpha}$ defined by

$$\tilde{\beta} = \frac{\bar{y}_2 - \bar{y}_1}{\bar{x}_2 - \bar{x}_1} \quad \text{and} \quad \tilde{\alpha} = \bar{y}_1 - \tilde{\beta} \bar{x}_1.$$

Are these estimators better or worse than the least squares estimators $\hat{\beta}$ and $\hat{\alpha}$? Explain.

8. (Section 10.2.6)

Consider a bivariate regression model $y_t = \alpha + \beta x_t + u_t$, $t = 1, 2, \ldots,$ 5, where $\{x_t\}$ are known constants and equal to $(2, 0, 2, 0, 4)$ and $\{u_t\}$ are i.i.d. with $Eu_t = 0$ and $Vu_t = \sigma^2$. We wish to predict y_5 on the basis of observations (y_1, y_2, y_3, y_4). We consider two predictors of y_5:

(1) $\hat{y}_5 = \hat{\alpha} + \hat{\beta} x_5$, where $\hat{\alpha}$ and $\hat{\beta}$ are the least squares estimators based on the first four observations on $\{x_t\}$ and $\{y_t\}$,

$$(2) \quad \tilde{y}_5 = \tilde{\alpha} + \tilde{\alpha}x_5, \quad \text{where} \quad \tilde{\alpha} = \frac{\sum_{t=1}^{4}(1 + x_t)y_t}{\sum_{t=1}^{4}(1 + x_t)^2}.$$

Obtain the mean squared prediction errors of the two predictors. For what values of α and β is $\tilde{y}_5$ preferred to $\hat{y}_5$?

9. (Section 10.3.1)

Test the hypothesis that there is no gender difference in the wage rate by estimating the regression model

$$y_i = \alpha + \beta x_i + u_i, \quad i = 1, 2, \ldots, n,$$

where y_i is the wage rate (dollars per hour) of the ith person and $x_i = 1$ or 0, depending on whether the ith person is male or female. We assume that $\{u_i\}$ are i.i.d. $N(0, \sigma^2)$. The data are given by the following table:

	Number of people	Sample mean of wage rate	Sample variance of wage rate
Male	20	5	3.75
Female	10	4	3.00

10. (Section 10.3.2)

The accompanying table gives the annual U.S. data on hourly wage rates (y) and labor productivity (x) in two periods: Period 1, 1972–1979; and Period 2, 1980–1986. (Source: *Economic Report of the President*, Government Printing Office, Washington, D.C., 1992.)

Period 1							
y:	3.70	3.94	4.24	4.53	4.86	5.25	5.69	6.16
x:	92.60	95.00	93.30	95.50	98.30	99.80	100.40	99.30

Period 2						
y:	6.66	7.25	7.68	8.02	8.32	8.57	8.76
x:	98.60	99.90	100.00	102.20	104.60	106.10	108.30

(a) Calculate the linear regression equations of y and x for each period and test whether the two lines differ in slope, assuming that the error variances are the same in both regressions.

(b) Test the equality of the error variances.

(c) Test the equality of the slope coefficients without assuming the equality of the variances.

11 | ELEMENTS OF MATRIX ANALYSIS

In Chapter 10 we discussed the bivariate regression model using summation notation. In this chapter we present basic results in matrix analysis. The multiple regression model with many independent variables can be much more effectively analyzed by using vector and matrix notation. Since our goal is to familiarize the reader with basic results, we prove only those theorems which are so fundamental that the reader can learn important facts from the process of proof itself. For the other proofs we refer the reader to Bellman (1970).

Symmetric matrices play a major role in statistics, and Bellman's discussion of them is especially good. Additional useful results, especially with respect to nonsymmetric matrices, may be found in a compact paperback volume, Marcus and Minc (1964). Graybill (1969) described specific applications in statistics. For concise introductions to matrix analysis see, for example, Johnston (1984, chapter 4), Anderson (1984, appendix), or Amemiya (1985, appendix).

11.1 DEFINITION OF BASIC TERMS

Matrix. A matrix, here denoted by a boldface capital letter, is a rectangular array of real numbers arranged as follows:

$$(11.1.1) \quad \mathbf{A} = \begin{bmatrix} a_{11} & a_{12} & \cdot & \cdot & \cdot & a_{1m} \\ a_{21} & a_{22} & \cdot & \cdot & \cdot & a_{2m} \\ \cdot & \cdot & & & & \\ \cdot & \cdot & & & & \\ a_{n1} & a_{n2} & \cdot & \cdot & \cdot & a_{nm} \end{bmatrix}.$$

A matrix such as **A** in (11.1.1), which has n rows and m columns, is called an $n \times m$ (read "n by m") matrix. Matrix **A** may also be denoted by the symbol $\{a_{ij}\}$, indicating that its i, jth element (the element in the ith row and jth column) is a_{ij}.

Transpose. Let **A** be as in (11.1.1). Then the transpose of **A**, denoted by **A**$'$, is defined as an $m \times n$ matrix whose i, jth element is equal to a_{ji}. For example,

$$\begin{bmatrix} 1 & 4 \\ 2 & 5 \\ 3 & 6 \end{bmatrix}' = \begin{bmatrix} 1 & 2 & 3 \\ 4 & 5 & 6 \end{bmatrix}.$$

Note that the transpose of a matrix is obtained by rewriting its columns as rows.

Square matrix. A matrix which has the same number of rows and columns is called a square matrix. Thus, **A** in (11.1.1) is a square matrix if $n = m$.

Symmetric matrix. If a square matrix **A** is the same as its transpose, **A** is called a symmetric matrix. In other words, a square matrix **A** is symmetric if **A**$' = $ **A**. For example,

$$\begin{bmatrix} 1 & 4 & 6 \\ 4 & 2 & 5 \\ 6 & 5 & 3 \end{bmatrix}$$

is a symmetric matrix.

Vector. An $n \times 1$ matrix is called an n-component column vector, and a $1 \times n$ matrix is called an n-component row vector. (A vector will be denoted by a boldface lowercase letter.) If **b** is a column vector, **b**$'$ (transpose of **b**) is a row vector. Normally, a vector with a prime (transpose sign) means a row vector and a vector without a prime signifies a column vector.

Diagonal matrix. Let **A** be as in (11.1.1) and suppose that $n = m$ (square matrix). Elements a_{11}, a_{22}, . . . , a_{nn} are called diagonal elements. The other elements are off-diagonal elements. A square matrix whose off-diagonal elements are all zero is called a diagonal matrix.

Identity matrix. An $n \times n$ diagonal matrix whose diagonal elements are all ones is called the identity matrix of size n and is denoted by $\mathbf{I}_n$. Sometimes it is more simply written as $\mathbf{I}$, if the size of the matrix is apparent from the context.

11.2 MATRIX OPERATIONS

Equality. If $\mathbf{A}$ and $\mathbf{B}$ are matrices of the same size and $\mathbf{A} = \{a_{ij}\}$ and $\mathbf{B} = \{b_{ij}\}$, then we write $\mathbf{A} = \mathbf{B}$ if and only if $a_{ij} = b_{ij}$ for every i and j.

Addition or subtraction. If $\mathbf{A}$ and $\mathbf{B}$ are matrices of the same size and $\mathbf{A} = \{a_{ij}\}$ and $\mathbf{B} = \{b_{ij}\}$, then $\mathbf{A} \pm \mathbf{B}$ is a matrix of the same size as $\mathbf{A}$ and $\mathbf{B}$ whose i, jth element is equal to $a_{ij} \pm b_{ij}$. For example, we have

$$\begin{bmatrix} a_{11} & a_{12} \\ a_{21} & a_{22} \end{bmatrix} \pm \begin{bmatrix} b_{11} & b_{12} \\ b_{21} & b_{22} \end{bmatrix} = \begin{bmatrix} a_{11} \pm b_{11} & a_{12} \pm b_{12} \\ a_{21} \pm b_{21} & a_{22} \pm b_{22} \end{bmatrix}.$$

Scalar multiplication. Let $\mathbf{A}$ be as in (11.1.1) and let c be a scalar (that is, a real number). Then, we define $c\mathbf{A}$ or $\mathbf{A}c$, the product of a scalar and a matrix, to be an $n \times m$ matrix whose i, jth element is ca_{ij}. In other words, every element of $\mathbf{A}$ is multiplied by c.

Matrix multiplication. Let $\mathbf{A}$ be an $n \times m$ matrix $\{a_{ij}\}$ as in (11.1.1) and let $\mathbf{B}$ be an $m \times r$ matrix $\{b_{ij}\}$. Then, $\mathbf{C} = \mathbf{AB}$ is an $n \times r$ matrix whose i, jth element c_{ij} is equal to $\Sigma_{k=1}^{m} a_{ik} b_{kj}$. From the definition it is clear that matrix multiplication is defined only when the number of columns of the first matrix is equal to the number of rows of the second matrix. The exception is when one of the matrices is a scalar—the case for which multiplication was previously defined. The following example illustrates the definition of matrix multiplication:

$$\begin{bmatrix} a_{11} & a_{12} & a_{13} \\ a_{21} & a_{22} & a_{23} \end{bmatrix} \begin{bmatrix} b_{11} & b_{12} \\ b_{21} & b_{22} \\ b_{31} & b_{32} \end{bmatrix} = \begin{bmatrix} a_{11}b_{11} + a_{12}b_{21} + a_{13}b_{31} & a_{11}b_{12} + a_{12}b_{22} + a_{13}b_{32} \\ a_{21}b_{11} + a_{22}b_{21} + a_{23}b_{31} & a_{21}b_{12} + a_{22}b_{22} + a_{23}b_{32} \end{bmatrix}.$$

If $\mathbf{A}$ and $\mathbf{B}$ are square matrices of the same size, both $\mathbf{AB}$ and $\mathbf{BA}$ are defined and are square matrices of the same size as $\mathbf{A}$ and $\mathbf{B}$. However, $\mathbf{AB}$ and $\mathbf{BA}$ are not in general equal. For example,

$$\begin{bmatrix} 1 & 2 \\ 0 & 1 \end{bmatrix} \begin{bmatrix} 3 & 1 \\ 1 & 2 \end{bmatrix} = \begin{bmatrix} 5 & 5 \\ 1 & 2 \end{bmatrix},$$

$$\begin{bmatrix} 3 & 1 \\ 1 & 2 \end{bmatrix} \begin{bmatrix} 1 & 2 \\ 0 & 1 \end{bmatrix} = \begin{bmatrix} 3 & 7 \\ 1 & 4 \end{bmatrix}.$$

In describing $\mathbf{AB}$, we may say either that $\mathbf{B}$ is premultiplied by $\mathbf{A}$, or that $\mathbf{A}$ is postmultiplied by $\mathbf{B}$.

Let $\mathbf{A}$ be an $n \times m$ matrix and let $\mathbf{I}_n$ and $\mathbf{I}_m$ be the identity matrices of size n and m, respectively. Then it is easy to show that $\mathbf{I}_n\mathbf{A} = \mathbf{A}$ and $\mathbf{AI}_m = \mathbf{A}$.

Let $\mathbf{a}'$ be a row vector $(a_1, a_2, \ldots, a_n)$ and let $\mathbf{b}$ be a column vector such that its transpose $\mathbf{b}' = (b_1, b_2, \ldots, b_n)$. Then, by the above rule of matrix multiplication, we have $\mathbf{a}'\mathbf{b} = \Sigma_{i=1}^n a_i b_i$, which is called the *vector product* of $\mathbf{a}$ and $\mathbf{b}$. Clearly, $\mathbf{a}'\mathbf{b} = \mathbf{b}'\mathbf{a}$. Vectors $\mathbf{a}$ and $\mathbf{b}$ are said to be *orthogonal* if $\mathbf{a}'\mathbf{b} = 0$. The vector product of $\mathbf{a}$ and itself, namely $\mathbf{a}'\mathbf{a}$, is called the *inner product* of $\mathbf{a}$.

The proof of the following useful theorem is simple and is left as an exercise.

THEOREM 11.2.1   If $\mathbf{AB}$ is defined, $(\mathbf{AB})' = \mathbf{B}'\mathbf{A}'$.

11.3   DETERMINANTS AND INVERSES

Throughout this section, all the matrices are square and $n \times n$.

Before we give a formal definition of the *determinant* of a square matrix, let us give some examples. The determinant of a 1×1 matrix, or a scalar, is the scalar itself. Consider a 2×2 matrix

$$\mathbf{A} = \begin{bmatrix} a_{11} & a_{12} \\ a_{21} & a_{22} \end{bmatrix}.$$

Its determinant, denoted by $|\mathbf{A}|$ or det $\mathbf{A}$, is defined by

(11.3.1) $|\mathbf{A}| = a_{11}a_{22} - a_{21}a_{12}.$

The determinant of a 3×3 matrix

$$\mathbf{A} = \begin{bmatrix} a_{11} & a_{12} & a_{13} \\ a_{21} & a_{22} & a_{23} \\ a_{31} & a_{32} & a_{33} \end{bmatrix}$$

is given by

$$
(11.3.2) \quad |\mathbf{A}| = a_{11} \begin{vmatrix} a_{22} & a_{23} \\ a_{32} & a_{33} \end{vmatrix} - a_{21} \begin{vmatrix} a_{12} & a_{13} \\ a_{32} & a_{33} \end{vmatrix} + a_{31} \begin{vmatrix} a_{12} & a_{13} \\ a_{22} & a_{23} \end{vmatrix}
$$

$$
= a_{11}a_{22}a_{33} - a_{11}a_{32}a_{23} - a_{21}a_{12}a_{33} + a_{21}a_{32}a_{13}
$$

$$
+ a_{31}a_{12}a_{23} - a_{31}a_{22}a_{13}.
$$

Now we present a formal definition, given inductively on the assumption that the *determinant* of an $(n - 1) \times (n - 1)$ matrix has already been defined.

DEFINITION 11.3.1   Let $\mathbf{A} = \{a_{ij}\}$ be an $n \times n$ matrix, and let $\mathbf{A}_{ij}$ be the $(n - 1) \times (n - 1)$ matrix obtained by deleting the ith row and the jth column from $\mathbf{A}$. Then we define the determinant of $\mathbf{A}$, denoted by $|\mathbf{A}|$, as

$$
(11.3.3) \quad |\mathbf{A}| = \sum_{i=1}^{n} (-1)^{i+j} a_{ij} |\mathbf{A}_{ij}|.
$$

The j above can be arbitrarily chosen as any integer 1 through n without changing the value of $|\mathbf{A}|$. The term $(-1)^{i+j}|\mathbf{A}_{ij}|$ is called the *cofactor* of the element a_{ij}.

Alternatively, the determinant may be defined as follows. First, we write $\mathbf{A}$ as a collection of its columns:

$$
(11.3.4) \quad \mathbf{A} = (\mathbf{a}_1, \mathbf{a}_2, \ldots, \mathbf{a}_n),
$$

where $\mathbf{a}_1, \mathbf{a}_2, \ldots, \mathbf{a}_n$ are $n \times 1$ column vectors. Consider a sequence of n numbers defined by the rule that the first number is an element of $\mathbf{a}_1$ (the first column of $\mathbf{A}$), the second number is an element of $\mathbf{a}_2$, and so on, chosen in such a way that none of the elements lie on the same row. One can define $n!$ distinct such sequences and denote the ith sequence, $i = 1$, $2, \ldots, n!$, by $[a_1(i), a_2(i), \ldots, a_n(i)]$. Let $r_1(i)$ be the row number of $a_1(i)$, and so on, and consider the sequence $[r_1(i), r_2(i), \ldots, r_n(i)]$. Let $N(i)$ be the smallest number of transpositions by which $[r_1(i), r_2(i), \ldots, r_n(i)]$ can be obtained from $[1, 2, \ldots, n]$. For example, in the case of a 3×3 matrix, $N = 0$ for the sequence (a_{11}, a_{22}, a_{33}), $N = 1$ for (a_{11}, a_{32}, a_{23}), and $N = 2$ for (a_{21}, a_{32}, a_{13}). Then we have

$$
(11.3.5) \quad |\mathbf{A}| = \sum_{i=1}^{n!} (-1)^{N(i)} a_1(i) a_2(i) \cdots a_n(i).
$$

Let us state several useful theorems concerning the determinant.

THEOREM 11.3.1 $|\mathbf{A}| = |\mathbf{A}'|$.

This theorem can be proved directly from (11.3.5). Because of the theorem, we may state all the results concerning the determinant in terms of the column vectors only as we have done in (11.3.3) and (11.3.5), since the same results would hold in terms of the row vectors.

THEOREM 11.3.2 If any column consists only of zeroes, the determinant is zero.

Theorem 11.3.2 follows immediately from (11.3.3). The determinant of a matrix in which any row is a zero vector is also zero because of Theorem 11.3.1.

THEOREM 11.3.3 If the two adjacent columns are interchanged, the determinant changes the sign.

The proof of this theorem is apparent from (11.3.5), since the effect of interchanging adjacent columns is either increasing or decreasing $N(i)$ by one. (As a corollary, we can easily prove the theorem without including the word "adjacent.")

THEOREM 11.3.4 If any two columns are identical, the determinant is zero.

This theorem follows immediately from Theorem 11.3.3.

THEOREM 11.3.5 $|\mathbf{AB}| = |\mathbf{A}|\,|\mathbf{B}|$ if $\mathbf{A}$ and $\mathbf{B}$ are square matrices of the same size.

The proof of Theorem 11.3.5 is rather involved, but can be directly derived from Definition 11.3.1.

We now define the inverse of a square matrix, but only for a matrix with a nonzero determinant.

DEFINITION 11.3.2 The *inverse* of a matrix $\mathbf{A}$, denoted by $\mathbf{A}^{-1}$, is the matrix defined by

$$(11.3.6) \qquad \mathbf{A}^{-1} = \frac{1}{|\mathbf{A}|} \{(-1)^{i+j}|\mathbf{A}_{ij}|\},$$

provided that $|\mathbf{A}| \neq 0$. Here $(-1)^{i+j}|\mathbf{A}_{ij}|$ is the cofactor of a_{ij} as given in Definition 11.3.1, and $\{(-1)^{i+j}|\mathbf{A}_{ij}|\}$ is the matrix whose i, jth element is $(-1)^{i+j}|\mathbf{A}_{ij}|$.

The use of the word "inverse" is justified by the following theorem.

THEOREM 11.3.6 $\mathbf{A}^{-1}\mathbf{A} = \mathbf{A}\mathbf{A}^{-1} = \mathbf{I}$ for any matrix $\mathbf{A}$ such that $|\mathbf{A}| \neq 0$.

This theorem can be easily proved from Definitions 11.3.1 and 11.3.2 and Theorem 11.3.4. It implies that if $\mathbf{AB} = \mathbf{I}$, then $\mathbf{B} = \mathbf{A}^{-1}$ and $\mathbf{B}^{-1} = \mathbf{A}$.

THEOREM 11.3.7 If $\mathbf{A}$ and $\mathbf{B}$ are square matrices of the same size such that $|\mathbf{A}| \neq 0$ and $|\mathbf{B}| \neq 0$, then $(\mathbf{AB})^{-1} = \mathbf{B}^{-1}\mathbf{A}^{-1}$.

The theorem follows immediately from the identity $\mathbf{ABB}^{-1}\mathbf{A}^{-1} = \mathbf{I}$.

THEOREM 11.3.8 Let $\mathbf{A}$, $\mathbf{B}$, $\mathbf{C}$, and $\mathbf{D}$ be matrices such that

$$\begin{bmatrix} \mathbf{A} & \mathbf{B} \\ \mathbf{C} & \mathbf{D} \end{bmatrix}$$

is square and $|\mathbf{D}| \neq 0$. (Note that $\mathbf{A}$ and $\mathbf{D}$ must be square, but $\mathbf{B}$ and $\mathbf{C}$ need not be.) Then

$$(11.3.7) \qquad \det \begin{bmatrix} \mathbf{A} & \mathbf{B} \\ \mathbf{C} & \mathbf{D} \end{bmatrix} = |\mathbf{D}| \, |\mathbf{A} - \mathbf{BD}^{-1}\mathbf{C}|.$$

Proof. We have

$$(11.3.8) \qquad \begin{bmatrix} \mathbf{I} & -\mathbf{BD}^{-1} \\ \mathbf{0} & \mathbf{I} \end{bmatrix} \begin{bmatrix} \mathbf{A} & \mathbf{B} \\ \mathbf{C} & \mathbf{D} \end{bmatrix} = \begin{bmatrix} \mathbf{A} - \mathbf{BD}^{-1}\mathbf{C} & \mathbf{0} \\ \mathbf{C} & \mathbf{D} \end{bmatrix},$$

where $\mathbf{0}$ denotes a matrix of appropriate size which consists entirely of zeroes. We can ascertain from (11.3.5) that the determinant of the first matrix of the left-hand side of (11.3.8) is unity and the determinant of the right-hand side of (11.3.8) is equal to $|\mathbf{A} - \mathbf{BD}^{-1}\mathbf{C}|\,|\mathbf{D}|$. Therefore, taking the determinant of both sides of (11.3.8) and using Theorem 11.3.5 yields (11.3.7). ❑

THEOREM 11.3.9

$$\begin{bmatrix} \mathbf{A} & \mathbf{B} \\ \mathbf{C} & \mathbf{D} \end{bmatrix}^{-1} = \begin{bmatrix} \mathbf{E}^{-1} & -\mathbf{E}^{-1}\mathbf{BD}^{-1} \\ -\mathbf{D}^{-1}\mathbf{CE}^{-1} & \mathbf{F}^{-1} \end{bmatrix},$$

where $\mathbf{E} = \mathbf{A} - \mathbf{BD}^{-1}\mathbf{C}$, $\mathbf{F} = \mathbf{D} - \mathbf{CA}^{-1}\mathbf{B}$, $\mathbf{E}^{-1} = \mathbf{A}^{-1} + \mathbf{A}^{-1}\mathbf{BF}^{-1}\mathbf{CA}^{-1}$, and $\mathbf{F}^{-1} = \mathbf{D}^{-1} + \mathbf{D}^{-1}\mathbf{CE}^{-1}\mathbf{BD}^{-1}$, provided that the inverse on the left-hand side exists.

Proof. To prove this theorem, simply premultiply both sides by

$$\begin{bmatrix} \mathbf{A} & \mathbf{B} \\ \mathbf{C} & \mathbf{D} \end{bmatrix}. \quad ❑$$

11.4 SIMULTANEOUS LINEAR EQUATIONS

Throughout this section, $\mathbf{A}$ will denote an $n \times n$ square matrix and $\mathbf{X}$ a matrix that is not necessarily square. Generally, we shall assume that $\mathbf{X}$ is $n \times K$ with $K \leq n$.

Consider the following n linear equations:

$$a_{11}x_1 + a_{12}x_2 + \cdots + a_{1n}x_n = y_1$$
$$a_{21}x_1 + a_{22}x_2 + \cdots + a_{2n}x_n = y_2$$

(11.4.1)

$$\cdot$$
$$\cdot$$
$$\cdot$$

$$a_{n1}x_1 + a_{n2}x_2 + \cdots + a_{nn}x_n = y_n$$

Define $\mathbf{x} = (x_1, x_2, \ldots, x_n)'$ and $\mathbf{y} = (y_1, y_2, \ldots, y_n)'$ and let $\mathbf{A}$ be as in (11.1.1) with $n = m$. Then (11.4.1) can be written in matrix notation as

(11.4.2) $\mathbf{Ax} = \mathbf{y}.$

A major goal of this section is to obtain a necessary and sufficient condition on **A** such that (11.4.2) can be solved in terms of **x** for any **y**. Using the notation $\exists$ (there exists), $\forall$ (for any), and s.t. (such that), we can express the last clause of the previous sentence as

$$\forall \, \mathbf{y} \; \exists \, \mathbf{x} \text{ s.t. } \mathbf{Ax} = \mathbf{y}.$$

Let us consider a couple of examples. The matrix

(11.4.3)
$$\begin{bmatrix} 1 & 2 \\ 2 & 4 \end{bmatrix}$$

does not satisfy the above-mentioned condition because there is clearly no solution to the linear system

(11.4.4)
$$\begin{bmatrix} 1 & 2 \\ 2 & 4 \end{bmatrix} \begin{bmatrix} x_1 \\ x_2 \end{bmatrix} = \begin{bmatrix} 1 \\ 1 \end{bmatrix}.$$

But there are infinite solutions to the system

(11.4.5)
$$\begin{bmatrix} 1 & 2 \\ 2 & 4 \end{bmatrix} \begin{bmatrix} x_1 \\ x_2 \end{bmatrix} = \begin{bmatrix} 1 \\ 2 \end{bmatrix},$$

since any point on the line $x_1 + 2x_2 = 1$ satisfies (11.4.5). In general, if **A** is such that $\mathbf{Ax} = \mathbf{y}$ has no solution for some **y**, it has infinite solutions for some other **y**.

Next consider

(11.4.6)
$$\begin{bmatrix} 1 & 1 \\ 1 & 2 \end{bmatrix}.$$

This matrix satisfies the condition because $x_1 = 2y_1 - y_2$, $x_2 = y_2 - y_1$ constitute the unique solution to

(11.4.7)
$$\begin{bmatrix} 1 & 1 \\ 1 & 2 \end{bmatrix} \begin{bmatrix} x_1 \\ x_2 \end{bmatrix} = \begin{bmatrix} y_1 \\ y_2 \end{bmatrix}$$

for any y_1 and y_2. It can be shown that if **A** satisfies the said condition, the solution to $\mathbf{Ax} = \mathbf{y}$ is unique.

We now embark on a general discussion, in which the major results are given as a series of definitions and theorems.

DEFINITION 11.4.1   A set of vectors $\mathbf{x}_1, \mathbf{x}_2, \ldots, \mathbf{x}_K$ is said to be *linearly independent* if $\Sigma_{i=1}^{K} c_i \mathbf{x}_i = 0$ implies $c_i = 0$ for all $i = 1, 2, \ldots, K$. Otherwise it is *linearly dependent*.

For example, the vectors $(1, 1)$ and $(1, 2)$ are linearly independent because

$$c_1 \begin{bmatrix} 1 \\ 1 \end{bmatrix} + c_2 \begin{bmatrix} 1 \\ 2 \end{bmatrix} = \begin{bmatrix} 0 \\ 0 \end{bmatrix}$$

only for $c_1 = c_2 = 0$. But $(1, 2)$ and $(2, 4)$ are linearly dependent because

$$c_1 \begin{bmatrix} 1 \\ 2 \end{bmatrix} + c_2 \begin{bmatrix} 2 \\ 4 \end{bmatrix} = \begin{bmatrix} 0 \\ 0 \end{bmatrix}$$

can be satisfied by setting $c_1 = -2$ and $c_2 = 1$.

DEFINITION 11.4.2 If the column vectors of a matrix (not necessarily square) are linearly independent, we say the matrix is *column independent* (abbreviated as CI); if the row vectors are linearly independent, we say the matrix is *row independent* (RI).

THEOREM 11.4.1 $\mathbf{A}$ is not CI $\Rightarrow |\mathbf{A}| = 0$.

Proof. Write $\mathbf{A} = (\mathbf{a}_1, \mathbf{a}_2, \ldots, \mathbf{a}_n)$ and $|\mathbf{A}| = F(\mathbf{a}_1, \mathbf{a}_2, \ldots, \mathbf{a}_n)$. Since $\mathbf{A}$ is not CI, there is a vector $\mathbf{x} \neq \mathbf{0}$ such that $\mathbf{Ax} = \mathbf{0}$. But $\mathbf{x} \neq \mathbf{0}$ means that at least one element of $\mathbf{x}$ is nonzero. Assume $x_1 \neq 0$ without loss of generality, where x_1 is the first element of $\mathbf{x}$. From Definition 11.3.1, we have

$$(11.4.8) \quad F(\mathbf{Ax}, \mathbf{a}_2, \ldots, \mathbf{a}_n) = x_1 |\mathbf{A}| + x_2 F(\mathbf{a}_2, \mathbf{a}_2, \mathbf{a}_3, \ldots, \mathbf{a}_n)$$
$$+ x_3 F(\mathbf{a}_3, \mathbf{a}_2, \mathbf{a}_3, \ldots, \mathbf{a}_n) + \cdots$$
$$+ x_n F(\mathbf{a}_n, \mathbf{a}_2, \mathbf{a}_3, \ldots, \mathbf{a}_n).$$

But the left-hand side of (11.4.8) is zero by Theorem 11.3.2 and the right-hand side is $x_1 |\mathbf{A}|$ by Theorem 11.3.4. Therefore $|\mathbf{A}| = 0$. ❑

The converse of Theorem 11.4.1, stated below as Theorem 11.4.5, is more difficult to prove; therefore, we prove three other theorems first.

THEOREM 11.4.2 If $\mathbf{X}'$ is $K \times n$, where $K < n$, $\mathbf{X}'$ is not CI.

Proof. Assume $K = n - 1$ without loss of generality, for otherwise we can affix $n - 1 - K$ row vectors of zeroes at the bottom of $\mathbf{X}'$. We prove the theorem by induction.

The theorem is clearly true for $n = 2$. Assume that it is true for n, and consider $n + 1$. Is there a vector $\mathbf{c} \neq \mathbf{0}$ such that $\mathbf{X'c} = \mathbf{0}$, where $\mathbf{X'}$ is $n \times (n + 1)$ and $\mathbf{c} = (c_1, c_2, \ldots, c_{n+1})'$? Write the nth row of $\mathbf{X'}$ as $(x_{n1}, x_{n2}, \ldots, x_{n,n+1})$ and assume without loss of generality that $x_{n,n+1} \neq 0$. Solving the last equation of $\mathbf{X'c} = \mathbf{0}$ for c_{n+1} and inserting its value into the remaining equations yields $n - 1$ equations for which the theorem was assumed to hold. So the prescribed $\mathbf{c}$ exists. $\square$

THEOREM 11.4.3 $\mathbf{A}$ is CI $\Rightarrow \forall\, \mathbf{y}\, \exists\, \mathbf{x}$ s.t. $\mathbf{Ax} = \mathbf{y}$.

Proof. Using the matrix $(\mathbf{A}, \mathbf{y})$ as $\mathbf{X'}$ in Theorem 11.4.2 shows that $(\mathbf{A}, \mathbf{y})$ is not CI. Therefore there exists $\mathbf{c} \neq \mathbf{0}$ such that $(\mathbf{A}, \mathbf{y})\mathbf{c} = \mathbf{0}$. Since $\mathbf{A}$ is CI, the coefficient on $\mathbf{y}$ in $\mathbf{c}$ is nonzero and solving for $\mathbf{y}$ yields $\mathbf{Ax} = \mathbf{y}$. $\square$

THEOREM 11.4.4 $|\mathbf{A}| \neq 0 \Leftrightarrow \forall\, \mathbf{y}\, \exists\, \mathbf{x}$ s.t. $\mathbf{Ax} = \mathbf{y}$.

Proof. ($\Rightarrow$) If $|\mathbf{A}| \neq 0$, $\mathbf{A}^{-1}$ exists by Definition 11.3.2. Set $\mathbf{x} = \mathbf{A}^{-1}\mathbf{y}$. Premultiplying both sides by $\mathbf{A}$ yields $\mathbf{Ax} = \mathbf{y}$ because of Theorem 11.3.6.
($\Leftarrow$) Let $\mathbf{e}_i$ be a column vector with 1 in the ith position and 0 everywhere else. Then $\mathbf{Ax}_1 = \mathbf{e}_1$, $\mathbf{Ax}_2 = \mathbf{e}_2, \ldots, \mathbf{Ax}_n = \mathbf{e}_n$ may be summarized as $\mathbf{AX} = \mathbf{I}$ by setting $\mathbf{X} = (\mathbf{x}_1, \mathbf{x}_2, \ldots, \mathbf{x}_n)$ and noting that $(\mathbf{e}_1, \mathbf{e}_2, \ldots, \mathbf{e}_n) = \mathbf{I}$. Since $|\mathbf{I}| = 1$, $|\mathbf{A}| \neq 0$ follows from Theorem 11.3.5. $\square$

Combining Theorems 11.4.3 and 11.4.4 immediately yields the converse of Theorem 11.4.1, namely,

THEOREM 11.4.5 $\mathbf{A}$ is CI $\Rightarrow |\mathbf{A}| \neq 0$.

From the results derived thus far, we conclude that the following five statements are equivalent:

$|\mathbf{A}| \neq 0$.

$\mathbf{A}^{-1}$ exists.

$\mathbf{A}$ is CI.

$\mathbf{A}$ is RI.

$\forall\, \mathbf{y}\, \exists\, \mathbf{x}$ s.t. $\mathbf{Ax} = \mathbf{y}$.

DEFINITION 11.4.3   If any of the above five statements holds, we say $\mathbf{A}$ is *nonsingular.*

If $\mathbf{A}$ is nonsingular, we can solve (11.4.2) for $\mathbf{x}$ as $\mathbf{x} = \mathbf{A}^{-1}\mathbf{y}$. An alternative solution is given by *Cramer's rule.* In this method x_i, the ith element of $\mathbf{x}$, is determined by

$$(11.4.9) \qquad x_i = \frac{|\mathbf{B}_i|}{|\mathbf{A}|},$$

where $\mathbf{B}_i$ is the $n \times n$ matrix obtained by replacing the ith column of $\mathbf{A}$ by the vector $\mathbf{y}$.

The remainder of this section is concerned with the relationship between nonsingularity and the concept called *full rank*; see Definition 11.4.5 below.

DEFINITION 11.4.4   For an arbitrary matrix $\mathbf{X}$, we denote the maximal number of linearly independent column vectors of $\mathbf{X}$ by $CR(\mathbf{X})$ (read "*column rank* of $\mathbf{X}$") and the maximal number of linearly independent row vectors of $\mathbf{X}$ by $RR(\mathbf{X})$ (read "*row rank* of $\mathbf{X}$").

THEOREM 11.4.6   Let an $n \times K$ matrix $\mathbf{X}$, where $K \leq n$, be CI. Then, $RR(\mathbf{X}) = K$.

Proof. $RR(\mathbf{X}) > K$ contradicts Theorem 11.4.2. If $RR(\mathbf{X}) < K$, there exists a vector $\boldsymbol{\alpha} \neq \mathbf{0}$ such that $\mathbf{X}\boldsymbol{\alpha} = \mathbf{0}$ because of Theorem 11.4.2; but this contradicts the assumption that $\mathbf{X}$ is CI.   ❑

THEOREM 11.4.7 $CR(\mathbf{X}) = RR(\mathbf{X})$.

Proof.   Suppose that $\mathbf{X}$ is $n \times K$, $K \leq n$, and $CR(\mathbf{X}) = r \leq K$. Let $\mathbf{X}_1$ consist of a subset of the column vectors of $\mathbf{X}$ such that $\mathbf{X}_1$ is $n \times r$ and CI. Then by Theorem 11.4.6, $RR(\mathbf{X}_1) = r$. Let $\mathbf{X}_{11}$ consist of a subset of the row vectors of $\mathbf{X}_1$ such that $\mathbf{X}_{11}$ is $r \times r$ and RI. Then $(\mathbf{X}_{11}, \mathbf{Y})$ is RI, where $\mathbf{Y}$ is an arbitrary $r \times (K - r)$ matrix. Therefore $RR(\mathbf{X}) \geq CR(\mathbf{X})$. By reversing the rows and columns in the above argument, we can similarly show $RR(\mathbf{X}) \leq CR(\mathbf{X})$.   ❑

DEFINITION 11.4.5 $CR(\mathbf{X})$ or, equivalently, $RR(\mathbf{X})$, is called the *rank* of $\mathbf{X}$. If $\text{rank}(\mathbf{X}) = \min(\text{number of rows, number of columns})$, we say $\mathbf{X}$ is *full rank.* Note that a square matrix is full rank if and only if it is nonsingular.

THEOREM 11.4.8 An $n \times K$ matrix $\mathbf{X}$, where $K \le n$, is full rank if and only if $\mathbf{X}'\mathbf{X}$ is nonsingular.

Proof. To prove the "only if" part, note that $\mathbf{X}'\mathbf{Xc} = \mathbf{0} \Rightarrow \mathbf{c}'\mathbf{X}'\mathbf{Xc} = 0$ $\Rightarrow \mathbf{c} = \mathbf{0}$. To prove the "if" part, note that $\mathbf{Xc} = \mathbf{0} \Rightarrow \mathbf{X}'\mathbf{Xc} = \mathbf{0} \Rightarrow \mathbf{c} = \mathbf{0}$. ❑

THEOREM 11.4.9 Let an $n \times K$ matrix $\mathbf{X}$ be full rank, where $K < n$. Then there exists an $n \times (n - K)$ matrix $\mathbf{Z}$ such that $(\mathbf{X}, \mathbf{Z})$ is nonsingular and $\mathbf{X}'\mathbf{Z} = \mathbf{0}$.

Proof. Because of Theorem 11.4.2, there exists a vector $\mathbf{z}_1 \ne \mathbf{0}$ such that $\mathbf{X}'\mathbf{z}_1 = \mathbf{0}$. By the same theorem, there exists a vector $\mathbf{z}_2 \ne \mathbf{0}$ such that $(\mathbf{X}, \mathbf{z}_1)'\mathbf{z}_2 = \mathbf{0}$, and so on. Collect these $n - K$ vectors and define $\mathbf{Z}$ as $(\mathbf{z}_1, \mathbf{z}_2, \dots, \mathbf{z}_{n-K})$. Clearly, $\mathbf{X}'\mathbf{Z} = \mathbf{0}$. We have

$$(11.4.10) \qquad \begin{bmatrix} \mathbf{X}' \\ \mathbf{Z}' \end{bmatrix} (\mathbf{X}, \mathbf{Z}) = \begin{bmatrix} \mathbf{X}'\mathbf{X} & \mathbf{0} \\ \mathbf{0} & \mathbf{D} \end{bmatrix},$$

where $\mathbf{D} = \mathbf{Z}'\mathbf{Z}$ is a diagonal matrix. Therefore, by Theorems 11.3.1 and 11.3.5,

$$(11.4.11) \qquad |(\mathbf{X}, \mathbf{Z})|^2 = |\mathbf{X}'\mathbf{X}| \, |\mathbf{D}|.$$

But since $|\mathbf{X}'\mathbf{X}| \ne 0$ and $|\mathbf{D}| \ne 0$, $|(\mathbf{X}, \mathbf{Z})| \ne 0$. ❑

THEOREM 11.4.10 Let $\mathbf{X}$ be a matrix not necessarily square, and suppose that there exists an $n \times (n - K)$ matrix $\mathbf{Z}$ of rank $n - K$ such that $\mathbf{Z}'\mathbf{X} = \mathbf{0}$. Then $\text{rank}(\mathbf{X}) \le K$. If $\mathbf{W}'\mathbf{X} = \mathbf{0}$ for some matrix $\mathbf{W}$ with n columns implies that $\text{rank}(\mathbf{W}) \le n - K$, then $\text{rank}(\mathbf{X}) = K$.

Proof. Suppose $\text{rank}(\mathbf{X}) = r > K$. Let $\mathbf{S}$ be r linearly independent columns of $\mathbf{X}$. Suppose $\mathbf{Sc} + \mathbf{Zd} = \mathbf{0}$ for some vectors $\mathbf{c}$ and $\mathbf{d}$. Premultiplying by $\mathbf{S}'$ yields $\mathbf{S}'\mathbf{Sc} = \mathbf{0}$. Therefore, by Theorem 11.4.8, $\mathbf{c} = \mathbf{0}$. Premultiplying by $\mathbf{Z}'$ yields $\mathbf{Z}'\mathbf{Zd} = \mathbf{0}$. Again by Theorem 11.4.8, $\mathbf{d} = \mathbf{0}$. Then $CR[(\mathbf{X}, \mathbf{Z})] > n$, which is a contradiction.

Next, suppose that $\text{rank}(\mathbf{X}) = r < K$. Let $\mathbf{S}$ be as defined above. Then, by Theorem 11.4.9, there exists an $n \times (n - r)$ matrix $\mathbf{W}$ such that $\mathbf{S'W} = \mathbf{0}$ and rank$(\mathbf{W}) = n - r$. But this contradicts the assumption of the theorem. Therefore, rank$(\mathbf{X}) = K$. ❑

THEOREM 11.4.11   For any matrix $\mathbf{X}$ not necessarily square, rank$(\mathbf{BX}) =$ rank$(\mathbf{X})$ if $\mathbf{B}$ is nonsingular (NS).

Proof.   Let rank$(\mathbf{BX})$ and rank$(\mathbf{X})$ be r_1 and r_2, respectively. By Theorem 11.4.9 there exists a full-rank $(n - r_1) \times n$ matrix $\mathbf{Z}'$ such that $\mathbf{Z'BX} = \mathbf{0}$. Since $\mathbf{B}$ is NS, $\mathbf{Z'B}$ is also full rank. (To see this, suppose that $\boldsymbol{\alpha}'\mathbf{Z'B} = \mathbf{0}$ for some $\boldsymbol{\alpha}$. Then $\boldsymbol{\alpha}'\mathbf{Z}' = \mathbf{0}$ because $\mathbf{B}$ is NS. But this implies that $\boldsymbol{\alpha} = \mathbf{0}$, since $\mathbf{Z}$ is full rank.) Therefore $r_2 \leq r_1$ by the first part of Theorem 11.4.10. Also by Theorem 11.4.9, there exists a full-rank $(n - r_2) \times n$ matrix $\mathbf{Y}'$ such that $\mathbf{Y'X} = \mathbf{0}$. We can write $\mathbf{Y'X} = \mathbf{Y'B}^{-1}\mathbf{BX}$. Clearly, $\mathbf{Y'B}^{-1}$ is full rank. Therefore $r_1 \leq r_2$ and $r_1 = r_2$. ❑

11.5 PROPERTIES OF THE SYMMETRIC MATRIX

Now we shall study the properties of symmetric matrices, which play a major role in multivariate statistical analysis. Throughout this section, $\mathbf{A}$ will denote an $n \times n$ symmetric matrix and $\mathbf{X}$ a matrix that is not necessarily square. We shall often assume that $\mathbf{X}$ is $n \times K$ with $K \leq n$.

The following theorem about the diagonalization of a symmetric matrix is central to this section.

THEOREM 11.5.1   For any symmetric matrix $\mathbf{A}$, there exists an *orthogonal matrix* $\mathbf{H}$ (that is, a square matrix satisfying $\mathbf{H'H} = \mathbf{I}$) such that

$$(11.5.1) \quad \mathbf{H'AH} = \boldsymbol{\Lambda},$$

where $\boldsymbol{\Lambda}$ is a diagonal matrix. The diagonal elements of $\boldsymbol{\Lambda}$ are called the *characteristic roots* (or *eigenvalues*) of $\mathbf{A}$. The ith column of $\mathbf{H}$ is called the *characteristic vector* (or *eigenvector*) of $\mathbf{A}$ corresponding to the characteristic root of $\mathbf{A}$, which is the ith diagonal element of $\boldsymbol{\Lambda}$.

Proof.   See Bellman (1970, p. 54).

Note that $\mathbf{H}$ and $\boldsymbol{\Lambda}$ are not uniquely determined for a given symmetric matrix $\mathbf{A}$, since $\mathbf{H'AH} = \boldsymbol{\Lambda}$ would still hold if we changed the order of the diagonal elements of $\boldsymbol{\Lambda}$ and the order of the corresponding columns of

H. The set of the characteristic roots of a given matrix is unique, however, if we ignore the order in which they are arranged.

Theorem 11.5.1 is important in that it establishes a close relationship between matrix operations and scalar operations. For example, the inverse of a matrix defined in Definition 11.3.2 is related to the usual inverse of a scalar in the following sense. Premultiplying and postmultiplying (11.5.1) by $\mathbf{H}$ and $\mathbf{H}'$ respectively, and noting that $\mathbf{HH}' = \mathbf{H}'\mathbf{H} = \mathbf{I}$, we obtain

(11.5.2) $\mathbf{A} = \mathbf{H\Lambda H}'.$

Inverting both sides of (11.5.2) and using Theorem 11.3.7 yields

(11.5.3) $\mathbf{A}^{-1} = \mathbf{H\Lambda}^{-1}\mathbf{H}',$

since $\mathbf{H}'\mathbf{H} = \mathbf{I}$ implies $\mathbf{H}^{-1} = \mathbf{H}'$. Denote $\mathbf{\Lambda}$ by $\mathbf{D}(\lambda_i)$, indicating that it is a diagonal matrix with λ_i in the ith diagonal position. Then clearly $\mathbf{\Lambda}^{-1} = \mathbf{D}(\lambda_i^{-1})$. Thus the orthogonal diagonalization (11.5.1) has enabled us to reduce the calculation of the matrix inversion to that of the ordinary scalar inversion.

More generally, a matrix operation $f(\mathbf{A})$ can be reduced to the corresponding scalar operation by the formula

(11.5.4) $f(\mathbf{A}) = \mathbf{H}\mathbf{D}[f(\lambda_i)]\mathbf{H}'.$

The reader should verify, for example, that

(11.5.5) $\mathbf{A}^2(\equiv\mathbf{AA}) = \mathbf{H}\mathbf{D}(\lambda_i^2)\mathbf{H}'.$

Given a symmetric matrix $\mathbf{A}$, how can we find $\mathbf{\Lambda}$ and $\mathbf{H}$? The following theorem will aid us.

THEOREM 11.5.2 Let λ be a characteristic root of $\mathbf{A}$ and let $\mathbf{h}$ be the corresponding characteristic vector. Then,

(11.5.6) $\mathbf{Ah} = \lambda\mathbf{h}$

and

(11.5.7) $|\mathbf{A} - \lambda\mathbf{I}| = 0.$

Proof. Premultiplying (11.5.1) by $\mathbf{H}$ yields

(11.5.8) $\mathbf{AH} = \mathbf{H\Lambda}.$

Singling out the ith column of both sides of (11.5.8) yields $\mathbf{Ah}_i = \lambda_i \mathbf{h}_i$, where λ_i is the ith diagonal element of $\mathbf{\Lambda}$ and $\mathbf{h}_i$ is the ith column of $\mathbf{H}$. This proves (11.5.6). Writing (11.5.6) as $(\mathbf{A} - \lambda \mathbf{I})\mathbf{h} = \mathbf{0}$ and using Theorem 11.4.1 proves (11.5.7).   ❑

Let us find the characteristic roots and vectors of the matrix

$$\begin{bmatrix} 1 & 2 \\ 2 & 1 \end{bmatrix}.$$

By (11.5.7) we have

$$\begin{vmatrix} 1-\lambda & 2 \\ 2 & 1-\lambda \end{vmatrix} = (1-\lambda)^2 - 4 = 0.$$

Therefore the characteristic roots are 3 and -1. Solving

$$\begin{bmatrix} 1 & 2 \\ 2 & 1 \end{bmatrix}\begin{bmatrix} x_1 \\ x_2 \end{bmatrix} = 3\begin{bmatrix} x_1 \\ x_2 \end{bmatrix} \quad \text{and} \quad x_1^2 + x_2^2 = 1$$

simultaneously for x_1 and x_2, we obtain $x_1 = x_2 = \sqrt{2}^{-1}$. Solving

$$\begin{bmatrix} 1 & 2 \\ 2 & 1 \end{bmatrix}\begin{bmatrix} y_1 \\ y_2 \end{bmatrix} = (-1)\begin{bmatrix} y_1 \\ y_2 \end{bmatrix} \quad \text{and} \quad y_1^2 + y_2^2 = 1$$

simultaneously for y_1 and y_2, we obtain $y_1 = \sqrt{2}^{-1}$ and $y_2 = -\sqrt{2}^{-1}$. ($y_1 = -\sqrt{2}^{-1}$ and $y_2 = \sqrt{2}^{-1}$ also constitute a solution.) The diagonalization (11.5.1) can be written in this case as

$$\begin{bmatrix} \dfrac{1}{\sqrt{2}} & \dfrac{1}{\sqrt{2}} \\ \dfrac{1}{\sqrt{2}} & -\dfrac{1}{\sqrt{2}} \end{bmatrix}\begin{bmatrix} 1 & 2 \\ 2 & 1 \end{bmatrix}\begin{bmatrix} \dfrac{1}{\sqrt{2}} & \dfrac{1}{\sqrt{2}} \\ \dfrac{1}{\sqrt{2}} & -\dfrac{1}{\sqrt{2}} \end{bmatrix} = \begin{bmatrix} 3 & 0 \\ 0 & -1 \end{bmatrix}.$$

The characteristic roots of any square matrix can be also defined by (11.5.7). From this definition some of the theorems presented below hold for general square matrices. Whenever we speak of the characteristic roots of a matrix, the reader may assume that the matrix in question is symmetric. Even when a theorem holds for a general square matrix, we shall prove it only for symmetric matrices.

The following are useful theorems concerning characteristic roots.

THEOREM 11.5.3 The rank of a square matrix is equal to the number of its nonzero characteristic roots.

Proof. We shall prove the theorem for an $n \times n$ symmetric matrix **A**. Suppose that n_1 of the roots are nonzero. Using (11.5.2), we have

$$\text{rank}(\mathbf{A}) = \text{rank}(\mathbf{H}\boldsymbol{\Lambda}\mathbf{H}')$$

$$= \text{rank}(\boldsymbol{\Lambda}\mathbf{H}') \quad \text{by Theorem 11.4.11}$$

$$= \text{rank}(\mathbf{H}\boldsymbol{\Lambda}) \quad \text{by Theorem 11.4.7}$$

$$= \text{rank}(\boldsymbol{\Lambda}) \quad \text{by Theorem 11.4.11}$$

$$= n_1. \quad \square$$

THEOREM 11.5.4 For any matrices **X** and **Y** not necessarily square, the nonzero characteristic roots of **XY** and **YX** are the same, whenever both **XY** and **YX** are defined.

Proof. See Bellman (1970, p. 96).

THEOREM 11.5.5 Let **A** and **B** be symmetric matrices of the same size. Then **A** and **B** can be diagonalized by the same orthogonal matrix if and only if **AB** = **BA**.

Proof. See Bellman (1970, p. 56).

THEOREM 11.5.6 Let λ_1 and λ_n be the largest and the smallest characteristic roots, respectively, of an $n \times n$ symmetric matrix **A**. Then for every nonzero n-component vector **x**,

$$(11.5.9) \quad \lambda_1 \geq \frac{\mathbf{x}'\mathbf{A}\mathbf{x}}{\mathbf{x}'\mathbf{x}} \geq \lambda_n.$$

Proof. Using (11.5.1) and $\mathbf{HH}' = \mathbf{I}$, we have

$$(11.5.10) \quad \frac{\mathbf{x}'\mathbf{A}\mathbf{x}}{\mathbf{x}'\mathbf{x}} = \frac{\mathbf{x}'\mathbf{HH}'\mathbf{AHH}'\mathbf{x}}{\mathbf{x}'\mathbf{HH}'\mathbf{x}} = \frac{\mathbf{z}'\boldsymbol{\Lambda}\mathbf{z}}{\mathbf{z}'\mathbf{z}},$$

where $z = H'x$. The inequalities (11.5.9) follow from $z'(\lambda_1 I - \Lambda)z \geq 0$ and $z'(\Lambda - \lambda_n I)z \geq 0$. ❑

Each characteristic root of a matrix can be regarded as a real function of the matrix which captures certain characteristics of that matrix. The determinant of a matrix, which we examined in Section 11.3, is another important scalar representation of a matrix. The following theorem establishes a close connection between the two concepts.

THEOREM 11.5.7 The determinant of a square matrix is the product of its characteristic roots.

Proof. We shall prove the theorem only for a symmetric matrix A. Taking the determinant of both sides of (11.5.2) and using Theorems 11.3.1 and 11.3.5 yields $|A| = |H|^2|\Lambda|$. Similarly, $H'H = I$ implies $|H| = 1$. Therefore $|A| = |\Lambda|$, which implies the theorem, since the determinant of a diagonal matrix is the product of the diagonal elements. ❑

We now define another important scalar representation of a square matrix called the *trace*.

DEFINITION 11.5.1 The trace of a square matrix, denoted by the notation tr, is defined as the sum of the diagonal elements of the matrix.

The following useful theorem can be proved directly from the definition of matrix multiplication.

THEOREM 11.5.8 Let X and Y be any matrices, not necessarily square, such that XY and YX are both defined. Then, tr XY = tr YX.

There is a close connection between the trace and the characteristic roots.

THEOREM 11.5.9 The trace of a square matrix is the sum of its characteristic roots.

Proof. We shall prove the theorem only for a symmetric matrix A. Using (11.5.2) and Theorem 11.5.8, we have

(11.5.11) $\operatorname{tr} \mathbf{A} = \operatorname{tr} \mathbf{H} \boldsymbol{\Lambda} \mathbf{H}' = \operatorname{tr} \boldsymbol{\Lambda} \mathbf{H}' \mathbf{H} = \operatorname{tr} \boldsymbol{\Lambda}.$ ❑

We now introduce an important concept called *positive definiteness*, which plays an important role in statistics. We deal only with symmetric matrices.

DEFINITION 11.5.2   If $\mathbf{A}$ is an $n \times n$ symmetric matrix, $\mathbf{A}$ is *positive definite* if $\mathbf{x}'\mathbf{A}\mathbf{x} > 0$ for every n-vector $\mathbf{x}$ such that $\mathbf{x} \neq \mathbf{0}$. If $\mathbf{x}'\mathbf{A}\mathbf{x} \geq 0$, we say that $\mathbf{A}$ is *nonnegative definite* or *positive semidefinite*. (*Negative definite* and *nonpositive definite* or *negative semidefinite* are similarly defined.)

If $\mathbf{A}$ is positive definite, we write $\mathbf{A} > \mathbf{0}$. The inequality symbol should not be regarded as meaning that every element of $\mathbf{A}$ is positive. (If $\mathbf{A}$ is diagonal, $\mathbf{A} > \mathbf{0}$ does imply that all the diagonal elements are positive.) More generally, if $\mathbf{A} - \mathbf{B}$ is positive definite, we write $\mathbf{A} > \mathbf{B}$. For nonnegative definiteness, we use the symbol $\geq$.

THEOREM 11.5.10   A symmetric matrix is positive definite if and only if its characteristic roots are all positive. (The theorem is also true if we change the word "positive" to "nonnegative," "negative," or "nonpositive.")

Proof. The theorem follows immediately from Theorem 11.5.6.   ❑

THEOREM 11.5.11 $\mathbf{A} > \mathbf{0} \Rightarrow \mathbf{A}^{-1} > \mathbf{0}.$

Proof. The theorem follows from Theorem 11.5.10, since the characteristic roots of $\mathbf{A}^{-1}$ are the reciprocals of the characteristic roots of $\mathbf{A}$ because of (11.5.3).   ❑

THEOREM 11.5.12   Let $\mathbf{A}$ be an $n \times n$ symmetric matrix and let $\mathbf{X}$ be an $n \times K$ matrix where $K \leq n$. Then $\mathbf{A} \geq \mathbf{0} \Rightarrow \mathbf{X}'\mathbf{A}\mathbf{X} \geq \mathbf{0}$. Moreover, if $\operatorname{rank}(\mathbf{X}) = K$, then $\mathbf{A} > \mathbf{0} \Rightarrow \mathbf{X}'\mathbf{A}\mathbf{X} > \mathbf{0}$.

Proof. Let $\mathbf{c}$ be an arbitrary nonzero vector of K components, and define $\mathbf{d} = \mathbf{X}\mathbf{c}$. Then $\mathbf{c}'\mathbf{X}'\mathbf{A}\mathbf{X}\mathbf{c} = \mathbf{d}'\mathbf{A}\mathbf{d}$. Since $\mathbf{A} \geq \mathbf{0}$ implies $\mathbf{d}'\mathbf{A}\mathbf{d} \geq 0$, we have $\mathbf{X}'\mathbf{A}\mathbf{X} \geq \mathbf{0}$. If $\mathbf{X}$ is full rank, then $\mathbf{d} \neq \mathbf{0}$. Therefore $\mathbf{A} > \mathbf{0}$ implies $\mathbf{d}'\mathbf{A}\mathbf{d} > 0$ and $\mathbf{X}'\mathbf{A}\mathbf{X} > \mathbf{0}$.   ❑

THEOREM 11.5.13 Let $\mathbf{A}$ and $\mathbf{B}$ be symmetric positive definite matrices of the same size. Then $\mathbf{A} \geq \mathbf{B} \Rightarrow \mathbf{B}^{-1} \geq \mathbf{A}^{-1}$, and $\mathbf{A} > \mathbf{B} \Rightarrow \mathbf{B}^{-1} > \mathbf{A}^{-1}$.

Proof. See Bellman (1970, p. 93).

Next we discuss application of the above theorems concerning a positive definite matrix to the theory of estimation of multiple parameters. Recall that in Definition 7.2.1 we defined the goodness of an estimator using the mean squared error as the criterion. The question we now pose is, How do we compare two vector estimators of a vector of parameters? The following is a natural generalization of Definition 7.2.1 to the case of vector estimation.

DEFINITION 11.5.3 Let $\hat{\boldsymbol{\theta}}$ and $\tilde{\boldsymbol{\theta}}$ be estimators of a vector parameter $\boldsymbol{\theta}$. Let $\mathbf{A}$ and $\mathbf{B}$ be their respective mean squared error matrix; that is, $\mathbf{A} = E(\hat{\boldsymbol{\theta}} - \boldsymbol{\theta})(\hat{\boldsymbol{\theta}} - \boldsymbol{\theta})'$ and $\mathbf{B} = E(\tilde{\boldsymbol{\theta}} - \boldsymbol{\theta})(\tilde{\boldsymbol{\theta}} - \boldsymbol{\theta})'$. Then we say that $\hat{\boldsymbol{\theta}}$ is better than $\tilde{\boldsymbol{\theta}}$ if $\mathbf{A} \leq \mathbf{B}$ for any parameter value and $\mathbf{A} \neq \mathbf{B}$ for at least one value of the parameter. (Both $\mathbf{A}$ and $\mathbf{B}$ can be shown to be nonnegative definite directly from Definition 11.5.2.)

Note that if $\hat{\boldsymbol{\theta}}$ is better than $\tilde{\boldsymbol{\theta}}$ in the sense of this definition, $\hat{\boldsymbol{\theta}}$ is at least as good as $\tilde{\boldsymbol{\theta}}$ for estimating any element of $\boldsymbol{\theta}$. More generally, it implies that $\mathbf{c}'\hat{\boldsymbol{\theta}}$ is at least as good as $\mathbf{c}'\tilde{\boldsymbol{\theta}}$ for estimating $\mathbf{c}'\boldsymbol{\theta}$ for an arbitrary vector $\mathbf{c}$ of the same size as $\boldsymbol{\theta}$. Thus we see that this definition is a reasonable generalization of Definition 7.2.1.

Unfortunately, we cannot always rank two estimators by this definition alone. For example, consider

$$(11.5.12) \quad \mathbf{A} = \begin{bmatrix} 1 & 0 \\ 0 & 1 \end{bmatrix} \quad \text{and} \quad \mathbf{B} = \begin{bmatrix} 2 & 0 \\ 0 & 0.5 \end{bmatrix},$$

or

$$(11.5.13) \quad \mathbf{A} = \begin{bmatrix} 2 & 1 \\ 1 & 2 \end{bmatrix} \quad \text{and} \quad \mathbf{B} = \begin{bmatrix} 2 & 0 \\ 0 & 2 \end{bmatrix}.$$

In neither example can we establish that $\mathbf{A} \geq \mathbf{B}$ or $\mathbf{B} \geq \mathbf{A}$. We must use some other criteria to rank estimators. The two most commonly used are the trace and the determinant. In (11.5.12), tr $\mathbf{A} <$ tr $\mathbf{B}$, and in (11.5.13),

$|\mathbf{A}| < |\mathbf{B}|$. Note that $\mathbf{A} < \mathbf{B}$ implies tr $\mathbf{A} <$ tr $\mathbf{B}$ because of Theorem 11.5.9. It can be also shown that $\mathbf{A} < \mathbf{B}$ implies $|\mathbf{A}| < |\mathbf{B}|$. The proof is somewhat involved and hence is omitted. In each case, the converse is not necessarily true.

In the remainder of this section we discuss the properties of a particular positive definite matrix of the form $\mathbf{P} \equiv \mathbf{X}(\mathbf{X}'\mathbf{X})^{-1}\mathbf{X}'$, where $\mathbf{X}$ is an $n \times K$ matrix of rank K. This matrix plays a very important role in the theory of the least squares estimator developed in Chapter 12.

THEOREM 11.5.14   An arbitrary n-dimensional vector $\mathbf{y}$ can be written as $\mathbf{y} = \mathbf{y}_1 + \mathbf{y}_2$ such that $\mathbf{P}\mathbf{y}_1 = \mathbf{y}_1$ and $\mathbf{P}\mathbf{y}_2 = \mathbf{0}$.

Proof.   By Theorem 11.4.9, there exists an $n \times (n - K)$ matrix $\mathbf{Z}$ such that $(\mathbf{X}, \mathbf{Z})$ is nonsingular and $\mathbf{X}'\mathbf{Z} = \mathbf{0}$. Since $(\mathbf{X}, \mathbf{Z})$ is nonsingular, there exists an n-vector $\mathbf{c}$ such that $\mathbf{y} = (\mathbf{X}, \mathbf{Z})\mathbf{c} \equiv \mathbf{X}\mathbf{c}_1 + \mathbf{Z}\mathbf{c}_2$. Set $\mathbf{y}_1 = \mathbf{X}\mathbf{c}_1$ and $\mathbf{y}_2 = \mathbf{Z}\mathbf{c}_2$. Then clearly $\mathbf{P}\mathbf{y}_1 = \mathbf{y}_1$ and $\mathbf{P}\mathbf{y}_2 = \mathbf{0}$.   ❑

It immediately follows from Theorem 11.5.14 that $\mathbf{P}\mathbf{y} = \mathbf{y}_1$. We call this operation the projection of $\mathbf{y}$ onto the space spanned by the columns of $\mathbf{X}$, since the resulting vector $\mathbf{y}_1 = \mathbf{X}\mathbf{c}_1$ is a linear combination of the columns of $\mathbf{X}$. Hence we call $\mathbf{P}$ a *projection matrix*. The projection matrix $\mathbf{M} \equiv \mathbf{Z}(\mathbf{Z}'\mathbf{Z})^{-1}\mathbf{Z}'$, where $\mathbf{Z}$ is as defined in the proof of Theorem 11.5.14, plays the opposite role from the projection matrix $\mathbf{P}$. Namely, $\mathbf{M}\mathbf{y} = \mathbf{y}_2$.

THEOREM 11.5.15 $\mathbf{I} - \mathbf{P} = \mathbf{M}$.

Proof.   We have

(11.5.14) $(\mathbf{I} - \mathbf{P} - \mathbf{M})(\mathbf{X}, \mathbf{Z}) = (\mathbf{X}, \mathbf{Z}) - (\mathbf{X}, \mathbf{0}) - (\mathbf{0}, \mathbf{Z}) = \mathbf{0}$.

Postmultiplying both sides of (11.5.14) by $(\mathbf{X}, \mathbf{Z})^{-1}$ yields the desired result.   ❑

THEOREM 11.5.16 $\mathbf{P} = \mathbf{P}' = \mathbf{P}^2$.

This can be easily verified. Any square matrix $\mathbf{A}$ for which $\mathbf{A} = \mathbf{A}^2$ is called an *idempotent matrix*. Theorem 11.5.16 states that $\mathbf{P}$ is a symmetric idempotent matrix.

THEOREM 11.5.17 rank$(\mathbf{P}) = K$.

Proof. As we have shown in the proof of Theorem 11.5.14, there exists an $n \times (n - K)$ full-rank matrix $\mathbf{Z}$ such that $\mathbf{PZ} = \mathbf{0}$. Suppose $\mathbf{PW} = \mathbf{0}$ for some matrix $\mathbf{W}$ with n rows. Since, by Theorem 11.5.14, $\mathbf{W} = \mathbf{XA} + \mathbf{ZB}$ for some matrices $\mathbf{A}$ and $\mathbf{B}$, $\mathbf{PW} = \mathbf{0}$ implies $\mathbf{XA} = \mathbf{0}$, which in turn implies $\mathbf{A} = \mathbf{0}$. Therefore $\mathbf{W} = \mathbf{ZB}$, which implies rank$(\mathbf{W}) \leq n - K$. Thus the theorem follows from Theorem 11.4.10. (An alternative proof is to use Theorem 11.5.3 and Theorem 11.5.18 below.) ❑

THEOREM 11.5.18 Characteristic roots of $\mathbf{P}$ consist of K ones and $n - K$ zeroes.

Proof. By Theorem 11.5.4 the nonzero characteristic roots of $\mathbf{X}(\mathbf{X}'\mathbf{X})^{-1}\mathbf{X}'$ and $(\mathbf{X}'\mathbf{X})^{-1}\mathbf{X}'\mathbf{X}$ are the same. But since the second matrix is the identity of size K, its characteristic roots are K ones. ❑

THEOREM 11.5.19 Let $\mathbf{X}$ be an $n \times K$ matrix of rank K. Partition $\mathbf{X}$ as $\mathbf{X} = (\mathbf{X}_1, \mathbf{X}_2)$ such that $\mathbf{X}_1$ is $n \times K_1$ and $\mathbf{X}_2$ is $n \times K_2$ and $K_1 + K_2 = K$. If we define $\mathbf{X}_2^* = [\mathbf{I} - \mathbf{X}_1(\mathbf{X}_1'\mathbf{X}_1)^{-1}\mathbf{X}_1']\mathbf{X}_2$, then we have $\mathbf{X}(\mathbf{X}'\mathbf{X})^{-1}\mathbf{X}' = \mathbf{X}_1(\mathbf{X}_1'\mathbf{X}_1)^{-1}\mathbf{X}_1' + \mathbf{X}_2^*(\mathbf{X}_2^{*\prime}\mathbf{X}_2^*)^{-1}\mathbf{X}_2^{*\prime}$.

Proof. The theorem follows from noting that

$$[\mathbf{X}(\mathbf{X}'\mathbf{X})^{-1}\mathbf{X}' - \mathbf{X}_1(\mathbf{X}_1'\mathbf{X}_1)^{-1}\mathbf{X}_1' - \mathbf{X}_2^*(\mathbf{X}_2^{*\prime}\mathbf{X}_2^*)^{-1}\mathbf{X}_2^{*\prime}][\mathbf{X}_1, \mathbf{X}_2, \mathbf{Z}] = \mathbf{0}. ❑$$

EXERCISES

1. (Section 11.2)
   Prove Theorem 11.2.1.

2. (Section 11.3)
   Using Theorem 11.3.3, prove its corollary obtained by deleting the word "adjacent" from the theorem.

3. (Section 11.3)
   Verify $|\mathbf{AB}| = |\mathbf{A}| \, |\mathbf{B}|$, where

$$A = \begin{bmatrix} 1 & 2 \\ 3 & 4 \end{bmatrix} \quad \text{and} \quad B = \begin{bmatrix} 2 & 1 \\ 1 & 1 \end{bmatrix}.$$

4. (Section 11.3)

   Prove $A^{-1} - (A + B)^{-1} = A^{-1}(A^{-1} + B^{-1})^{-1}A^{-1}$ whenever all the inverses exist. If you cannot prove it, verify it for the A and B given in Exercise 3 above.

5. (Section 11.4)

   Solve the following equations for x_1 for x_2; first, by using the inverse of the matrix, and second, by using Cramer's rule:

   $$\begin{bmatrix} 1 & 2 \\ 3 & 4 \end{bmatrix} \begin{bmatrix} x_1 \\ x_2 \end{bmatrix} = \begin{bmatrix} 2 \\ 1 \end{bmatrix}.$$

6. (Section 11.4)

   Solve the following equations for x_1, x_2, and x_3; first, by using the inverse of the matrix, and second, by using Cramer's rule:

   $$\begin{bmatrix} 1 & -2 & 3 \\ 1 & 1 & -1 \\ 2 & 1 & 2 \end{bmatrix} \begin{bmatrix} x_1 \\ x_2 \\ x_3 \end{bmatrix} = \begin{bmatrix} 1 \\ 0 \\ 1 \end{bmatrix}.$$

7. (Section 11.4)

   Find the rank of the matrix

   $$\begin{bmatrix} 1 & 1 & 1 \\ 2 & 3 & 1 \\ 2 & 1 & 3 \end{bmatrix}.$$

8. (Section 11.4)

   Find the rank of the matrix

   $$\begin{bmatrix} 1 & 2 & 1 & 2 \\ 1 & 2 & 3 & 4 \\ 1 & 2 & 5 & 6 \\ 2 & 4 & 0 & 2 \end{bmatrix}.$$

9. (Section 11.5)

   Find the characteristic vectors and roots of

$$\mathbf{A} = \begin{bmatrix} 3 & \sqrt{2} \\ \sqrt{2} & 2 \end{bmatrix}$$

and compute $\mathbf{A}^{0.5}$.

10. (Section 11.5)
    Compute
    $$\begin{bmatrix} 5 & 2 \\ 2 & 2 \end{bmatrix}^{-0.5}.$$

11. (Section 11.5)
    Prove Theorem 11.5.8.

12. (Section 11.5)
    Let $\mathbf{A}$ be a symmetric matrix whose characteristic roots are less than one in absolute value. Show that
    $$(\mathbf{I} - \mathbf{A})^{-1} = \mathbf{I} + \mathbf{A} + \mathbf{A}^2 + \dots .$$

13. (Section 11.5)
    Suppose that $\mathbf{A}$ and $\mathbf{B}$ are symmetric positive definite matrices of the same size. Show that if $\mathbf{AB}$ is symmetric, it is positive definite.

14. (Section 11.5)
    Find the inverse of the matrix $\mathbf{I} + \mathbf{xx}'$ where $\mathbf{x}$ is a vector of the same dimension as $\mathbf{I}$.

15. (Section 11.5)
    Define
    $$\mathbf{X} = \begin{bmatrix} 1 & 1 \\ 1 & 1 \\ 1 & -2 \end{bmatrix}.$$

    Compute $\mathbf{X}(\mathbf{X}'\mathbf{X})^{-1}\mathbf{X}$ and its characteristic vectors and roots.

12 | MULTIPLE REGRESSION MODEL

12.1 INTRODUCTION

In Chapter 10 we considered the bivariate regression model—the regression model with one dependent variable and one independent variable. In this chapter we consider the *multiple regression model*—the regression model with one dependent variable and many independent variables. The multiple regression model should be distinguished from the *multivariate regression model*, which refers to a set of many regression equations.

Most of the results of this chapter are multivariate generalizations of those in Chapter 10, except for the discussion of F tests in Section 12.4. The organization of this chapter is similar to that of Chapter 10.

The results of Chapter 11 on matrix analysis will be used extensively. As before, a boldface capital letter will denote a matrix and a boldface lowercase letter will denote a vector. We define the multiple linear regression model as follows:

$$(12.1.1) \qquad y_t = \sum_{i=1}^{K} \beta_i x_{ti} + u_t, \qquad t = 1, 2, \ldots, T,$$

where $\{y_t\}$ are observable random variables; $\{x_{ti}\}$, $i = 1, 2, \ldots, K$ and $t = 1, 2, \ldots, T$ are known constants; $\{u_t\}$ are unobservable random variables which are i.i.d. with $Eu_t = 0$ and $Vu_t = \sigma^2$; and $\beta_1, \beta_2, \ldots, \beta_K$ and σ^2 are unknown parameters that we wish to estimate. We shall state the assumption on $\{x_{ti}\}$ later, after we rewrite (12.1.1) in matrix notation. The linear regression model with these assumptions is called the *classical regression model*.

We shall rewrite (12.1.1) in vector and matrix notation in two steps. Define the K-dimensional row vector $\mathbf{x}_t' = (x_{t1}, x_{t2}, \ldots, x_{tK})$ and the K-dimensional column vector $\boldsymbol{\beta} = (\beta_1, \beta_2, \ldots, \beta_K)'$. Then (12.1.1) can be written as

(12.1.2) $y_t = \mathbf{x}_t'\boldsymbol{\beta} + u_t, \quad t = 1, 2, \ldots, T.$

Although we have simplified the notation by going from (12.1.1) to (12.1.2), the real advantage of matrix notation is that we can write the T equations in (12.1.2) as a single vector equation.

Define the column vectors $\mathbf{y} = (y_1, y_2, \ldots, y_T)'$ and $\mathbf{u} = (u_1, u_2, \ldots, u_T)'$ and define the $T \times K$ matrix $\mathbf{X}$ whose tth row is equal to $\mathbf{x}_t'$ so that $\mathbf{X}' = (\mathbf{x}_1, \mathbf{x}_2, \ldots, \mathbf{x}_T)$. Then we can rewrite (12.1.2) as

(12.1.3) $\mathbf{y} = \mathbf{X}\boldsymbol{\beta} + \mathbf{u}$, where $\mathbf{X} = \begin{bmatrix} x_{11} & x_{12} & \cdot & \cdot & x_{1K} \\ x_{21} & x_{22} & \cdot & \cdot & x_{2K} \\ \cdot & \cdot & & & \\ \cdot & \cdot & & & \\ \cdot & \cdot & & & \\ x_{T1} & x_{T2} & \cdot & \cdot & x_{TK} \end{bmatrix}.$

We assume rank$(\mathbf{X}) = K$. Note that in the bivariate regression model this assumption is equivalent to assuming that x_t is not constant for all t.

We denote the columns of $\mathbf{X}$ by $\mathbf{x}_{(1)}, \mathbf{x}_{(2)}, \ldots, \mathbf{x}_{(K)}$. Thus, $\mathbf{X} = [\mathbf{x}_{(1)}, \mathbf{x}_{(2)}, \ldots, \mathbf{x}_{(K)}]$. The assumption rank$(\mathbf{X}) = K$ is equivalent to assuming that $\mathbf{x}_{(1)}, \mathbf{x}_{(2)}, \ldots, \mathbf{x}_{(K)}$ are linearly independent. Another way to express this assumption is to state that $\mathbf{X}'\mathbf{X}$ is nonsingular. (See Theorem 11.4.8.)

The assumption that $\mathbf{X}$ is full rank is not restrictive, because of the following observation. Suppose rank$(\mathbf{X}) = K_1 < K$. Then, by Definition 11.4.4, we can find a subset of K_1 columns of $\mathbf{X}$ which are linearly independent. Without loss of generality assume that the subset consists of the first K_1 columns of $\mathbf{X}$ and partition $\mathbf{X} = (\mathbf{X}_1, \mathbf{X}_2)$, where $\mathbf{X}_1$ is $T \times K_1$ and $\mathbf{X}_2$, $T \times K_2$. Then we can write $\mathbf{X}_2 = \mathbf{X}_1\mathbf{A}$ for some $K_1 \times K_2$ matrix $\mathbf{A}$, and hence $\mathbf{X} = \mathbf{X}_1(\mathbf{I}, \mathbf{A})$. Therefore we can rewrite the regression equation (12.1.3) as

$\mathbf{y} = \mathbf{X}_1\boldsymbol{\beta}_1 + \mathbf{u},$

where $\boldsymbol{\beta}_1 = (\mathbf{I}, \mathbf{A})\boldsymbol{\beta}$ and $\mathbf{X}_1$ is full rank.

In practice, $\mathbf{x}_{(1)}$ is usually taken to be the vector consisting of T ones. But we shall not make this assumption specifically as part of the linear regression model, for most of our results do not require it.

Our assumptions on $\{u_t\}$ imply in terms of the vector $\mathbf{u}$

$$(12.1.4) \quad E\mathbf{u} = \mathbf{0}$$

and

$$(12.1.5) \quad E\mathbf{u}\mathbf{u}' = \sigma^2\mathbf{I}.$$

In (12.1.4), $\mathbf{0}$ denotes a column vector consisting of T zeroes. We shall denote a vector consisting of only zeroes and a matrix consisting of only zeroes by the same symbol $\mathbf{0}$. The reader must infer what $\mathbf{0}$ represents from the context. To understand (12.1.5) fully, the reader should write out the elements of the $T \times T$ matrix $\mathbf{u}\mathbf{u}'$. The identity matrix on the right-hand side of (12.1.5) is of the size T, which the reader should also infer from the context. Note that $\mathbf{u}'\mathbf{u}$, a row vector times a column vector, is a scalar and can be written in the summation notation as $\Sigma_{t=1}^{T}u_t^2$. Taking the trace of both sides of (12.1.5) and using Theorem 11.5.8 yields $E\mathbf{u}'\mathbf{u} = \sigma^2 T$.

12.2 LEAST SQUARES ESTIMATORS

12.2.1 Definition

The *least squares estimators* of the regression coefficients $\{\beta_i\}$, $i = 1, 2, \ldots,$ K, in the multiple regression model (12.1.1) are defined as the values of $\{\beta_i\}$ which minimize the sum of squared residuals

$$(12.2.1) \quad S(\boldsymbol{\beta}) = \sum_{t=1}^{T}\left(y_t - \sum_{i=1}^{K}\beta_i x_{ti}\right)^2.$$

Differentiating (12.2.1) with respect to β_k and equating the partial derivative to 0, we obtain

$$(12.2.2) \quad \frac{\partial S}{\partial \beta_k} = -2\sum_{t=1}^{T}\left(y_t - \sum_{i=1}^{K}\beta_i x_{ti}\right)x_{tk} = 0, \quad k = 1, 2, \ldots, K.$$

The least squares estimators $\{\hat{\beta}_i\}$, $i = 1, 2, \ldots, K$, are the solutions to the K equations in (12.2.2). We put $\beta_i = \hat{\beta}_i$ in (12.2.2) and rewrite it as

(12.2.3)

$$\hat{\beta}_1 \Sigma x_{t1}^2 \quad + \quad \hat{\beta}_2 \Sigma x_{t1} x_{t2} \quad + \cdots + \quad \hat{\beta}_K \Sigma x_{t1} x_{tK} \; = \; \Sigma x_{t1} y_t,$$

$$\hat{\beta}_1 \Sigma x_{t2} x_{t1} \quad + \quad \hat{\beta}_2 \Sigma x_{t2}^2 \quad + \cdots + \quad \hat{\beta}_K \Sigma x_{t2} x_{tK} \; = \; \Sigma x_{t2} y_t,$$

$$\hat{\beta}_1 \Sigma x_{tK} x_{t1} \quad + \quad \hat{\beta}_2 \Sigma x_{tK} x_{t2} \quad + \cdots + \quad \hat{\beta}_K \Sigma x_{tK}^2 \; = \; \Sigma x_{tK} y_t,$$

where Σ should be understood to mean $\Sigma_{t=1}^{T}$, unless otherwise noted. Using the vector and matrix notation defined in Section 12.1, we can write (12.2.3) as

(12.2.4) $\mathbf{X'X\hat{\beta}} = \mathbf{X'y}$,

where we have defined $\hat{\boldsymbol{\beta}} = (\hat{\beta}_1, \hat{\beta}_2, \ldots, \hat{\beta}_K)'$. Premultiplying (12.2.4) by $(\mathbf{X'X})^{-1}$ yields

(12.2.5) $\hat{\boldsymbol{\beta}} = (\mathbf{X'X})^{-1}\mathbf{X'y}$,

since we have assumed the nonsingularity of $\mathbf{X'X}$.

We now show how to obtain the same result without using the summation notation at all. We can write (12.2.1) in vector notation as

(12.2.6) $S(\boldsymbol{\beta}) = (\mathbf{y} - \mathbf{X\boldsymbol{\beta}})'(\mathbf{y} - \mathbf{X\boldsymbol{\beta}}) = \mathbf{y'y} - 2\mathbf{y'X\boldsymbol{\beta}} + \boldsymbol{\beta}'\mathbf{X'X\boldsymbol{\beta}}$.

Define the vector of partial derivatives

(12.2.7) $\dfrac{\partial S}{\partial \boldsymbol{\beta}} = \left(\dfrac{\partial S}{\partial \beta_1}, \dfrac{\partial S}{\partial \beta_2}, \ldots, \dfrac{\partial S}{\partial \beta_k} \right)'.$

Then

(12.2.8) $\dfrac{\partial S}{\partial \boldsymbol{\beta}} = -2\mathbf{X'y} + 2\mathbf{X'X\boldsymbol{\beta}}$.

The reader should verify (12.2.8) by noting that it is equivalent to (12.2.2). Equating (12.2.8) to $\mathbf{0}$ and solving for $\boldsymbol{\beta}$ yields (12.2.5).

Let $\mathbf{1} = (1, 1, \ldots, 1)'$ be the vector of T ones and define $\mathbf{x} = (x_1, x_2, \ldots, x_T)'$. If we assume $K = 2$ and put $\mathbf{x}_{(1)} = \mathbf{1}$ and $\mathbf{x}_{(2)} = \mathbf{x}$, the multiple regression model is reduced to the bivariate regression model discussed in Chapter 10. The reader should verify that making the same substitution in (12.2.5) gives the least squares estimators $\hat{\alpha}$ and $\hat{\beta}$ defined in Section 10.2.

As a generalization of (10.2.6) we define the *least squares predictor* of the vector $\mathbf{y}$, denoted by $\hat{\mathbf{y}}$, as

(12.2.9) $\quad \hat{\mathbf{y}} = \mathbf{X}\hat{\boldsymbol{\beta}}.$

As a generalization of (10.2.7) the vector of the *least squares residuals* is defined by

(12.2.10) $\quad \hat{\mathbf{u}} = \mathbf{y} - \hat{\mathbf{y}}.$

Defining $\mathbf{P} = \mathbf{X}(\mathbf{X'X})^{-1}\mathbf{X'}$ and $\mathbf{M} = \mathbf{I} - \mathbf{P}$, we can rewrite (12.2.9) and (12.2.10) respectively as

(12.2.11) $\quad \hat{\mathbf{y}} = \mathbf{Py}$

and

(12.2.12) $\quad \hat{\mathbf{u}} = \mathbf{My}.$

The $\mathbf{P}$ and $\mathbf{M}$ above are projection matrices, whose properties were discussed in Section 11.5. Note that the decomposition of $\mathbf{y}$ defined by

(12.2.13) $\quad \mathbf{y} = \hat{\mathbf{y}} + \hat{\mathbf{u}}$

is the same as that explained in Theorem 11.5.14. Premultiplying (12.2.12) by $\mathbf{X'}$ and noting that $\mathbf{X'M} = \mathbf{0}$, we obtain

(12.2.14) $\quad \mathbf{X'\hat{u}} = \mathbf{0},$

which signifies the orthogonality between the regressors and the least squares residuals and is a generalization of equations (10.2.8) and (10.2.9). Equation (12.2.13) represents the decomposition of $\mathbf{y}$ into the vector which is spanned by the columns of $\mathbf{X}$ and the vector which is orthogonal to the columns of $\mathbf{X}$.

It is useful to derive from (12.2.4) an explicit formula for a subvector of $\hat{\boldsymbol{\beta}}$. Suppose we partition $\hat{\boldsymbol{\beta}}' = (\hat{\boldsymbol{\beta}}_1', \hat{\boldsymbol{\beta}}_2')$ where $\hat{\boldsymbol{\beta}}_1$ is a K_1-vector and $\hat{\boldsymbol{\beta}}_2$ is a K_2-vector such that $K_1 + K_2 = K$. Partition $\mathbf{X}$ conformably as $\mathbf{X} = (\mathbf{X}_1, \mathbf{X}_2)$. Then we can write (12.2.4) as

(12.2.15) $\quad \mathbf{X}_1' \mathbf{X}_1\hat{\boldsymbol{\beta}}_1 + \mathbf{X}_1' \mathbf{X}_2\hat{\boldsymbol{\beta}}_2 = \mathbf{X}_1' \mathbf{y}$

and

(12.2.16) $\quad \mathbf{X}_2' \mathbf{X}_1\hat{\boldsymbol{\beta}}_1 + \mathbf{X}_2' \mathbf{X}_2\hat{\boldsymbol{\beta}}_2 = \mathbf{X}_2' \mathbf{y}.$

Solving (12.2.16) for $\hat{\boldsymbol{\beta}}_2$ and inserting it into (12.2.15) yields

(12.2.17) $\hat{\boldsymbol{\beta}}_1 = (\mathbf{X}_1' \, \mathbf{M}_2\mathbf{X}_1)^{-1}\mathbf{X}_1' \, \mathbf{M}_2\mathbf{y},$

where $\mathbf{M}_2 = \mathbf{I} - \mathbf{X}_2(\mathbf{X}_2' \, \mathbf{X}_2)^{-1}\mathbf{X}_2'$. Similarly,

(12.2.18) $\hat{\boldsymbol{\beta}}_2 = (\mathbf{X}_2' \, \mathbf{M}_1\mathbf{X}_2)^{-1}\mathbf{X}_2' \, \mathbf{M}_1\mathbf{y},$

where $\mathbf{M}_1 = \mathbf{I} - \mathbf{X}_1(\mathbf{X}_1' \, \mathbf{X}_1)^{-1}\mathbf{X}_1'$. In the special case where $\mathbf{X}_1 = \mathbf{1}$, the vector of T ones, and $\mathbf{X}_2 = \mathbf{x}$, formulae (12.2.17) and (12.2.18) are reduced to (10.2.16) and (10.2.12), respectively.

12.2.2 Finite Sample Properties of $\hat{\boldsymbol{\beta}}$

We shall obtain the mean and the variance-covariance matrix of the least squares estimator $\hat{\boldsymbol{\beta}}$.

Inserting (12.1.3) into the right-hand side of (12.2.5), we obtain

(12.2.19) $\hat{\boldsymbol{\beta}} = (\mathbf{X}'\mathbf{X})^{-1}\mathbf{X}'(\mathbf{X}\boldsymbol{\beta} + \mathbf{u}) = \boldsymbol{\beta} + (\mathbf{X}'\mathbf{X})^{-1}\mathbf{X}'\mathbf{u}.$

Since $\mathbf{X}$ is a matrix of constants (a nonstochastic matrix) and $E\mathbf{u} = \mathbf{0}$ by the assumptions of our model, from Theorem 4.1.6,

(12.2.20) $E\hat{\boldsymbol{\beta}} = \boldsymbol{\beta} + (\mathbf{X}'\mathbf{X})^{-1}\mathbf{X}'E\mathbf{u} = \boldsymbol{\beta}.$

In other words, the least squares estimator $\hat{\boldsymbol{\beta}}$ is unbiased.

Define the variance-covariance matrix of $\hat{\boldsymbol{\beta}}$, denoted as $V\hat{\boldsymbol{\beta}}$, by

(12.2.21) $V\hat{\boldsymbol{\beta}} = E(\hat{\boldsymbol{\beta}} - E\hat{\boldsymbol{\beta}})(\hat{\boldsymbol{\beta}} - E\hat{\boldsymbol{\beta}})'.$

Then, using (12.2.19) and (12.2.20), we have

(12.2.22) $V\hat{\boldsymbol{\beta}} = E(\hat{\boldsymbol{\beta}} - \boldsymbol{\beta})(\hat{\boldsymbol{\beta}} - \boldsymbol{\beta})'$

$\qquad\qquad = E(\mathbf{X}'\mathbf{X})^{-1}\mathbf{X}'\mathbf{u}\mathbf{u}'\mathbf{X}(\mathbf{X}'\mathbf{X})^{-1}$

$\qquad\qquad = (\mathbf{X}'\mathbf{X})^{-1}\mathbf{X}'(E\mathbf{u}\mathbf{u}')\mathbf{X}(\mathbf{X}'\mathbf{X})^{-1}$

$\qquad\qquad = \sigma^2(\mathbf{X}'\mathbf{X})^{-1}.$

The third equality above follows from Theorem 4.1.6, since each element of the matrix $(\mathbf{X}'\mathbf{X})^{-1}\mathbf{X}'\mathbf{u}\mathbf{u}'\mathbf{X}(\mathbf{X}'\mathbf{X})^{-1}$ is a linear combination of the T^2 elements of the matrix $\mathbf{u}\mathbf{u}'$. The fourth equality follows from the assumption $E\mathbf{u}\mathbf{u}' = \sigma^2\mathbf{I}$.

The ith diagonal element of the variance-covariance matrix $V\hat{\boldsymbol{\beta}}$ is equal to $V\hat{\beta}_i$, the variance of the ith element of $\hat{\beta}$. The i, jth element of $V\hat{\beta}$ is equal to $\text{Cov}(\hat{\beta}_i, \hat{\beta}_j)$, the covariance between $\hat{\beta}_i$ and $\hat{\beta}_j$. Note that $V\hat{\beta}$ is symmetric, as every variance-covariance matrix should be. The reader should verify that setting $\mathbf{X} = (1, \mathbf{x})$ in (12.2.22) yields the variances $V\hat{\alpha}$ and $V\hat{\beta}$ given, respectively, in (10.2.24) and (10.2.23) as the diagonal elements of the 2×2 variance-covariance matrix. The off-diagonal element yields $\text{Cov}(\hat{\alpha}, \hat{\beta})$, which was obtained in (10.2.25).

Since we have assumed the nonsingularity of $\mathbf{X}'\mathbf{X}$ in our model, the variance-covariance matrix (12.2.22) exists and is finite. If $\mathbf{X}'\mathbf{X}$ is nearly singular, or more exactly, if the determinant $\mathbf{X}'\mathbf{X}$ is nearly zero, the elements of $V\hat{\beta}$ are large, as we can see from the definition of the inverse given in Definition 11.3.2. We call this largeness of the elements of $V\hat{\beta}$ due to the near-singularity of $\mathbf{X}'\mathbf{X}$ the problem of *multicollinearity*. Next we shall prove that the least squares estimator $\hat{\beta}$ is the best linear unbiased estimator of $\boldsymbol{\beta}$.

We define the class of linear estimators of $\boldsymbol{\beta}$ to be the class of estimators which can be written as $\mathbf{C}'\mathbf{y}$ for some $T \times K$ constant matrix $\mathbf{C}$. We define the class of linear unbiased estimators as a subset of the class of linear estimators which are unbiased. That is, we impose

(12.2.23) $E\mathbf{C}'\mathbf{y} = \boldsymbol{\beta}.$

By inserting (12.1.3) into the left-hand side of (12.2.23), we note that (12.2.23) is equivalent to

(12.2.24) $\mathbf{C}'\mathbf{X} = \mathbf{I}.$

Thus the class of linear unbiased estimators is the class of estimators which can be written as $\mathbf{C}'\mathbf{y}$, where $\mathbf{C}$ is a $T \times K$ constant matrix satisfying (12.2.24).

The least squares estimator $\hat{\beta}$ is a member of this class where $\mathbf{C}' = (\mathbf{X}'\mathbf{X})^{-1}\mathbf{X}'$.

The theorem derived below shows that $\hat{\beta}$ is the *best linear unbiased estimator* (BLUE), where we have used the word *best* in the sense of Definition 11.5.3.

THEOREM 12.2.1 (Gauss-Markov) Let $\boldsymbol{\beta}^* = \mathbf{C}'\mathbf{y}$ where $\mathbf{C}$ is a $T \times K$ constant matrix such that $\mathbf{C}'\mathbf{X} = \mathbf{I}$. Then, $\hat{\beta}$ is better than $\boldsymbol{\beta}^*$ if $\boldsymbol{\beta}^* \neq \hat{\beta}$.

Proof. Since $\boldsymbol{\beta}^* = \boldsymbol{\beta} + \mathbf{C}'\mathbf{u}$ because of (12.2.24), we have

(12.2.25) $V\boldsymbol{\beta}* = E\mathbf{C}'\mathbf{u}\mathbf{u}'\mathbf{C}$

$\qquad\qquad = \mathbf{C}'(E\mathbf{u}\mathbf{u}')\mathbf{C}$

$\qquad\qquad = \sigma^2\mathbf{C}'\mathbf{C}$

$\qquad\qquad = \sigma^2(\mathbf{X}'\mathbf{X})^{-1} + \sigma^2[\mathbf{C}' - (\mathbf{X}'\mathbf{X})^{-1}\mathbf{X}'][\mathbf{C} - \mathbf{X}(\mathbf{X}'\mathbf{X})^{-1}].$

To verify the last equality, multiply out the four terms within the square brackets above and use (12.2.24). The last term above can be written as $\sigma^2\mathbf{Z}'\mathbf{Z}$ by setting $\mathbf{Z} = \mathbf{C} - \mathbf{X}(\mathbf{X}'\mathbf{X})^{-1}$. But $\mathbf{Z}'\mathbf{Z} \geq \mathbf{0}$, meaning that $\mathbf{Z}'\mathbf{Z}$ is a nonnegative definite matrix, by Theorem 11.5.12. Therefore $V\boldsymbol{\beta}* \geq \sigma^2(\mathbf{X}'\mathbf{X})^{-1}$, meaning that $V\boldsymbol{\beta}* - \sigma^2(\mathbf{X}'\mathbf{X})^{-1}$ is a nonnegative definite matrix. Finally, the theorem follows from observing that $\sigma^2(\mathbf{X}'\mathbf{X})^{-1} = V\hat{\boldsymbol{\beta}}$ and using Definition 11.5.3. □

Suppose we wish to estimate an arbitrary linear combination of the regression coefficients, say $\mathbf{d}'\boldsymbol{\beta}$. From the discussion following Definition 11.5.3, we note that Theorem 12.2.1 implies that $\mathbf{d}'\hat{\boldsymbol{\beta}}$ is better (in the sense of smaller mean squared error) than any other linear unbiased estimator $\mathbf{d}'\boldsymbol{\beta}*$. In particular, by choosing $\mathbf{d}$ to be the vector consisting of one in the ith position and zero elsewhere, we see that $\hat{\beta}_i$ is the better estimator of β_i than β_i^*. Thus the best linear unbiasedness of $\hat{\alpha}$ and $\hat{\beta}$ proved in Section 10.2.2 follows as a special case of Theorem 12.2.1.

As we demonstrated in Section 7.2 regarding the sample mean, there are biased or nonlinear estimators that are better than the least squares for certain values of the parameters. An example is the *ridge estimator* defined as $(\mathbf{X}'\mathbf{X} + \gamma\mathbf{I})^{-1}\mathbf{X}'\mathbf{y}$ for an appropriately chosen constant γ. The estimator, although biased, is better than the least squares for certain values of the parameters because the addition of $\gamma\mathbf{I}$ reduces the variance. The improvement is especially noteworthy when $\mathbf{X}'\mathbf{X}$ is nearly singular. (For further discussion of the ridge and related estimators, see Amemiya, 1985, chapter 2.)

12.2.3 Estimation of σ^2

As in Section 10.2.3, we define the least squares estimator $\hat{\sigma}^2$ as

(12.2.26) $\hat{\sigma}^2 = \dfrac{\hat{\mathbf{u}}'\hat{\mathbf{u}}}{T},$

using the least squares residuals $\hat{\mathbf{u}}$ defined in (12.2.12). In deriving $E\hat{\sigma}^2$ it is useful to note that

(12.2.27) $\hat{\mathbf{u}} = \mathbf{My} = \mathbf{M}(\mathbf{X\boldsymbol{\beta}} + \mathbf{u}) = \mathbf{Mu}.$

From (12.2.27) we obtain

(12.2.28) $E\hat{\mathbf{u}}'\hat{\mathbf{u}} = E\mathbf{u}'\mathbf{Mu}$ since $\mathbf{M}^2 = \mathbf{M}$

$\qquad\qquad = E \operatorname{tr} \mathbf{u}'\mathbf{Mu}$ since $\mathbf{u}'\mathbf{Mu}$ is a scalar

$\qquad\qquad = E \operatorname{tr} \mathbf{Muu}'$ by Theorem 11.5.8

$\qquad\qquad = \operatorname{tr} \mathbf{M}(E\mathbf{uu}')$ by Theorem 4.1.6

$\qquad\qquad = \sigma^2 \operatorname{tr} \mathbf{M}$ since $E\mathbf{uu}' = \sigma^2\mathbf{I}$

$\qquad\qquad = \sigma^2(T - K)$ by Theorem 11.5.18.

Therefore, $E\hat{\sigma}^2 = T^{-1}(T - K)\sigma^2$; hence $\hat{\sigma}^2$ is a biased estimator of σ^2. Note, however, that the bias diminishes to zero as T goes to infinity. An unbiased estimator of σ^2 is defined by

(12.2.29) $\tilde{\sigma}^2 = \dfrac{\hat{\mathbf{u}}'\hat{\mathbf{u}}}{T - K} .$

See Section 12.4 for the distribution of $\hat{\mathbf{u}}'\hat{\mathbf{u}}$ under the assumption that $\{u_t\}$ are normally distributed.

Using $\hat{\sigma}^2$ defined in (12.2.26), we can define R^2 by the same formula as equation (10.2.46). If we define a $T \times T$ matrix

(12.2.30) $\mathbf{L} = \mathbf{I} - \dfrac{\mathbf{11}'}{T} ,$

where $\mathbf{1}$ is the vector of T ones, we can write $s_y^2 = T^{-1}\mathbf{y}'\mathbf{Ly}$. Note that $\mathbf{L}$ is the projection matrix which projects any vector onto the space orthogonal to $\mathbf{1}$. In other words, the premultiplication of a vector by $\mathbf{L}$ subtracts the average of the elements of the vector from each element. Using (12.2.27) and (12.2.30), we can rewrite (10.2.46) as

(12.2.31) $R^2 = \dfrac{\mathbf{y}'(\mathbf{L} - \mathbf{M})\mathbf{y}}{\mathbf{y}'\mathbf{Ly}} .$

Suppose that the first column of $\mathbf{X}$ is the vector of ones, and partition $\mathbf{X} = (\mathbf{1}, \mathbf{X}_2)$. Then, by Theorem 11.5.19,

(12.2.32) $\mathbf{L} - \mathbf{M} = \mathbf{LX}_2(\mathbf{X}_2'\,\mathbf{LX}_2)^{-1}\mathbf{X}_2'\mathbf{L}.$

Therefore,

(12.2.33) $R^2 = \dfrac{\mathbf{y}'\mathbf{LX}_2(\mathbf{X}_2'\mathbf{LX}_2)^{-1}\mathbf{X}_2'\mathbf{Ly}}{\mathbf{y}'\mathbf{Ly}}.$

We now seek an interpretation of (12.2.33) that generalizes the intepretation given by (10.2.52). For this purpose define $\mathbf{y}^* = \mathbf{Ly}$, $\mathbf{X}_2^* = \mathbf{LX}_2$, and

(12.2.34) $\hat{\mathbf{y}}^* = \mathbf{X}_2^*(\mathbf{X}_2^{*\prime}\mathbf{X}_2^*)^{-1}\mathbf{X}_2^{*\prime}\mathbf{y}^*.$

Note that (12.2.34) defines the least squares predictor of $\mathbf{y}^*$ based on $\mathbf{X}_2^*$. So we can rewrite (12.2.33) as

(12.2.35) $R^2 = \dfrac{(\mathbf{y}^{*\prime}\hat{\mathbf{y}}^*)^2}{(\mathbf{y}^{*\prime}\mathbf{y}^*) \cdot (\hat{\mathbf{y}}^{*\prime}\hat{\mathbf{y}}^*)},$

which is the square of the sample correlation coefficient between $\mathbf{y}^*$ and $\hat{\mathbf{y}}^*$. Because of (12.2.35) we sometimes call R, the square root of R^2, the *multiple correlation coefficient*.

See Section 12.5 for a discussion of the necessity to modify R^2 in order to use it as a criterion for choosing a regression equation.

12.2.4 Asymptotic Properties of Least Squares Estimators

In this section we prove the consistency and the asymptotic normality of $\hat{\boldsymbol{\beta}}$ and the consistency of $\hat{\sigma}^2$ under suitable assumptions on the regressor matrix $\mathbf{X}$.

THEOREM 12.2.2 In the multiple regression model (12.1.1), the least squares estimator $\hat{\boldsymbol{\beta}}$ is a consistent estimator of $\boldsymbol{\beta}$ if $\lambda_s(\mathbf{X}'\mathbf{X}) \to \infty$, where $\lambda_s(\mathbf{X}'\mathbf{X})$ denotes the smallest characteristic root of $\mathbf{X}'\mathbf{X}$.

Proof. Equation (11.5.3) shows that the characteristic roots of $(\mathbf{X}'\mathbf{X})^{-1}$ are the reciprocals of the characteristic roots of $\mathbf{X}'\mathbf{X}$. Therefore $\lambda_s(\mathbf{X}'\mathbf{X}) \to \infty$ implies $\lambda_l[(\mathbf{X}'\mathbf{X})^{-1}] \to 0$, where λ_l denotes the largest characteristic root. Since the characteristic roots of $(\mathbf{X}'\mathbf{X})^{-1}$ are all positive, $\lambda_l[(\mathbf{X}'\mathbf{X})^{-1}] \to 0$ implies tr $(\mathbf{X}'\mathbf{X})^{-1} \to 0$ because the trace is the sum of the characteristic roots by Theorem 11.5.9. Since $V\hat{\boldsymbol{\beta}} = \sigma^2(\mathbf{X}'\mathbf{X})^{-1}$, as we obtained in (12.2.22), tr $(\mathbf{X}'\mathbf{X})^{-1} \to 0$ implies tr $V\hat{\boldsymbol{\beta}} \to 0$, which in turn implies

$V\hat{\beta}_i \to 0$ for $i = 1, 2, \ldots, K$. Our theorem follows from Theorem 6.1.1.
❑

Note that the assumption $\lambda_s(\mathbf{X}'\mathbf{X}) \to \infty$ implies that every diagonal element of $\mathbf{X}'\mathbf{X}$ goes to infinity as T goes to infinity. We can prove this as follows. Let $\mathbf{e}_i$ be the T-vector that has 1 in the ith position and 0 elsewhere. Then, the ith diagonal element of $\mathbf{X}'\mathbf{X}$, $\mathbf{x}'_{(i)}\mathbf{x}_{(i)}$ can be written as

$$(12.2.36) \quad \mathbf{x}'_{(i)}\mathbf{x}_{(i)} = \frac{\mathbf{e}'_i\mathbf{X}'\mathbf{X}\mathbf{e}_i}{\mathbf{e}'_i\mathbf{e}_i}.$$

But the right-hand side of (12.2.36) is greater than or equal to $\lambda_s(\mathbf{X}'\mathbf{X})$ by Theorem 11.5.6. Therefore $\lambda_s(\mathbf{X}'\mathbf{X}) \to \infty$ implies $\mathbf{x}'_{(i)}\mathbf{x}_{(i)} \to \infty$.

The converse of this result is not true, as we show below. Suppose $\mathbf{X}$ has two columns, the first of which consists of T ones and the second of which has zero in the first position and one elsewhere. Then, we have

$$(12.2.37) \quad \mathbf{X}'\mathbf{X} = \begin{bmatrix} T & T-1 \\ T-1 & T \end{bmatrix}$$

so that $\mathbf{x}'_{(i)}\mathbf{x}_{(i)} \to \infty$, $i = 1, 2$. Solving

$$(12.2.38) \quad \det \begin{bmatrix} T-\lambda & T-1 \\ T-1 & T-\lambda \end{bmatrix} = 0$$

for λ, we find that the characteristic roots of $\mathbf{X}'\mathbf{X}$ are 1 and $2T - 1$. Therefore we do not have $\lambda_s(\mathbf{X}'\mathbf{X}) \to \infty$. Using the results of Section 11.3, we have from (12.2.37)

$$(12.2.39) \quad (\mathbf{X}'\mathbf{X})^{-1} = \frac{1}{2T-1} \begin{bmatrix} T & 1-T \\ 1-T & T \end{bmatrix}.$$

Thus, in this example, the variance of the least squares estimator of each of the two parameters converges to $\sigma^2/2$ as T goes to infinity.

THEOREM 12.2.3 In the multiple regression model (12.1.1), $\hat{\sigma}^2$ as defined in (12.2.26) is a consistent estimator of σ^2.

Proof. From (12.2.26) and (12.2.27) we have

$$(12.2.40) \quad \hat{\sigma}^2 = \frac{\mathbf{u}'\mathbf{u}}{T} - \frac{\mathbf{u}'\mathbf{P}\mathbf{u}}{T},$$

where $\mathbf{P} = \mathbf{X}(\mathbf{X}'\mathbf{X})^{-1}\mathbf{X}'$ as before. As we showed in equation (10.2.67),

(12.2.41) $\text{plim } \dfrac{\mathbf{u}'\mathbf{u}}{T} = \sigma^2.$

By a derivation similar to (12.2.28), we have $E\mathbf{u}'\mathbf{P}\mathbf{u} = \sigma^2 K$. Therefore, by Chebyshev's inequality (6.1.2), we have for any ϵ^2

(12.2.42) $P\left(\dfrac{\mathbf{u}'\mathbf{P}\mathbf{u}}{T} > \epsilon^2\right) \leq \dfrac{\sigma^2 K}{\epsilon^2 T},$

which implies

(12.2.43) $\text{plim } \dfrac{\mathbf{u}'\mathbf{P}\mathbf{u}}{T} = 0.$

The consistency of $\hat{\sigma}^2$ follows from (12.2.40), (12.2.41), and (12.2.43) because of Theorem 6.1.3. ❏

Let $\mathbf{x}_{(i)}$ be the ith column of $\mathbf{X}$ and let $\mathbf{X}_{(-i)}$ be the $T \times (K - 1)$ submatrix of $\mathbf{X}$ obtained by removing $\mathbf{x}_{(i)}$ from $\mathbf{X}$. Define

$$\mathbf{M}_{(-i)} = \mathbf{I} - \mathbf{X}_{(-i)}[\mathbf{X}'_{(-i)}\mathbf{X}_{(-i)}]^{-1}\mathbf{X}'_{(-i)} \quad \text{and} \quad \mathbf{x}^*_{(i)} = \mathbf{M}_{(-i)}\mathbf{x}_{(i)}.$$

Using (12.2.17), we can write the ith element of $\hat{\boldsymbol{\beta}}$ as

(12.2.44) $\hat{\beta}_i = \dfrac{\mathbf{x}^{*\prime}_{(i)}\mathbf{y}}{\mathbf{x}^{*\prime}_{(i)}\mathbf{x}^*_{(i)}}.$

Inserting (12.1.3) into the right-hand side of (12.2.44) and noting that $\mathbf{M}_{(-i)}\mathbf{X}_{(-i)} = \mathbf{0}$, we have

(12.2.45) $\hat{\beta}_i - \beta_i = \dfrac{\mathbf{x}^{*\prime}_{(i)}\mathbf{u}}{\mathbf{x}^{*\prime}_{(i)}\mathbf{x}^*_{(i)}}.$

Note that (12.2.45) is a generalization of equations (10.2.19) and (10.2.21). Since (12.2.45) has the same form as the expression (10.2.68), the sufficient condition for the asymptotic normality of (12.2.45) can be obtained from Theorem 10.2.2.

The following theorem generalizes Theorem 10.2.2 and shows that the elements of $\hat{\boldsymbol{\beta}}$ are jointly asymptotically normal under the given assumptions. (For proof of the theorem, see Amemiya, 1985, chapter 3).

THEOREM 12.2.4 In the multiple regression model (12.1.1), assume that

$$(12.2.46) \quad \lim_{T\to\infty} \frac{\max_{1\le t\le T} x_{ti}^2}{\mathbf{x}_{(i)}'\mathbf{x}_{(i)}} = 0, \quad i = 1, 2, \ldots, K.$$

Define $\mathbf{Z} = \mathbf{XS}^{-1}$, where $\mathbf{S}$ is the $K \times K$ diagonal matrix with $[\mathbf{x}_{(i)}'\mathbf{x}_{(i)}]^{1/2}$ as its ith diagonal element, and assume that $\lim_{T\to\infty} \mathbf{Z}'\mathbf{Z} \equiv \mathbf{R}$ exists and is nonsingular. Then $\mathbf{S}(\hat{\boldsymbol{\beta}} - \boldsymbol{\beta}) \to N(0, \sigma^2\mathbf{R}^{-1})$.

12.2.5 Maximum Likelihood Estimators

In this section we show that if we assume the normality of $\{u_t\}$ in the model (12.1.1), the least squares estimators $\hat{\boldsymbol{\beta}}$ and $\hat{\sigma}^2$ are also the maximum likelihood estimators. We also show that $\hat{\boldsymbol{\beta}}$ is the best unbiased estimator in this case.

Using the multivariate normal density (5.4.1), the likelihood function of the parameters $\boldsymbol{\beta}$ and σ^2 can be written in vector notation as

$$(12.2.47) \quad L = (2\pi\sigma^2)^{-T/2} \exp\left[-\frac{1}{2\sigma^2} (\mathbf{y} - \mathbf{X}\boldsymbol{\beta})'(\mathbf{y} - \mathbf{X}\boldsymbol{\beta})\right],$$

which is a generalization of equation (10.2.77). Taking the natural logarithm of (12.2.47) yields

$$(12.2.48) \quad \log L = -\frac{T}{2} \log 2\pi - \frac{T}{2} \log \sigma^2 - \frac{1}{2\sigma^2} (\mathbf{y} - \mathbf{X}\boldsymbol{\beta})'(\mathbf{y} - \mathbf{X}\boldsymbol{\beta}).$$

From (12.2.48) it is apparent that the maximum likelihood estimator of $\boldsymbol{\beta}$ is identical to the least squares estimator $\hat{\boldsymbol{\beta}}$. To show that the maximum likelihood estimator of σ^2 is the $\hat{\sigma}^2$ defined in (12.2.26), the reader should follow the discussion in Section 10.2.5 by regarding the $\hat{u}_t$ that appears in equations (10.2.80) and (10.2.81) as that defined in (12.2.12).

To show that $\hat{\boldsymbol{\beta}}$ is best unbiased under the normality assumption of $\mathbf{u}$, we need the following vector generalization.

THEOREM 12.2.5 (Cramér-Rao) Let $\boldsymbol{\theta}^*$ be any unbiased estimator of a vector parameter $\boldsymbol{\theta}$ and let $V\boldsymbol{\theta}^*$ be its variance-covariance matrix. Suppose that $\partial^2 \log L/\partial\boldsymbol{\theta}\partial\boldsymbol{\theta}'$ denotes a matrix whose i, jth element is equal to $\partial^2 \log L/\partial\theta_i\partial\theta_j$. Then we have

(12.2.49) $V\boldsymbol{\theta}^* \geq -\left[E\dfrac{\partial^2 \log L}{\partial\boldsymbol{\theta}\partial\boldsymbol{\theta}'}\right]^{-1},$

where $\geq$ is in the sense given in connection with Definition 11.5.2. The right-hand side of (12.2.49) is called the *Cramér-Rao (matrix) lower bound*.

We put $\boldsymbol{\theta} = (\boldsymbol{\beta}', \sigma^2)'$ and calculate the Cramér-Rao lower bound for the log L given in (12.2.48). We have

(12.2.50) $\dfrac{\partial \log L}{\partial\boldsymbol{\beta}} = \dfrac{1}{\sigma^2}(\mathbf{X}'\mathbf{y} - \mathbf{X}'\mathbf{X}\boldsymbol{\beta}),$

(12.2.51) $\dfrac{\partial \log L}{\partial(\sigma^2)} = -\dfrac{T}{2\sigma^2} + \dfrac{1}{2\sigma^4}(\mathbf{y} - \mathbf{X}\boldsymbol{\beta})'(\mathbf{y} - \mathbf{X}\boldsymbol{\beta}),$

(12.2.52) $\dfrac{\partial^2 \log L}{\partial\boldsymbol{\beta}\partial\boldsymbol{\beta}'} = -\dfrac{1}{\sigma^2}\mathbf{X}'\mathbf{X},$

(12.2.53) $\dfrac{\partial^2 \log L}{\partial(\sigma^2)^2} = \dfrac{T}{2\sigma^4} - \dfrac{1}{\sigma^6}(\mathbf{y} - \mathbf{X}\boldsymbol{\beta})'(\mathbf{y} - \mathbf{X}\boldsymbol{\beta}),$

(12.2.54) $\dfrac{\partial^2 \log L}{\partial\boldsymbol{\beta}\partial(\sigma^2)} = -\dfrac{1}{\sigma^4}(\mathbf{X}'\mathbf{y} - \mathbf{X}'\mathbf{X}\boldsymbol{\beta}).$

From (12.2.52), (12.2.53), and (12.2.54) we obtain

(12.2.55) $-\left[E\dfrac{\partial^2 \log L}{\partial\boldsymbol{\theta}\partial\boldsymbol{\theta}'}\right]^{-1} = \begin{bmatrix} \sigma^2(\mathbf{X}'\mathbf{X})^{-1} & 0 \\ 0 & \dfrac{2\sigma^4}{T} \end{bmatrix}.$

From (12.2.49) and (12.2.55) we conclude that if $\boldsymbol{\beta}^*$ is any unbiased estimator of $\boldsymbol{\beta}$,

(12.2.56) $V\boldsymbol{\beta}^* \geq \sigma^2(\mathbf{X}'\mathbf{X})^{-1}.$

But since the right-hand side of (12.2.56) is the variance-covariance matrix of $\hat{\boldsymbol{\beta}}$, we have proved the following generalization of Example 7.4.2.

THEOREM 12.2.6 If **u** is normal in the model (12.1.1), the least squares estimator $\hat{\boldsymbol{\beta}}$ is best unbiased.

12.2.6 Prediction

As in Section 10.2.6, we affix the following "prediction period" equation to the model (12.1.1):

$$(12.2.57) \quad y_p = \mathbf{x}_p' \boldsymbol{\beta} + u_p,$$

where y_p and u_p are both unobservable and $\mathbf{x}_p$ is a K-vector of known constants. We assume that u_p is distributed independently of the vector **u**, and $Eu_p = 0$ and $Vu_p = \sigma^2$. Note that $\boldsymbol{\beta}$ and σ^2 are the same as in (12.1.1).

Let $\tilde{\boldsymbol{\beta}}$ be an arbitrary estimator of $\boldsymbol{\beta}$ based on **y** and define the predictor $\tilde{y}_p$ of y_p by

$$(12.5.58) \quad \tilde{y}_p = \mathbf{x}_p'\tilde{\boldsymbol{\beta}}.$$

We obtain the mean squared prediction error of $\tilde{y}_p$ conditional upon $\mathbf{x}_p$ as

$$(12.2.59) \quad E(y_p - \tilde{y}_p)^2 = E[u_p - \mathbf{x}_p'(\tilde{\boldsymbol{\beta}} - \boldsymbol{\beta})]^2$$
$$= \sigma^2 + \mathbf{x}_p'E(\tilde{\boldsymbol{\beta}} - \boldsymbol{\beta})(\tilde{\boldsymbol{\beta}} - \boldsymbol{\beta})'\mathbf{x}_p.$$

The second equality follows from the independence of u_p and **u** in view of Theorem 3.5.1.

Equation (12.2.59) establishes a close relationship between the criterion of prediction and the criterion of estimation. In particular, it shows that if an estimator $\tilde{\boldsymbol{\beta}}$ is better than an estimator $\boldsymbol{\beta}^*$ in the sense of Definition 11.5.3, the corresponding predictor $\tilde{y}_p \equiv \mathbf{x}_p'\tilde{\boldsymbol{\beta}}$ is better than $y_p^* \equiv \mathbf{x}_p'\boldsymbol{\beta}^*$ in the sense that the former has the smaller mean squared prediction error. Thus, by restricting $\tilde{\boldsymbol{\beta}}$ to the class of linear unbiased estimators, we immediately see that the least squares predictor $\hat{y}_p \equiv \mathbf{x}_p'\hat{\boldsymbol{\beta}}$ is the best linear unbiased predictor of y_p.

Let $\tilde{\boldsymbol{\beta}}$ and $\boldsymbol{\beta}^*$ be the two estimators of $\boldsymbol{\beta}$. In Section 11.5 we demonstrated that we may not be always able to show either

$$E(\tilde{\boldsymbol{\beta}} - \boldsymbol{\beta})(\tilde{\boldsymbol{\beta}} - \boldsymbol{\beta})' \leq E(\boldsymbol{\beta}^* - \boldsymbol{\beta})(\boldsymbol{\beta}^* - \boldsymbol{\beta})'$$

or the reverse inequality; if not, we can rank the two estimators by the trace or the determinant of the mean squared error matrix. The essential part of the mean squared prediction error (12.2.59),

$$\mathbf{x}_p' E(\tilde{\boldsymbol{\beta}} - \boldsymbol{\beta})(\tilde{\boldsymbol{\beta}} - \boldsymbol{\beta})' \mathbf{x}_p,$$

provides another scalar criterion by which we can rank estimators. One weakness of this criterion is that $\mathbf{x}_p$ may not always be known at the time when we must choose the estimator.

In practice, we must often predict $\mathbf{x}_p$ before we can predict y_p. Accordingly we now treat $\mathbf{x}_p$ as a random vector and take the expectation of $\mathbf{x}_p' E(\tilde{\boldsymbol{\beta}} - \boldsymbol{\beta})(\tilde{\boldsymbol{\beta}} - \boldsymbol{\beta})' \mathbf{x}_p$. We assume that

$$(12.2.60) \quad E\mathbf{x}_p\mathbf{x}_p' = \frac{1}{T} \mathbf{X}'\mathbf{X},$$

which means that the second moments of the regressors remain the same from the sample period to the prediction period. Using (12.2.58), we obtain

$$(12.2.61) \quad E^*\mathbf{x}_p' E(\tilde{\boldsymbol{\beta}} - \boldsymbol{\beta})(\tilde{\boldsymbol{\beta}} - \boldsymbol{\beta})' \mathbf{x}_p = \text{tr } E(\tilde{\boldsymbol{\beta}} - \boldsymbol{\beta})(\tilde{\boldsymbol{\beta}} - \boldsymbol{\beta})' E^*\mathbf{x}_p\mathbf{x}_p'$$

$$= \frac{1}{T} \text{tr } E(\tilde{\boldsymbol{\beta}} - \boldsymbol{\beta})(\tilde{\boldsymbol{\beta}} - \boldsymbol{\beta})' \mathbf{X}'\mathbf{X}$$

$$= \frac{1}{T} E (\tilde{\boldsymbol{\beta}} - \boldsymbol{\beta})' \mathbf{X}'\mathbf{X}(\tilde{\boldsymbol{\beta}} - \boldsymbol{\beta}),$$

where E^* denotes the expectation taken with respect to $\mathbf{x}_p$. The right-hand side of (12.2.61) is a useful criterion by which to choose an estimator in situations where the best estimator in the sense of Definition 11.5.3 cannot be found. We shall call (12.2.61) plus σ^2 the *unconditional mean squared prediction error.*

12.3 CONSTRAINED LEAST SQUARES ESTIMATORS

In this section we consider the estimation of the parameters $\boldsymbol{\beta}$ and σ^2 in the model (12.1.1) when there are certain linear constraints about the elements of $\boldsymbol{\beta}$. We assume that the constraints are of the form

$$(12.3.1) \quad \mathbf{Q}'\boldsymbol{\beta} = \mathbf{c},$$

where $\mathbf{Q}$ is a $K \times q$ matrix of known constants and $\mathbf{c}$ is q-vector of known constants. We assume $q < K$ and $\text{rank}(\mathbf{Q}) = q$.

Constraints of the form (12.3.1) embody many common constraints which occur in practice. For example, if $\mathbf{Q}' = (\mathbf{I}, \mathbf{0})$ where $\mathbf{I}$ is the identity matrix of size K_1 and $\mathbf{0}$ is the $K_1 \times K_2$ matrix of zeroes such that $K_1 + K_2 = K$, the constraints mean that a K_1-component subset of $\boldsymbol{\beta}$ is specified to take certain values, whereas the remaining K_2 elements are allowed to vary freely. As another example, the case where $\mathbf{Q}'$ is a row vector of ones and $c = 1$ corresponds to the restriction that the sum of the regression parameters is unity.

The study of this subject is useful for its own sake; it also provides a basis for the next section, where we shall discuss tests of the linear hypothesis (12.3.1).

The *constrained least squares (CLS) estimator* of $\boldsymbol{\beta}$, denoted $\boldsymbol{\beta}^+$, is defined to be the value of $\boldsymbol{\beta}$ that minimizes the sum of the squared residuals:

(12.3.2) $S(\boldsymbol{\beta}) = (\mathbf{y} - \mathbf{X}\boldsymbol{\beta})'(\mathbf{y} - \mathbf{X}\boldsymbol{\beta}),$

subject to the constraints specified in (12.3.1). In Section 12.2.1 we showed that (12.3.2) is minimized without constraint at the least squares estimator $\hat{\boldsymbol{\beta}}$. Writing $S(\hat{\boldsymbol{\beta}})$ for the sum of the squares of the least squares residuals, we can rewrite (12.3.2) as

(12.3.3) $S(\boldsymbol{\beta}) = S(\hat{\boldsymbol{\beta}}) + (\hat{\boldsymbol{\beta}} - \boldsymbol{\beta})'\mathbf{X}'\mathbf{X}(\hat{\boldsymbol{\beta}} - \boldsymbol{\beta}).$

Instead of directly minimizing (12.3.2) subject to (12.3.1), we minimize (12.3.3) under (12.3.1), which is mathematically simpler.

Put $\hat{\boldsymbol{\beta}} - \boldsymbol{\beta} = \boldsymbol{\delta}$ and $\mathbf{Q}'\hat{\boldsymbol{\beta}} - \mathbf{c} = \boldsymbol{\gamma}$. Then the problem is equivalent to the minimization of $\boldsymbol{\delta}'\mathbf{X}'\mathbf{X}\boldsymbol{\delta}$ subject to $\mathbf{Q}'\boldsymbol{\delta} = \boldsymbol{\gamma}$. The solution is obtained by equating the derivatives of

(12.3.4) $\boldsymbol{\delta}'\mathbf{X}'\mathbf{X}\boldsymbol{\delta} + 2\boldsymbol{\lambda}'(\mathbf{Q}'\boldsymbol{\delta} - \boldsymbol{\gamma})$

with respect to $\boldsymbol{\delta}$ and a q-vector of Lagrange multipliers $\boldsymbol{\lambda}$ to zero. Thus,

(12.3.5) $\mathbf{X}'\mathbf{X}\boldsymbol{\delta} + \mathbf{Q}\boldsymbol{\lambda} = \mathbf{0}$

and

(12.3.6) $\mathbf{Q}'\boldsymbol{\delta} = \boldsymbol{\gamma}.$

Solving (12.3.5) for $\boldsymbol{\delta}$ gives

(12.3.7) $\boldsymbol{\delta} = -(\mathbf{X}'\mathbf{X})^{-1}\mathbf{Q}\boldsymbol{\lambda}.$

Inserting (12.3.7) into (12.3.6) and solving for $\boldsymbol{\lambda}$, we get

(12.3.8) $\boldsymbol{\lambda} = -[\mathbf{Q}'(\mathbf{X}'\mathbf{X})^{-1}\mathbf{Q}]^{-1}\boldsymbol{\gamma}.$

Finally, inserting (12.3.8) back into (12.3.5) and solving for $\boldsymbol{\delta}$, we obtain

(12.3.9) $\boldsymbol{\delta} = (\mathbf{X}'\mathbf{X})^{-1}\mathbf{Q}[\mathbf{Q}'(\mathbf{X}'\mathbf{X})^{-1}\mathbf{Q}]^{-1}\boldsymbol{\gamma}.$

Transforming $\boldsymbol{\delta}$ and $\boldsymbol{\gamma}$ into the original variables, we can write the solution as

(12.3.10) $\boldsymbol{\beta}^+ = \hat{\boldsymbol{\beta}} - (\mathbf{X}'\mathbf{X})^{-1}\mathbf{Q}[\mathbf{Q}'(\mathbf{X}'\mathbf{X})^{-1}\mathbf{Q}]^{-1}(\mathbf{Q}'\hat{\boldsymbol{\beta}} - \mathbf{c}).$

The corresponding estimator of σ^2 is given by

(12.3.11) $\sigma^{2+} = \dfrac{1}{T}(\mathbf{y} - \mathbf{X}\boldsymbol{\beta}^+)'(\mathbf{y} - \mathbf{X}\boldsymbol{\beta}^+).$

Taking the expectation of (12.3.10) under the assumption that (12.3.1) is true, we immediately see that $E\boldsymbol{\beta}^+ = \boldsymbol{\beta}$. We can evaluate $V\boldsymbol{\beta}^+$ from (12.3.10) as

(12.3.12) $V\boldsymbol{\beta}^+ = \sigma^2\{(\mathbf{X}'\mathbf{X})^{-1} - (\mathbf{X}'\mathbf{X})^{-1}\mathbf{Q}[\mathbf{Q}'(\mathbf{X}'\mathbf{X})^{-1}\mathbf{Q}]^{-1}\mathbf{Q}'(\mathbf{X}'\mathbf{X})^{-1}\}.$

Since the second term within the braces above is nonnegative definite, we have $V\boldsymbol{\beta}^+ \leq V\hat{\boldsymbol{\beta}}$. We should expect this result, for $\hat{\boldsymbol{\beta}}$ ignores the constraints. It can be shown that if (12.3.1) is true, the CLS $\boldsymbol{\beta}^+$ is the best linear unbiased estimator.

If $\{u_t\}$ are normal in the model (12.1.1) and if (12.3.1) is true, the constrained least squares estimators $\boldsymbol{\beta}^+$ and σ^{2+} are the maximum likelihood estimators.

We can give an alternative derivation of the CLS $\boldsymbol{\beta}^+$. Theorem 11.4.9 assures us that we can find a $K \times (K - q)$ matrix $\mathbf{R}$ such that, first, $(\mathbf{Q}, \mathbf{R})$ is nonsingular and, second, $\mathbf{R}'\mathbf{Q} = \mathbf{0}$. The $\mathbf{R}$ is not unique; any value that satisfies these conditions will do. Finding $\mathbf{R}$ is easy for the following reason. Suppose we find a $K \times (K - q)$ matrix $\mathbf{S}$ such that $(\mathbf{Q}, \mathbf{S})$ is nonsingular. Then $\mathbf{R}$ defined by $\mathbf{R} = [\mathbf{I} - \mathbf{Q}(\mathbf{Q}'\mathbf{Q})^{-1}\mathbf{Q}']\mathbf{S}$ satisfies our two conditions.

Now define $\mathbf{A} = (\mathbf{Q}, \mathbf{R})'$. Using $\mathbf{A}$ we can transform equation (12.1.3) as follows:

(12.3.13) $\mathbf{y} = \mathbf{X}\boldsymbol{\beta} + \mathbf{u}$

$\qquad\quad = \mathbf{X}\mathbf{A}^{-1}\mathbf{A}\boldsymbol{\beta} + \mathbf{u}$

$$= \mathbf{Z}\begin{bmatrix} \mathbf{c} \\ \mathbf{\alpha} \end{bmatrix} + \mathbf{u}$$

$$= \mathbf{Z}_1\mathbf{c} + \mathbf{Z}_2\mathbf{\alpha} + \mathbf{u},$$

where $\mathbf{Z} = \mathbf{XA}^{-1}$, $\mathbf{\alpha} = \mathbf{R}'\mathbf{\beta}$, $\mathbf{Z}_1$ consists of the first q columns of $\mathbf{Z}$, and $\mathbf{Z}_2$ consists of the last $K - q$ columns of $\mathbf{Z}$. From (12.3.13),

(12.3.14) $\mathbf{y} - \mathbf{Z}_1\mathbf{c} = \mathbf{Z}_2\mathbf{\alpha} + \mathbf{u}.$

Since $\mathbf{Z}_1$, $\mathbf{Z}_2$ and $\mathbf{c}$ are all known constants, equation (12.3.14) represents a multiple regression model in which $\mathbf{y} - \mathbf{Z}_1\mathbf{c}$ is the vector of dependent variables and a $(K - q)$-vector $\mathbf{\alpha}$ constitutes the unknown regression coefficients. Thus, by the transformation of (12.3.13), we have reduced the problem of estimating K parameters subject to q constraints to the problem of estimating $K - q$ parameters without constraint.

We can apply the least squares method to (12.3.14) to obtain

(12.3.15) $\hat{\mathbf{\alpha}} = (\mathbf{Z}_2'\mathbf{Z}_2)^{-1}\mathbf{Z}_2'(\mathbf{y} - \mathbf{Z}_1\mathbf{c})$

and then estimate $\mathbf{\beta}$ by

(12.3.16) $\mathbf{\beta}^+ = \mathbf{A}^{-1}\begin{bmatrix} \mathbf{c} \\ \hat{\mathbf{\alpha}} \end{bmatrix}$

$$= \mathbf{R}(\mathbf{R}'\mathbf{X}'\mathbf{XR})^{-1}\mathbf{R}'\mathbf{X}'\mathbf{y} + [\mathbf{I} - \mathbf{R}(\mathbf{R}'\mathbf{X}'\mathbf{XR})^{-1}\mathbf{R}'\mathbf{X}'\mathbf{X}]\mathbf{Q}(\mathbf{Q}'\mathbf{Q})^{-1}\mathbf{c}.$$

In (12.3.16) we have used the same symbol as the CLS $\mathbf{\beta}^+$ because the right-hand side of (12.3.16) can be shown to be identical to the right-hand side of (12.3.10) if $\mathbf{X}'\mathbf{X}$ is nonsingular. (The proof can be found in Amemiya, 1985, chapter 1.)

12.4 TESTS OF HYPOTHESES

12.4.1 Introduction

In this section we regard the linear constraints of (12.3.1) as a testable hypothesis and develop testing procedures. We shall call (12.3.1) the null hypothesis. Throughout the section we assume the multiple regression model (12.1.1) with the normality of $\mathbf{u}$, since the distribution of the test statistics we use is derived under the normality assumption. We discuss

Student's t test, the F test, and a test for structural change (a special case of the F test), in that order.

As preliminaries, we derive the distribution of $\hat{\boldsymbol{\beta}}$ and $\hat{\mathbf{u}}'\hat{\mathbf{u}}$ and related results.

Applying Theorem 5.4.2 to $\hat{\boldsymbol{\beta}}$ defined in (12.2.5), we immediately see that $\hat{\boldsymbol{\beta}}$ is normally distributed if $\mathbf{y}$ is normal. Using the mean and variance obtained in Section 12.2.2, we obtain

(12.4.1) $\hat{\boldsymbol{\beta}} \sim N[\boldsymbol{\beta}, \sigma^2(\mathbf{X}'\mathbf{X})^{-1}]$.

THEOREM 12.4.1 Let $\hat{\mathbf{u}}$ be as defined in (12.2.12). In the model (12.1.1), with the normality of $\mathbf{u}$ we have

(12.4.2) $\dfrac{\hat{\mathbf{u}}'\hat{\mathbf{u}}}{\sigma^2} \sim \chi^2_{T-K}$.

Proof. If we define $\mathbf{v} = \sigma^{-1}\mathbf{u}$, we have $\mathbf{v} \sim N(\mathbf{0}, \mathbf{I})$. Since $\hat{\mathbf{u}}'\hat{\mathbf{u}} = \mathbf{u}'\mathbf{M}\mathbf{u}$ from (12.2.27), we can write

(12.4.3) $\dfrac{\hat{\mathbf{u}}'\hat{\mathbf{u}}}{\sigma^2} = \mathbf{v}'\mathbf{M}\mathbf{v}$.

Because of Theorem 11.5.18, there exists a $T \times T$ matrix $\mathbf{H}$ such that $\mathbf{H}'\mathbf{H} = \mathbf{I}$ and

(12.4.4) $\mathbf{H}'\mathbf{M}\mathbf{H} = \begin{bmatrix} \mathbf{I} & \mathbf{0} \\ \mathbf{0} & \mathbf{0} \end{bmatrix}$,

where the right-hand side of (12.4.4) denotes a diagonal matrix that has one in the first $T - K$ diagonal positions and zero elsewhere. Therefore,

(12.4.5) $\mathbf{v}'\mathbf{M}\mathbf{v} = \mathbf{v}'\mathbf{H}\mathbf{H}'\mathbf{M}\mathbf{H}\mathbf{H}'\mathbf{v}$

$$= \mathbf{w}'\begin{bmatrix} \mathbf{I} & \mathbf{0} \\ \mathbf{0} & \mathbf{0} \end{bmatrix}\mathbf{w}$$

$$= \sum_{i=1}^{T-K} w_i^2,$$

where $\mathbf{w} = \mathbf{H}'\mathbf{v}$ and w_i is the ith element of $\mathbf{w}$. Since $\mathbf{w} \sim N(\mathbf{0}, \mathbf{I})$, $\sum_{i=1}^{T-K} w_i^2 \sim \chi^2_{T-K}$ by Definition 1 of the Appendix. ❑

Next, let us show the independence of (12.4.1) and (12.4.2).

THEOREM 12.4.2 In the model (12.1.1) with the normality of **u**, the random variables defined in (12.4.1) and (12.4.2) are independent.

Proof. We need only show the independence of $\hat{\boldsymbol{\beta}}$ and $\hat{\mathbf{u}}$ because of Theorem 3.5.1. But since $\hat{\boldsymbol{\beta}}$ and $\hat{\mathbf{u}}$ are jointly normally distributed by Theorem 5.4.2, we need only show that $\hat{\boldsymbol{\beta}}$ and $\hat{\mathbf{u}}$ are uncorrelated. This follows from

$$
\begin{aligned}
(12.4.6) \qquad E(\hat{\boldsymbol{\beta}} - \boldsymbol{\beta})\hat{\mathbf{u}}' &= E(\mathbf{X}'\mathbf{X})^{-1}\mathbf{X}'\mathbf{u}\mathbf{u}'\mathbf{M} \\
&= (\mathbf{X}'\mathbf{X})^{-1}\mathbf{X}'(E\mathbf{u}\mathbf{u}')\mathbf{M} \\
&= \sigma^2(\mathbf{X}'\mathbf{X})^{-1}\mathbf{X}'\mathbf{M} \\
&= \mathbf{0}. \qquad \square
\end{aligned}
$$

12.4.2 Student's *t* Test

The *t* test is ideal when we have a single constraint, that is, $q = 1$. The *F* test, discussed in the next section, must be used if $q > 1$.

Since $\hat{\boldsymbol{\beta}}$ is normal as shown above, we have

$$
(12.4.7) \qquad \mathbf{Q}'\hat{\boldsymbol{\beta}} \sim N[c, \sigma^2\mathbf{Q}'(\mathbf{X}'\mathbf{X})^{-1}\mathbf{Q}]
$$

under the null hypothesis (that is, if $\mathbf{Q}'\boldsymbol{\beta} = c$). Note that here $\mathbf{Q}'$ is a row vector and c is a scalar. Therefore,

$$
(12.4.8) \qquad \frac{\mathbf{Q}'\hat{\boldsymbol{\beta}} - c}{\sigma\sqrt{\mathbf{Q}'(\mathbf{X}'\mathbf{X})^{-1}\mathbf{Q}}} \sim N(0, 1).
$$

The random variables defined in (12.4.2) and (12.4.8) are independent because of Theorem 12.4.2. Hence, by Definition 2 of the Appendix, we have

$$
(12.4.9) \qquad \frac{\mathbf{Q}'\hat{\boldsymbol{\beta}} - c}{\tilde{\sigma}\sqrt{\mathbf{Q}'(\mathbf{X}'\mathbf{X})^{-1}\mathbf{Q}}} \sim t_{T-K},
$$

Student's *t* with $T - K$ degrees of freedom, where $\tilde{\sigma}$ is the square root of the unbiased estimator of σ^2 defined in equation (12.2.29). Note that the denominator in (12.4.9) is an estimate of the standard deviation of the numerator. The null hypothesis $\mathbf{Q}'\boldsymbol{\beta} = c$ can be tested by the statistic (12.4.9). We use a one-tail or two-tail test, depending on the alternative hypothesis.

The following are some of the values of $\mathbf{Q}$ and c that frequently occur in practice:

The ith element of $\mathbf{Q}$ is unity and all other elements are zero. Then the null hypothesis is simply $\beta_i = c$.

The ith and jth elements of $\mathbf{Q}$ are 1 and -1, respectively, and $c = 0$. Then the null hypothesis becomes $\beta_i = \beta_j$.

$\mathbf{Q}$ is a K-vector of ones. Then the null hypothesis becomes $\sum_{i=1}^{K} \beta_i = c$.

12.4.3 The F Test

In this section we consider the test of the null hypothesis $\mathbf{Q}'\boldsymbol{\beta} = \mathbf{c}$ against the alternative hypothesis $\mathbf{Q}'\boldsymbol{\beta} \neq \mathbf{c}$ when it involves more than one constraint (that is, $q > 1$). In this case the t test cannot be used.

Again $\mathbf{Q}'\hat{\boldsymbol{\beta}} - \mathbf{c}$ will play a central role in the test statistic. The distribution of $\mathbf{Q}'\hat{\boldsymbol{\beta}}$ given in (12.4.7) is valid even if $q > 1$ because of Theorem 5.4.2. Therefore, by Theorem 9.7.1,

$$(12.4.10) \quad \frac{(\mathbf{Q}'\hat{\boldsymbol{\beta}} - \mathbf{c})'[\mathbf{Q}'(\mathbf{X}'\mathbf{X})^{-1}\mathbf{Q}]^{-1}(\mathbf{Q}'\hat{\boldsymbol{\beta}} - \mathbf{c})}{\sigma^2} \sim \chi_q^2.$$

If σ^2 were known, we could use the test statistic (12.4.10) right away and reject the null hypothesis if the left-hand side were greater than a certain value. The reader will recall from Section 9.7 that this would be the likelihood ratio test if $\hat{\boldsymbol{\beta}}$ were normal and the generalized Wald test if $\hat{\boldsymbol{\beta}}$ were only asymptotically normal.

Since $\hat{\boldsymbol{\beta}}$ and $\hat{\mathbf{u}}$ are independent as shown in the argument leading to Theorem 12.4.2, the chi-square variables (12.4.2) and (12.4.10) are independent. Therefore, by Definition 3 of the Appendix, we have

$$(12.4.11) \quad \eta \equiv \frac{T-K}{q} \cdot \frac{(\mathbf{Q}'\hat{\boldsymbol{\beta}} - \mathbf{c})'[\mathbf{Q}'(\mathbf{X}'\mathbf{X})^{-1}\mathbf{Q}]^{-1}(\mathbf{Q}'\hat{\boldsymbol{\beta}} - \mathbf{c})}{\hat{\mathbf{u}}'\hat{\mathbf{u}}} \sim F(q, T-K).$$

The null hypothesis $\mathbf{Q}'\boldsymbol{\beta} = \mathbf{c}$ is rejected if $\eta > d$, where d is determined so that $P(\eta > d)$ is equal to a certain prescribed significance level under the null hypothesis.

Comparing (12.4.9) and (12.4.11), we see that if $q = 1$ (and therefore $\mathbf{Q}'$ is a row vector), the F statistic (12.4.11) is the square of the t statistic (12.4.9). This fact indicates that if $q = 1$ we must use the t test rather than the F test, since a one-tail test is possible only with the t test.

The F statistic can be alternatively written as follows. From equation (12.3.3) we have

(12.4.12) $S(\boldsymbol{\beta}^+) - S(\hat{\boldsymbol{\beta}}) = (\hat{\boldsymbol{\beta}} - \boldsymbol{\beta}^+)'\mathbf{X}'\mathbf{X}(\hat{\boldsymbol{\beta}} - \boldsymbol{\beta}^+).$

From equations (12.3.10) and (12.4.12) we have

(12.4.13) $S(\boldsymbol{\beta}^+) - S(\hat{\boldsymbol{\beta}}) = (\mathbf{Q}'\hat{\boldsymbol{\beta}} - \mathbf{c})'[\mathbf{Q}'(\mathbf{X}'\mathbf{X})^{-1}\mathbf{Q}](\mathbf{Q}'\hat{\boldsymbol{\beta}} - \mathbf{c}).$

Therefore we can write (12.4.11) alternatively as

(12.4.14) $\eta = \dfrac{T-K}{q} \cdot \dfrac{S(\boldsymbol{\beta}^+) - S(\hat{\boldsymbol{\beta}})}{S(\hat{\boldsymbol{\beta}})} \sim F(q, T-K).$

Note that $S(\boldsymbol{\beta}^+) - S(\hat{\boldsymbol{\beta}})$ is always nonnegative by the definition of $\boldsymbol{\beta}^+$ and $\hat{\boldsymbol{\beta}}$, and the closer $\mathbf{Q}'\boldsymbol{\beta}$ is to $\mathbf{c}$, the smaller $S(\boldsymbol{\beta}^+) - S(\hat{\boldsymbol{\beta}})$ becomes. Also note that (12.4.14) provides a more convenient form for computation than (12.4.11) if constrained least squares residuals can be easily computed.

The result (12.4.14) may be directly verified. Using the regression equation (12.3.13), we have

(12.4.15) $S(\hat{\boldsymbol{\beta}}) \equiv \mathbf{u}'[\mathbf{I} - \mathbf{Z}(\mathbf{Z}'\mathbf{Z})^{-1}\mathbf{Z}']\mathbf{u} \sim \chi^2_{T-K}$

and

(12.4.16) $S(\boldsymbol{\beta}^+) \equiv \mathbf{u}'[\mathbf{I} - \mathbf{Z}_2(\mathbf{Z}_2'\mathbf{Z}_2)^{-1}\mathbf{Z}_2']\mathbf{u} \sim \chi^2_{T-K+q}.$

Therefore, by Theorem 11.5.19,

(12.4.17) $S(\boldsymbol{\beta}^+) - S(\hat{\boldsymbol{\beta}}) = \mathbf{u}'\bar{\mathbf{Z}}_1(\bar{\mathbf{Z}}_1'\bar{\mathbf{Z}}_1)^{-1}\bar{\mathbf{Z}}_1'\mathbf{u},$

where $\bar{\mathbf{Z}}_1 = [\mathbf{I} - \mathbf{Z}_2(\mathbf{Z}_2'\mathbf{Z}_2)^{-1}\mathbf{Z}_2']\mathbf{Z}_1$. Finally, (12.4.15) and (12.4.17) are independent because $[\mathbf{I} - \mathbf{Z}(\mathbf{Z}'\mathbf{Z})^{-1}\mathbf{Z}']\bar{\mathbf{Z}}_1 = \mathbf{0}$.

The F statistic η given in (12.4.11) takes on a variety of forms as we insert specific values into $\mathbf{Q}$ and $\mathbf{c}$. Consider the case where the $\boldsymbol{\beta}$ is partitioned as $\boldsymbol{\beta}' = (\boldsymbol{\beta}_1', \boldsymbol{\beta}_2')$, where $\boldsymbol{\beta}_1$ is a K_1-vector and $\boldsymbol{\beta}_2$ is a K_2-vector such that $K_1 + K_2 = K$, and the null hypothesis specifies $\boldsymbol{\beta}_2 = \bar{\boldsymbol{\beta}}_2$ and leaves $\boldsymbol{\beta}_1$ unspecified. This hypothesis can be written in the form $\mathbf{Q}'\boldsymbol{\beta} = \mathbf{c}$ by putting $\mathbf{Q}' = (\mathbf{0}, \mathbf{I})$, where $\mathbf{0}$ is the $K_2 \times K_1$ matrix of zeroes, $\mathbf{I}$ is the identity matrix of size K_2, and $\mathbf{c} = \bar{\boldsymbol{\beta}}_2$. Inserting these values into (12.4.11) yields

(12.4.18) $\eta = \dfrac{T-K}{K_2} \cdot \dfrac{(\hat{\boldsymbol{\beta}}_2 - \bar{\boldsymbol{\beta}}_2)'[(\mathbf{0}, \mathbf{I})(\mathbf{X}'\mathbf{X})^{-1}(\mathbf{0}, \mathbf{I})']^{-1}(\hat{\boldsymbol{\beta}}_2 - \bar{\boldsymbol{\beta}}_2)}{\hat{\mathbf{u}}'\hat{\mathbf{u}}}$

$\sim F(K_2, T-K).$

We can simplify (12.4.18) somewhat. Partition $\mathbf{X}$ as $\mathbf{X} = (\mathbf{X}_1, \mathbf{X}_2)$ conformably with the partition of β, and define $\mathbf{M}_1 = \mathbf{I} - \mathbf{X}_1(\mathbf{X}_1'\,\mathbf{X}_1)^{-1}\mathbf{X}_1'$. Then, by Theorem 11.3.9, we have

(12.4.19) $[(\mathbf{0}, \mathbf{I})(\mathbf{X}'\mathbf{X})^{-1}(\mathbf{0}, \mathbf{I})']^{-1} = \mathbf{X}_2'\,\mathbf{M}_1\mathbf{X}_2.$

Therefore, we can rewrite (12.4.18) as

(12.4.20) $\eta = \dfrac{T - K}{K_2} \cdot \dfrac{(\hat{\boldsymbol{\beta}}_2 - \bar{\boldsymbol{\beta}}_2)'\mathbf{X}_2'\mathbf{M}_1\mathbf{X}_2(\hat{\boldsymbol{\beta}}_2 - \bar{\boldsymbol{\beta}}_2)}{\hat{\mathbf{u}}'\hat{\mathbf{u}}} \sim F(K_2, T - K).$

Of particular interest is a special case of (12.4.20) where $K_1 = 1$, so that β_1 is a scalar coefficient on the first column of $\mathbf{X}$, which we assume to be the vector of ones (denoted by $\mathbf{1}$). Furthermore, we assume $\bar{\boldsymbol{\beta}}_2 = \mathbf{0}$. Then $\mathbf{M}_1$ in (12.4.19) becomes $\mathbf{L} = \mathbf{I} - T^{-1}\mathbf{1}\mathbf{1}'$. Also, we have from equation (12.2.14),

(12.4.21) $\hat{\boldsymbol{\beta}}_2 = (\mathbf{X}_2'\mathbf{L}\mathbf{X}_2)^{-1}\mathbf{X}_2'\mathbf{L}\mathbf{y}.$

Therefore (12.4.20) can now be written as

(12.4.22) $\eta = \dfrac{T - K}{K - 1} \cdot \dfrac{\mathbf{y}'\mathbf{L}\mathbf{X}_2(\mathbf{X}_2'\mathbf{L}\mathbf{X}_2)^{-1}\mathbf{X}_2'\mathbf{L}\mathbf{y}}{\hat{\mathbf{u}}'\hat{\mathbf{u}}} \sim F(K - 1, T - K).$

Using the definition of R^2 given in (12.2.33), we further rewrite (12.2.22) as

(12.4.23) $\eta = \dfrac{T - K}{K - 1} \cdot \dfrac{R^2}{1 - R^2} \sim F(K - 1, T - K),$

since $\hat{\mathbf{u}}'\hat{\mathbf{u}} = \mathbf{y}'\mathbf{L}\mathbf{y} - \mathbf{y}'\mathbf{L}\mathbf{X}_2(\mathbf{X}_2'\mathbf{L}\mathbf{X}_2)^{-1}\mathbf{X}_2'\mathbf{L}\mathbf{y}$ by (12.2.32).

12.4.4 Tests for Structural Change

Suppose we have two regression regimes

(12.4.24) $\mathbf{y}_1 = \mathbf{X}_1\boldsymbol{\beta}_1 + \mathbf{u}_1$

and

(12.4.25) $\mathbf{y}_2 = \mathbf{X}_2\boldsymbol{\beta}_2 + \mathbf{u}_2,$

where the vectors and matrices in (12.4.24) have T_1 rows and those in (12.4.25) have T_2 rows; $\mathbf{X}_1$ is a $T_1 \times K^*$ matrix and $\mathbf{X}_2$ is a $T_2 \times K^*$ matrix; and $\mathbf{u}_1$ and $\mathbf{u}_2$ are normally distributed with zero means and the variance-covariance matrix

$$E \begin{bmatrix} \mathbf{u}_1 \\ \mathbf{u}_2 \end{bmatrix} (\mathbf{u}_1', \mathbf{u}_2') = \begin{bmatrix} \sigma_1^2 \mathbf{I}_{T_1} & 0 \\ 0 & \sigma_2^2 \mathbf{I}_{T_2} \end{bmatrix}.$$

We want to test the null hypothesis $\boldsymbol{\beta}_1 = \boldsymbol{\beta}_2$ assuming $\sigma_1^2 = \sigma_2^2 \ (\equiv \sigma^2)$. This test can be handled as a special case of the F test presented in the preceding section.

To apply the F test to the problem, combine equations (12.4.24) and (12.4.25) as

(12.4.26) $\mathbf{y} = \mathbf{X}\boldsymbol{\beta} + \mathbf{u}$,

where

$$\mathbf{y} = \begin{bmatrix} \mathbf{y}_1 \\ \mathbf{y}_2 \end{bmatrix}, \quad \mathbf{X} = \begin{bmatrix} \mathbf{X}_1 & 0 \\ 0 & \mathbf{X}_2 \end{bmatrix}, \quad \boldsymbol{\beta} = \begin{bmatrix} \boldsymbol{\beta}_1 \\ \boldsymbol{\beta}_2 \end{bmatrix}, \quad \mathbf{u} = \begin{bmatrix} \mathbf{u}_1 \\ \mathbf{u}_2 \end{bmatrix}.$$

Since $\sigma_1^2 = \sigma_2^2 \ (\equiv \sigma^2)$, (12.4.26) is the same as the model (12.1.1) with normality. We can represent our hypothesis $\boldsymbol{\beta}_1 = \boldsymbol{\beta}_2$ as a standard linear hypothesis of the form (12.3.1) by putting $T = T_1 + T_2$, $K = 2K^*$, $q = K^*$, $\mathbf{Q}' = (\mathbf{I}, -\mathbf{I})$, and $\mathbf{c} = \mathbf{0}$. Inserting these values into (12.4.11) yields the test statistic

(12.4.27) $\eta = \dfrac{T_1 + T_2 - 2K^*}{K^*}$

$$\cdot \frac{(\hat{\boldsymbol{\beta}}_1 - \hat{\boldsymbol{\beta}}_2)' [\mathbf{X}_1'\mathbf{X}_1)^{-1} + (\mathbf{X}_2'\mathbf{X}_2)^{-1}]^{-1}(\hat{\boldsymbol{\beta}}_1 - \hat{\boldsymbol{\beta}}_2)}{\mathbf{y}'[\mathbf{I} - \mathbf{X}(\mathbf{X}'\mathbf{X})^{-1}\mathbf{X}']\mathbf{y}}$$

$$\sim F(K^*, T_1 + T_2 - 2K^*),$$

where $\hat{\boldsymbol{\beta}}_1 = (\mathbf{X}_1'\mathbf{X}_1)^{-1}\mathbf{X}_1'\mathbf{y}_1$ and $\hat{\boldsymbol{\beta}}_2 = (\mathbf{X}_2'\mathbf{X}_2)^{-1}\mathbf{X}_2'\mathbf{y}_2$.

We can obtain the same result using (12.4.14). In (12.4.26) we combined equations (12.4.24) and (12.4.25) without making use of the hypothesis $\boldsymbol{\beta}_1 = \boldsymbol{\beta}_2$. If we do use it, we can combine the two equations as

(12.4.28) $\mathbf{y} = \mathbf{Z}\boldsymbol{\beta}_1 + \mathbf{u}$,

where we have defined $\mathbf{Z} = (\mathbf{X}_1', \mathbf{X}_2')'$. Let $S(\hat{\boldsymbol{\beta}})$ be the sum of the squared residuals from (12.4.26), that is,

(12.4.29) $S(\hat{\boldsymbol{\beta}}) = \mathbf{y}'[\mathbf{I} - \mathbf{X}(\mathbf{X}'\mathbf{X})^{-1}\mathbf{X}']\mathbf{y}$, and let $S(\boldsymbol{\beta}^+)$ be the sum of the squared residuals from (12.4.28), that is,

(12.4.30) $S(\boldsymbol{\beta}^+) = \mathbf{y}'[\mathbf{I} - \mathbf{Z}(\mathbf{Z}'\mathbf{Z})^{-1}\mathbf{Z}']\mathbf{y}.$

Then using (12.4.14), we have

(12.4.31) $\eta = \dfrac{T_1 + T_2 - 2K^*}{K^*} \cdot \dfrac{S(\boldsymbol{\beta}^+) - S(\hat{\boldsymbol{\beta}})}{S(\hat{\boldsymbol{\beta}})} \sim F(K^*, T_1 + T_2 - 2K^*).$

Even though (12.4.31) and (12.4.27) look very different, they can be shown to be equivalent in the same way that we showed the equivalence between (12.4.11) and (12.4.14).

The hypothesis $\boldsymbol{\beta}_1 = \boldsymbol{\beta}_2$ is merely one of the many linear hypotheses that can be imposed on the $\boldsymbol{\beta}$ of the model (12.4.26). There may be a situation where we want to test the equality of a subset of $\boldsymbol{\beta}_1$ to the corresponding subset of $\boldsymbol{\beta}_2$. For example, if the subset consists of the first K_1^* elements of both $\boldsymbol{\beta}_1$ and $\boldsymbol{\beta}_2$, we put $T = T_1 + T_2$ and $K = 2K^*$ as before, but $q = K_1^*$, $\mathbf{Q}' = (\mathbf{I}, \mathbf{0}, -\mathbf{I}, \mathbf{0})$, and $\mathbf{c} = \mathbf{0}$.

If, however, we wish to test the equality of a single element of $\boldsymbol{\beta}_1$ to the corresponding element of $\boldsymbol{\beta}_2$, we use the t test rather than the F test for the reason given in the last section. We do not discuss this t test here, since it is analogous to the one discussed in Section 10.3.2.

So far we have considered the test of the hypothesis $\boldsymbol{\beta}_1 = \boldsymbol{\beta}_2$ under the assumption that $\sigma_1^2 = \sigma_2^2$. We may wish to test the hypothesis $\sigma_1^2 = \sigma_2^2$. before performing the F test discussed above. Under the null hypothesis that $\sigma_1^2 = \sigma_2^2$ ($\equiv \sigma^2$) we have

(12.4.32) $\dfrac{\mathbf{y}_1'\mathbf{M}_1\mathbf{y}_1}{\sigma^2} \sim \chi_{T_1-K^*}^2$

and

(12.4.33) $\dfrac{\mathbf{y}_2'\mathbf{M}_2\mathbf{y}_2}{\sigma^2} \sim \chi_{T_2-K^*}^2.$

Since these two chi-square variables are independent by the assumption of the model, we have by Definition 3 of the Appendix

(12.4.34) $\dfrac{T_2 - K^*}{T_1 - K^*} \cdot \dfrac{\mathbf{y}_1'\mathbf{M}_1\mathbf{y}_1}{\mathbf{y}_2'\mathbf{M}_2\mathbf{y}_2} \sim F(T_1 - K^*, T_2 - K^*).$

Unlike the F test developed in Section 12.3, we should use a two-tail test here, since either a large or a small value of the statistic in (12.4.34) is a reason for rejecting the null hypothesis.

In Section 10.3.2 we presented Welch's method of testing the equality of regression coefficients without assuming the equality of variances in the bivariate regression model. Unfortunately, Welch's approximate t test does not effectively generalize to the multiple regression model. So we shall mention two simple procedures that can be used when the variances are unequal. Both procedures are valid only asymptotically, that is, when the sample size is large.

The first is the likelihood ratio test. The likelihood function of the model defined by (12.4.24) and (12.4.25) is given by

$$(12.4.35) \quad L = (2\pi)^{-(T_1+T_2)/2}(\sigma_1^2)^{-T_1/2}(\sigma_2^2)^{-T_2/2}$$

$$\cdot \exp\left[-\frac{1}{2\sigma_1^2}(\mathbf{y}_1 - \mathbf{X}_1\boldsymbol{\beta}_1)'(\mathbf{y}_1 - \mathbf{X}_1\boldsymbol{\beta}_1)\right]$$

$$\cdot \exp\left[-\frac{1}{2\sigma_2^2}(\mathbf{y}_2 - \mathbf{X}_2\boldsymbol{\beta}_2)'(\mathbf{y}_2 - \mathbf{X}_2\boldsymbol{\beta}_2)\right].$$

The value of L attained when it is maximized without constraint, denoted by $\hat{L}$, can be obtained by evaluating the parameters of L at

$$\boldsymbol{\beta}_1 = \hat{\boldsymbol{\beta}}_1, \quad \boldsymbol{\beta}_2 = \hat{\boldsymbol{\beta}}_2,$$

$$\sigma_1^2 = \hat{\sigma}_1^2 \equiv T_1^{-1}(\mathbf{y}_1 - \mathbf{X}_1\hat{\boldsymbol{\beta}}_1)'(\mathbf{y}_1 - \mathbf{X}_1\hat{\boldsymbol{\beta}}_1),$$

and $\qquad \sigma_2^2 = \hat{\sigma}_2^2 \equiv T_2^{-1}(\mathbf{y}_2 - \mathbf{X}_2\hat{\boldsymbol{\beta}}_2)'(\mathbf{y}_2 - \mathbf{X}_2\hat{\boldsymbol{\beta}}_2).$

The value of L attained when it is maximized subject to the constraints $\boldsymbol{\beta}_1 = \boldsymbol{\beta}_2$, denoted by $\tilde{L}$, can be obtained by evaluating the parameters of L at the constrained maximum likelihood estimates: $\tilde{\boldsymbol{\beta}}_1 = \tilde{\boldsymbol{\beta}}_2 \ (\equiv \tilde{\boldsymbol{\beta}})$, and $\tilde{\sigma}_1^2$, and $\tilde{\sigma}_2^2$. These may be obtained as follows:

Step 1. Calculate

$$\tilde{\boldsymbol{\beta}} = (\hat{\sigma}_1^{-2}\mathbf{X}_1'\mathbf{X}_1 + \hat{\sigma}_2^{-2}\mathbf{X}_2'\mathbf{X}_2)^{-1}(\hat{\sigma}_1^{-2}\mathbf{X}_1'\mathbf{y}_1 + \hat{\sigma}_2^{-2}\mathbf{X}_2'\mathbf{y}_2).$$

Step 2. Calculate

$$\tilde{\sigma}_1^2 = T_1^{-1}(\mathbf{y}_1 - \mathbf{X}_1\tilde{\boldsymbol{\beta}})'(\mathbf{y}_1 - \mathbf{X}_1\tilde{\boldsymbol{\beta}})$$

and

$$\tilde{\sigma}_2^2 = T_2^{-1}(\mathbf{y}_2 - \mathbf{X}_2\tilde{\boldsymbol{\beta}})'(\mathbf{y}_2 - \mathbf{X}_2\tilde{\boldsymbol{\beta}}).$$

Step 3. Repeat step 1, substituting $\tilde{\sigma}_1^2$ and $\tilde{\sigma}_2^2$ for $\hat{\sigma}_1^2$ and $\hat{\sigma}_2^2$, respectively.

Step 4. Repeat step 2, substituting the estimates of $\boldsymbol{\beta}$ obtained in step 3 for $\tilde{\boldsymbol{\beta}}$.

Continue this process until the estimates converge. In practice, the estimates obtained at the end of step 1 and step 2 may be used without changing the asymptotic result (12.4.36) given below.

By Theorem 9.4.1, we have asymptotically (that is, approximately, when both T_1 and T_2 are large)

$$(12.4.36) \quad -2 \log \frac{\tilde{L}}{\hat{L}} = T_1 \log \frac{\tilde{\sigma}_1^2}{\hat{\sigma}_1^2} + T_2 \log \frac{\tilde{\sigma}_2^2}{\hat{\sigma}_2^2} \sim \chi_{K^*}^2.$$

The null hypothesis $\boldsymbol{\beta}_1 = \boldsymbol{\beta}_2$ is rejected when the statistic in (12.4.36) is large.

The second test is derived by the following simple procedure. First, estimate σ_1^2 and σ_2^2 by $\hat{\sigma}_1^2$ and $\hat{\sigma}_2^2$, respectively, and define $\hat{\rho} = \hat{\sigma}_1/\hat{\sigma}_2$. Second, multiply both sides of (12.4.25) by $\hat{\rho}$ and define the new equation

$$(12.4.37) \quad \mathbf{y}_2^* = \mathbf{X}_2^* \boldsymbol{\beta}_2 + \mathbf{u}_2^*,$$

where $\mathbf{y}_2^* = \hat{\rho} \mathbf{y}_2$, $\mathbf{X}_2^* = \hat{\rho} \mathbf{X}_2$, and $\mathbf{u}_2^* = \hat{\rho} \mathbf{u}_2$. Finally, treat (12.4.24) and (12.4.37) as the given equations, and perform the F test (12.4.27) on them. The method works asymptotically because the variance of $\mathbf{u}_2^*$ is approximately the same as that of $\mathbf{u}_1$ when T_1 and T_2 are large, since $\hat{\rho}$ is a consistent estimator of σ_1/σ_2.

12.5 SELECTION OF REGRESSORS

In Section 10.2.3 we briefly discussed the problem of choosing between two bivariate regression equations with the same dependent variable. We stated that, other things being equal, it makes sense to choose the equation with the higher R^2. Here, we consider choosing between two multiple regression equations

$$(12.5.1) \quad \mathbf{y} = \mathbf{X}\boldsymbol{\beta} + \mathbf{u}_1$$

and

$$(12.5.2) \quad \mathbf{y} = \mathbf{S}\boldsymbol{\gamma} + \mathbf{u}_2,$$

where each equation satisfies the assumptions of model (12.1.3). Suppose the vectors $\boldsymbol{\beta}$ and $\boldsymbol{\gamma}$ have K and H elements, respectively. If $H \neq K$, it no longer makes sense to choose the equation with the higher R^2, because the greater the number of regressors, the larger R^2 tends to be. In the extreme case where the number of regressors equals the number of observations, $R^2 = 1$. So if we are to use R^2 as a criterion for choosing a regression equation, we need to adjust it somehow for the degrees of freedom.

Theil (1961, p. 213) proposed one such adjustment. *Theil's corrected R^2*, denoted $\bar{R}^2$, is defined by

$$(12.5.3) \quad 1 - \bar{R}^2 = \frac{T}{T - K}(1 - R^2),$$

where K is the number of regressors. Theil proposed choosing the equation with the largest $\bar{R}^2$, other things being equal. Since, from (12.2.31),

$$(12.5.4) \quad 1 - R^2 = \frac{\mathbf{y'My}}{\mathbf{y'Ly}},$$

choosing the equation with the largest $\bar{R}^2$ is equivalent to choosing the equation with the smallest $\tilde{\sigma}^2$, defined in (12.2.29).

Theil offers the following justification for his corrected $\bar{R}^2$. Let $\tilde{\sigma}_1^2$ and $\tilde{\sigma}_2^2$ be the unbiased estimators of the error variances in regression equations (12.5.1) and (12.5.2), respectively. That is,

$$\tilde{\sigma}_1^2 = \mathbf{y'}[\mathbf{I} - \mathbf{X(X'X)}^{-1}\mathbf{X'}]\mathbf{y}\,/\,(T - K)$$

and

$$\tilde{\sigma}_2^2 = \mathbf{y'}[\mathbf{I} - \mathbf{S(S'S)}^{-1}\mathbf{S'}]\mathbf{y}\,/\,(T - H).$$

Then, he shows that

$$(12.5.5) \quad E(\tilde{\sigma}_1^2 - \tilde{\sigma}_2^2) > 0$$

if the expectation is taken assuming that (12.5.2) is the true model. The justification is merely intuitive and not very strong.

An important special case of the problem considered above is when $\mathbf{S}$ is a subset of $\mathbf{X}$. Without loss of generality, assume $\mathbf{X} = (\mathbf{X_1, X_2})$ and $\mathbf{S} = \mathbf{X_1}$. Partition $\boldsymbol{\beta}$ conformably as $\boldsymbol{\beta'} = (\boldsymbol{\beta_1'}, \boldsymbol{\beta_2'})$. Then, choosing (12.5.2) over (12.5.1) is equivalent to accepting the hypothesis $\boldsymbol{\beta_2} = \mathbf{0}$. But the F test of the hypothesis accepts it if $\eta < c$, where η is as given in (12.4.20) with $\bar{\boldsymbol{\beta}}_2$ set equal to $\mathbf{0}$. Therefore, any decision rule can be made equivalent to the choice of a particular value of c. It can be shown that the use of Theil's $\bar{R}^2$ is equivalent to $c = 1$.

Mallows (1964), Akaike (1973), and Sawa and Hiromatsu (1973) obtained solutions to this problem on the basis of three different principles and arrived at similar recommendations, in which the value of c ranges roughly from 1.8 to 2. These results suggest that Theil's $\bar{R}^2$, though an improvement over the unadjusted R^2, still tends to favor a regression equation with more regressors.

What value of c is implied by the customary choice of the 5% significance level? The answer depends on the degrees of freedom of the F test: $K - H$ and $T - K$. Note that $K - H$ appears as K_2 in (12.4.20). Table 12.1 gives the value of c for selected values of the degrees of freedom. The table is calculated by solving for c in $P[F(K - H, T - K) < c] = 0.05$. The results cast some doubt on the customary choice of 5%.

TABLE 12.1 Critical values of F test implied by 5% significance level

$K - H$	$T - K$	c
1	30	0.465
3	30	0.807
1	100	0.458
5	100	0.867

EXERCISES

1. (Section 12.2.2)

    Consider the regression model $\mathbf{y} = \mathbf{X}\boldsymbol{\beta} + \mathbf{u}$, where $E\mathbf{u} = \mathbf{0}$, $E\mathbf{u}\mathbf{u}' = \mathbf{I}_4$, and

    $$\mathbf{X}' = \begin{bmatrix} 1 & 1 & 1 & 1 \\ 1 & 2 & 1 & -1 \end{bmatrix}.$$

    Let $\hat{\boldsymbol{\beta}} = (\mathbf{X}'\mathbf{X})^{-1}\mathbf{X}'\mathbf{y}$ and $\tilde{\boldsymbol{\beta}} = (\mathbf{S}'\mathbf{X})^{-1}\mathbf{S}'\mathbf{y}$, where

    $$\mathbf{S}' = \begin{bmatrix} 1 & 1 & 1 & 1 \\ 1 & 2 & 3 & 4 \end{bmatrix}.$$

    Show directly that $\hat{\boldsymbol{\beta}}$ is a better estimator than $\tilde{\boldsymbol{\beta}}$, without using Theorem 12.2.1.

2. (Section 12.2.2)

   Consider the regression model $\mathbf{y} = \beta \mathbf{x} + \mathbf{u}$, where β is a scalar unknown parameter, $\mathbf{x}$ is a T-vector consisting entirely of ones, $\mathbf{u}$ is a T-vector such that $E\mathbf{u} = \mathbf{0}$ and $E\mathbf{u}\mathbf{u}' = \sigma^2 \mathbf{I}_T$. Obtain the mean squared errors of the following two estimators:

$$\hat{\beta} = \frac{\mathbf{x}'\mathbf{y}}{\mathbf{x}'\mathbf{x}} \quad \text{and} \quad \tilde{\beta} = \frac{\mathbf{z}'\mathbf{y}}{\mathbf{z}'\mathbf{x}},$$

   where $\mathbf{z}' = (1, 0, 1, 0, \ldots, 1, 0)$. Assume that T is even. Which estimator is preferred? Answer directly, without using Theorem 12.2.1.

3. (Section 12.2.5)

   Suppose the joint distribution of X and Y is given by the following table:

X \ Y	1	0	
1	α	β	
0	$0.5 - \alpha$	$0.5 - \beta$	$0 \le \alpha,\ \beta \le 0.5$

   (a) Derive an explicit formula for the maximum likelihood estimator of α based on i.i.d. sample $\{X_i, Y_i\}$, $i = 1, 2, \ldots, n$, and derive its asymptotic distribution directly, without using the Cramér-Rao lower bound.

   (b) Derive the Cramér-Rao lower bound.

4. (Section 12.2.6)

   In the model $\mathbf{y} = \mathbf{X}\boldsymbol{\beta} + \mathbf{u}$ and $y_p = \mathbf{x}_1'\boldsymbol{\beta} + u_p$, obtain the unconditional mean squared prediction errors of the predictors $\mathbf{x}_p'\hat{\boldsymbol{\beta}}$ and $\mathbf{x}_{1p}'\boldsymbol{\beta}_1^+$, where $\hat{\boldsymbol{\beta}} = (\mathbf{X}'\mathbf{X})^{-1}\mathbf{X}'\mathbf{y}$ and $\boldsymbol{\beta}_1^+ = (\mathbf{X}_1'\mathbf{X}_1)^{-1}\mathbf{X}_1'\mathbf{y}$. We have defined $\mathbf{X}_1$ as the first K_1 columns of $\mathbf{X}$ and $\mathbf{x}_{1p}'$ as the first K_1 elements of $\mathbf{x}_p'$. Under what circumstances can the second predictor be regarded as superior to the first?

5. (Section 12.3)

   Show that $\mathbf{R}$ defined in the paragraphs before (12.3.13) satisfies the two conditions given there.

6. (Section 12.4.2)

   Consider the regression model

$$y = \beta_1 \begin{bmatrix} 1 \\ 1 \\ 1 \\ 1 \end{bmatrix} + \beta_2 \begin{bmatrix} 1 \\ -1 \\ 1 \\ -1 \end{bmatrix} + u,$$

where β_1 and β_2 are scalar unknown parameters and $u \sim N(0, \sigma^2 I_4)$. Assuming that the observed values of y' are $(2, 0, 1, -1)$, test the null hypothesis $\beta_2 = \beta_1$ against the alternative hypothesis $\beta_2 > \beta_1$ at the 5% significance level.

7. (Section 12.4.3)
   Consider the regression model $y = X\beta + u$, where y and u are eight-component vectors, X is an 8×3 matrix, and β is a three-component vector of unknown parameters. We want to test hypotheses on the elements of β, which we write as β_1, β_2, and β_3. The data are given by

$$X'X = \begin{bmatrix} 2 & 0 & 0 \\ 0 & 3 & 1 \\ 0 & 1 & 3 \end{bmatrix}, \quad X'y = \begin{bmatrix} 4 \\ 5 \\ 3 \end{bmatrix}, \quad y'y = 22.$$

   (a) Test $\beta_2 = \beta_1$ against $\beta_2 > \beta_1$ at the 5% significance level.
   (b) Test $\beta_1 = \beta_2 = \beta_3$ at the 5% significance level.

8. (Section 12.4.3)
   Consider three bivariate regression models, each consisting of four observations:

$$y_1 = \alpha_1 1 + \beta_1 x_1 + u_1,$$

$$y_2 = \alpha_2 1 + \beta_2 x_2 + u_2,$$

$$y_3 = \alpha_3 1 + \beta_3 x_3 + u_3,$$

   where 1 is a four-component vector consisting only of ones, and the elements of u_1, u_2, and u_3 are independent normal with zero mean and constant variance. The data are as follows:

$$x_1 = \begin{bmatrix} 1 \\ 0 \\ 1 \\ 0 \end{bmatrix}, \quad x_2 = \begin{bmatrix} 1 \\ 1 \\ 0 \\ 0 \end{bmatrix}, \quad x_3 = \begin{bmatrix} 1 \\ 0 \\ 0 \\ -1 \end{bmatrix},$$

$$\mathbf{y}_1 = \begin{bmatrix} 1 \\ 1 \\ 0 \\ 0 \end{bmatrix}, \quad \mathbf{y}_2 = \begin{bmatrix} 1 \\ 0 \\ 1 \\ 0 \end{bmatrix}, \quad \mathbf{y}_3 = \begin{bmatrix} 0 \\ 1 \\ 0 \\ 1 \end{bmatrix}.$$

Test the null hypothesis "$\alpha_1 = \alpha_2 = \alpha_3$ and $\beta_1 = \beta_2 = \beta_3$" at the 5% significance level.

9. (Section 12.4.3)

In the following regression model, test H_0: $\alpha_1 + \beta_1 = \alpha_2 + \beta_2$ and $\beta_2 = 0$ versus H_1: not H_0.

$$\mathbf{y}_1 = \alpha_1 \mathbf{x}_1 + \beta_1 \mathbf{z}_1 + \mathbf{u}_1 \quad \text{and} \quad \mathbf{y}_2 = \alpha_2 \mathbf{x}_2 + \beta_2 \mathbf{z}_2 + \mathbf{u}_2,$$

where $\mathbf{u}_1$ and $\mathbf{u}_2$ are independent of each other and distributed as $N(\mathbf{0}, \sigma^2 \mathbf{I}_5)$. Use the 5% significance level. The data are given as follows:

$$\mathbf{y}_1 = \begin{bmatrix} 2 \\ 1 \\ 3 \\ 1 \\ 3 \end{bmatrix}, \quad \mathbf{y}_2 = \begin{bmatrix} 2 \\ 2 \\ 3 \\ 2 \\ 3 \end{bmatrix}, \quad \mathbf{x}_1 = \mathbf{x}_2 = \begin{bmatrix} 1 \\ 1 \\ 1 \\ 1 \\ 1 \end{bmatrix}, \quad \mathbf{z}_1 = \mathbf{z}_2 = \begin{bmatrix} 1 \\ -1 \\ 1 \\ -2 \\ 1 \end{bmatrix}.$$

10. (Section 12.4.3)

Solve Exercise 35 of Chapter 9 in a regression framework.

11. (Section 12.4.3)

We want to estimate a Cobb-Douglas production function

$$\log Q_t = \beta_1 + \beta_2 \log K_t + \beta_3 \log L_t + u_t, \quad t = 1, 2, \ldots, T,$$

in each of three industries A, B, and C and test the hypothesis that β_2 is the same for industries A and B and β_3 is the same for industries B and C (jointly, not separately). We assume that β_1 varies among the three industries. Write detailed instructions on how to perform such a test. You may assume that the u_t are normal with mean zero and their variance is constant for all t and for all three industries, and that the K_t and L_t are distributed independently of the u_t.

13 | ECONOMETRIC MODELS

The multiple regression model studied in Chapter 12 is by far the most frequently used statistical model in all the applied disciplines, including econometrics. It is also the basic model from which various other models can be derived. For these reasons the model is sometimes called the *classical regression model* or the *standard regression model*. In this chapter we study various other models frequently used in applied research. The models discussed in Sections 13.1 through 13.4 may be properly called *regression models* (models in which the conditional mean of the dependent variable is specified as a function of the independent variables), whereas those discussed in Sections 13.5 through 13.7 are more general models. We have given them the common term "econometric models," but all of them have been used by researchers in other disciplines as well.

The models of Section 13.1 arise as the assumption of independence or *homoscedasticity* (constant variance) is removed from the classical regression model. The models of Sections 13.2 and 13.3 arise as the assumption of exogeneity of the regressors is removed. Finally, the models of Section 13.4 arise as the linearity assumption is removed. The models of Sections 13.5, 13.6, and 13.7 are more general than regression models.

Our presentation will focus on the fundamental results. For a more detailed study the reader is referred to Amemiya (1985).

13.1 GENERALIZED LEAST SQUARES

In this section we consider the regression model

$$(13.1.1) \quad \mathbf{y} = \mathbf{X}\boldsymbol{\beta} + \mathbf{u},$$

where we assume that $\mathbf{X}$ is a full-rank $T \times K$ matrix of known constants and $\mathbf{u}$ is a T-dimensional vector of random variables such that $E\mathbf{u} = \mathbf{0}$ and

(13.1.2) $\quad E\mathbf{u}\mathbf{u}' = \boldsymbol{\Sigma}$.

We assume only that $\boldsymbol{\Sigma}$ is a positive definite matrix. This model differs from the classical regression model only in its general specification of the variance-covariance matrix given in (13.1.2).

13.1.1 Known Variance-Covariance Matrix

In this subsection we develop the theory of generalized least squares under the assumption that $\boldsymbol{\Sigma}$ is known (known up to a scalar multiple, to be precise); in the remaining subsections we discuss various ways the elements of $\boldsymbol{\Sigma}$ are specified as a function of a finite number of parameters so that they can be consistently estimated.

Since $\boldsymbol{\Sigma}$ is symmetric, by Theorem 11.5.1 we can find an orthogonal matrix $\mathbf{H}$ which diagonalizes $\boldsymbol{\Sigma}$ as $\mathbf{H}'\boldsymbol{\Sigma}\mathbf{H} = \boldsymbol{\Lambda}$, where $\boldsymbol{\Lambda}$ is the diagonal matrix consisting of the characteristic roots of $\boldsymbol{\Sigma}$. Moreover, since $\boldsymbol{\Sigma}$ is positive definite, the diagonal elements of $\boldsymbol{\Lambda}$ are positive by Theorem 11.5.10. Using (11.5.4), we define $\boldsymbol{\Sigma}^{-1/2} = \mathbf{H}\boldsymbol{\Lambda}^{-1/2}\mathbf{H}'$, where $\boldsymbol{\Lambda}^{-1/2} = D\{\lambda_i^{-1/2}\}$, where λ_i is the ith diagonal element of $\boldsymbol{\Lambda}$. Premultiplying (13.1.1) by $\boldsymbol{\Sigma}^{-1/2}$, we obtain

(13.1.3) $\quad \mathbf{y}^* = \mathbf{X}^*\boldsymbol{\beta} + \mathbf{u}^*$,

where $\mathbf{y}^* = \boldsymbol{\Sigma}^{-1/2}\mathbf{y}$, $\mathbf{X}^* = \boldsymbol{\Sigma}^{-1/2}\mathbf{X}$, and $\mathbf{u}^* = \boldsymbol{\Sigma}^{-1/2}\mathbf{u}$. Then, by Theorem 4.1.6, $E\mathbf{u}^* = \mathbf{0}$ and

$$
\begin{aligned}
(13.1.4) \quad E\mathbf{u}^*\mathbf{u}^{*\prime} &= E\boldsymbol{\Sigma}^{-1/2}\mathbf{u}\mathbf{u}'(\boldsymbol{\Sigma}^{-1/2})' \\
&= \boldsymbol{\Sigma}^{-1/2}\boldsymbol{\Sigma}(\boldsymbol{\Sigma}^{-1/2})' \qquad \text{by Theorem 4.1.6} \\
&= \boldsymbol{\Sigma}^{-1/2}\boldsymbol{\Sigma}^{1/2}\boldsymbol{\Sigma}^{1/2}\boldsymbol{\Sigma}^{-1/2} \\
&= \mathbf{I}.
\end{aligned}
$$

(The reader should verify that $\boldsymbol{\Sigma}^{1/2}\boldsymbol{\Sigma}^{1/2} = \boldsymbol{\Sigma}$, that $\boldsymbol{\Sigma}^{-1/2}\boldsymbol{\Sigma}^{1/2} = \mathbf{I}$, and that $(\boldsymbol{\Sigma}^{-1/2})' = \boldsymbol{\Sigma}^{-1/2}$ from the definitions of these matrices.) Therefore (13.1.3) is a classical regression model, and hence the least squares estimator applied to (13.1.3) has all the good properties derived in Chapter

12. We call it the *generalized least squares (GLS) estimator* applied to the original model (13.1.1). Denoting it by $\hat{\boldsymbol{\beta}}_G$, we have

(13.1.5) $\hat{\boldsymbol{\beta}}_G = (\mathbf{X}^{*\prime}\mathbf{X}^*)^{-1}\mathbf{X}^{*\prime}\mathbf{y}^*$

$= (\mathbf{X}'\boldsymbol{\Sigma}^{-1/2}\boldsymbol{\Sigma}^{-1/2}\mathbf{X})^{-1}\mathbf{X}'\boldsymbol{\Sigma}^{-1/2}\boldsymbol{\Sigma}^{-1/2}\mathbf{y}$

$= (\mathbf{X}'\boldsymbol{\Sigma}^{-1}\mathbf{X})^{-1}\mathbf{X}'\boldsymbol{\Sigma}^{-1}\mathbf{y}.$

(Suppose $\boldsymbol{\Sigma}$ is known up to a scalar multiple. That is, suppose $\boldsymbol{\Sigma} = \alpha\mathbf{Q}$, where α is a scalar positive unknown parameter and $\mathbf{Q}$ is a known positive definite matrix. Then α drops out of formula (13.1.5) and we have $\hat{\boldsymbol{\beta}}_G = (\mathbf{X}'\mathbf{Q}^{-1}\mathbf{X})^{-1}\mathbf{X}'\mathbf{Q}^{-1}\mathbf{y}$. The classical regression model is a special case, in which $\alpha = \sigma^2$ and $\mathbf{Q} = \mathbf{I}$.)

Inserting (13.1.1) into the final term of (13.1.5) and using Theorem 4.1.6, we can readily show that

(13.1.6) $E\hat{\boldsymbol{\beta}}_G = \boldsymbol{\beta}$

and

(13.1.7) $V\hat{\boldsymbol{\beta}}_G = (\mathbf{X}'\boldsymbol{\Sigma}^{-1}\mathbf{X})^{-1}.$

It is important to study the properties of the least squares estimator applied to the model (13.1.1) because the researcher may use the LS estimator under the mistaken assumption that his model is (at least approximately) the classical regression model. We have, using Theorem 4.1.6,

(13.1.8) $E\hat{\boldsymbol{\beta}} = \boldsymbol{\beta}$

and

(13.1.9) $V\hat{\boldsymbol{\beta}} = E(\mathbf{X}'\mathbf{X})^{-1}\mathbf{X}'\mathbf{u}\mathbf{u}'\mathbf{X}(\mathbf{X}'\mathbf{X})^{-1}$

$= (\mathbf{X}'\mathbf{X})^{-1}\mathbf{X}'\boldsymbol{\Sigma}\mathbf{X}(\mathbf{X}'\mathbf{X})^{-1}.$

Thus the LS estimator is unbiased even under the model (13.1.1). Its variance-covariance matrix, however, is different from either (13.1.7) or (12.2.22). Since the GLS estimator is the best linear unbiased estimator under the model (13.1.1) and the LS estimator is a linear estimator, it follows from Theorem 12.2.1 that

(13.1.10) $(\mathbf{X}'\mathbf{X})^{-1}\mathbf{X}'\boldsymbol{\Sigma}\mathbf{X}(\mathbf{X}'\mathbf{X})^{-1} \geq (\mathbf{X}'\boldsymbol{\Sigma}^{-1}\mathbf{X})^{-1}.$

The above can also be directly verified using theorems in Chapter 11.

Although strict inequality generally holds in (13.1.10), there are cases where equality holds. (See Amemiya, 1985, section 6.1.3.)

The consistency and the asymptotic normality of the GLS estimator follow from Section 12.2.4. The LS estimator can be also shown to be consistent and asymptotically normal under general conditions in the model (13.1.1).

If Σ is unknown, its elements cannot be consistently estimated unless we specify them to be functions of a finite number of parameters. In the next three subsections we consider various parameterizations of Σ. Let θ be a vector of unknown parameters of a finite dimension. In each of the models to be discussed, we shall indicate how θ can be consistently estimated. Denoting the consistent estimator by $\hat{\theta}$, we can define the *feasible generalized least squares (FGLS) estimator,* denoted by $\hat{\beta}_F$, by

$$(13.1.11) \quad \hat{\beta}_F = [X'\Sigma(\hat{\theta})^{-1}X]^{-1}X'\Sigma(\hat{\theta})^{-1}y,$$

where the dependence of Σ on θ is expressed by the symbol $\Sigma(\theta)$. Under general conditions, $\hat{\beta}_F$ is consistent, and $\sqrt{T}(\hat{\beta}_F - \beta)$ has the same limit distribution as $\sqrt{T}(\hat{\beta}_G - \beta)$.

13.1.2 Heteroscedasticity

In the classical regression model it is assumed that the variance of the error term is constant (homoscedastic). Here we relax this assumption and specify more generally that

$$(13.1.12) \quad Vu_t = \sigma_t^2, \quad t = 1, 2, \ldots, T.$$

This assumption of nonconstant variances is called *heteroscedasticity.* The other assumptions remain the same. If the variances are known, this model is a special case of the model discussed in Section 13.1.1. In the present case, Σ is a diagonal matrix whose tth diagonal element is equal to σ_t^2. The GLS estimator in this case is given a special name, the *weighted least squares estimator.*

If the variances are unknown, we must specify them as depending on a finite number of parameters. There are two main methods of parameterization.

In the first method, the variances are assumed to remain at a constant value, say, σ_1^2, in the period $t = 1, 2, \ldots, T_1$ and then change to a new constant value of σ_2^2 in the period $t = T_1 + 1, T_1 + 2, \ldots, T$. If T_1 is known, this is the same as (12.4.26). There we suggested how to estimate

σ_1^2 and σ_2^2. Using these estimates, we can define the FGLS estimator by the formula (13.1.11). If T_1 is unknown, T_1 as well as σ_1^2 and σ_2^2 can be still estimated, but the computation and the statistical inference become much more complex. See Goldfeld and Quandt (1976) for further discussion of this case. It is not difficult to generalize to the case where the variances assume more than two values.

In the second method, it is specified that

$$(13.1.13) \quad \sigma_t^2 = g(\mathbf{z}_t' \boldsymbol{\alpha}),$$

where $g(\cdot)$ is a known function, $\mathbf{z}_t$ is a vector of known constants, not necessarily related to $\mathbf{x}_t$, and $\boldsymbol{\alpha}$ is a vector of unknown parameters. Goldfeld and Quandt (1972) considered the case where $g(\cdot)$ is a linear function and proposed estimating $\boldsymbol{\alpha}$ consistently by regressing $\hat{u}_t^2$ on $\mathbf{z}_t$, where $\{\hat{u}_t\}$ are the least squares residuals defined in (12.2.12). If $g(\cdot)$ is nonlinear, $\hat{u}_t^2$ must be treated as the dependent variable of a nonlinear regression model—see Section 13.4 below.

Even if we do not specify σ_t^2 as a function of a finite number of parameters, we can consistently estimate the variance-covariance matrix of the LS estimator given by (13.1.9). Let $\{\hat{u}_t\}$ be the least squares residuals, and define the diagonal matrix $\mathbf{D}$ whose tth diagonal element is equal to $\hat{u}_t^2$. Then the *heteroscedasticity-consistent estimator* of (13.1.9) is defined by

$$(13.1.14) \quad \hat{V}\hat{\boldsymbol{\beta}} = (\mathbf{X}'\mathbf{X})^{-1}\mathbf{X}'\mathbf{D}\mathbf{X}(\mathbf{X}'\mathbf{X})^{-1}.$$

Under general conditions $T\hat{V}\hat{\boldsymbol{\beta}}$ can be shown to converge to $TV\hat{\boldsymbol{\beta}}$. See Eicker (1963) and White (1980).

13.1.3 Serial Correlation

In this section we allow a nonzero correlation between u_t and u_s for $s \neq t$ in the model (12.1.1). Correlation between the values at different periods of a time series is called *serial correlation* or *autocorrelation*. It can be specified in infinitely various ways; here we consider one particular form of serial correlation associated with the *stationary first-order autoregressive model*. It is defined by

$$(13.1.15) \quad u_t = \rho u_{t-1} + \varepsilon_t, \qquad t = 1, 2, \ldots, T,$$

where $\{\varepsilon_t\}$ are i.i.d. with $E\varepsilon_t = 0$ and $V\varepsilon_t = \sigma^2$, and u_0 is independent of $\varepsilon_1, \varepsilon_2, \ldots, \varepsilon_T$ with $Eu_0 = 0$ and $Vu_0 = \sigma^2/(1 - \rho^2)$.

Taking the expectation of both sides of (13.1.15) for $t = 1$ and using our assumptions, we see that $Eu_1 = \rho Eu_0 + E\varepsilon_1 = 0$. Repeating the same procedure for $t = 2, 3, \ldots, T$, we conclude that

$$(13.1.16) \quad Eu_t = 0 \quad \text{for all } t.$$

Next we evaluate the variances and covariances of $\{u_t\}$. Taking the variance of both sides of (13.1.15) for $t = 1$, we obtain

$$Vu_1 = \rho^2 \cdot \frac{\sigma^2}{1 - \rho^2} + \sigma^2 = \frac{\sigma^2}{1 - \rho^2}.$$

Repeating the process for $t = 2, 3, \ldots, T$, we conclude that

$$(13.1.17) \quad Vu_t = \frac{\sigma^2}{1 - \rho^2} \quad \text{for all } t.$$

Multiplying both sides of (13.1.15) by u_{t-1} and taking the expectation, we obtain

$$(13.1.18) \quad Eu_t u_{t-1} = \frac{\sigma^2 \rho}{1 - \rho^2} \quad \text{for all } t$$

because of (13.1.17) and because u_{t-1} and ε_t are independent. Next, multiplying both sides of (13.1.15) by u_{t-2} and taking the expectation, we obtain

$$(13.1.19) \quad Eu_t u_{t-2} = \frac{\sigma^2 \rho^2}{1 - \rho^2} \quad \text{for all } t.$$

Repeating this process, we obtain

$$(13.1.20) \quad Eu_t u_{t-j} = \frac{\sigma^2 \rho^j}{1 - \rho^2}, \quad t = 1, 2, \ldots, T; \ j = 0, 1, \ldots, t - 1.$$

Note that (13.1.20) contains (13.1.17), (13.1.18), and (13.1.19) as special cases. Conditions (13.1.16) and (13.1.20) constitute *stationarity* (more precisely, *weak stationarity*).

In matrix notation, (13.1.16) can be written as $E\mathbf{u} = \mathbf{0}$ and (13.1.20) is equivalent to

$$(13.1.21) \quad \Sigma \, (\equiv E\mathbf{uu'}) = \frac{\sigma^2}{1 - \rho^2}
\begin{bmatrix}
1 & \rho & \rho^2 & \cdot & \cdot & \rho^{T-1} \\
\rho & 1 & \rho & \cdot & \cdot & \rho^{T-2} \\
\rho^2 & \rho & 1 & \cdot & \cdot & \rho^{T-3} \\
\cdot & & & & & \\
& & & & & \\
\cdot & & & & & \\
\rho^{T-1} & \rho^{T-2} & \cdot & \cdot & \cdot & 1
\end{bmatrix}$$

It can be shown that

$$(13.1.22) \quad \Sigma^{-1} = \frac{1}{\sigma^2}
\begin{bmatrix}
1 & -\rho & 0 & 0 & \cdot & 0 \\
-\rho & 1 + \rho^2 & -\rho & 0 & \cdot & 0 \\
0 & -\rho & 1 + \rho^2 & \cdot & \cdot & \cdot \\
\cdot & \cdot & \cdot & \cdot & \cdot & \cdot \\
\cdot & \cdot & \cdot & -\rho & 1 + \rho^2 & -\rho \\
\cdot & \cdot & \cdot & 0 & -\rho & 1
\end{bmatrix}$$

If ρ is known, we can compute the GLS estimator of $\boldsymbol{\beta}$ by inserting Σ^{-1} obtained above into (13.1.5). Note that σ^2 need not be known because it drops out of the formula (13.1.5).

The computation of the GLS estimator is facilitated by noting that

$$(13.1.23) \quad \Sigma^{-1} = \frac{1}{\sigma^2} \mathbf{R'R},$$

where

$$(13.1.24) \quad \mathbf{R} = \begin{bmatrix} \sqrt{1 - \rho^2} & 0 & 0 & \cdot & \cdot & 0 \\ -\rho & 1 & 0 & \cdot & \cdot & 0 \\ 0 & -\rho & 1 & \cdot & \cdot & \cdot \\ \cdot & & \cdot & \cdot & \cdot & \cdot \\ \cdot & \cdot & 0 & -\rho & 1 & 0 \\ 0 & \cdot & \cdot & 0 & -\rho & 1 \end{bmatrix}.$$

Using $\mathbf{R}$, we can write the GLS estimator (13.1.5) as

$$(13.1.25) \quad \hat{\boldsymbol{\beta}}_G = (\mathbf{X}'\mathbf{R}'\mathbf{R}\mathbf{X})^{-1}\mathbf{X}'\mathbf{R}'\mathbf{R}\mathbf{y}.$$

Except for the first row, premultiplication of a T-vector $\mathbf{z} = (z_1, z_2, \ldots, z_T)'$ by $\mathbf{R}$ performs the operation $z_t - \rho z_{t-1}$, $t = 2, 3, \ldots, T$. Thus the GLS estimator is computed as the LS estimator after this operation is performed on the dependent and the independent variables. The asymptotic distribution of the GLS estimator is unchanged if the first row of $\mathbf{R}$ is deleted in defining the estimator by (13.1.25).

Many economic variables exhibit a pattern of serial correlation similar to that in (13.1.20). Therefore the first-order autoregressive model (13.1.15) is an empirically useful model to the extent that the error term of the regression may be regarded as the sum of the omitted independent variables. If, however, we believe that $\{u_t\}$ follow a higher-order autoregressive process, we should appropriately modify the definition of $\mathbf{R}$ used in (13.1.25). For example, if we suppose that $\{u_t\}$ follow a *pth order autoregressive model*

$$(13.1.26) \quad u_t = \sum_{j=1}^{p} \rho_j u_{t-j} + \varepsilon_t,$$

we should perform the operation $z_t - \sum_{j=1}^{p} \rho_j z_{t-j}$ on both the dependent and independent variables and then apply the LS method.

Another important process that gives rise to serial correlation is the *moving-average process*. It is defined by

$$(13.1.27) \quad u_t = \sum_{j=0}^{q} \alpha_j \varepsilon_{t-j},$$

where $\{\varepsilon_t\}$ are i.i.d. as before. Computation of the GLS estimator is still possible in this case, but with more difficulty than for an autoregressive process. Nevertheless, a moving-average process can be well approximated by an autoregressive process as long as its order is taken high enough.

We consider next the estimation of ρ in the regression model defined by (12.1.1) and (13.1.15). If $\{u_t\}$, $t = 1, 2, \ldots, T$, were observable, we could estimate ρ by the LS estimator applied to (13.1.15). Namely,

$$(13.1.28) \quad \tilde{\rho} = \frac{\displaystyle\sum_{t=2}^{T} u_t u_{t-1}}{\displaystyle\sum_{t=2}^{T} u_{t-1}^2}.$$

Since (13.1.15) itself cannot be regarded as the classical regression model because u_{t-1} cannot be regarded as nonstochastic, $\tilde{\rho}$ does not possess all the properties of the LS estimator under the classical regression model. For example, it can be shown that $\tilde{\rho}$ is generally biased. But it can also be shown that $\tilde{\rho}$ is consistent and its asymptotic distribution is given by

$$(13.1.29) \quad \sqrt{T} \, (\tilde{\rho} - \rho) \to N(0, 1 - \rho^2).$$

Since $\{u_t\}$ are in fact unobservable, it should be reasonable to replace them in (13.1.28) by the LS residuals $\hat{u}_t \equiv y_t - \mathbf{x}_t'\hat{\boldsymbol{\beta}}$, where $\hat{\boldsymbol{\beta}}$ is the LS estimator, and define

$$(13.1.30) \quad \hat{\rho} = \frac{\displaystyle\sum_{t=2}^{T} \hat{u}_t \hat{u}_{t-1}}{\displaystyle\sum_{t=2}^{T} \hat{u}_{t-1}^2}.$$

It can be shown that $\hat{\rho}$ is consistent and has the same asymptotic distribution as $\tilde{\rho}$ given in (13.1.29). Finally, inserting $\hat{\rho}$ into $\mathbf{R}$ in (13.1.24), we can compute the FGLS estimator.

In the remainder of this section, we consider the test of independence against serial correlation. In particular, we take the classical regression model as the null hypothesis and the model defined by (12.1.1) and (13.1.15) as the alternative hypothesis. This test is equivalent to testing H_0: $\rho = 0$ versus H_1: $\rho \neq 0$ in (13.1.15). Therefore it would be reasonable to use (13.1.30) as the test statistic. It is customary, however, to use the *Durbin-Watson statistic*

$$(13.1.31) \quad d = \frac{\sum_{t=2}^{T} (\hat{u}_t - \hat{u}_{t-1})^2}{\sum_{t=1}^{T} \hat{u}_t^2},$$

which is approximately equal to $2 - 2\hat{\rho}$, because its distribution can be more easily computed than that of $\hat{\rho}$. Before the days of modern computer technology, researchers used the table of the upper and lower bounds of the statistic compiled by Durbin and Watson (1951). Today, however, the exact p-value of the statistic can be computed.

13.1.4 Error Components Model

The *error components model* is useful when we wish to pool time-series and cross-section data. For example, we may want to estimate production functions using data collected on the annual inputs and outputs of many firms, of demand functions using data on the quantities and prices collected monthly from many consumers. By pooling time-series and cross-section data, we hope to be able to estimate the parameters of a relationship such as a production function or a demand function more efficiently than by using two sets of data separately. Still, we should not treat time-series and cross-section data homogeneously. At the least, we should try to account for the difference by introducing the specific effects of time and cross-section into the error term of the regression, as follows:

$$(13.1.32) \quad y_{it} = \mathbf{x}_{it}'\boldsymbol{\beta} + u_u$$

and

$$(13.1.33) \quad u_{it} = \mu_i + \lambda_t + \varepsilon_{it}, \quad i = 1, 2, \ldots, N; t = 1, 2, \ldots, T,$$

where μ_i and λ_t are the cross-section specific and time-specific components.

In the simplest version of such a model, we assume that the sequence $\{\mu_i\}$, $\{\lambda_t\}$, and $\{\varepsilon_{it}\}$ are i.i.d. random variables with zero mean and are mutually independent with the variances σ_μ^2, σ_λ^2, and σ_ε^2, respectively. In order to find the variance-covariance matrix $\boldsymbol{\Sigma}$ of this model, we must first decide how to write (13.1.32) in the form of (13.1.1). In defining the vector **y**, for example, it is customary to arrange the observations in the following way: $\mathbf{y}' = (y_{11}, y_{12}, \ldots, y_{1T}, y_{21}, y_{22}, \ldots, y_{2T}, \ldots, y_{N1}, y_{N2}, \ldots, y_{NT})$. If we define **X** and **u** similarly, we can write (13.1.32) in the form of (13.1.1). To facilitate the derivation of $\boldsymbol{\Sigma}$, we need the following definition.

DEFINITION 13.1.1   Let $\mathbf{A} = \{a_{ij}\}$ be a $K \times L$ matrix and let **B** be an $M \times N$ matrix. Then the *Kronecker product* $\mathbf{A} \otimes \mathbf{B}$ is a $KM \times LN$ matrix defined by

$$\mathbf{A} \otimes \mathbf{B} = \begin{bmatrix} a_{11}\mathbf{B} & a_{12}\mathbf{B} & \cdot & \cdot & \cdot & a_{1L}\mathbf{B} \\ a_{21}\mathbf{B} & a_{22}\mathbf{B} & \cdot & \cdot & \cdot & a_{2L}\mathbf{B} \\ & \cdot & & & & \\ & \cdot & & & & \\ & \cdot & & & & \\ a_{K1}\mathbf{B} & a_{K2}\mathbf{B} & \cdot & \cdot & \cdot & a_{KL}\mathbf{B} \end{bmatrix}.$$

Let $\mathbf{J}_K$ be the $K \times K$ matrix consisting entirely of ones. Then we have

(13.1.34) $\boldsymbol{\Sigma} = \sigma_\mu^2 \mathbf{A} + \sigma_\lambda^2 \mathbf{B} + \sigma_\varepsilon^2 \mathbf{I}_{NT}$,

where $\mathbf{A} = \mathbf{I}_N \otimes \mathbf{J}_T$ and $\mathbf{B} = \mathbf{J}_N \otimes \mathbf{I}_T$. Its inverse can be shown to be

(13.1.35) $\boldsymbol{\Sigma}^{-1} = \dfrac{1}{\sigma_\varepsilon^2} (\mathbf{I}_{NT} - \gamma_1 \mathbf{A} - \lambda_2 \mathbf{B} + \gamma_3 \mathbf{J}_{NT})$,

where

$$\gamma_1 = \sigma_\mu^2 (\sigma_\varepsilon^2 + T\sigma_\mu^2)^{-1},$$
$$\gamma_2 = \sigma_\lambda^2 (\sigma_\varepsilon^2 + N\sigma_\lambda^2)^{-1},$$
$$\gamma_3 = \gamma_1 \gamma_2 (2\sigma_\varepsilon^2 + T\sigma_\mu^2 + N\sigma_\lambda^2)(\sigma_\varepsilon^2 + T\sigma_\mu^2 + N\sigma_\lambda^2)^{-1}.$$

From the above, $\boldsymbol{\beta}$ can be estimated by the GLS estimator (13.1.5), or more practically by the FGLS estimator (13.1.11), using the consistent estimators of γ_1, γ_2, and γ_3. Alternatively, we can estimate $\boldsymbol{\beta}$ by the so-called *transformation estimator*

(13.1.36) $\hat{\boldsymbol{\beta}}_Q = (\mathbf{X}'\mathbf{Q}\mathbf{X})^{-1}\mathbf{X}'\mathbf{Q}\mathbf{y}$,

where

(13.1.37) $\mathbf{Q} = \mathbf{I} - \dfrac{1}{T}\mathbf{A} - \dfrac{1}{N}\mathbf{B} + \dfrac{1}{NT}\mathbf{J}_{NT}.$

This estimator is computationally simpler than the FGLS estimator, because it does not require estimation of the γ's, yet is consistent and has the same asymptotic distribution as FGLS.

Remember that if we arrange the observations in a different way, we need a different formula for $\boldsymbol{\Sigma}$.

13.2 TIME SERIES REGRESSION

In this section we consider the pth order autoregressive model

(13.2.1) $y_t = \displaystyle\sum_{j=1}^{p} \rho_j\, y_{t-j} + \varepsilon_t, \qquad t = p+1,\, p+2,\, \ldots,\, T,$

where $\{\varepsilon_t\}$ are i.i.d. with $E\varepsilon_t = 0$ and $V\varepsilon_t = \sigma^2$, and $(y_1, y_2, \ldots, y_p)$ are independent of $(\varepsilon_{p+1}, \varepsilon_{p+2}, \ldots, \varepsilon_T)$. This model differs from (13.1.26) only in that the $\{y_t\}$ are observable, whereas the $\{u_t\}$ in the earlier equation are not. We can write (13.2.1) in matrix notation as

(13.2.2) $\mathbf{y} = \mathbf{Y}\boldsymbol{\rho} + \boldsymbol{\varepsilon}$

by defining

$$\mathbf{y} = (y_{p+1}, y_{p+2}, \ldots, y_T)',$$

$$\boldsymbol{\varepsilon} = (\varepsilon_{p+1}, \varepsilon_{p+2}, \ldots, \varepsilon_T)',$$

$$\boldsymbol{\rho} = (\rho_1, \rho_2, \ldots, \rho_p)',$$

$$\mathbf{Y} = \begin{bmatrix} y_p & y_{p-1} & \cdot & \cdot & y_1 \\ y_{p+1} & y_p & \cdot & \cdot & y_2 \\ \cdot & & & & \cdot \\ \cdot & & & & \cdot \\ \cdot & \cdot & & & \cdot \\ y_{T-1} & y_{T-2} & \cdot & \cdot & y_{T-p} \end{bmatrix}.$$

Although the model superficially resembles (12.1.3), it is not a classical regression model because $\mathbf{Y}$ cannot be regarded as a nonstochastic matrix.

The LS estimator $\hat{\boldsymbol{\rho}} = (\mathbf{Y'Y})^{-1}\mathbf{Y'y}$ is generally biased but is consistent with the asymptotic distribution

(13.2.3) $\hat{\boldsymbol{\rho}} \overset{A}{\sim} N[\boldsymbol{\rho}, \sigma^2(\mathbf{Y'Y})^{-1}]$.

Since Theorem 12.2.4 implies that $\hat{\boldsymbol{\beta}} \overset{A}{\sim} N[\boldsymbol{\beta}, \sigma^2(\mathbf{X'X})^{-1}]$, the above result shows that even though (13.2.2) is not a classical regression model, we can asymptotically treat it as if it were. Note that (13.1.29), obtained earlier, is a special case of (13.2.3).

It is useful to generalize (13.2.2) by including the independent variables on the right-hand side as

(13.2.4) $\mathbf{y} = \mathbf{Y}\boldsymbol{\rho} + \mathbf{Z}\boldsymbol{\gamma} + \boldsymbol{\varepsilon}$,

where $\mathbf{Z}$ is a known nonstochastic matrix. Essentially the same asymptotic results hold for this model as for (13.2.2), although the results are more difficult to prove. That is, we can asymptotically treat (13.2.4) as if it were a classical regression model with the combined regressors $\mathbf{X} = (\mathbf{Y}, \mathbf{Z})$. Economists call this model the *distributed-lag model*. See a survey of the topic by Griliches (1967).

We now consider a simple special case of (13.2.4),

(13.2.5) $y_t = \rho y_{t-1} + \gamma z_t + \varepsilon_t$.

This model can be equivalently written as

(13.2.6) $y_t = \gamma \sum_{j=0}^{\infty} \rho^j z_{t-j} + w_t$,

where $w_t = \rho w_{t-1} + \varepsilon_t$. The transformation from (13.2.5) to (13.2.6) is called the *inversion of the autoregressive process*. The reverse transformation is the inversion of the moving-average process. A similar transformation is possible for a higher-order process. The term "distributed lag" describes the manner in which the coefficients on z_{t-j} in (13.2.6) are distributed over j. This particular lag distribution is referred to as the *geometric lag*, or the *Koyck lag*, as it originated in the work of Koyck (1954).

The estimation of ρ and γ in (13.2.5) presents a special problem if $\{\varepsilon_t\}$ are serially correlated. In this case, plim $T^{-1} \sum_{t=2}^{T} y_{t-1}\varepsilon_t \neq 0$, and therefore the LS estimators of ρ and γ are not consistent.

In general, this problem arises whenever plim $T^{-1}\mathbf{X'u} \neq \mathbf{0}$ in the regression model $\mathbf{y} = \mathbf{X}\boldsymbol{\beta} + \mathbf{u}$. We shall encounter another such example in

Section 13.3. In such a case we can consistently estimate $\boldsymbol{\beta}$ by the *instrumental variables (IV) estimator* defined by

(13.2.7) $\hat{\boldsymbol{\beta}}_{IV} = (\mathbf{S}'\mathbf{X})^{-1}\mathbf{S}'\mathbf{y},$

where $\mathbf{S}$ is a known nonstochastic matrix of the same dimension as $\mathbf{X}$, such that plim $T^{-1}\mathbf{S}'\mathbf{X}$ is a nonsingular matrix. It should be noted that the nonstochasticness of $\mathbf{S}$ assures plim $T^{-1}\mathbf{S}'\mathbf{u} = \mathbf{0}$ under fairly general assumptions on $\mathbf{u}$ in spite of the fact that the $\mathbf{u}$ are serially correlated. Then, under general conditions, we have

(13.2.8) $\hat{\boldsymbol{\beta}}_{IV} \overset{A}{\sim} N[\boldsymbol{\beta}, (\mathbf{S}'\mathbf{X})^{-1}\mathbf{S}'\boldsymbol{\Sigma}\mathbf{S}(\mathbf{X}'\mathbf{S})^{-1}],$

where $\boldsymbol{\Sigma} = E\mathbf{u}\mathbf{u}'$. The asymptotic variance-covariance matrix above suggests that, loosely speaking, the more $\mathbf{S}$ is correlated with $\mathbf{X}$, the better.

To return to the specific model (13.2.5), the above consideration suggests that z_t and z_{t-1} constitute a reasonable set of instrumental variables. For a more efficient set of instrumental variables, see Amemiya and Fuller (1967).

13.3 SIMULTANEOUS EQUATIONS MODEL

A study of the *simultaneous equations model* was initiated by the researchers of the Cowles Commission at the University of Chicago in the 1940s. The model was extensively used by econometricians in the 1950s and 1960s. Although it was more frequently employed in macroeconomic analysis, we shall illustrate it by a supply and demand model. Consider

(13.3.1) $\mathbf{y}_1 = \gamma_1\mathbf{y}_2 + \mathbf{X}_1\boldsymbol{\beta}_1 + \mathbf{u}_1$

and

(13.3.2) $\mathbf{y}_2 = \gamma_2\mathbf{y}_1 + \mathbf{X}_2\boldsymbol{\beta}_2 + \mathbf{u}_2,$

where $\mathbf{y}_1$ and $\mathbf{y}_2$ are T-dimensional vectors of dependent variables, $\mathbf{X}_1$ and $\mathbf{X}_2$ are known nonstochastic matrices, and $\mathbf{u}_1$ and $\mathbf{u}_2$ are unobservable random variables such that $E\mathbf{u}_1 = E\mathbf{u}_2 = \mathbf{0}$, $V\mathbf{u}_1 = \sigma_1^2\mathbf{I}$, $V\mathbf{u}_2 = \sigma_2^2\mathbf{I}$, and $E\mathbf{u}_1\mathbf{u}_2' = \sigma_{12}\mathbf{I}$. We give these equations the following interpretation.

A buyer comes to the market with the schedule (13.3.1), which tells him what price ($\mathbf{y}_1$) he should offer for each amount ($\mathbf{y}_2$) of a good he is to buy at each time period t, corresponding to the tth element of the vector. A seller comes to the market with the schedule (13.3.2), which tells her how much (y_2) she should sell at each value (y_1) of the price offered at each t. Then, by some kind of market mechanism (for example, the help of an auctioneer, or trial and error), the values of y_1 and y_2 that satisfy both equations simultaneously—namely, the equilibrium price and quantity—are determined.

Solving the above two equations for y_1 and y_2, we obtain (provided that $\gamma_1\gamma_2 \neq 1$):

$$(13.3.3) \qquad y_1 = \frac{1}{1 - \gamma_1\gamma_2} (X_1\beta_1 + X_2\gamma_1\beta_2 + u_1 + \gamma_1 u_2)$$

and

$$(13.3.4) \qquad y_2 = \frac{1}{1 - \gamma_1\gamma_2} (X_2\beta_2 + X_1\gamma_2\beta_1 + u_2 + \gamma_2 u_1).$$

We call (13.3.1) and (13.3.2) the *structural equations* and (13.3.3) and (13.3.4) the *reduced-form equations*. A structural equation describes the behavior of an economic unit such as a buyer or a seller, whereas a reduced-form equation represents a purely statistical relatic...ship.

A salient feature of a structural equation is that the LS estimator is inconsistent because of the correlation between the dependent variable that appears on the right-hand side of a regression equation and the error term. For example, in (13.3.1) y_2 is correlated with u_1 because y_2 depends on u_1, as we can see in (13.3.4).

Next, we consider the consistent estimation of the parameters of structural equations. Rewrite the reduced-form equations as

$$(13.3.5) \qquad y_1 = X\pi_1 + v_1$$

and

$$(13.3.6) \qquad y_2 = X\pi_2 + v_2,$$

where X consists of the distinct columns of X_1 and X_2 after elimination of any redundant vector and π_1, π_2, v_1, and v_2 are appropriately defined. Note that π_1 and π_2 are functions of γ's and β's. Express that fact as

$$(13.3.7) \qquad (\pi_1, \pi_2) = g(\gamma_1, \gamma_2, \beta_1, \beta_2).$$

Since a reduced-form equation constitutes a classical regression model, the LS estimator applied to (13.3.5) or (13.3.6) yields a consistent estimator of π_1 or π_2. If mapping $g(\cdot)$ is one-to-one, we can uniquely determine the estimates of γ's and β's from the LS estimators of π_1 and π_2, and the resulting estimators are expected to possess desirable properties. If mapping $g(\cdot)$ is many-to-one, however, any solution to the equation $(\hat{\pi}_1, \hat{\pi}_2)$ $= g(\gamma_1, \gamma_2, \beta_1, \beta_2)$, where $\hat{\pi}_1$ and $\hat{\pi}_2$ are the LS estimators, is still consistent but in general not efficient. If, for example, we assume the joint normality of u_1 and u_2, and hence of v_1 and v_2, we can derive the likelihood function from equations (13.3.5) and (13.3.6). Maximizing that function with respect to γ's, β's, and σ's yields a consistent and asymptotically efficient estimator, known as the *full information maximum likelihood estimator.*

A simple consistent estimator of γ's and β's is provided by the instrumental variables method, discussed in Section 13.2. Consider the estimation of γ_1 and β_1 in (13.3.1). For this purpose, rewrite the equation as

(13.3.8) $\quad \mathbf{y}_1 = \mathbf{Z}\boldsymbol{\alpha} + \mathbf{u}_1,$

where $\mathbf{Z} = (\mathbf{y}_2, \mathbf{X})$ and $\boldsymbol{\alpha} = (\gamma_1, \beta_1)'$. Let $\mathbf{S}$ be a known nonstochastic matrix of the same size as $\mathbf{Z}$ such that plim $T^{-1}\mathbf{S}'\mathbf{Z}$ is nonsingular. Then the instrumental variables (IV) estimator of $\boldsymbol{\alpha}$ is defined by

(13.3.9) $\quad \hat{\boldsymbol{\alpha}}_{IV} = (\mathbf{S}'\mathbf{Z})^{-1}\mathbf{S}'\mathbf{y}_1.$

Under general conditions it is consistent and asymptotically

(13.3.10) $\quad \hat{\boldsymbol{\alpha}}_{IV} \overset{A}{\sim} N[\boldsymbol{\alpha}, \sigma_1^2 (\mathbf{S}'\mathbf{Z})^{-1}\mathbf{S}'\mathbf{S}(\mathbf{Z}'\mathbf{S})^{-1}].$

Let $\mathbf{X}$ be as defined after (13.3.6), and define the projection matrix $\mathbf{P}$ $= \mathbf{X}(\mathbf{X}'\mathbf{X})^{-1}\mathbf{X}'$. If we insert $\mathbf{S} = \mathbf{PZ}$ on the right-hand side of (13.3.9), we obtain the *two-stage least squares (2SLS) estimator*

(13.3.11) $\quad \hat{\boldsymbol{\alpha}}_{2S} = (\mathbf{Z}'\mathbf{PZ})^{-1}\mathbf{Z}'\mathbf{Py}_1.$

This estimator was proposed by Theil (1953). It is consistent and asymptotically

(13.3.12) $\quad \hat{\boldsymbol{\alpha}}_{2S} \overset{A}{\sim} N[\boldsymbol{\alpha}, \sigma_1^2(\mathbf{Z}'\mathbf{PZ})^{-1}].$

It can be shown that

(13.3.13) $\quad$ plim $T(\mathbf{Z}'\mathbf{PZ})^{-1} \leq$ plim $T(\mathbf{S}'\mathbf{Z})^{-1}\mathbf{S}'\mathbf{S}(\mathbf{Z}'\mathbf{S})^{-1}.$

In other words, the two-stage least squares estimator is asymptotically more efficient than any instrumental variables estimator.

Nowadays the simultaneous equations model is not so frequently used as in the 1950s and 1960s. One reason is that a multivariate time series model has proved to be more useful for prediction than the simultaneous equations model, especially when data with time intervals finer than annual are used. Another reason is that a disequilibrium model is believed to be more realistic than an equilibrium model. Let us illustrate, again with the supply and demand model. Consider

$$(13.3.14) \quad D_t = \gamma_1 P_t + \mathbf{x}'_{1t}\boldsymbol{\beta}_1 + u_{1t}$$

and

$$(13.3.15) \quad S_t = \gamma_2 P_t + \mathbf{x}'_{2t}\boldsymbol{\beta}_2 + u_{2t},$$

where D_t is the quantity the buyer desires to buy at price P_t, and S_t is the quantity the seller desires to sell at price P_t. We do not observe D_t or S_t, but instead observe the actually traded amount Q_t, which is defined by

$$(13.3.16) \quad Q_t = \min (D_t, S_t).$$

This is the *disequilibrium model* proposed by Fair and Jaffee (1972). The parameters of this model can be consistently and efficiently estimated by the maximum likelihood estimator. There are two different likelihood functions, depending on whether the research knows which of the two variables D_t or S_t is smaller. The case when the researcher knows is called *sample separation*; when the researcher does not know, we have the case of no sample separation. The computation of the maximum likelihood estimator in the second instance is cumbersome. Note that replacing (13.3.16) with the equilibrium condition $D_t = S_t$ leads to a simultaneous equations model similar to (13.3.1) and (13.3.2).

Although the simultaneous equations model is of limited use, estimators such as the instrumental variables and the two-stage least squares are valuable because they can be effectively used whenever a correlation between the regressors and the error term exists. We have already seen one such example in Section 13.2. Another example is the *error-in-variables model*. See Chapter 11, Exercise 5, for the simplest such model and Fuller (1987) for a discussion in depth.

13.4 NONLINEAR REGRESSION MODEL

The *nonlinear regression model* is defined by

$$(13.4.1) \quad y_t = f_t(\boldsymbol{\beta}) + u_t, \quad t = 1, 2, \ldots, T,$$

where $f_t(\cdot)$ is a known function, $\boldsymbol{\beta}$ is a K-vector of unknown parameters, and $\{u_t\}$ are i.i.d. with $Eu_t = 0$ and $Vu_t = \sigma^2$. In practice we often specify $f_t(\boldsymbol{\beta}) = f(\mathbf{x}_t, \boldsymbol{\beta})$, where $\mathbf{x}_t$ is a vector of exogenous variables which, unlike the linear regression model, may not necessarily be of the same dimension as $\boldsymbol{\beta}$.

An example of the nonlinear regression model is the *Cobb-Douglas production function* with an additive error term,

$$(13.4.2) \qquad Q_t = \beta_1 K_t^{\beta_2} L_t^{\beta_3} + u_t,$$

where Q, K, and L denote output, capital input, and labor input, respectively. Another example is the CES production function (see Arrow et al., 1961):

$$(13.4.3) \qquad Q_t = \beta_1 [\beta_2 K_t^{\beta_2} + (1 - \beta_2) L_t^{-\beta_3}]^{-\beta_4/\beta_3} + u_t.$$

We can write (13.4.1) in vector notation as

$$(13.4.4) \qquad \mathbf{y} = \mathbf{f}(\boldsymbol{\beta}) + \mathbf{u},$$

where $\mathbf{y}$, $\mathbf{f}$, and $\mathbf{u}$ are T-vectors having y_t, f_t, and u_t, respectively, for the tth element.

The *nonlinear least squares (NLLS) estimator* of $\boldsymbol{\beta}$ is defined as the value of $\boldsymbol{\beta}$ that minimizes

$$(13.4.5) \qquad S_T(\boldsymbol{\beta}) = \sum_{t=1}^{T} [y_t - f_t(\boldsymbol{\beta})]^2.$$

Denoting the NLLS estimator by $\hat{\boldsymbol{\beta}}$, we can estimate σ^2 by

$$(13.4.6) \qquad \hat{\sigma}^2 = \frac{1}{T} S_T(\hat{\boldsymbol{\beta}}).$$

The estimators $\hat{\boldsymbol{\beta}}$ and $\hat{\sigma}^2$ can be shown to be the maximum likelihood estimators if $\{u_t\}$ are assumed to be jointly normal. The derivation is analogous to the linear case given in Section 12.2.5.

The minimization of $S_T(\boldsymbol{\beta})$ must generally be done by an iterative method. The Newton-Raphson method described in Section 7.3.3 can be used for this purpose. Another iterative method, the *Gauss-Newton method*, is specifically designed for the nonlinear regression model. Let $\hat{\boldsymbol{\beta}}_1$ be the initial value, be it an estimator or a mere guess. Expand $f_t(\boldsymbol{\beta})$ in a Taylor series around $\boldsymbol{\beta} = \hat{\boldsymbol{\beta}}_1$ as

$$(13.4.7) \qquad f_t(\boldsymbol{\beta}) \cong f_t(\hat{\boldsymbol{\beta}}_1) + \frac{\partial f_t}{\partial \boldsymbol{\beta}'}\bigg|_{\hat{\boldsymbol{\beta}}_1} (\boldsymbol{\beta} - \hat{\boldsymbol{\beta}}_1),$$

where $\partial f_t / \partial \boldsymbol{\beta}'$ is a K-dimensional row vector whose jth element is the derivative of f_t with respect to the jth element of $\boldsymbol{\beta}$. Note that (13.4.7) holds approximately because the derivatives are evaluated by $\hat{\boldsymbol{\beta}}_1$. Inserting (13.4.7) into the right-hand side of (13.4.1) and rearranging terms, we obtain:

$$(13.4.8) \quad y_t - f_t(\hat{\boldsymbol{\beta}}_1) + \left.\frac{\partial f_t}{\partial \boldsymbol{\beta}'}\right|_{\hat{\boldsymbol{\beta}}_1} \hat{\boldsymbol{\beta}}_1 \cong \left.\frac{\partial f_t}{\partial \boldsymbol{\beta}'}\right|_{\hat{\boldsymbol{\beta}}_1} \boldsymbol{\beta} + u_t.$$

The second-round estimator of the iteration, $\hat{\boldsymbol{\beta}}_2$, is obtained as the LS estimator applied to (13.4.8), treating the entire left-hand side as the dependent variable and $\partial f_t/\partial \boldsymbol{\beta}'|_{\hat{\boldsymbol{\beta}}_1}$ as the vector of regressors. The iteration is repeated until it converges. It is simpler than the Newton-Raphson method because it requires computation of only the first derivatives of f_t, whereas Newton-Raphson requires the second derivatives as well.

We can show that under general assumptions the NLLS estimator $\hat{\boldsymbol{\beta}}$ is consistent and

$$(13.4.9) \quad \sqrt{T}(\hat{\boldsymbol{\beta}} - \boldsymbol{\beta}) \to N\left(\mathbf{0}, \sigma^2 \operatorname{plim} T\left[\frac{\partial \mathbf{f}'}{\partial \boldsymbol{\beta}} \frac{\partial \mathbf{f}}{\partial \boldsymbol{\beta}'}\right]^{-1}\right).$$

The above result is analogous to the asymptotic normality of the LS estimator given in Theorem 12.2.4. Note that $\partial \mathbf{f}/\partial \boldsymbol{\beta}'$ above is just like $\mathbf{X}$ in Theorem 12.2.4. The difference is that $\partial \mathbf{f}/\partial \boldsymbol{\beta}'$ depends on the unknown parameter $\boldsymbol{\beta}$ and hence is unknown, whereas $\mathbf{X}$ is assumed to be known. The practical implication of (13.4.9) is that

$$(13.4.10) \quad \hat{\boldsymbol{\beta}} \overset{A}{\sim} N\left(\boldsymbol{\beta}, \sigma^2 \left[\left.\frac{\partial \mathbf{f}'}{\partial \boldsymbol{\beta}}\right|_{\hat{\boldsymbol{\beta}}} \left.\frac{\partial \mathbf{f}}{\partial \boldsymbol{\beta}'}\right|_{\hat{\boldsymbol{\beta}}}\right]^{-1}\right).$$

The asymptotic variance-covariance matrix above is comparable to formula (12.2.22) for the LS estimator. We can test hypotheses about $\boldsymbol{\beta}$ in the nonlinear regression model by the methods presented in Section 12.4, provided that we use $\partial \mathbf{f}/\partial \boldsymbol{\beta}'|_{\hat{\boldsymbol{\beta}}}$ for $\mathbf{X}$.

13.5 QUALITATIVE RESPONSE MODEL

The *qualitative response model* or *discrete variables model* is the statistical model that specifies the probability distribution of one or more discrete dependent variables as a function of independent variables. It is analogous to a regression model in that it characterizes a relationship between two sets of variables, but differs from a regression model in that not all of the information of the model is fully captured by specifying conditional means and variances of the dependent variables, given the independent variables. The same remark holds for the models of the subsequent two sections.

The qualitative response model originated in the biometric field, where it was used to analyze phenomena such as whether a patient was cured by a medical treatment, or whether insects died after the administration of an insecticide. Recently the model has gained great popularity among econometricians, as extensive sample survey data describing the behavior of individuals have become available. Many of these data are discrete. The following are some examples: whether or not a consumer buys a car in a given year, whether or not a worker is unemployed at a given time, how many cars a household owns, what type of occupation a person's job is considered, and by what mode of transportation during what time interval a commuter travels to his workplace. The first two examples are binary; the next two, multinomial; and the last, multivariate.

In this book we consider only models that involve a single dependent variable. In Section 13.5.1 we examine the binary model, where the dependent variable takes two values, and in Section 13.5.2 we look at the multinomial model, where the dependent variable takes more than two values. The multivariate model, as well as many other issues not dealt with here, are discussed at an introductory level in Amemiya (1981) and at a more advanced level in Amemiya (1985, chapter 9).

13.5.1 Binary Model

We formally define the *univariate binary model* by

$$(13.5.1) \qquad P(y_i = 1) = F(\mathbf{x}_i'\boldsymbol{\beta}), \qquad i = 1, 2, \ldots, n,$$

where we assume that y_i takes the values 1 or 0, F is a known distribution function, $\mathbf{x}_i$ is a known nonstochastic vector, and $\boldsymbol{\beta}$ is a vector of unknown parameters.

If, for example, we apply the model to study whether or not a person buys a car in a given year, $y_i = 1$ represents the fact that the ith person buys a car, and the vector $\mathbf{x}_i$ will include among other factors the price of the car and the person's income. As in a regression model, however, the $\mathbf{x}_i$ need not be the original variables such as price and income; they could be functions of the original variables. The assumption that y takes the values 1 or 0 is made for mathematical convenience. The essential features of the model are unchanged if we choose any other pair of distinct real numbers.

Model (13.5.1) can be derived from the principle of utility maximization as follows. Let U_{1i} and U_{0i} be the ith person's utilities associated with the alternatives 1 and 0, respectively. We assume that

$$(13.5.2) \quad U_{1i} = \mathbf{x}'_{1i}\boldsymbol{\beta} + u_{1i} \text{ and } U_{0i} = \mathbf{x}'_{0i}\boldsymbol{\beta} + u_{0i},$$

where $\mathbf{x}_{1i}$ and $\mathbf{x}_{0i}$ are nonstochastic and known, and (u_{1i}, u_{0i}) are bivariate i.i.d. random variables, which may be regarded as the omitted independent variables known to the decision maker but unobservable to the statistician. We assume that the ith person chooses alternative 1 if and only if $U_{1i} > U_{0i}$. Thus we have

$$(13.5.3) \quad P(y_i = 1) = P(U_{1i} > U_{0i})$$
$$= P[u_{0i} - u_{1i} < (\mathbf{x}_{1i} - \mathbf{x}_{0i})'\boldsymbol{\beta}].$$

We obtain model (13.5.1) if we assume that the distribution function of $u_{0i} - u_{1i}$ is F and define $\mathbf{x}_i = \mathbf{x}_{1i} - \mathbf{x}_{0i}$.

The following two distribution functions are most frequently used: standard normal Φ and logistic Λ. The *standard normal distribution function* (see Section 5.2) is defined by

$$(13.5.4) \quad \Phi(x) = \int_{-\infty}^{x} \frac{1}{\sqrt{2\pi}} \exp(-z^2/2)dz$$

and the *logistic distribution function* is defined by

$$(13.5.5) \quad \Lambda(x) = \frac{e^x}{1 + e^x}.$$

When Φ is used in (13.5.1), the model is called *probit*; when Λ is used, the model is called *logit*. The two distribution functions have similar shapes, except that the logistic has a slightly fatter tail than the standard normal.

To the extent that the econometrician experiments with various transformations of the original independent variables, as he normally would in a regression model, the choice of F is not crucial. To see this, suppose that the true distribution function is G, but the econometrician assumed it to be F. Then, by choosing a function $h(\cdot)$ appropriately, he can always satisfy $G(\mathbf{x}'_i\boldsymbol{\beta}) = F[h(\mathbf{x}'_i\boldsymbol{\beta})]$.

It is important to remember that in model (13.5.1) the regression coefficients β do not have any intrinsic meaning. The important quantity is, rather, the vector $\partial F/\partial \mathbf{x}_i$. If one researcher fits a given set of data using a probit model and another researcher fits the same data using a logit model, it would be meaningless to compare the two estimates of β. We must instead compare $\partial \Phi/\partial \mathbf{x}_i$ with $\partial \Lambda/\partial \mathbf{x}_i$. In most cases these two derivatives will take very similar values.

The best way to estimate model (13.5.1) is by the maximum likelihood method. The likelihood function of the model is given by

$$(13.5.6) \qquad L = \prod_{i=1}^{n} F(\mathbf{x}_i'\beta)^{y_i}[1 - F(\mathbf{x}_i'\beta)]^{1-y_i}.$$

When F is either Φ or Λ, the likelihood function is *globally concave* in β. Therefore, maximizing L with respect to β by any standard iterative method such as the Newton-Raphson (see Section 7.3.3) is straightforward. Although we do not have the i.i.d. sample here because $\mathbf{x}_i$ varies with i, we can prove the consistency and the asymptotic normality of the maximum likelihood estimator by an argument similar to the one presented in Sections 7.4.2 and 7.4.3. The asymptotic distribution of the maximum likelihood estimator $\hat{\beta}$ is given by

$$(13.5.7) \qquad \sqrt{T}(\hat{\beta} - \beta) \to N(0, \mathbf{A}^{-1}),$$

where

$$\mathbf{A} = \lim \frac{1}{n} \sum_{i=1}^{n} \frac{f_i^2}{F_i(1 - F_i)} \mathbf{x}_i\mathbf{x}_i',$$

where f is the density function of F.

13.5.2 Multinomial Model

We illustrate the multinomial model by considering the case of three alternatives, which for convenience we associate with three integers 1, 2, and 3. One example of the three-response model is the commuter's choice of mode of transportation, where the three alternatives are private car, bus, and train. Another example is the worker's choice of three types of employment: being fully employed, partially employed, and self-employed.

We extend (13.5.2) to the case of three alternatives as

(13.5.8) $U_{1i} = \mathbf{x}'_{1i}\boldsymbol{\beta} + u_{1i}$

$U_{2i} = \mathbf{x}'_{2i}\boldsymbol{\beta} + u_{2i}$

$U_{3i} = \mathbf{x}'_{3i}\boldsymbol{\beta} + u_{3i}$,

where (u_{1i}, u_{2i}, u_{3i}) are i.i.d. It is assumed that the individual chooses the alternative with the largest utility. Therefore, if we represent the ith person's discrete choice by the variable y_i, our model is defined by

$$P(y_i = 1) = P(U_{1i} > U_{2i}, U_{1i} > U_{3i})$$

$$P(y_i = 2) = P(U_{2i} > U_{1i}, U_{2i} > U_{3i}), \quad 1, 2, \ldots, n.$$

If we specify the joint distribution of (u_{1i}, u_{2i}, u_{3i}) up to an unknown parameter vector $\boldsymbol{\theta}$, we can express the above probabilities as a function of $\boldsymbol{\beta}$ and $\boldsymbol{\theta}$. If we define binary variables y_{ji} by $y_{ji} = 1$ if $y_i = j$, $j = 1, 2$, the likelihood function of the model is given by

$$(13.5.10) \quad L = \prod_{i=1}^{n} P_{1i}^{y_{1i}} P_{2i}^{y_{2i}} (1 - P_{1i} - P_{2i})^{1 - y_{1i} - y_{2i}},$$

where $P_{1i} = P(y_i = 1)$ and $P_{2i} = P(y_i = 2)$. An iterative method must be used for maximizing the above with respect to $\boldsymbol{\beta}$ and $\boldsymbol{\theta}$.

One way to specify the distribution of the u's would be to assume them to be jointly normal. We can assume without loss of generality that their means are zeroes and one of the variances is unity. The former assumption is possible because the nonstochastic part can absorb nonzero means, and the latter because multiplication of the three utilities by an identical positive constant does not change their ranking. We should generally allow for nonzero correlation among the three error terms. An analogous model based on the normality assumption was estimated by Hausman and Wise (1978). In the normal model we must evaluate the probabilities as definite integrals of a joint normal density. This is cumbersome if the number of alternatives is larger than five, although an advance in the simulation method (see McFadden, 1989) has made the problem more manageable than formerly.

McFadden (1974) proposed a joint distribution of the errors that makes possible an explicit representation of the probabilities. He assumed that the errors are mutually independent (in addition to being independent across i) and that each is distributed as

(13.5.11) $F(u) = \exp(-e^{-u})$.

This was called the *Type I extreme-value distribution* by Johnson and Kotz (1970, p. 272). The probabilities are explicitly given by

(13.5.12) $P(y_i = j) = \dfrac{\exp(\mathbf{x}'_{ji}\,\boldsymbol{\beta})}{\exp(\mathbf{x}'_{1i}\,\boldsymbol{\beta}) + \exp(\mathbf{x}'_{2i}\,\boldsymbol{\beta}) + \exp(\mathbf{x}'_{3i}\,\boldsymbol{\beta})}$,

$$j = 1, 2, 3;\ i = 1, 2, \ldots, n.$$

This model is called the *multinomial logit model*. Besides the advantage of having explicit formulae for the probabilities, this model has the computational advantage of a globally concave likelihood function.

It is easy to criticize the multinomial logit model from a theoretical point of view. First, no economist is ready to argue that the utility should be distributed according to the Type I extreme-value distribution. Second, the model implies *independence from irrelevant alternatives*, which can be mathematically stated as

(13.5.13) $P(U_3 > U_1) = P(U_3 > U_1 \,|\, U_3 > U_2 \text{ or } U_1 > U_2)$

and similar equalities involving the two other possible pairs of utilities. (We have suppressed the subscript i above to simplify the notation.) The equality (13.5.13) means that the information that a person has not chosen alternative 2 does not alter the probability that the person prefers 3 to 1. Let us consider whether or not this assumption is reasonable in the two examples we mentioned at the beginning of this section.

In the first example, suppose that alternatives 1, 2, and 3 correspond to bus, train, and private car, respectively, and suppose that a person is known to have chosen either bus or car. It is perhaps reasonable to surmise that the nonselection of train indicates the person's dislike of public transportation. Given this information, we might expect her to be more likely to choose car over bus. If this reasoning is correct, we should expect inequality $<$ to hold in the place of equality in (13.5.13). This argument would be more convincing if alternatives 1 and 2 corresponded to blue bus and red bus, instead of bus and train, to cite McFadden's well-known example. Given that a person has not chosen red bus, it is likely that she will also prefer car to blue bus (unless she happens to abhor the color red).

In the second example, suppose that alternatives 1, 2, and 3 correspond to fully employed, partially employed, and self-employed. Again, we would expect inequality $<$ in (13.5.13), to the extent that the nonselection of "partially employed" can be taken to mean an aversion to work for others.

If, however, we view (13.5.12) as a purely statistical model, not necessarily derived from utility maximization, it is much more general than it appears, precisely for the same reason that the choice of F does not matter much in (13.5.1) as long as the researcher experiments with various transformations of the independent variables. Any multinomial model can be approximated by a multinomial logit model if the researcher is allowed to manipulate the nonstochastic parts of the utilities.

It is possible to generalize the multinomial logit model in such a way that the assumption of independence from irrelevant alternatives is removed, yet the probabilities can be explicitly derived. We shall explain the *nested logit model* proposed by McFadden (1977) in the model of three alternatives. Suppose that u_3 is distributed as (13.5.11) and independent of u_1 and u_2, but u_1 and u_2 follow the joint distribution

$$(13.5.14) \quad F(u_1, u_2) = \exp\{-[e^{-u_1/\rho} + e^{-u_2/\rho}]^\rho\}, \quad 0 < \rho \le 1.$$

The joint distribution was named *Gumbel's Type B bivariate extreme-value distribution* by Johnson and Kotz (1972, p. 256). By taking either u_1 or u_2 to infinity, we can readily see that each marginal distribution is the same as (13.5.11). The parameter ρ measures the (inverse) degree of association between u_1 and u_2 such that $\rho = 1$ implies independence. Clearly, if $\rho = 1$ the model is reduced to the multinomial logit model. Therefore it is useful to estimate this model and test the hypothesis $\rho = 1$.

In a given practical problem the researcher must choose a priori which two alternatives should be paired in the nested logit model. In the aforementioned examples, it is natural to pair bus and train or fully employed and partially employed.

For generalization of the nested logit model to the case of more than three alternatives and to the case of higher-level nesting, see McFadden (1981) or Amemiya (1985, sections 9.3.5 and 9.3.6).

The probabilities of the above three-response nested logit model are specified by

$$(13.5.15) \quad P(y_i = 1 \mid y_i = 1 \text{ or } 2) = \Lambda[(\mathbf{x}_{1i} - \mathbf{x}_{2i})'\boldsymbol{\beta}/\rho]$$

and

(13.5.16) $P(y_i = 1 \text{ or } 2) = \Lambda[(\mathbf{x}_{2i} - \mathbf{x}_{3i})'\boldsymbol{\beta} + \rho \log z_i]$,

where

$$z_i = \exp[(\mathbf{x}_{1i} - \mathbf{x}_{2i})'\boldsymbol{\beta}/\rho] + 1.$$

13.6 CENSORED OR TRUNCATED REGRESSION MODEL (TOBIT MODEL)

Tobin (1958) proposed the following important model:

(13.6.1) $y_i^* = \mathbf{x}_i'\boldsymbol{\beta} + u_i$

and

(13.6.2) $y_i = \mathbf{x}_i'\boldsymbol{\beta} + u_i \qquad \text{if } y_i^* > 0$

$\qquad\qquad\quad = 0 \qquad\qquad\quad \text{if } y_i^* > 0, \qquad i = 1, 2, \ldots, n,$

where $\{u_i\}$ are assumed to be i.i.d. $N(0, \sigma^2)$ and $\mathbf{x}_i$ is a known nonstochastic vector. It is assumed that $\{y_i\}$ and $\{\mathbf{x}_i\}$ are observed for all i, but $\{y_i^*\}$ are unobserved if $y_i^* \leq 0$. This model is called the *censored regression model* or the *Tobit model* (after Tobin, in analogy to probit). If the observations corresponding to $y_i^* \leq 0$ are totally lost, that is, if $\{\mathbf{x}_i\}$ are not observed whenever $y_i^* \leq 0$, and if the researcher does not know how many observations exist for which $y_i^* \leq 0$, the model is called the *truncated regression model*.

Tobin used this model to explain a household's expenditure (y) on a durable good in a given year as a function of independent variables ($\mathbf{x}$), including the price of the durable good and the household's income. The above model is necessitated by the fact that there are likely to be many households for which the expenditure is zero. The variable y_i^* may be interpreted as the desired amount of expenditure, and it is hypothesized that a household does not buy the durable good if the desired expenditure is zero or negative (a negative expenditure is not possible). The Tobit model has been used in many areas of economics. Amemiya (1985), p. 365, lists several representative applications.

If there is a single independent variable x, the observed data on y and x in the Tobit model will normally look like Figure 13.1. It is apparent there that the LS estimator of the slope coefficient obtained by regressing

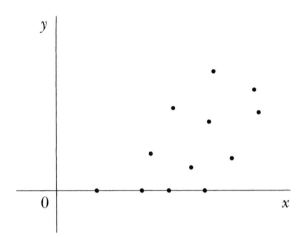

FIGURE 13.1   An example of censored data

all the y's (including those that are zeroes) on x will be biased and inconsistent. Although not apparent from the figure, it can further be shown that the LS estimator using only the positive y's is also biased and inconsistent.

The consistent and asymptotically efficient estimator of $\boldsymbol{\beta}$ and σ^2 in the Tobit model is obtained by the maximum likelihood estimator. The likelihood function of the model is given by

$$(13.6.3) \qquad L = \prod_0 [1 - \Phi(\mathbf{x}'_i\boldsymbol{\beta}/\sigma)] \prod_1 \sigma^{-1}\phi[(y_i - \mathbf{x}'_i\boldsymbol{\beta})/\sigma],$$

where Φ and ϕ are the standard normal distribution and density functions and Π_0 and Π_1 stand for the product over those i for which $y_i = 0$ and $y_i > 0$, respectively. It is a peculiar product of a probability and a density, yet the maximum likelihood estimator can be shown to be consistent and asymptotically normal. For the proof, see Amemiya (1973). Olsen (1978) proved the global concavity of (13.6.3).

The likelihood function of the truncated regression model can be written as

$$(13.6.4) \qquad L = \prod_1 \Phi(\mathbf{x}'_i\boldsymbol{\beta}/\sigma)^{-1}\sigma^{-1}\phi[(y_i - \mathbf{x}'_i\boldsymbol{\beta})/\sigma].$$

Amemiya (1973) proved the consistency and the asymptotic normality of this model as well.

The Tobit maximum likelihood estimator is consistent even when $\{u_i\}$ are serially correlated (see Robinson, 1982). It loses its consistency, however, when the true distribution of $\{u_i\}$ is either nonnormal or heteroscedastic. For discussion of these cases, see Amemiya (1985, section 10.5).

Many generalizations of the Tobit model have been used in empirical research. Amemiya (1985, section 10.6) classifies them into five broad types, of which we shall discuss only Types 2 and 5.

Type 2 Tobit is the simplest natural generalization of the Tobit model (Type 1) and is defined by

$$(13.6.5) \qquad y_{1i}^* = \mathbf{x}_{1i}'\boldsymbol{\beta}_1 + u_{1i}$$

$$y_{2i}^* = \mathbf{x}_{2i}'\boldsymbol{\beta}_2 + u_{2i}$$

and

$$(13.6.6) \qquad y_{2i} = y_{2i}^* \quad \text{if } y_{1i}^* > 0$$

$$= 0 \quad \text{if } y_{1i}^* \leq 0, \qquad i = 1, 2, \ldots, n,$$

where (u_{1i}, u_{2i}) are i.i.d. drawings from a bivariate normal distribution with zero means, variances σ_1^2 and σ_2^2. and covariance σ_{12}. It is assumed that only the sign of y_{1i}^* is observed and that y_{2i}^* is observed only when $y_{1i}^* > 0$. It is assumed that $\mathbf{x}_{1i}$ are observed for all i but that $\mathbf{x}_{2i}$ need not be observed for those i such that $y_{1i}^* \leq 0$.

The likelihood function of this model is given by

$$(13.6.7) \qquad L = \prod_0 P(y_{1i}^* \leq 0) \prod_1 f(y_{2i} \mid y_{1i}^* > 0)P(y_{1i}^* > 0),$$

where Π_0 and Π_1 stand for the product over those i for which $y_{2i} = 0$ and $y_{2i} \neq 0$, respectively, and $f(\cdot \mid y_{1i}^* > 0)$ stands for the conditional density of y_{2i}^* given $y_{1i}^* > 0$.

The Tobit model (Type 1) is a special case of the Type 2 Tobit, in which $y_{1i}^* = y_{2i}^*$. Since a test of Type 1 versus Type 2 cannot be translated as a test about the parameters of the Type 2 Tobit model, the choice between the two models must be made in a nonclassical way. Another special case of Type 2 is when u_{1i} and u_{2i} are independent. In this case the LS regression of the positive y_{2i} on $\mathbf{x}_{2i}$ yields the maximum likelihood estimators of $\boldsymbol{\beta}_2$ and σ_2^2, while the probit maximum likelihood estimator applied to the first equation of (13.6.5) yields the maximum likelihood estimator of $\boldsymbol{\beta}_1/\sigma_1$.

In the work of Gronau (1973), y_1^* represents the offered wage minus the *reservation wage* (the lowest wage the worker is willing to accept) and y_2^* represents the offered wage. Only when the offered wage exceeds the reservation wage do we observe the actual wage, which is equal to the offered wage. In the work of Dudley and Montmarquette (1976), y_{1i}^* signifies the measure of the U.S. inclination to give aid to the ith country, so that aid is given if y_{1i}^* is positive, and y_{2i}^* determines the actual amount of aid.

Type 5 Tobit is defined by

$$(13.6.8) \quad y_{ji}^* = \mathbf{x}_{ji}'\boldsymbol{\beta}_j + u_{ji},$$

$$z_{ji}^* = \mathbf{s}_{ji}'\boldsymbol{\gamma}_j + v_{ji},$$

$$y_i = y_{ki}^* \text{ if } z_{ki}^* = \max_j z_{ji}^*, \quad j = 1, 2, \ldots, J; i = 1, 2, \ldots, n,$$

where y_i, $\mathbf{x}_{ji}$, $\mathbf{s}_{ji}$ are observed. It is assumed that (u_{ji}, v_{ji}) are i.i.d. across i but may be correlated across j, and for each i and j the two random variables may be correlated with each other. Their joint distribution is variously specified by researchers. In some applications the maximum in (13.6.8) can be replaced by the minimum without changing the essential features of the model.

The likelihood function of the model is given by

$$(13.6.9) \quad L = \prod_1 f(y_{1i}^* \mid z_{1i}^* \text{ is the maximum})P_{1i}$$

$$\times \prod_2 f(y_{2i}^* \mid z_{2i}^* \text{ is the maximum })P_{2i} \ldots$$

$$\times \prod_J f(y_{Ji}^* \mid z_{Ji}^* \text{ is the maximum})P_{Ji},$$

where $\prod_j$ is the product over those i for which z_{ji}^* is the maximum and $P_{ji} = P(z_{ji}^* \text{ is the maximum})$.

In the model of Lee (1978), $J = 2$, $y = z$, and z_{1i}^* represents the wage rate of the ith worker in case he joins the union and z_{2i}^* in case he does not. The researcher observes the actual wage rate y_i, which is the greater of the two. (We have slightly simplified Lee's model.) The disequilibrium model defined by (13.3.14), (13.3.15), and (13.3.16) becomes this type if we assume sample separation. In the model of Duncan (1980), z_{ji}^* is the net profit accruing to the ith firm from the plant to be built in the jth location, and $\mathbf{y}_{ji}^*$ is the input-output vector at the jth location. In the model of Dubin and McFadden (1984), z_{ji}^* is the utility of the jth portfolio of the electric and gas appliances of the ith household, and $\mathbf{y}_{ji}^*$ (vector) consists of the gas and electricity consumption associated with the jth portfolio in the ith household.

13.7 DURATION MODEL

The *duration model* purports to explain the distribution function of a duration variable as a function of independent variables. The duration variable may be human life, how long a patient lives after an operation, the life of a machine, or the duration of unemployment. As is evident from these examples, the duration model is useful in many disciplines, including medicine, engineering, and economics. Introductory books on duration analysis emphasizing each of the areas of application mentioned above are Kalbfleisch and Prentice (1980), Miller (1981), and Lancaster (1990).

We shall initially explain the basic facts about the duration model in the setting of the i.i.d. sample, then later introduce the independent variables.

Denoting the duration variable by T, we can completely characterize the duration model in the i.i.d. case by specifying the distribution function

$$(13.7.1) \quad F(t) = P(T < t).$$

In duration analysis the concept known as *hazard* plays an important role. We define

$$(13.7.2) \quad \text{Hazard}(t, t + \Delta t) = P(t < T < t + \Delta t \mid T > t)$$

and call it the hazard of the interval $(t, t + \Delta t)$. If T refers to the life of a person, the above signifies the probability that she dies in the time interval $(t, t + \Delta t)$, given that she has lived up to time t. Assuming that the density function $f(t)$ exists to simplify the analysis, we have from (13.7.2)

$$(13.7.3) \quad \text{Hazard}(t, t + \Delta t) \cong \frac{f(t)}{1 - F(t)} \Delta t,$$

where the approximation gets better as Δt gets smaller. We define the *hazard function*, denoted $\lambda(t)$, by

$$(13.7.4) \quad \lambda(t) = \frac{f(t)}{1 - F(t)}.$$

There is a one-to-one correspondence between $F(t)$ and $\lambda(t)$. Since $f(t) = \partial F(t)/\partial t$, (13.7.4) shows that $\lambda(t)$ is known once $F(t)$ is known. The next equation shows the converse:

$$(13.7.5) \quad F(t) = 1 - \exp\left[-\int_0^t \lambda(s)ds\right].$$

Therefore $\lambda(t)$ contains no new information beyond what is contained in $F(t)$. Nevertheless, it is useful to define this concept because sometimes the researcher has a better feel for the hazard function than for the distribution function; hence it is easier for him to specify the former than the latter.

The simplest duration model is the one for which the hazard function is constant:

$$(13.7.6) \quad \lambda(t) = \lambda.$$

This is called the *exponential model*. From (13.7.5) we have for this model $F(t) = 1 - e^{-\lambda t}$ and $f(t) = \lambda e^{-\lambda t}$. This model would not be realistic to use for human life, for it would imply that the probability a person dies within the next minute, say, is the same for persons of every age. The exponential model for the life of a machine implies that the machine is always like new, regardless of how old it may be. A more realistic model for human life would be the one in which $\lambda(t)$ has a U shape, remaining high for age 0 to 1, attaining a minimum at youth, and then rising again with age. For some other applications (for example, the duration of a marriage) an inverted U shape may be more realistic.

The simplest generalization of the exponential model is the *Weibull model*, in which the hazard function is specified as

$$(13.7.7) \quad \lambda(t) = \lambda \alpha t^{\alpha - 1}.$$

When $\alpha = 1$, the Weibull model is reduced to the exponential model. Therefore, the researcher can test exponential versus Weibull by testing $\alpha = 1$ in the Weibull model. Differentiating (13.7.7) with respect to t, we obtain

$$(13.7.8) \quad \alpha \begin{array}{c} > \\ = \\ < \end{array} 1 \Leftrightarrow \frac{\partial \lambda}{\partial t} \begin{array}{c} > \\ = \\ < \end{array} 0.$$

Thus the Weibull model can accommodate an increasing or decreasing hazard function, but neither a U-shaped nor an inverted U-shaped hazard function.

Lancaster (1979) estimated a Weibull model of unemployment duration. He introduced independent variables into the model by specifying the hazard function of the ith unemployed worker as

(13.7.9) $\lambda_i(t) = \exp(\mathbf{x}_i'\boldsymbol{\beta})\alpha t^{\alpha-1}$.

The vector $\mathbf{x}_i$ contains log age, log unemployment rate of the area, and log replacement (unemployment benefit divided by earnings from the last job). Lancaster was interested in testing $\alpha = 1$, because economic theory does not clearly indicate whether α should be larger or smaller than 1. He found, curiously, that his maximum likelihood estimator of α approached 1 from below as he kept adding the independent variables, starting with the constant term only.

As Lancaster showed, this phenomenon is due to the fact that even if the hazard function is constant over time for each individual, if different individuals are associated with different levels of the hazard function, an aggregate estimate of the hazard function obtained by treating all the individuals homogeneously will exhibit a declining hazard function (that is, $\partial\lambda/\partial t < 0$). We explain this fact by the illustrative example in Table 13.1. In this example three groups of individuals are associated with three levels of the hazard rate—0.5, 0.2, and 0.1. Initially there are 1000 people in each group. The first row shows, for example, that 500 people remain at the end of period 1 and the beginning of period 2, and so on. The last row indicates the ratio of the aggregate number of people who die in each period to the number of people who remain at the beginning of the period.

The heterogeneity of the sample may not be totally explained by all the independent variables that the researcher can observe. In such a case it would be advisable to introduce into the model an unobservable random variable, known as the *unobserved heterogeneity*, which acts as a surrogate for the omitted independent variables.

In one of his models Lancaster (1979) specified the hazard function as

(13.7.10) $\lambda_i(t) = \exp(\mathbf{x}_i'\boldsymbol{\beta} + v_i)\alpha t^{\alpha-1}$,

where $\{v_i\}$ are i.i.d. gamma. If $L_i(v_i)$ denotes the conditional likelihood function for the ith person, given v_i, the likelihood function of the model with the unobserved heterogeneity is given by

(13.7.11) $L = \prod_{i=1}^{n} EL_i(v_i)$,

TABLE 13.1 An illustrative example of a declining aggregate hazard

Individual hazard rate	Period 1		Period 2		Period 3	
	Remain	Die	Remain	Die	Remain	Die
0.5	1000	500	500	250	250	125
0.2	1000	200	800	160	640	128
0.1	1000	100	900	90	810	81
Total	3000	800	2200	500	1700	334
Total hazard rate	0.267		0.227		0.196	

where the expectation is taken with respect to the distribution of v_i. (The likelihood function of the model without the unobserved heterogeneity will be given later.) As Lancaster introduced the unobserved heterogeneity, his estimate of α further approached 1. The unobserved heterogeneity can be used with a model more general than Weibull. Heckman and Singer (1984) studied the properties of the maximum likelihood estimator of the distribution of the unobserved heterogeneity without parametrically specifying it in a general duration model. They showed that the maximum likelihood estimator of the distribution is discrete.

A hazard function with independent variables may be written as

$$(13.7.12) \quad \lambda_i(t) = \lambda_0(t)\exp(\mathbf{x}_{it}'\boldsymbol{\beta}).$$

where $\lambda_0(t)$ is referred to as the *baseline hazard function*. This formulation is more general than (13.7.9), first, in the sense that $\mathbf{x}$ depends on time t as well as on individual i, and, second, in the sense that the baseline hazard function is general. Some examples of the baseline hazard functions which have been used in econometric applications are as follows:

$$(13.7.13) \quad \lambda_0(t) = \exp\left[\gamma_0 + \gamma_1 \frac{t^{\lambda_1} - 1}{\lambda_1} + \gamma_2 \frac{t^{\lambda_2} - 1}{\lambda_2}\right].$$

Flinn and Heckman (1982)

$$(13.7.14) \quad \lambda_0(t) = \frac{\rho k t^{k-1}}{1 + \rho t^k}. \quad \text{Gritz (1993)}$$

$$(13.7.15) \quad \lambda_0(t) = \lambda \exp(\gamma_1 t + \gamma_2 t^2). \quad \text{Sturm (1991)}$$

Next we consider the derivation of the likelihood function of the duration model with the hazard function of the form (13.7.12). The first step is to obtain the distribution function by the formula (13.7.5) as

$$(13.7.16) \quad F_i(t) = 1 - \exp\left[-\int_0^t \lambda_0(s)\exp(\mathbf{x}_{is}'\boldsymbol{\beta})ds\right]$$

and then the density function, by differentiating the above as

$$(13.7.17) \quad f_i(t) = \lambda_0(t)\exp(\mathbf{x}_{it}'\boldsymbol{\beta})\exp\left[-\int_0^t \lambda_0(s)\exp(\mathbf{x}_{is}'\boldsymbol{\beta})ds\right].$$

The computation of the integral in the above two formulae presents a problem in that we must specify the independent variable vector $\mathbf{x}_{is}$ as a continuous function of s. It is customary in practice to divide the sample period into intervals and assume that $\mathbf{x}_{is}$ remains constant within each interval. This assumption simplifes the integral considerably.

The likelihood function depends on a sampling scheme. As an illustration, let us assume that our data consist of the survival durations of all those who had heart transplant operations at Stanford University from the day of the first such operation there until December 31, 1992. There are two categories of data: those who died before December 31, 1992, and those who were still living on that date. The contribution of a patient in the first category to the likelihood function is the density function evaluated at the observed survival duration, and the contribution of a patient in the second category is the probability that he lived at least until December 31, 1992. Thus the likelihood function is given by

$$(13.7.18) \quad L = \prod_0 f_i(t_i) \prod_1 [1 - F_i(t_i)],$$

where Π_0 is the product over those individuals who died before December 31, 1992, and Π_1 is the product over those individuals who were still living on that date. Note that for patients of the first category t_i refers to the time from the operation to the death, whereas for patients of the second category t_i refers to the time from the operation to December 31, 1992. The survival durations of the patients still living on the last day of observation (in this example December 31, 1992) are said to be *right censored*.

Note a similarity between the above likelihood function and the likelihood function of the Tobit model given in (13.6.3). In fact, the two models are mathematically equivalent.

Now consider another sampling scheme with the same heart transplant data. Suppose we observe only those patients who either had their operations between January 1, 1980, and December 31, 1992, or those who had their operations before January 1, 1980, but were still living on that date. Then (13.7.18) is no longer the correct likelihood function. Maximizing it would overestimate the survival duration, because this sampling scheme tends to include more long-surviving patients than short-surviving patients among those who had their operations before January 1, 1980. The survival durations of the patients who had their operations before the first day of observation (in this example January 1, 1980) and were still living on that date are said to be *left censored*. In order to obtain consistent estimates of the parameters of this model, we must either maximize the correct likelihood function or eliminate from the sample all the patients living on January 1, 1980. For the correct likelihood function of the second sampling scheme with left censoring, see Amemiya (1991).

We have deliberately chosen the heart transplant example to illustrate two sampling schemes. With data such as unemployment spells, the first sampling scheme is practically impossible because the history of unemployment goes back very far.

We mentioned earlier a problem of computing the integral in (13.7.16) or (13.7.17), which arises when we specify the hazard function generally as (13.7.12). The problem does not arise if we assume

$$(13.7.19) \quad \lambda_i(t) = \lambda_0(t)\exp(\mathbf{x}_i'\boldsymbol{\beta}).$$

The duration model with the hazard function that can be written as a product of the term that depends only on t and the term that depends only on i, as above, is called the *proportional hazard model*. Note that Lancaster's model (13.7.9) is a special case of such a model. Cox (1972) showed that in the proportional hazard model $\boldsymbol{\beta}$ can be estimated without specifying the baseline hazard $\lambda_0(t)$. This estimator of $\boldsymbol{\beta}$ is called the *partial maximum likelihood estimator.* The baseline hazard $\lambda_0(t)$ can be nonparametrically estimated by the *Kaplan-Meier estimator* (1958). For an econometric application of these estimators, see Lehrer (1988).

The general model with the hazard function (13.7.12) may be estimated by a discrete approximation. In this case $\lambda_i(t)$ must be interpreted as the probability that the spell of the ith person ends in the interval $(t, t + 1)$. The contribution to the likelihood function of the spell that ends after k periods is $\prod_{t=1}^{k-1}[1 - \lambda_i(t)]\lambda_i(k)$, whereas the contribution to the likelihood function of the spell that lasts at least for k periods is $\prod_{t=1}^{k}[1 - \lambda_i(t)]$. See Moffitt (1985) for the maximum likelihood estimator of a duration model using a discrete approximation.

Next we demonstrate how the exponential duration model can be derived from utility maximization in a simple *job-search model.* We do so first in the case of discrete time, and second in the case of continuous time.

Consider a particular unemployed worker. In every period there is a probability λ that a wage offer will arrive, and if it does arrive, its size is distributed i.i.d. as G. If the worker accepts the offer, he will receive the same wage forever. If he rejects it, he incurs the search cost c until he is employed. The discount rate is δ. Let $V(t)$ be the maximum utility at time t. Then the *Bellman equation* is

(13.7.20) $V(t) = \lambda \max[\delta^{-1}W(t), (1 - \delta)EV(t + 1) - c]$

$$+ (1 - \lambda)[(1 - \delta)EV(t + 1) - c].$$

Taking the expectation of both sides and setting $EV(t) \equiv V$ because of stationarity,

(13.7.21) $V = \delta^{-1}\lambda E[\max(W, R)] + \delta^{-1}(1 - \lambda)R,$

where $R = \delta[(1 - \delta)V - c]$ and $W(t)$ has been written simply as W because of our i.i.d. assumption. Note that

(13.7.22) $E[\max(W, R)] = \int_R^\infty w dG(w) + RG(R).$

Note further that V appears in both sides of (13.7.21). Solve for V, call the solution V^*, and define $R^* = \delta[(1 - \delta)V^* - c]$, the *reservation wage*. The worker should accept the wage offer if and only if $W > R^*$. Define $P = P(w > R^*)$. Then the likelihood function of the worker who accepted the wage in the $(t + 1)$st period is

(13.7.23) $L = (1 - \lambda P)^t \lambda P.$

Many extensions of this basic model have been estimated in econometric applications, of which we mention only two. The model of Wolpin (1987) introduces the following extensions: first, the planning horizon is finite; second, the wage is observed with an error. A new feature in the model of Pakes (1986), in which W is the net return from the renewal of a patent, is that $W(t)$ is serially correlated. This feature makes solution of the Bellman equation considerably more cumbersome.

The next model we consider is the continuous time version of the previous model. A fuller discussion of the model can be found, for example, in Lippman and McCall (1976). The duration T until the wage offer arrives is distributed exponentially with the rate λ: that is, $P(T > t) = \exp(-\lambda t)$. When it arrives, the wage is distributed i.i.d. as G. We define c and δ as before. The Bellman equation is given by

(13.7.24) $V(t) = \max[\delta^{-1}W(t), K],$

where

(13.7.25) $K = \int_t^\infty \{\exp[-\delta(s-t)]EV(s) - c\int_0^{s-t}\exp(-\delta\tau)d\tau\}\lambda\exp[-\lambda(s-t)]ds.$

Taking the expectation of both sides and putting $EV(t) \equiv V$ because of stationarity, we have

(13.7.26) $V = \delta^{-1}E[\max(W, R)],$

where $R = \delta K$. Solve (13.7.26) for V, call the solution V^*, and define R^* accordingly. It is easy to show that R^* satisfies

(13.7.27) $R^* = -c + \delta^{-1}\lambda\int_{R^*}^\infty (w - R^*)dG(w).$

Let $f(t)$ be the density function of the unemployment duration. Then we have

(13.7.28) $f(t) = \lambda P \exp(-\lambda Pt),$

where $P = P(W > R^*)$. Thus we have obtained the exponential model. For a small value of λP, (13.7.28) is approximately equal to (13.7.23).

APPENDIX:
DISTRIBUTION THEORY

DEFINITION 1 (Chi-square Distribution) Let $\{Z_i\}$, $i = 1, 2, \ldots, n$, be i.i.d. as $N(0, 1)$. Then the distribution of $\sum_{i=1}^{n} Z_i^2$ is called the *chi-square distribution*, with n degrees of freedom and denoted by χ_n^2 .

THEOREM 1 If $X \sim \chi_n^2$ and $Y \sim \chi_m^2$ and if X and Y are independent, then $X + Y \sim \chi_{n+m}^2$.

THEOREM 2 If $X \sim \chi_n^2$, then $EX = n$ and $VX = 2n$.

THEOREM 3 Let $\{X_i\}$ be i.i.d. as $N(\mu, \sigma^2)$, $i = 1, 2, \ldots, n$. Define $\bar{X}_n = n^{-1} \sum_{i=1}^{n} X_i$. Then

$$\frac{\sum_{i=1}^{n} (X_i - \bar{X}_n)^2}{\sigma^2} \sim \chi_{n-1}^2.$$

Proof. Define $Z_i = (X_i - \mu)/\sigma$. Then $Z_i \sim N(0, 1)$ and

$$(1) \qquad \frac{1}{\sigma^2} \sum_{i=1}^{n} (X_i - \bar{X}_n)^2 = \sum_{i=1}^{n} (Z_i - \bar{Z}_n)^2.$$

We shall show $\sum_{i=1}^{n} (Z_i - \bar{Z}_n)^2 \sim \chi_{n-1}^2$ by induction. First, consider the case $n = 2$. We have

$$(2) \qquad \sum_{i=1}^{2} (Z_i - \bar{Z}_2)^2 = \left[\frac{Z_1 - Z_2}{\sqrt{2}} \right]^2 .$$

But since $(Z_1 - Z_2)/\sqrt{2} \sim N(0, 1)$, the right-hand side of (2) is χ_1^2 by Definition 1. Therefore, the theorem is true for $n = 2$. Second, assume it is true for n and consider $n + 1$. We have

$$(3) \qquad \sum_{i=1}^{n+1} (Z_i - \bar{Z}_{n+1})^2 = \sum_{i=1}^{n} (Z_i - \bar{Z}_n)^2 + \left[\frac{\sqrt{n}}{\sqrt{n+1}} (Z_{n+1} - \bar{Z}_n) \right]^2.$$

But the first and second terms of the right-hand side above are independent because

$$(4) \qquad E(Z_i - \bar{Z}_n)(Z_{n+1} - \bar{Z}_n) = 0.$$

Moreover, we can easily verify

$$(5) \qquad \frac{\sqrt{n}}{\sqrt{n+1}} (Z_{n+1} - \bar{Z}_n) \sim N(0, 1),$$

which implies by Definition 1 that the square of (5) is χ_1^2. Therefore, by Theorem 1, the left-hand side of (3) is χ_n^2. $\square$

THEOREM 4 Let $\{X_i\}$ and $\bar{X}_n$ be as defined in Theorem 3. Then

$$\frac{1}{n} \sum_{i=1}^{n} (X_i - \bar{X}_n)^2 \stackrel{A}{\sim} N\left(\sigma^2, \frac{2\sigma^4}{n} \right).$$

DEFINITION 2 (Student's t Distribution) Let Y be $N(0, 1)$ and independent of a chi-square variable χ_n^2. Then the distribution of $\sqrt{n}Y/\sqrt{\chi_n^2}$ is called the *Student's t distribution* with n degrees of freedom. We shall denote this distribution by t_n.

THEOREM 5 Let $\{X_i\}$ be i.i.d. as $N(0, 1)$, $i = 1, 2, \ldots, n$. Define $\bar{X} = n^{-1}\Sigma_{i=1}^n X_i$ and $S^2 = n^{-1}\Sigma_{i=1}^n (X_i - \bar{X})^2$. Then

$$\frac{(\bar{X} - \mu)\sqrt{n - 1}}{S} \sim t_{n-1}.$$

Proof. Since $\bar{X} \sim N(\mu, n^{-1}\sigma^2)$, we have

$$(6) \qquad Y \equiv \frac{(\bar{X} - \mu)\sqrt{n}}{\sigma} \sim N(0, 1).$$

Also, we have

(7) $\text{Cov}[(X_i - \bar{X}), \bar{X}] = E(X_i - \bar{X})\bar{X} = EX_i\bar{X} - E\bar{X}^2$

$$= \frac{1}{n}EX_i^2 - \frac{1}{n^2}\sum_{i=1}^{n}EX_i^2 = 0.$$

Since $X_i - \bar{X}$ and $\bar{X}$ are jointly normal, (7) implies that these two terms are independent by virtue of Theorem 5.3.4. Therefore, by Theorem 3.5.1,

(8) S^2 and Y are independent.

But we have by Theorem 3

(9)
$$\frac{\sum_{i=1}^{n}(X_i - \bar{X}_n)^2}{\sigma^2} \sim \chi_{n-1}^2.$$

Therefore, the theorem follows from (6), (8), and (9) because of Definition 2. $\square$

THEOREM 6   Let $\{X_i\}$ be i.i.d. as $N(\mu_X, \sigma_X^2)$, $i = 1, 2, \ldots, n_X$ and let $\{Y_i\}$ be i.i.d. as $N(\mu_Y, \sigma_Y^2)$, $i = 1, 2, \ldots, n_Y$. Assume that $\{X_i\}$ are independent of $\{Y_i\}$. Let $\bar{X}$ and $\bar{Y}$ be the sample means and S_X^2 and S_Y^2 be the sample variances. Then if $\sigma_X^2 = \sigma_Y^2$,

$$\frac{(\bar{X} - \bar{Y}) - (\mu_X - \mu_Y)}{(n_X S_X^2 + n_Y S_Y^2)^{1/2}} \cdot \left[\frac{n_X n_Y(n_X + n_Y - 2)}{n_X + n_Y}\right]^{1/2} \sim t_{n_X + n_Y - 2}.$$

Proof. We have

(10)
$$\frac{(\bar{X} - \bar{Y}) - (\mu_X - \mu_Y)}{\left(\dfrac{\sigma_X^2}{n_X} + \dfrac{\sigma_Y^2}{n_Y}\right)^{1/2}}$$

and

(11)
$$\frac{\sum_{i=1}^{n_X}(X_i - \bar{X})^2}{\sigma_X^2} + \frac{\sum_{i=1}^{n_Y}(Y_i - \bar{Y})^2}{\sigma_Y^2} \sim \chi_{n_X + n_Y - 2}^2,$$

where (11) follows from Theorems 1 and 3. Moreover, (10) and (11) are independent for the same reason that (8) holds. Therefore, by Definition 2,

$$(12) \qquad \frac{(\bar{X} - \bar{Y}) - (\mu_X - \mu_Y)}{\left(\dfrac{\sigma_X^2}{n_X} + \dfrac{\sigma_Y^2}{n_Y} \right)^{1/2}} \cdot \frac{\sqrt{n_X + n_Y - 2}}{\left(\dfrac{n_X S_X^2}{\sigma_X^2} + \dfrac{n_Y S_Y^2}{\sigma_Y^2} \right)^{1/2}} \sim t_{n_X + n_Y - 2}.$$

Finally, the theorem follows from inserting $\sigma_X^2 = \sigma_Y^2$ into (12). $\square$

DEFINITION 3 (F Distribution) If $X \sim \chi_n^2$ and $Y \sim \chi_m^2$ and if X and Y are independent, then $(X/n)/(Y/m)$ is distributed as F with n and m degrees of freedom and denoted $F(n, m)$. This is known as the F *distribution*. Here n is called the numerator degrees of freedom, and m the denominator degrees of freedom.

REFERENCES

Akaike, H. 1973. "Information Theory and an Extension of the Maximum Likelihood Principle," in B. N. Petrov and F. Csaki, eds., *Second International Symposium on Information Theory*, pp. 267–281. Budapest: Akademiai Kiado.

Amemiya, T. 1973. "Regression Analysis When the Dependent Variable Is Truncated Normal." *Econometrica* 41: 997–1016.

—— 1981. "Qualitative Response Models: A Survey." *Journal of Economic Literature* 19: 1483–1536.

—— 1985. *Advanced Econometrics*. Cambridge, Mass.: Harvard University Press.

—— 1991. "A Note on Left Censoring." Technical Paper no. 235, CEPR, Stanford University, Calif.

Amemiya, T., and W. A. Fuller. 1967. "A Comparative Study of Alternative Estimators in a Distributed-Lag Model." *Econometrica* 35: 509–529.

Anderson, T. W. 1984. *Introduction to Multivariate Statistical Analysis*, 2nd ed. New York: John Wiley & Sons.

Apostol, T. M. 1974. *Mathematical Analysis*, 2nd ed. Reading, Mass.: Addison-Wesley.

Arrow, K. J. 1965. *Aspects of the Theory of Risk-Bearing*. Helsinki: Academic Book Store.

Arrow, K. J., H. B. Chenery, B. S. Minhas, and R. M. Solow. 1961. "Capital-Labor Substitution and Economic Efficiency." *Review of Economics and Statistics* 43: 225–250.

Bellman, R. 1970. *Introduction to Matrix Analysis*, 2nd ed. New York: McGraw-Hill.

Birnbaum, A. 1962. "On the Foundations of Statistical Inference." *Journal of the American Statistical Association* 57: 269–326 (with discussion).

Box, G. E. P., and D. R. Cox. 1964. "An Analysis of Transformations." *Journal of the Royal Statistical Society*, ser. B, 26: 211–252 (with discussion).

Chung, K. L. 1974. *A Course in Probability Theory*, 2nd ed. New York: Academic Press.

Cox, D. R. 1972. "Regression Models and Life Tables." *Journal of the Royal Statistical Society*, ser. B, 34: 187–220 (with discussion).

DeGroot, M. H. 1970. *Optimal Statistical Decisions*. New York: McGraw-Hill.

Dubin, J. A., and D. McFadden. 1984. "An Econometric Analysis of Residential Electric Appliance Holdings and Consumption." *Econometrica* 52: 345–362.

Dudley, L., and C. Montmarquette. 1976. "A Model of the Supply of Bilateral Foreign Aid." *American Economic Review* 66: 132–142.

Duncan, G. M. 1980. "Formulation and Statistical Analysis of the Mixed, Continuous/Discrete Dependent Variable Model in Classical Production Theory." *Econometrica* 48: 839–852.

Durbin, J., and G. S. Watson. 1951. "Testing for Serial Correlation in Least Squares Regression, II." *Biometrika* 38: 159–178.

Eicker, F. 1963. "Asymptotic Normality and Consistency of the Least Squares Estimators for Families of Linear Regressions." *Annals of Mathematical Statistics* 34: 447–456.

Fair, R. C., and D. M. Jaffee. 1972. "Methods of Estimation for Markets in Disequilibrium." *Econometrica* 40: 497–514.

Ferguson, T. S. 1967. *Mathematical Statistics*. New York: Academic Press.

Flinn, C. J., and J. J. Heckman. 1982. "Models for the Analysis of Labor Force Dynamics." *Advances in Econometrics* 1: 35–95.

Fuller, W. A. 1987. *Measurement Error Models*. New York: John Wiley & Sons.

Goldfeld, S. M., and R. E. Quandt. 1972. *Nonlinear Methods in Econometrics*. Amsterdam: North-Holland Publishing.

———— 1976. "Techniques for Estimating Switching Regressions," in S. M. Goldfeld and R. E. Quandt, eds., *Studies in Nonlinear Estimation*, pp. 3–35. Cambridge, Mass.: Ballinger Publishing.

Graybill, F. A. 1969. *Introduction to Matrices with Applications in Statistics*. Belmont, Calif.: Wadsworth Publishing.

Griliches, Z. 1967. "Distributed Lag Models: A Survey." *Econometrica* 35: 16–49.

Gritz, M. 1993. "The Impact of Training on the Frequency and Duration of Employment." *Journal of Econometrics*, 57: 21–51.

Gronau, R. 1973. "The Effects of Children on the Household's Value of Time." *Journal of Political Economy* 81: S168–S199.

Hausman, J. A., and D. A. Wise. 1978. "A Conditional Probit Model for Qualitative Choice: Discrete Decisions Recognizing Interdependence and Heterogeneous Preferences." *Econometrica* 46: 403–426.

Heckman, J. J., and B. Singer. 1984. "A Method for Minimizing the Impact of Distributional Assumptions in Econometric Models for Duration Data." *Econometrica* 52: 271–320.

Hoel, P. G. 1984. *Introduction to Mathematical Statistics*, 5th ed. New York: John Wiley & Sons.

Huang, C., and R. H. Litzenberger. 1988. *Foundations for Financial Economics*. Amsterdam: North-Holland Publishing.

Hwang, J. J. 1985. "Universal Domination and Stochastic Domination: Estimation Simultaneously under a Broad Class of Loss Functions." *Annals of Statistics* 13: 295–314.

Johnson, N. L., and S. Kotz. 1970. *Continuous Univariate Distributions—1.* Boston: Houghton Mifflin.

———— 1972. *Distributions in Statistics: Continuous Multivariate Distributions.* New York: John Wiley & Sons.

Johnston, J. 1984. *Econometric Methods,* 3rd ed. New York: McGraw-Hill.

Kalbfleisch, J. D., and R. L. Prentice. 1980. *Statistical Analysis of Failure Time Data.* New York: John Wiley & Sons.

Kaplan, E., and P. Meier. 1958. "Nonparametric Estimation from Incomplete Observations." *Journal of the American Statistical Association* 53: 457–481.

Kendall, M. G., and A. Stuart. 1973. *The Advanced Theory of Statistics,* vol. 2, 3rd ed. New York: Hafner Press.

Koyck, L. M. 1954. *Distributed Lags and Investment Analysis.* Amsterdam: North-Holland Publishing.

Lancaster, T. 1979. "Econometric Methods for the Duration of Unemployment." *Econometrica* 47: 939–956.

———— 1990. *The Econometric Analysis of Transition Data.* New York: Cambridge University Press.

Lee, L. F. 1978. "Unionism and Wage Rates: A Simultaneous Equations Model with Qualitative and Limited Dependent Variables." *International Economic Review* 19: 415–433.

Lehrer, E. L. 1988. "Determinants of Marital Instability: A Cox Regression Model." *Applied Economics* 20: 195–210.

Lippman, S. A., and J. J. McCall. 1976. "The Economics of Job Search: A Survey." *Economic Inquiry* 14: 155–189.

McFadden, D. 1974. "Conditional Logit Analysis of Qualitative Choice Behavior," in P. Zarembka, ed., *Frontiers in Econometrics,* pp. 105–142. New York: Academic Press.

———— 1977. "Qualitative Methods for Analyzing Travel Behavior of Individuals: Some Recent Developments." Cowles Foundation Discussion Paper no. 474.

———— 1981. "Econometric Models of Probabilistic Choice," in C. F. Manski and D. McFadden, eds., *Structural Analysis of Discrete Data with Econometric Applications,* pp. 198-272. Cambridge, Mass.: MIT Press.

———— 1989. "A Method of Simulated Moments for Estimation of Discrete Response Models without Numerical Integration." *Econometrica* 57: 995–1026.

Mallows, C. L. 1964. "Choosing Variables in a Linear Regression: A Graphical Aid." Paper presented at the Central Region Meeting of the Institute of Mathematical Statistics, Manhattan, Kans.

Marcus, M., and H. Minc. 1964. *A Survey of Matrix Theory and Matrix Inequalities.* Boston: Prindle, Weber & Schmidt.

Miller, R. G., Jr. 1981. *Survival Analysis.* New York: John Wiley & Sons.

Moffitt, R. 1985. "Unemployment Insurance and the Distribution of Unemployment Spells." *Journal of Econometrics* 28: 85–101.

Olsen, R. J. 1978. "Note on the Uniqueness of the Maximum Likelihood Estimator for the Tobit Model." *Econometrica* 46: 1211–15.

Pakes, A. 1986. "Patents as Options: Some Estimates of the Value of Holding European Patent Stocks." *Econometrica* 54: 755–784.

Rao, C. R. 1973. *Linear Statistical Inference and Its Applications*, 2nd ed. New York: John Wiley & Sons.

Robinson, P. M. 1982. "On the Asymptotic Properties of Estimators of Models Containing Limited Dependent Variables." *Econometrica* 50: 27–41.

Sawa, T., and T. Hiromatsu. 1973. "Minimax Regret Significance Points for a Preliminary Test in Regression Analysis." *Econometrica* 41: 1093–1101.

Serfling, R. J. 1980. *Approximate Theorems of Mathematical Statistics*. New York: John Wiley & Sons.

Silverman, B. W. 1986. *Density Estimation for Statistics and Data Analysis*. London: Chapman & Hall.

Sturm, R. 1991. "Reliability and Maintenance in European Nuclear Power Plants: A Structural Analysis of a Controlled Stochastic Process." Ph. D. dissertation, Stanford University.

Theil, H. 1953. "Repeated Least Squares Applied to Complete Equation Systems." Mimeographed paper. Central Planning Bureau, The Hague.

——— 1961. *Economic Forecasts and Policy*, 2nd ed. Amsterdam: North-Holland Publishing.

Tobin, J. 1958. "Estimation of Relationships for Limited Dependent Variables." *Econometrica* 26: 24–36.

Welch, B. L. 1938. "The Significance of the Difference between Two Means When the Population Variances Are Unequal." *Biometrika* 29: 350–362.

White, H. 1980. "A Heteroscedasticity-Consistent Covariance Matrix Estimator and a Direct Test for Heteroscedasticity." *Econometrica* 48: 817–838.

Wolpin, K. I. 1987. "Estimating a Structural Search Model: The Transition from School to Work." *Econometrica* 55: 801–817.

Zellner, A. 1971. *An Introduction to Bayesian Inference in Econometrics*. New York: John Wiley & Sons.

NAME INDEX

SUBJECT INDEX